THE FABER BOOK OF WAR POETRY

The Faber Book of WAR POETRY

edited by KENNETH BAKER

faber and faber

First published in Great Britain in 1996
by Faber and Faber Limited
3 Queen Square London WC1N 3AU

Phototypeset by Wilmaset Ltd, Wirral
Printed in England by Clays Ltd, St Ives plc

This collection © Kenneth Baker, 1996

Kenneth Baker is hereby identified as editor of this
work in accordance with Section 77 of the Copyright,
Designs and Patents Act 1988

A CIP record for this book
is available from the British Library

ISBN 0-571-17453-1

10 9 8 7 6 5 4 3 2 1

Contents

Introduction xxiii

Dulce et Decorum Est

To the Earl of Oxford JONATHAN SWIFT 1
from Amours de Voyage A. H. CLOUGH 2
Dulce et Decorum Est WILFRED OWEN 3
Death Valley SORLEY MACLEAN 4

The Patriotic Imperative

from Henry V WILLIAM SHAKESPEARE 6
Robert Bruce's Address to His Army ROBERT BURNS 8
The Minstrel-Boy THOMAS MOORE 9
Heart of Oak DAVID GARRICK 9
from McDermott's War Song G. W. HUNT 10

Off to the Wars

from The Treachery of Asmund ANONYMOUS
    (Old Norse) 11
A War Song BERTRAND DE BORN 12
from An Epistle to a Friend BEN JONSON 13
Into Battle JULIAN GRENFELL 13
'O what is that sound which so thrills the ear'
    W. H. AUDEN 15
The Waltz of the Twenty-Year-Olds LOUIS ARAGON 16
Ball's Bluff HERMAN MELVILLE 18
'Oh stay at home, my lad, and plough' A. E. HOUSMAN 19

Martial Music

from A Song for St Cecilia's Day JOHN DRYDEN 20
Fife Tune JOHN MANIFOLD 21

Pibroch of Donald Dhu WALTER SCOTT 22
Cha Till MacCruimein EWART ALAN MACKINTOSH 23
Beat! Beat! Drums! WALT WHITMAN 24
The Drum JOHN SCOTT 25
The British Grenadiers ANONYMOUS 26

A New Mistress

To Lucasta, Going to the Wars RICHARD LOVELACE 27
The Soldier Going to the Field WILLIAM DAVENANT 28
The Dashing White Sergeant JOHN BURGOYNE 29
A Soldier's Farewell ROBERT BURNS 29
The Last Evening RAINER MARIA RILKE 30
Goll Mac Morna Parts from His Wife ANONYMOUS
    (Irish) 31
from The Iliad, Book VI HOMER 33
The Colonel's Soliloquy THOMAS HARDY 36
At Parting ANNE RIDLER 37

The Women Left Behind

from Lysistrata ARISTOPHANES 38
Penelope DOROTHY PARKER 41
In Westminster Abbey JOHN BETJEMAN 41
Munition Wages MADELINE IDA BEDFORD 43
Far Away ANONYMOUS 44
Vergissmeinicht KEITH DOUGLAS 45

Recruiting

from A Posie of Gilliflowers WILLIAM GIFFORD 47
Over the Hills and Far Away ANONYMOUS 49
from Ode to St Crispin's Day R. H. ELLIS 49
Arthur McBride ANONYMOUS 50
'Become as little children' SYLVIA TOWNSEND WARNER 52
I Don't Want to Be a Soldier ANONYMOUS 52

Impressment and Conscription

High Germany ANONYMOUS 53
'Oh cruel was the press-gang' ANONYMOUS 54
The Forced Recruit ELIZABETH BARRETT BROWNING 55
The Song of the Dead Soldier CHRISTOPHER LOGUE 56

Mercenaries

To Captain Hungry BEN JONSON 59
from The Mercenary Soldier ANONYMOUS 60
Epitaph on an Army of Mercenaries A. E. HOUSMAN 62
Another Epitaph on an Army of Mercenaries
    HUGH MACDIARMID 62

The Training of Conscripts

Bayonet Training VERNON SCANNELL 63
Naming of Parts HENRY REED 65
Gas Drill TOM RAWLING 67
Drill's the Thing ANONYMOUS 67
Tatton Parachute Training School ANONYMOUS 68
1941 ROBERT GARIOCH 69

Military Justice and Punishment

from Henry V WILLIAM SHAKESPEARE 71
Hazel OLIVER REYNOLDS 72
The Lay of the Lash ANONYMOUS 73
The Deserter ANONYMOUS 73
The Deserter GILBERT FRANKAU 74
Danny Deever RUDYARD KIPLING 75
The Last Rhyme and Testament of Tony Lumpkin
    HARRY MORANT 76
from Cells RUDYARD KIPLING 77
Sergeant-Major Money ROBERT GRAVES 78

The Spirit of the Fighting Man

'Because we're here' ANONYMOUS 79
Roman Wall Blues W. H. AUDEN 79
Song of the Bowmen of Shu BUNNO 80
Tommy RUDYARD KIPLING 81
'I see a Soldiers service is forgot' PETER WOODHOUSE 83
from Citizen BOR Speaking H. H. TILLEY 83
Soldiers ANONYMOUS 84

Unlikely Soldiers

The Scholar Recruit PAO CHAO 85
from Henry IV, Part I WILLIAM SHAKESPEARE 86
The College Colonel HERMAN MELVILLE 87
Gentlemen-Rankers RUDYARD KIPLING 88
The Bohemians IVOR GURNEY 90

Women Warriors

from Boädicea ALFRED, LORD TENNYSON 91
from Jerusalem Delivered, Canto XX TORQUATO TASSO 93
from Henry VI, Part III WILLIAM SHAKESPEARE 96
Sweet Polly Oliver ANONYMOUS 98
My Sodger Laddie ANONYMOUS 98
Morse Lesson JOY CORFIELD 99

Rest and Recreation

The Ladies RUDYARD KIPLING 102
Concert Party: Busseboom EDMUND BLUNDEN 104
Messdeck ALAN ROSS 105
Tripoli PETER A. SANDERS 105
Officers' Mess GAVIN EWART 106
Minutiae 3 PAUL WIDDOWS 107
Shari Wag El Burka ANONYMOUS 108
Leave in Mid-Winter JOHN SHORT 108

The Consolations of Obscenity

Oh! Fucking Halkirk ANONYMOUS 110
Generals Ride in Cars ANONYMOUS 111
The Twats in the Ops Room ANONYMOUS 112
No Balls at All ANONYMOUS 112
The Army Dance ANONYMOUS 113

Home Thoughts

The Soldier JOHN CLARE 115
Drake's Drum HENRY NEWBOLT 116
The Private of the Buffs F. H. DOYLE 117
Vitaï Lampada HENRY NEWBOLT 118
The Soldier RUPERT BROOKE 119
Drummer Hodge THOMAS HARDY 120

Useful Tips

from The Young British Soldier RUDYARD KIPLING 121
Insensibility WILFRED OWEN 122
Lament of a Desert Rat N. J. TRAPNELL 125

Views of Death

I Have a Rendezvous with Death ALAN SEEGER 126
A Terre WILFRED OWEN 127
The Leveller ROBERT GRAVES 129
Breakfast WILFRED GIBSON 130
L.R.D.G. J. G. MEDDEMMEN 130
'Death is a matter of mathematics'
    BARRY CONRAD AMIEL 131

Gallantry and Heroism

from The Iliad, Book XII HOMER 134
Horatius THOMAS BABINGTON, LORD MACAULAY 135

from The Song of Roland ANONYMOUS (Old French) 156
from Othello WILLIAM SHAKESPEARE 160
from The Conquest of Granada JOHN DRYDEN 162
from The Dynasts, Part I THOMAS HARDY 162
An Irish Airman Foresees His Death W. B. YEATS 163
The Volunteer HERBERT ASQUITH 163
David and Goliath ROBERT GRAVES 164
Aristocrats KEITH DOUGLAS 165
Heroes SORLEY MACLEAN 166
from War and Hell ERNEST CROSBY 168

Killing

from War Music CHRISTOPHER LOGUE 169
from War Music CHRISTOPHER LOGUE 170
The Happy Warrior HERBERT READ 171
Outposts F. W. D. BENDALL 171
How to Kill KEITH DOUGLAS 172
The Taking of the Koppie UYS KRIGE 173

Leadership

The Ideal General ARCHILOCHUS 175
from Troilus and Cressida WILLIAM SHAKESPEARE 175
from Henry V WILLIAM SHAKESPEARE 176
1805 ROBERT GRAVES 178
from Don Juan, Canto IX GEORGE GORDON,
    LORD BYRON 179
Officers and Gentlemen Down Under JOHN BROOKES 180

Napoleon

The Grenadiers   HEINRICH HEINE 183
Russia 1812 VICTOR HUGO 184
Napoleon W. M. THACKERAY 187
from Antwerp FORD MADOX FORD 187
A St Helena Lullaby RUDYARD KIPLING 188

Donkeys

from Henry IV, Part I WILLIAM SHAKESPEARE 190
The General's Plaque HO XUAN HONG 192
The Crimean Heroes W. S. LANDOR 192
The General (1917) SIEGFRIED SASSOON 192
Mesopotamia 1917 RUDYARD KIPLING 193
Base Details SIEGFRIED SASSOON 194
A Bas la Gloire! EDWARD TENNANT 194
The Old Barbed Wire ANONYMOUS 196

Statesmen, Politicians and Profiteers

from Agamemnon AESCHYLUS 198
from Night CHARLES CHURCHILL 199
from The Task WILLIAM COWPER 200
A Dead Statesman RUDYARD KIPLING 200
Elegy in a Country Churchyard G. K. CHESTERTON 201
Almería PABLO NERUDA 201
'The hand that signed the paper felled a city'
    DYLAN THOMAS 202
Ultima Ratio Regum STEPHEN SPENDER 203
Judas and the Profiteer OSBERT SITWELL 204
'The Minister has all his notes in place' RICHARD HELLER 204

Armour

from The Iliad, Book XI HOMER 206
from The Iliad, Book XIX HOMER 207
from Sir Gawain and the Green Knight
    ANONYMOUS (Middle English) 208
from Marmion WALTER SCOTT 209
Children in Armour GEOFFREY ADKINS 212

Weapons

from The Song of the Sword W. E. HENLEY 213
Song of the English Bowmen ANONYMOUS 215

A Ballad of the Bayonet ERNEST BRYLL 216
'Brown Bess' RUDYARD KIPLING 217
Careless Love STANLEY KUNITZ 218
Every Bullet Has Its Billet ANONYMOUS 219
Grenade FRANCIS SCARFE 220
Metrum Parhemiacum Tragicum EUGENIUS VULGARIUS 221

Artillery and Big Bombs

from Paradise Lost, Book VI JOHN MILTON 222
The Origin of Naval Artillery THOMAS DIBDIN 227
Screw-Guns RUDYARD KIPLING 228
The Maxim Gun HILAIRE BELLOC 230
from War and Hell ERNEST CROSBY 230
Bombardment D. H. LAWRENCE 231
Post Card GUILLAUME APOLLINAIRE 231
Opening of an Offensive HAMISH HENDERSON 232
The Streets of Laredo LOUIS MACNEICE 233
from The Rhyme of the Flying Bomb MERVYN PEAKE 234
Unseen Fire R. N. CURREY 236
from Time YEHUDA AMICHAI 237
Flames TOGE SANKICHI 238
War Games CONNIE BENSLEY 240

Fortifications

from Tamburlaine the Great, Part II
    CHRISTOPHER MARLOWE 241
from The Dynasts, Part II THOMAS HARDY 242

Climate and Circumstances

from Henry V WILLIAM SHAKESPEARE 246
Rain   EDWARD THOMAS 246
from The Sentry WILFRED OWEN 247
Sand JOHN JARMAIN 248
Property ROBERT GARIOCH 249

Jungle Night 'K' 250
The Bitter Mangoes GEORGE SCURFIELD 251
from The Jungle ALUN LEWIS 253
Winter Warfare EDGELL RICKWORD 254
Destroyers in the Arctic ALAN ROSS 254
from Agamemnon AESCHYLUS 256

Fellow Creatures

The Rooks ARTHUR RIMBAUD 257
The Kite ALEXANDER BLOK 258
God of the Flies JOHN RIMINGTON 259
Louse Hunting ISAAC ROSENBERG 259
from In Parenthesis DAVID JONES 260

Night Scenes

The Night Patrol ARTHUR GRAEME WEST 262
Watch GIUSEPPE UNGARETTI 264
The Burial of Sir John Moore after Corunna
     CHARLES WOLFE 265
from The Dynasts, Part III THOMAS HARDY 266
from Childe Harold's Pilgrimage, Canto III
     GEORGE GORDON, LORD BYRON 268

Spying

from The Iliad, Book X HOMER 270
The Spies' March RUDYARD KIPLING 275

Victories

The Destruction of Sennacherib GEORGE GORDON,
     LORD BYRON 278
Battle of Brunanburh ALFRED, LORD TENNYSON 280
A Ballad of Agincourt MICHAEL DRAYTON 284
Lepanto G. K. CHESTERTON 288

The Battle of Naseby THOMAS BABINGTON,
LORD MACAULAY 293
Borodino MIKHAIL LERMONTOV 295

Disasters

The Charge of the Light Brigade ALFRED,
LORD TENNYSON 299
Isandula HUME NISBET 301
Night at Dunkirk LOUIS ARAGON 302
from The Fruits of War GEORGE GASCOIGNE 304

Hard Fighting

from The Iliad, Book XI HOMER 311
from The Iliad, Book XIII HOMER 312
from War Music CHRISTOPHER LOGUE 313
from Homer Travestie THOMAS BRIDGES 313
from Macbeth WILLIAM SHAKESPEARE 315
from The Battle of Otterbourne ANONYMOUS 317
from The Lusiads, Canto IV LUIS CAMOENS 319
The Charge at Waterloo WALTER SCOTT 323

Death in Action

from The Iliad, Book XVI HOMER 325
from The Song of Roland ANONYMOUS 327
from The Dynasts, Part I THOMAS HARDY 331
Song of the Dying Gunner AA1 CHARLES CAUSLEY 333
The Conscript Goes W. S. GRAHAM 333
Under the Greenwood Tree HUGH MACDIARMID 336

Naval Engagements

A Burnt Ship JOHN DONNE 337
from The Victory Obtained by Blake
ANDREW MARVELL 338
from Annus Mirabilis JOHN DRYDEN 341
from The Jervis Bay MICHAEL THWAITES 344

Old Ships

from The Building of the Ship HENRY WADSWORTH
LONGFELLOW 348
The *Temeraire* HERMAN MELVILLE 348
HMS *Glory* CHARLES CAUSLEY 350

Sieges

from The Aeneid, Book II VIRGIL 353
from The Aeneid, Book II VIRGIL 354
from Dido, Queen of Carthage CHRISTOPHER MARLOWE 356
from The Destruction of Jerusalem THOMAS DELONY 358
from Henry V WILLIAM SHAKESPEARE 361
The Pipes at Lucknow J. G. WHITTIER 362
from The Pulkovo Meridian VERA INBER 365

Nursing and Medicine

from The Iliad, Book IV HOMER 367
Santa Filomena HENRY WADSWORTH LONGFELLOW 368
from The Wound-Dresser WALT WHITMAN 369
War EDGAR WALLACE 371
Cholera Camp RUDYARD KIPLING 373
Gut Catcher STAN PLATKE 375
Mellow on Morphine DANA SHUSTER 375

Psychological Wounds

Suicide in the Trenches SIEGFRIED SASSOON 377
In the Ambulance WILFRED GIBSON 378
The Mad Soldier EDWARD TENNANT 378

Prisoners

In Prison WILLIAM MORRIS 380
Prisoners of War JOHN JARMAIN 381
Half-Ballad of Waterval RUDYARD KIPLING 382
The Performance JAMES DICKEY 383

Civilian Victims

Lidice ERNST WALDINGER 385
A Refusal to Mourn the Death, by Fire, of a Child in
    London DYLAN THOMAS 386
How Did They Kill My Grandmother? BORIS SLUTSKY 387
Green Beret HO THIEN 388
Two Villages GRACE PALEY 390
from Time YEHUDA AMICHAI 391
The Minutes of Hasiba HOLGER TESCHKE 392

The Holocaust

from Ten Songs W. H. AUDEN 393
A Camp in the Prussian Forest RANDALL JARRELL 394
Shemà PRIMO LEVI 396
September Song GEOFFREY HILL 397

The Distant View

from Fears in Solitude S. T. COLERIDGE 398
A Thousand Killed BERNARD SPENCER 399
To Whom It May Concern ADRIAN MITCHELL 400
Bosnia Tune JOSEPH BRODSKY 401
The Newscast IAN HAMILTON 402
from The Mystery of the Charity of Charles Péguy
    GEOFFREY HILL 403
Phooie! ROBERT GARIOCH 403

Eye-Witness

from Amours de Voyage A. H. CLOUGH 405
Dead Soldiers JAMES FENTON 407

Whims and Fates of the Conquerors

Alexander at Thebes ANNA AKHMATOVA 409
from The Rival Queens NATHANIEL LEE 410

from Tamburlaine the Great, Part I
CHRISTOPHER MARLOWE 414
from Tamburlaine the Great, Part II
CHRISTOPHER MARLOWE 415
from The Poem of the Cid ANONYMOUS (Spanish) 415
from Satires JUVENAL 418
from The Vanity of Human Wishes SAMUEL JOHNSON 419
'The world laid low, and the wind blew like a dust'
ANONYMOUS 421

Plunder and Spoils

from Tamburlaine the Great, Part II
CHRISTOPHER MARLOWE 422
A Personal Footnote GAVIN EWART 424
The Winning of Cales ANONYMOUS 424
The War Song of Dinas Vawr THOMAS LOVE PEACOCK 427
The Cycles of Donji Vakuf TONY HARRISON 428

The Defeated

Cleopatra ANNA AKHMATOVA 430
When the Troops Were Returning from Milan
NICCOLO DEGLI ALBIZZI 431
Dunbar, 1650 SIDNEY KEYES 431
'My Portion is Defeat – today –' EMILY DICKINSON 432
The City of Beggars ALFRED HAYES 433
The Invaders BERNARD SPENCER 434
Waiting for the Barbarians C. P. CAVAFY 435

Returning from War

The Returned Soldier JOHN CLARE 437
Johnny, I Hardly Knew Ye ANONYMOUS 438
What's the News? W. S. GRAHAM 440
Sons of War SAMIH AL-QASIM 441
The Beau Ideal JESSIE POPE 441

Basket Case BASIL T. PACQUET 442
'On the idle hill of summer' A. E. HOUSMAN 443
from Henry V WILLIAM SHAKESPEARE 444

Survivors

Disabled WILFRED OWEN 445
Strange Hells IVOR GURNEY 447
Out TED HUGHES 448
Arthur GEOFFREY ADKINS 450
En Route ALAN ROSS 451
For Services Rendered F. G. BUTTERFIELD 452
The Absent-Minded Beggar RUDYARD KIPLING 452
The Maunding Soldier MARTIN PARKER 454
The Man with the Wooden Leg
        KATHERINE MANSFIELD 457

Enemies as Brothers

Strange Meeting WILFRED OWEN 459
The Man He Killed THOMAS HARDY 460
Truce PAUL MULDOON 461
On the Relative Merit of Friend and Foe, Being Dead
        DONALD THOMPSON 462
The Enemy Dead BERNARD GUTTERIDGE 463
Love Letters of the Dead DOUGLAS STREET 463
Brothers HEINRICH LERSCH 464
German Prisoners JOSEPH LEE 465
The Dead RENÉ ARCOS 465
Ninth Elegy: Fort Capuzzo HAMISH HENDERSON 466
Juan Lopez and John Ward JORGE LUIS BORGES 467
Reconciliation WALT WHITMAN 468

The Bereaved

from 2 Samuel 2 ANONYMOUS (Hebrew) 469
from The Iliad, Book XVIII HOMER 470

from All Is Vanity ANNE FINCH,
    COUNTESS OF WINCHILSEA 471
Lament for Culloden ROBERT BURNS 472
The Soldier's Wife ROBERT SOUTHEY 473
Come Up from the Fields Father WALT WHITMAN 474
'Do not weep, maiden, for war is kind' STEPHEN CRANE 475
Glory of Women SIEGFRIED SASSOON 476
To L. H. B. (1894–1915) KATHERINE MANSFIELD 477
from Antwerp FORD MADOX FORD 478
Passed On BERNARD SPENCER 479
Familial JACQUES PRÉVERT 480
Heroes KATHLEEN RAINE 481

The Fruits of War

Sonnet 25 WILLIAM SHAKESPEARE 482
Rome JOACHIM DU BELLAY 483
from The Fruits of War GEORGE GASCOIGNE 483
from Ajax and Ulysses JAMES SHIRLEY 485
from Paradise Regained, Book III JOHN MILTON 486
War EBENEZER ELLIOTT 487
'War begets Poverty' EDWARD FITZGERALD 487
What Did the Nazi Send His Wife? BERTOLT BRECHT 487
Dead Cow Farm ROBERT GRAVES 489
from Phases WALLACE STEVENS 489
The End of the War IOAN ALEXANDRU 490

Civil War

from Henry VI, Part III WILLIAM SHAKESPEARE 492

War Poets

To a Certain Civilian WALT WHITMAN 495
On Being Asked for a War Poem W. B. YEATS 496
These Poems JOHN JARMAIN 496
When I'm Killed ROBERT GRAVES 497

Magpies in Picardy T. P. CAMERON WILSON 497
War Poet SIDNEY KEYES 499
The Poet DALE R. CARVER 499
The Volunteer's Reply to the Poet ROY CAMPBELL 500
First World War Poets EDWARD BOND 502
Trench Poets EDGELL RICKWORD 503

The Epic

from The Aeneid, Book I VIRGIL 505
from The Lusiads, Canto I LUIS CAMOENS 506
from Don Juan, Canto VII GEORGE GORDON,
    LORD BYRON 508
from Aurora Leigh ELIZABETH BARRETT BROWNING 509

Arguments for War

'What is the cause, why states, that war and win'
    FULKE GREVILLE, LORD BROOKE 512
from Phases WALLACE STEVENS 513

Pacifism

The Pacifist HILAIRE BELLOC 514
The White Feather Legion T. W. H. CROSLAND 515
The Non-Combatant HENRY NEWBOLT 515
Conscientious Objector EDNA ST VINCENT MILLAY 516
The Conchie R. F. PALMER 517
Letter to an American Visitor ALEX COMFORT 518
As One Non-Combatant to Another GEORGE ORWELL 523
'i sing of Olaf glad and big' E. E. CUMMINGS 527
The Military Creed ERNEST CROSBY 529
'One to destroy, is murder by the law' EDWARD YOUNG 530

The Religious Blessing

from Exodus 15 ANONYMOUS (Hebrew) 531

from The Defeat of the Norsemen
    SEDULIUS SCOTTUS 532
from The Poem of the Cid ANONYMOUS (Spanish) 533
from The Lusiads, Canto I LUIS CAMOENS 534
Hymn before Action RUDYARD KIPLING 537
The Soldier GERARD MANLEY HOPKINS 538
from War against War in South Africa W. T. STEAD 539
The Only Way W. N. EWER 540
May God Go with You, Son C. WRIGHT 541

Gods and Spirits of Warfare

Nike ERNEST BRYLL 543
Evil ARTHUR RIMBAUD 544
Fire, Famine and Slaughter S. T. COLERIDGE 545
'War is the mistress of enormity' JOSHUA SYLVESTER 547
from The Knight's Tale GEOFFREY CHAUCER 548
from The Iliad, Book IV HOMER 549
from The Iliad, Book II HOMER 550

Old Battlefields Revisited

An Arrowhead from the Ancient Battlefield of Ch'ang-p'ing
    LI HO 552
from Briggflatts BASIL BUNTING 553
The Battle of Blenheim ROBERT SOUTHEY 554
In Flanders Fields JOHN MCCRAE 557
High Wood PHILIP JOHNSTONE 557
El Alamein JOHN JARMAIN 558
Grass CARL SANDBURG 559

The Dead

The Greek Dead at Thermopylae SIMONIDES 561
The Due of the Dead W. M. THACKERAY 562
from When Lilacs Last in the Dooryard Bloom'd
    WALT WHITMAN 563

'It feels a shame to be Alive' EMILY DICKINSON 565
'When you see millions of the mouthless dead'
     CHARLES HAMILTON SORLEY 566
Blossoms in the Wind VICE-ADMIRAL OHNISHI 566
Hymn to the Fallen ANONYMOUS 567
The English Graves G. K. CHESTERTON 568
Albuera THOMAS HARDY 569
Dead on the War Path ANONYMOUS (Pueblo Indian) 570
Corporal Stare ROBERT GRAVES 570
Missing – Believed Drowned MICHAEL GREENING 571

Remembrance

Ashes of Soldiers WALT WHITMAN 573
from Poems for the Fallen LAWRENCE BINYON 575
Anthem for Doomed Youth WILFRED OWEN 575
MCMXIV PHILIP LARKIN 576
Simplify Me When I'm Dead KEITH DOUGLAS 577
The Distant Fury of Battle GEOFFREY HILL 578
Reasons for Refusal MARTIN BELL 579
Peacetime TOM PAULIN 581
from In 1940 ANNA AKHMATOVA 582
Courage BORIS PASTERNAK 582
Hamra Night SA'DI YUSUF 584

Peace

from Micah 4 ANONYMOUS (Hebrew) 585
The Vote RALPH KNEVET 585
from To Henry IV JOHN GOWER 586
'A soldier stood at the pearly gate' ANONYMOUS 587

Acknowledgements 589

Index of Authors 596

Introduction

The Purple Testament of Bleeding War

War and the business of fighting have occasioned, if not more poetry than any other activity of mankind, then a large part of what has endured across the ages and continues to matter to us. What I have tried to do, in this anthology, is to show how poets have responded to the subject of war in different centuries and in different countries. I wanted to paint a broad picture which would include the horrors and suffering as well as the heroism and excitement of fighting; the courage and the cowardice; victory and defeat; and not just the blunders of the generals and politicians, but also those many things which, in spite of them, have helped to sustain the morale of the fighting man: his sense of discipline and comradeship, his relationship to his weapons, all the routines and rituals of service life. This anthology is divided into sixty-six sections, each dealing with a distinct aspect of warfare, and I have introduced each one with a brief commentary.

Although many well-known war poems have concentrated on the horrors and suffering, and so been used as evidence in the powerful arguments against war, it would be untrue to say that this is the purpose of most of the poetry written about it. Certainly, the great poets of the First World War, who described the misery and futility of trench warfare, lent considerable strength to the pacifist movement of the 1920s and 1930s, but the poets of earlier wars, from the Trojan to the Napoleonic, were less apt to be merely appalled by the horrors. Fighting was accepted as part of the condition of mankind, and the poets' view of things allowed room for a celebration of heroic leadership and the courage of those fighting men who, following Horace's exhortation (page 1), believed that there was no better way to die than in the defence of one's country.

The poetry of the Second World War is different again from that of the First, because the nature and scale of the war were different too. The 1939–45 conflict was fought, not on any single front, but in a wide variety of theatres – Europe, North Africa, Burma and the Pacific, among others – and sea and air battles were as significant as those on land. The geographical spread and fluidity of the various campaigns did not bring about the intensity of experience felt by those soldiers who had been confined to the mud of Flanders. Nor did Second World War poets turn against their generals as Sassoon, Kipling and Chesterton had done. Churchill was not accused of having betrayed the young; and Montgomery, Rommel and Patton were never ridiculed as 'donkeys'. Another big difference is that the most memorable poets of the First World War – Owen, Sassoon and Graves – were of a particular social rank, classically educated and steeped in a great literary tradition, which was not necessarily the case with earlier and later poets. Some of the most interesting poetry of the Second World War, which has been splendidly preserved and published by the Salamander Oasis Trust, was written by men and women who had had no especially privileged upbringing, but who, finding themselves caught up in the great drama of war, discovered, perhaps for the only time in their lives, the gift of poetry as a means of recording their experiences and voicing their emotions.

One of the most significant consequences of war is that it shapes a nation's identity. The power of the Greek states and of Imperial Rome depended first and foremost on military supremacy, and the national pride engendered by it is reflected in their poetry, whether it be on the small scale of Simonides's elegy for the Spartans who died at Thermopylae (page 561), or the vast one of Virgil's epic of the founding of Rome (pages 353, 354 and 505). Myths concerning a nation's past are refined and embellished by its poets and used to galvanize the spirit of its people when faced with foreign aggression. Francis Bacon wrote: 'War towns, stored arsenals, and armouries, goodly races of horses, chariots of war, elephants, ordnance and artillery, and the like, all this is but a sheep in a lion skin except the breed and dispositions of the people be stout and warlike.'

So medieval France needed its *Song of Roland*, and expansionist Portugal its *Lusiads*. When a similar need arose in Elizabethan England, Shakespeare obliged by producing his history plays, chronicles of strife and bloodshed, loyalty and treachery, courage and cowardice; and he served the Tudor regime well by presenting its ancestors, the Lancastrians, and particularly Henry V, not only as successful warriors, but as the forgers of a united country. Henry V was a national hero, at one with St George and England, but his son, Henry VI, was a tragic failure because his weakness led to a bloody civil war.

If Shakespeare was the myth-maker of a specifically English patriotism, later poets also helped to shape the 'Britishness' of the British nation. Intermittently, for almost half the period between 1707, the year of the Act of Union, and 1837, the year of the accession of Queen Victoria, the United Kingdom of England, Scotland, Wales and Ireland was at war with France, and patriotic songs such as 'Rule, Britannia' and 'Heart of Oak' were a product of this belligerence. The country was often under threat of invasion and an army and navy had to be kept replenished for its defences. Recruiting officers prowled the land and press-gangs were busy. At the beginning of a war, the call to arms may have its glamorous attractions; and even if John Scott, writing in the middle of this period, declared 'I hate that drum's discordant sound,/ Parading round, and round, and round,' poets from Lovelace to Julian Grenfell (pages 27 and 13) have shown what it is to be elated by the challenge of war and its dangers. As hostilities continue, however, and conscripts are required, a different mood must find its outlet, and the vernacular tradition is rich in laments for loved ones seized and sent to fight for obscure causes in distant lands: 'O, cruel was the press-gang . . .' (page 54).

There have, of course, been people like the Quakers, as well as poets, who have opposed fighting on principle, and I have put together a substantial section on the debate over pacifism, even though the philosophy of conscientious objection has developed formally only within the last hundred years. It requires courage to refuse to fight on grounds of conscience, and at the time of the Boer and First World Wars it was not uncommon for young men who did not join up to be physically attacked or sent symbolic white feathers. Many who were not prepared to bear arms went willingly to serve as stretcher-bearers and medical orderlies, in which roles they often displayed quite exceptional bravery.

The nature of bravery, and other questions relating to the psychology of the fighting man, are addressed from a variety of angles in many different sections of this book. Poets of earlier periods chose the feats of legendary leaders and superhuman, sometimes semi-divine heroes like Achilles, Aeneas, Roland and El Cid, as their themes; but even here, as Homer in particular demonstrates, it is the poet's imaginative grasp of the actualities of warfare that keeps the writing lively. This realistic strain, which sometimes amounts to a document-ary factualness, is what I have looked for in choosing poems to illustrate many of my topics, whether it be a question of the develop-ment of weaponry through the ages; of the peculiarities of military justice; of how the fighting man finds his rest and recreation; of the part played by climatic conditions in the fortunes of war; or of what happens in the field of action itself. Wars are caused by the failure of politicians, and yet they are sustained through the participation of quite ordinary people; Kipling was their most inspired representative, but many have spoken for themselves and it is their experience that I have particularly drawn upon.

Poets have sung both the joys of victory and the bitterness of defeat, but the aftermath of war is another complex concern. The fate of the physically or psychologically wounded, of the civilian victim, of the bereaved, of the soldier returning home to find what usually turns out not to be the promised 'land fit for heroes' – these things and more are considered in later pages. And finally, there is our duty, both national and personal, to acknowledge the debt owed to those who have fought and died on our behalf, and to keep their memory fresh. Even this question is fraught with problems, as the sometimes acrimonious tone introduced by contributors to the section on the 'War Poets' themselves makes plain. Shelley called poets the 'unacknowledged legislators of mankind', but it hardly needs saying that no law or pronouncement of theirs has ever prevented a war. Since 1945, indeed, there has been not a single year without its violent conflict, and it has been estimated that in this century alone over 108 million people, military and civilians, have died as a result of war. All the more reason, then, why the poet should not shirk the responsibility to add his or her witness to what Shakespeare called 'The purple testament of bleeding war', and why, when he or she has done so, we must take note and remember. I hope the poems that follow will prove the point.

Dulce et Decorum Est

Horace himself had served as a soldier in the civil war that followed Julius Caesar's assassination and, having committed himself to Brutus, he had been on the losing side at the battle of Philippi (42 BC). The ode of his which contains the words *Dulce et decorum est pro patria mori* is the classic expression of the most noble justification for war. It was a duty to die for one's country, for the nation was greater than the individual. The Latin line has been chiselled into innumerable war memorials and paraphrased by leaders throughout history, both to encourage men to make the supreme sacrifice and to console the bereaved. Swift's translation of part of the ode captures the spirit of heroic disdain. Other poets have used Horace's words to show that death in battle is not in the least *dulce* or *decorum* and that the ultimate sacrifice is so often futile.

JONATHAN SWIFT

To the Earl of Oxford

after Horace, *Odes, Book III, 2*

How blest is he, who for his Country dies;
Since Death pursues the Coward as he flies.
The Youth, in vain, would fly from Fate's Attack,
With trembling Knees, and Terror at his Back;
Though Fear should lend him Pinions like the Wind,
Yet swifter Fate will seize him from behind.

   Virtue repuls't, yet knows not to repine;
But shall with unattainted Honour shine;
Nor stoops to take the Staff, nor lays it down,
Just as the Rabble please to smile or frown.

Virtue, to crown her Fav'rites, loves to try
Some new unbeaten Passage to the Sky;
Where Jove a Seat among the Gods will give
To those who die, for meriting to live.

Next, faithful Silence hath a sure Reward:
Within our Breast be ev'ry Secret barr'd:
He who betrays his Friend, shall never be
Under one Roof, or in one Ship with me.
For, who with Traytors would his Safety trust,
Lest with the Wicked, Heaven involve the Just?
And, though the Villain 'scape a while, he feels
Slow Vengeance, like a Blood-hound at his Heels.

A. H. CLOUGH

from Amours de Voyage, Canto II

Dulce it is, and *decorum*, no doubt, for the country to fall, – to
Offer one's blood an oblation to Freedom, and die for the
    Cause; yet
Still, individual culture is also something, and no man
Finds quite distinct the assurance that he of all others is called
    on,
Or would be justified even, in taking away from the world that
Precious creature, himself. Nature sent him here to abide here;
Else why send him at all? Nature wants him still, it is likely;
On the whole, we are meant to look after ourselves; it is certain
Each has to eat for himself, digest for himself, and in general
Care for his own dear life, and see to his own preservation;
Nature's intentions, in most things uncertain, in this are
    decisive;
Which, on the whole, I conjecture the Romans will follow, and
    I shall.
So we cling to our rocks like limpets; Ocean may bluster,

Over and under and round us; we open our shells to imbibe
    our
Nourishment, close them again, and are safe, fulfilling the
    purpose
Nature intended, – a wise one, of course, and a noble, we
    doubt not.
Sweet it may be and decorous, perhaps, for the country to die;
    but,
On the whole, we conclude the Romans won't do it, and I
    sha'n't.

WILFRED OWEN

Dulce et Decorum Est

Bent double, like old beggars under sacks,
Knock-kneed, coughing like hags, we cursed through sludge,
Till on the haunting flares we turned our backs,
And towards our distant rest began to trudge.
Men marched asleep. Many had lost their boots,
But limped on, blood-shod. All went lame, all blind;
Drunk with fatigue; deaf even to the hoots
Of gas-shells dropping softly behind.

Gas! Gas! Quick boys! – An ecstasy of fumbling,
Fitting the clumsy helmets just in time,
But someone still was yelling out and stumbling
And floundering like a man in fire or lime. –
Dim through the misty panes and thick green light,
As under a green sea, I saw him drowning.
In all my dreams, before my helpless sight,
He plunges at me, guttering, choking, drowning.

If in some smothering dreams, you too could pace
Behind the wagon that we flung him in,
And watch the white eyes writhing in his face,

His hanging face, like a devil's sick of sin;
If you could hear, at every jolt, the blood
Come gargling from the froth-corrupted lungs,
Obscene as cancer, bitter as the cud
Of vile, incurable sores on innocent tongues, –
My friend, you would not tell with such high zest
To children ardent for some desperate glory,
The old Lie: *Dulce et decorum est*
Pro patria mori.

SORLEY MACLEAN

Death Valley

Some Nazi or other has said that the Führer had restored to German
manhood the 'right and joy of dying in battle'.

Sitting dead in Death Valley
below Ruweisat Ridge
a boy with his forelock down about his cheek
and his face slate-grey.

I thought of the right and the joy
that he got from his Führer,
of falling in the field of slaughter
to rise no more;

of the pomp and the fame
that he had, not alone,
though he was the most piteous to see
in a valley gone to seed

with flies about grey corpses
on a dun sand
dirty yellow and full of the rubbish
and fragments of battle.

Was the boy of the band
who abused the Jews
and Communists, or of the greater
band of those

led, from the beginning of generations,
unwillingly to the trial
and mad delirium of every war
for the sake of rulers?

Whatever his desire or mishap,
his innocence or malignity,
he showed no pleasure in his death
below Ruweisat Ridge.

The Patriotic Imperative

Shakespeare did much to fashion English patriotism, and Henry V's address to his troops before Agincourt is still inspiring stuff. The poems from Scotland and Ireland in this section illustrate the universal appeal of the national pride, love of liberty and defiance of oppression that have led men to take up arms at all times and in all places. Perhaps the most exaggerated and debased expression of the sentiment is to be found in 'McDermott's War Song', composed in 1878 and performed in the music halls just as Britain was squaring up to Russia to stop her grabbing parts of the collapsing Ottoman Empire. Whatever purpose it served then, the song added a useful new word to the English language.

WILLIAM SHAKESPEARE

from Henry V (Act 4, Scene iii)

Westmoreland: O that we now had here
But one ten thousand of those men in England
That do no work to-day!
   King Henry: What's he that wishes so?
My cousin Westmoreland? No, my fair cousin:
If we are mark'd to die, we are enow
To do our country loss; and if to live,
The fewer men, the greater share of honour.
God's will! I pray thee, wish not one man more.
By Jove, I am not covetous for gold,
Nor care I who doth feed upon my cost;
It yearns me not if men my garments wear;
Such outward things dwell not in my desires:
But if it be a sin to covet honour,
I am the most offending soul alive.

No, faith, my coz, wish not a man from England:
God's peace! I would not lose so great an honour
As one man more, methinks, would share from me
For the best hope I have. O, do not wish one more!
Rather proclaim it, Westmoreland, through my host,
That he which hath no stomach to this fight,
Let him depart; his passport shall be made
And crowns for convoy put into his purse:
We would not die in that man's company
That fears his fellowship to die with us.
This day is call'd the feast of Crispian:
He that outlives this day, and comes safe home,
Will stand a tip-toe when this day is named,
And rouse him at the name of Crispian.
He that shall live this day, and see old age,
Will yearly on the vigil feast his neighbours,
And say, 'To-morrow is Saint Crispian:'
Then will he strip his sleeve and show his scars,
And say 'These wounds I had on Crispin's day.'
Old men forget; yet all shall be forgot,
But he'll remember with advantages
What feats he did that day: then shall our names,
Familiar in his mouth as household words,
Harry the king, Bedford and Exeter,
Warwick and Talbot, Salisbury and Gloucester,
Be in their flowing cups freshly remember'd.
This story shall the good man teach his son;
And Crispin Crispian shall ne'er go by,
From this day to the ending of the world,
But we in it shall be remembered;
We few, we happy few, we band of brothers;
For he to-day that sheds his blood with me
Shall be my brother; be he ne'er so vile,
This day shall gentle his condition:
And gentlemen in England now a-bed
Shall think themselves accursed they were not here,

And hold their manhoods cheap whiles any speaks
That fought with us upon Saint Crispin's day.

ROBERT BURNS

Robert Bruce's Address to His Army

Scots, wha hae wi' Wallace bled,
Scots, wham Bruce has aften led,
Welcome to your gory bed,
    Or to victorie!

Now's the day and now's the hour:
See the front o' battle lour:
See approach proud Edward's pow'r –
    Chains and slaverie!

Wha will be a traitor-knave?
Wha can fill a coward's grave?
Wha sae base as be a slave?
    Let him turn and flee!

Wha for Scotland's King and law
Freedom's sword will strongly draw,
Freeman stand, or freeman fa',
    Let him follow me!

By oppression's woes and pains!
By our sons in servile chains!
We will drain our dearest veins,
    But they shall be free!

Lay the proud usurpers low!
Tyrants fall in every foe!
Liberty's in every blow! –
    Let us do or die!

THOMAS MOORE

The Minstrel-Boy

The Minstrel-boy to the war is gone,
    In the ranks of death you'll find him;
His father's sword he has girded on,
    And his wild harp slung behind him.
'Land of Song!' said the warrior-bard,
    'Though all the world betrays thee,
One sword, at least, thy rights shall guard,
    One faithful harp shall praise thee.'

The Minstrel fell! but the foeman's chain
    Could not bring his proud soul under;
The harp he loved ne'er spoke again,
    For he tore its chords asunder;
And said, 'No chains shall sully thee,
    Thou soul of love and bravery!
Thy songs were made for the brave and free
    They shall never sound in slavery!'

DAVID GARRICK

Heart of Oak

Come, cheer up, my lads! 'tis to glory we steer,
To add something more to this wonderful year;
To honour we call you, not press you like slaves –
For who are so free as we sons of the waves?
    Heart of oak are our ships,
    Heart of oak are our men;
    We always are ready;
    Steady, boys, steady;
We'll fight and we'll conquer again and again.

We ne'er see our foes but we wish 'em to stay,
They never see us but they wish us away;
If they run, why, we follow, and run 'em ashore,
For if they won't fight us, we cannot do more.
    Heart of oak, etc.

They swear they'll invade us, these terrible foes,
They frighten our women, our children and beaux;
But should their flat-bottoms in darkness get o'er,
Still Britons they'll find to receive them on shore.
    Heart of oak, etc.

We'll still make 'em run, and we'll still make 'em sweat,
In spite of the devil and Brussels Gazette;
Then cheer up, my lads, with one heart let us sing,
Our soldiers, our sailors, our statesmen, and King.
    Heart of oak, etc.

G. W. HUNT

from McDermott's War Song

The 'Dogs of War' are loose and the rugged Russian Bear
Full bent on blood and robbery, has crawled out of his lair
It seems a thrashing now and then, will never help to tame,
That brute, and so he's out upon the 'Same old Game.'
The Lion did his best to find him some excuse,
To crawl back to his den again, all efforts were no use,
He hungered for his victim, he's pleased when blood is shed,
But let us hope his crimes may all recoil on his own head.

Chorus
We don't want to fight, yet by jingo when we do,
We've got the ships, we've got the men, and got the money too,
We've fought the Bear before, and the Turks have proved so
    true,
The Russians can't get near Constantinople!

Off to the Wars

For many, going to war has been a joyous and uplifting business.
Ben Jonson reminds a friend that fighting revives 'Man's buried
honour'. Julian Grenfell, who was to be killed by shrapnel in May
1915, wrote to his mother about his own experience of fighting: 'I
adore war. It is like a big picnic. I have never been so well or so
happy.' Even after five months in the trenches, warfare had kept
for him the air of a knightly adventure; but for most that spirit was
soon to sink beneath the mud of Flanders.

In the American Civil War, Herman Melville sees four regiments
of Union troops marching out of town, 'With fifes, and flags in
mottoed pageantry . . . like the gods sublime.' These same soldiers,
packed into boats on the Potomac river, were attacked by
Confederate forces at Ball's Bluff: pinned against a hundred-foot
cliff, a thousand were killed.

ANONYMOUS

from The Treachery of Asmund

'There is smoke above the hawks in the Hall of the king;
Wax from our sword-points soon will drip.
It is time for the gold, the twinkling gems,
And the helmets to be offered to Half's warriors.

'Awake, Half! All about us
Your grim-minded kin have kindled fires;
Jewels of flame are the gems they offer,
Pleasing presents you must pay back.

'Finish, friends, the foaming ale,
The stout pillars are starting to crack.
Men shall remember while men live
The march of our host to the maker-of-war.

'Go boldly forward nor fall back:
Our foes shall learn to fear our sword-play;
Cruel scars they shall carry hence,
Bloody limbs before the battle ends.

'Brave youths, break through the wall
Of glowing fire with our gallant prince;
No man is allowed to live forever:
The furnisher of rings will not flinch at death.'

Translated from the Old Norse (possibly 10th century)
by W. H. Auden and Paul B. Taylor

BERTRAND DE BORN

A War Song

Well pleaseth me the sweet time of Easter
That maketh the leaf and the flower come out.
And it pleaseth me when I hear the clamor
Of the birds, their song through the wood;
And it pleaseth me when I see through the meadows
The tents and pavilions set up, and great joy have I
When I see o'er the campagna knights armed and horses
    arrayed.

And it pleaseth me when the scouts set in flight the folk with
    their goods;
And it pleaseth me when I see coming together after them an
    host of armed men.
And it pleaseth me to the heart when I see strong castles
    besieged,

And barriers broken and riven, and I see the host on the shore
    all about shut in with ditches,
And closed in with lisses of strong piles.

    Translated from the Provençal by Ezra Pound

BEN JONSON

from An Epistle to a Friend, to perswade him to the Warres

Wake, friend, from forth thy lethargy; the drum
Beats brave and loud in Europe, and bids come
All that dare rouse, or are not loath to quit
Their vicious ease and be o'erwhelmed with it.
It is a call to keep the spirits alive
That gasp for action, and would yet revive
Man's buried honour in his sleepy life,
Quickening dead nature to her noblest strife.
All other acts of worldlings are but toil
In dreams, begun in hope, and end in spoil.

JULIAN GRENFELL

Into Battle

The naked earth is warm with Spring,
    And with green grass and bursting trees
Leans to the sun's gaze glorying,
    And quivers in the sunny breeze;

And Life is Colour and Warmth and Light,
    And a striving evermore for these;
And he is dead who will not fight;
    And who dies fighting has increase.

The fighting man shall from the sun
   Take warmth, and life from the glowing earth;
Speed with the light-foot winds to run,
   And with the trees to newer birth;
And find, when fighting shall be done,
   Great rest, and fullness after dearth.

All the bright company of Heaven
   Hold him in their high comradeship,
The Dog-Star and the Sisters Seven,
   Orion's Belt and sworded hip.

The woodland trees that stand together,
   They stand to him each one a friend;
They gently speak in the windy weather;
   They guide to valley and ridges' end.

The kestrel hovering by day,
   And the little owls that call by night,
Bid him be swift and keen as they,
   As keen of ear, as swift of sight.

The blackbird sings to him, 'Brother, brother,
   'If this be the last song you shall sing
'Sing well, for you may not sing another;
   'Brother, sing.'

In dreary doubtful waiting hours,
   Before the brazen frenzy starts,
The horses show him nobler powers;
   O patient eyes, courageous hearts!

And when the burning moment breaks,
   And all things else are out of mind,
And only Joy-of-Battle takes
   Him by the throat, and makes him blind.

Through joy and blindness he shall know,
   Not caring much to know, that still

Nor lead nor steel shall reach him, so
    That it be not the Destined Will.

The thundering line of battle stands,
    And in the air Death moans and sings;
But Day shall clasp him with strong hand,
    And night shall fold him in soft wings.

W. H. AUDEN

'O what is that sound which so thrills the ear'

O what is that sound which so thrills the ear
    Down in the valley drumming, drumming?
Only the scarlet soldiers, dear,
    The soldiers coming.

O what is that light I see flashing so clear
    Over the distance brightly, brightly?
Only the sun on their weapons, dear,
    As they step lightly.

O what are they doing with all that gear,
    What are they doing this morning, this morning?
Only the usual manœuvres, dear,
    Or perhaps a warning.

O why have they left the road down there,
    Why are they suddenly wheeling, wheeling?
Perhaps a change in the orders, dear.
    Why are you kneeling?

O haven't they stopped for the doctor's care,
    Haven't they reined their horses, their horses?
Why, they are none of them wounded, dear,
    None of these forces.

O is it the parson they want with white hair,
  Is it the parson, is it, is it?
No they are passing his gateway, dear,
  Without a visit.

O it must be the farmer who lives so near.
  It must be the farmer so cunning, so cunning?
They have passed the farm already, dear,
  And now they are running.

O where are you going? stay with me here!
  Were the vows you swore deceiving, deceiving?
No, I promised to love you dear,
  But I must be leaving.

O it's broken the lock and splintered the door,
  O it's the gate where they're turning, turning;
Their feet are heavy on the floor
  And their eyes are burning.

LOUIS ARAGON

The Waltz of the Twenty-Year-Olds

Good for the wind, good for the night, good for the cold
Good for the march and the bullets and the mud
Good for legends, good for the stations of the cross
Good for absence and long evenings. Funny ball
At which I danced and, children, you will dance
To the same dehumanized orchestral score
Good for fear, good for machine guns, good for rats
Good as good bread and good as simple salad

But here is the rising of the conscript sun
The waltz of the twenty-year-olds sweeps over Paris

Good for a shot of brandy at dawn and the anguish before the
    attack
Good for the waiting, the storm and the patrols
Good for night silence under rocket flares
Good for youth passing and the rusting heart
Good for love and death, good to be forgotten
In the rain and shadow cloaking the battlefields
Child soldiers trundled in no other bed
But the ditch already tailored to their measure

The twenty-year-old waltz sweeps through the bistros
And breaks like a laugh at the entrance to the Métro

Army classes of yesterday, vanished dreams
Fourteen, Fifteen, Sixteen: listen. They hum
Like us the trite refrain, like us believe it
And like us in those days, may God forgive them
They value more than their lives a single moment
Of drunkenness, of folly, of delight
What do they know of the world? Does living mean
Quite simply, Mother, to die very young?

Good for this, good for that. My good friends I am leaving
Twenty years old. Good for the armed forces.

Ah, the waltz begins and the dancer buys the same
Eternal trinkets from the Arab peddlers
But this time sings the daughter of Madelon
I have used up forty years. Their twenty are coming close
Boulevard Saint-Germain and Rue Saint-Honoré
With flags in their lapels the class of Forty
Hears the word Good repeated in golden English
I want to believe with them that life is swell

I will forget, I will forget, forget, forget
The waltz of the twenty-year-olds will sweep away
        My forty years in the year 1940.

Translated from the French by Rolf Humphries and Malcolm Cowley

HERMAN MELVILLE

Ball's Bluff

A Reverie

One noonday, at my window in the town,
　I saw a sight – saddest that eyes can see –
　Young soldiers marching lustily
　　　　Unto the wars,
With fifes, and flags in mottoed pageantry;
　　　　While all the porches, walks, and doors
Were rich with ladies cheering royally.

They moved like Juny morning on the wave,
　Their hearts were fresh as clover in its prime
　(It was the breezy summer time),
　　　　Life throbbed so strong,
How should they dream that Death in a rosy clime
　　　　Would come to thin their shining throng?
Youth feels immortal, like the gods sublime.

Weeks passed; and at my window, leaving bed,
　By night I mused, of easeful sleep bereft,
　On those brave boys (Ah War! thy theft);
　　　　Some marching feet
Found pause at last by cliffs Potomac cleft;
　　　　Wakeful I mused, while in the street
Far footfalls died away till none were left.

(October 1861)

A. E. HOUSMAN

'Oh stay at home, my lad, and plough'

Oh stay at home, my lad, and plough
  The land and not the sea,
And leave the soldiers at their drill,
And all about the idle hill
  Shepherd your sheep with me.

Oh stay with company and mirth
  And daylight and the air;
Too full already is the grave
Of fellows that were good and brave
  And died because they were.

Martial Music

From the beginning, armies have marched to the sound of horns, gongs, pipes, trumpets, fifes, cymbals and drums. Musical instruments lift the spirits and sustain the rhythm of an advance. I cannot read of any battle in Scotland's history, or of any engagement in which Scottish regiments played their part, without hearing the skirl of the bagpipes.

Bands still form an important part of the military machine. They are the very heart of ceremonial parades, and today, as in the eighteenth century, they encourage recruitment. The drum is to the Army what the bell is to the Church – both summon the faithful, cheer the spirit and accompany mourning for the dead.

In the 1770s, John Scott blamed the drum's compelling power for much of the suffering of war. He reflected, probably without knowing it, Voltaire's dismissal of 'murderers clothed in scarlet and wearing caps two foot high, who enlist citizens by a noise made with two little sticks on an ass's skin extended'.

JOHN DRYDEN

from A Song for St Cecilia's Day, 1687

The TRUMPETS loud Clangor
   Excites us to Arms
With shrill Notes of Anger
   And mortal Alarms.
The double double double beat
   Of the thundring DRUM
Cryes, heark the Foes come;
Charge, Charge, 'tis too late to retreat.

JOHN MANIFOLD

Fife Tune

(6/8) for 6 Platoon, 308th ITC

One morning in Spring
We marched from Devizes
All shapes and all sizes
Like beads on a string,
But yet with a swing
We trod the bluemetal
And full of high fettle
We started to sing.

She ran down the stair
A twelve-year-old darling
And laughing and calling
She tossed her bright hair;
Then silent to stare
At the men flowing past her –
These were all she could master
Adoring her there.

It's seldom I'll see
A sweeter or prettier;
I doubt we'll forget her
In two years or three,
And lucky he'll be
She takes for a lover
While we are far over
The treacherous sea.

WALTER SCOTT

Pibroch of Donald Dhu

Pibroch of Donuil Dhu,
  Pibroch of Donuil,
Wake thy wild voice anew,
  Summon Clan Conuil.
Come away, come away,
  Hark to the summons!
Come in your war array,
  Gentles and commons.

Come from deep glen, and
  From mountain so rocky,
The war-pipe and pennon
  Are at Inverlocky.
Come every hill-plaid, and
  True heart that wears one,
Come every steel blade, and
  Strong hand that bears one.

Leave untended the herd,
  The flock without shelter;
Leave the corpse uninterr'd,
  The bride at the altar;
Leave the deer, leave the steer,
  Leave nets and barges:
Come with your fighting gear,
  Broadswords and targes.

Come as the winds come, when
  Forests are rended;
Come as the waves come, when
  Navies are stranded:
Faster come, faster come,
  Faster and faster,

Chief, vassal, page and groom,
    Tenant and master.

Fast they come, fast they come;
    See how they gather!
Wide waves the eagle plume,
    Blended with heather.
Cast your plaids, draw your blades,
    Forward each man set!
Pibroch of Donuil Dhu,
    Knell for the onset!

EWART ALAN MACKINTOSH

Cha Till MacCruimein

Departure of the 4th Camerons

The pipes in the streets were playing bravely,
    The marching lads went by,
With merry hearts and voices singing
    My friends marched out to die;
But I was hearing a lonely pibroch
    Out of an older war,
'Farewell, farewell, farewell, MacCrimmon,
    MacCrimmon comes no more.'

And every lad in his heart was dreaming
    Of honour and wealth to come,
And honour and noble pride were calling
    To the tune of the pipes and drum:
But I was hearing a woman singing
    On dark Dunvegan shore,
'In battle or peace, with wealth or honour,
    MacCrimmon comes no more.'

And there in front of the men were marching,
　　With feet that made no mark,
The grey old ghosts of the ancient fighters
　　Come back again from the dark;
And in front of them all MacCrimmon piping
　　A weary tune and sore,
'On the gathering day, for ever and ever,
　　MacCrimmon comes no more.'

WALT WHITMAN

Beat! Beat! Drums!

Beat! beat! drums! – blow! bugles! blow!
Through the windows – through doors – burst like a ruthless
　　　force,
Into the solemn church, and scatter the congregation,
Into the school where the scholar is studying;
Leave not the bridegroom quiet – no happiness must he have
　　　now with his bride,
Nor the peaceful farmer any peace, ploughing his field or
　　　gathering his grain,
So fierce you whirr and pound you drums – so shrill you bugles
　　　blow.

Beat! beat! drums! – blow! bugles! blow!
Over the traffic of cities – over the rumble of wheels in the
　　　streets;
Are beds prepared for sleepers at night in the houses? no
　　　sleepers must sleep in those beds,
No bargainers' bargains by day – no brokers or speculators –
　　　would they continue?
Would the talkers be talking? would the singer attempt to
　　　sing?

Would the lawyer rise in the court to state his case before the
 judge?
Then rattle quicker, heavier drums – you bugles wilder blow.

Beat! beat! drums! – blow! bugles! blow!
Make no parley – stop for no expostulation,
Mind not the timid – mind not the weeper or prayer,
Mind not the old man beseeching the young man,
Let not the child's voice be heard, nor the mother's entreaties,
Make even the trestles to shake the dead where they lie
 awaiting the hearses,
So strong you thump O terrible drums – so loud you bugles
 blow.

JOHN SCOTT

The Drum

I hate that drum's discordant sound,
Parading round, and round, and round:
To thoughtless youth it pleasure yields,
And lures from cities and from fields,
To sell their liberty for charms
Of tawdry lace, and glittering arms;
And when Ambition's voice commands,
To march, and fight, and fall, in foreign lands.

I hate that drum's discordant sound,
Parading round, and round, and round:
To me it talks of ravag'd plains,
And burning towns, and ruin'd swains,
And mangled limbs, and dying groans,
And widows' tears, and orphans' moans;
And all that Misery's hand bestows,
To fill the catalogue of human woes.

ANONYMOUS

The British Grenadiers

Some talk of Alexander, and some of Hercules.
Of Hector and Lysander, and such great names as these;
But of all the world's brave heroes, there's none that can
     compare,
With a tow, row row, row row, row row, to the British
     Grenadier.

Those heroes of antiquity ne'er saw a cannon ball,
Or knew the force of powder to slay their foes withal;
But our brave boys do know it, and banish all their fears,
Sing tow, row row, row row, row row, to the British
     Grenadiers.

Then Jove, the god of thunder, and Mars, the god of war,
Brave Neptune with his trident, Apollo in his car,
And all the gods celestial, descending from their sphere,
Behold with admiration the British Grenadier.

Whene'er we are commanded to storm the palisades;
Our leaders march with fusees, and we with hand-grenades,
We throw them from the glacis, about the Frenchmen's ears,
With a tow, row row, row row, row row, for the British
     Grenadiers.

And when the siege is over, we to the town repair,
The townsmen cry huzza, boys, here comes a grenadier,
Here come the grenadiers, my boys, who know no doubts or
     fears,
Then sing tow, row row, row row, row row, for the British
     Grenadiers.

A New Mistress

The pang of departure, and of leaving behind a wife or a loved one, was most poignantly dramatized by Homer in the scene between Hector, the hero of Troy, and his wife, Andromache. This is the first passage that I have included from Homer's *Iliad*, the greatest poem about war ever written. In choosing passages, I have drawn from several translations, and the extract here is by George Chapman who published his version in 1611.

Gentleman Johnny Burgoyne was in the cavalier tradition of Richard Lovelace and William Davenant, but unlike other poets he actually led a British army – unfortunately to one of its most humiliating surrenders, to the American colonial forces at Saratoga Springs in 1777. There was nothing dashing about that.

RICHARD LOVELACE

To Lucasta, Going to the Wars

Tell me not, Sweet, I am unkind,
   That from the nunnery
Of thy chaste breast and quiet mind
   To war and arms I fly.

True, a new mistress now I chase,
   The first foe in the field;
And with a stronger faith embrace
   A sword, a horse, a shield.

Yet this inconstancy is such
   As thou too shalt adore;
I could not love thee, Dear, so much,
   Loved I not Honour more.

WILLIAM DAVENANT

The Soldier Going to the Field

Preserve thy sighs, unthrifty girl,
  To purify the air;
Thy tears to thread instead of pearl
  On bracelets of thy hair.

The trumpet makes the echo hoarse
  And wakes the louder drum;
Expense of grief gains no remorse
  When sorrow should be dumb.

For I must go where lazy Peace
  Will hide her drowsy head,
And, for the sport of Kings, increase
  The number of the dead.

But first I'll chide thy cruel theft:
  Can I in war delight,
Who being of my heart bereft
  Can have no heart to fight?

Thou know'st the sacred Laws of old
  Ordained a thief should pay,
To quit him of his theft, sevenfold
  What he had stolen away.

Thy payment shall but double be;
  O then with speed resign
My own seducèd heart to me,
  Accompanied with thine.

JOHN BURGOYNE

The Dashing White Sergeant

If I had a beau
For a soldier who'd go,
Do you think I'd say no?
    No, no, not I!
When his red coat I saw,
Not a tear would it draw,
But I'd give him eclat
    For his bravery!
If an army of Amazons e'er came in play,
As a dashing white sergeant I'd march away.

When my soldier is gone,
Do you think I'd take on,
Or sit moping forlorn?
    No, no, not I!
His fame my concern,
How my bosom would burn,
When I saw him return
    Crown'd with victory!
If an army of Amazons e'er came in play,
As a dashing white sergeant I'd march away.

ROBERT BURNS

A Soldier's Farewell

Go fetch to me a pint of wine,
    And fill it in a silver tassie;
That I may drink before I go
    A service to my bonnie lassie:

The boat rocks at the pier of Leith,
    Fu' loud the wind blaws frae the Ferry,
The ship rides by the Berwick-law,
    And I maun leave my bonnie Mary.

The trumpets sound, the banners fly,
    The glittering spears are rankèd ready;
The shouts o' war are heard afar,
    The battle closes thick and bloody;
But it's not the roar of sea or shore
    Wad make me langer wish to tarry;
Nor shouts of war that's heard afar –
    It's leaving thee, my bonnie Mary.

RAINER MARIA RILKE

The Last Evening

Night and the distant rumbling; for the train
of the whole army passed by the estate.
But still he raised his eyes and played again
the clavichord and gazed at her . . . and waited

almost like a man looking in a mirror
which was completely filled with his young face,
knowing how his features bore his sorrow,
more beautifully seductive with the grace

of music. The scene faded out. Instead,
wearily at the window, in her trouble,
she held the violent thumping of her heart.

He finished. The dawn wind was blowing hard.
And strangely alien on the mirror table
stood the black shako with its white death's-head.

Translated from the German by C. F. MacIntyre

ANONYMOUS

Goll Mac Morna Parts from His Wife

Goll: Take my tunic, woman.
    Rise up, and leave me here.
    Leave me — red-cheeked and pure —
    now before I am killed.

Wife: Goll, where can I go?
    I have few friends, alas.
    What luck has any lady
    without her head and lord?

Goll: Find Finn's camp, and the Fian,
    here in the Westward quarter.
    Lie there — red-lipped and sweet —
    with some fine fitting man.

Wife: What man should I lie with there,
    great Goll who have guarded me?
    West or east where will I find
    one for my bed like you?

Goll: Take Finn's son Oisín,
    or Aonghus, Aodh Rinn's son,
    or handsome blood-stained Cairell,
    or fleet-foot Corr the hundred-killer.

Wife: And my father Conall of Cruachan!
    I, fostered with Conn of the Hundred Battles!
    With Céidghein, Conall Red-Hand's son,
    in the north land for my brother!

    It is harder now to leave
    my chosen cheerful man
    now that seven brave years have passed
    since you took me to bed, my husband.

From that night until this
you were not hard-hearted ever.
And from this night I will take
ease with no man on earth.

Thirty days without food, alive
– was there ever your like before?
A hundred heroes, Goll, by your hand
fell on the narrow rock.

Goll: Wide is the ocean round us
and I on a narrow rock.
By hunger I am beaten,
by thirst I am undone.

And though it is hunger beats me,
though fierce this war of five battalions
my cheeks are faded more
through drinking the bitter brine.

If one of the Fian slew
my nine and twenty brothers
I would make my peace with him
if it eased my thirst one night!

Wife: Goll Mac Morna from Maon Plain
eat one of those corpses near you.
After that meat I will ease your thirst:
you can drink the milk from my breasts.

Goll: Conall's daughter, I will tell no lie,
it is wretched the tale turned out.
But I never followed, north or south,
woman's counsel, and never will.

Wife: Goll, it was a cruel case:
five battalions or six against you
and you in an angle of hard rock
high and bare and cold.

Goll: My only fear on land or wave
      (red mouth that were once so sweet)
      was Finn and his Fian in pursuit
      and I starved in a narrow crack.

      I reddened my spears rightly
      in the bodies of Tréanmór's tribe!
      Trouble and strife I gave them.
      I killed Cumhall of the mighty shaft!

      Munster's men I brought to grief
      that Tuesday on Léan Plain.
      I waged a lovely war
      that morning on Eanach Plain!

      Eochaidh Red-Limb, son of Mál,
      proud-faced High King of Ulster
      – I mixed my spear in that hero!
      I brought him to grief, woman!

    Translated from the Irish (10th or 11th century) by Thomas Kinsella

HOMER

from The Iliad, Book VI

      To this, great Hector said:
'Be well assured, wife, all these things in my kind cares are
    weighed.
But what a shame, and fear, it is to think how Troy would
    scorn
(Both in her husbands and her wives, whom long-train'd
    gowns adorn)
That I should cowardly fly off! The spirit I first did breath
Did never teach me that; much less, since the contempt of
    death
Was settled in me, and my mind knew what a worthy was

Whose office is to lead in fight, and give no danger pass
Without improvement. In this fire must Hector's trial shine;
Here must his country, father, friends, be, in him, made divine.
And such a stormy day shall come (in mind and soul I know)
When sacred Troy shall shed her tow'rs for tears of overthrow,
When Priam, all his birth and pow'r, shall in those tears be
    drown'd.
But neither Troy's posterity so much my soul doth wound,
Priam, nor Hecuba herself, nor all my brothers' woes,
(Who though so many, and so good, must all be food for foes)
As thy sad state, when some rude Greek shall lead thee
    weeping hence,
These free days clouded, and a night of captive violence
Loading thy temples, out of which thine eyes must never see,
But spin the Greek wives' webs of task, and their fetch-water
    be
To Argos, from Messeides, or clear Hyperia's spring;
Which howsoever thou abhorr'st, Fate's such a shrewish thing
She will be mistress; whose curs'd hands, when they shall
    crush out cries
From thy oppressions (being beheld by other enemies)
Thus they will nourish thy extremes: "This dame was Hector's
    wife,
A man that, at the wars of Troy, did breathe the worthiest life
Of all their army." This again will rub thy fruitful wounds,
To miss the man that to thy bands could give such narrow
    bounds.
But that day shall not wound mine eyes; the solid heap of night
Shall interpose, and stop mine ears against thy plaints, and
    plight.'
    This said, he reach'd to take his son, who, of his arms afraid,
And then the horse-hair plume, with which he was so overlaid,
Nodded so horribly, he cling'd back to his nurse, and cried.
Laughter affected his great sire, who doff'd, and laid aside,
His fearful helm, that on the earth cast round about it light,
Then took and kiss'd his loving son, and (balancing his weight

In dancing him) these loving vows to living Jove he us'd,
And all the other bench of Gods: 'O you that have infus'd
Soul to this infant, now set down this blessing on his star; —
Let his renown be clear as mine; equal his strength in war;
And make his reign so strong in Troy, that years to come may
    yield
His facts this fame, when, rich in spoils, he leaves the
    conquer'd field
Sown with his slaughters: "These high deeds exceed his
    father's worth."
And let this echo'd praise supply the comforts to come forth
Of his kind mother with my life.' This said, th' heroic sire
Gave him his mother, whose fair eyes fresh streams of love's
    salt fire
Billow'd on her soft cheeks, to hear the last of Hector's
    speech,
In which his vows compris'd the sum of all he did beseech
In her wish'd comfort. So she took into her odorous breast
Her husband's gift; who, mov'd to see her heart so much
    oppress'd,
He dried her tears, and thus desir'd: 'Afflict me not, dear wife,
With these vain griefs. He doth not live that can disjoin my life
And this firm bosom, but my fate; and fate, whose wings can
    fly?
Noble, ignoble, fate controls. Once born, the best must die.
Go home, and set thy housewifery on these extremes of
    thought;
And drive war from them with thy maids; keep them from
    doing nought;
These will be nothing; leave the cares of war to men, and me
In whom of all the Ilion race they take their high'st degree.'
    On went his helm; his princess home, half cold with kindly
       fears,
When every fear turn'd back her looks, and every look shed
    tears.

Translated from the Greek by George Chapman

THOMAS HARDY

The Colonel's Soliloquy

Southampton Docks, October 1899

'The quay recedes. Hurrah! Ahead we go! . . .
It's true I've been accustomed now to home,
And joints get rusty, and one's limbs may grow
          More fit to rest than roam.

'But I can stand as yet fair stress and strain;
There's not a little steel beneath the rust;
My years mount somewhat, but here's to't again!
          And if I fall, I must.

'God knows that for myself I have scanty care;
Past scrimmages have proved as much to all;
In Eastern lands and South I have had my share
          Both of the blade and ball.

'And where those villains ripped me in the flitch
With their old iron in my early time,
I'm apt at change of wind to feel a twitch,
          Or at a change of clime.

'And what my mirror shows me in the morning
Has more of blotch and wrinkle than of bloom;
My eyes, too, heretofore all glasses scorning,
          Have just a touch of rheum. . . .

'Now sounds "The Girl I've left behind me", – Ah,
The years, the ardours, wakened by that tune!
Time was when, with the crowd's farewell "Hurrah!"
          'Twould lift me to the moon.

'But now it's late to leave behind me one
Who if, poor soul, her man goes underground,

Will not recover as she might have done
          In days when hopes abound.

'She's waving from the wharfside, palely grieving,
As down we draw. . . . Her tears make little show,
Yet now she suffers more than at my leaving
          Some twenty years ago!

'I pray those left at home will care for her;
I shall come back; I have before; though when
The Girl you leave behind you is a grandmother,
          Things may not be as then.'

ANNE RIDLER

At Parting

Since we through war awhile must part
Sweetheart, and learn to lose
Daily use
Of all that satisfied our heart:
Lay up those secrets and those powers
Wherewith you pleased and cherished me these two years:

Now we must draw, as plants would,
On tubers stored in a better season,
Our honey and heaven;
Only our love can store such food.
Is this to make a god of absence?
A new-born monster to steal our sustenance?

We cannot quite cast out lack and pain.
Let him remain – what he may devour
We can well spare:
He never can tap this, the true vein.
I have no words to tell you what you were,
But when you are sad, think, Heaven could give no more.

The Women Left Behind

Women are the first casualties of war. Penelope, the wife of Ulysses and archetype of the warrior's patient consort, the woman left behind, waited twenty years for her husband to return from the Trojan Wars. She fended off suitors by saying that she would not consider their advances until she had finished weaving a shroud. Each night, she unpicked the work she had done during the day so that it was never finished. As Dorothy Parker acidly says, for this, 'They will call him brave'.

Lysistrata, in Aristophanes' play, adopted a rather more practical line. She urged her friends to deny their husbands and lovers any sexual pleasure until they stopped fighting – a forlorn hope.

Many women left behind have often been recruited to help in the war effort. In the First World War, one in three munitions workers in Britain was a woman, which certainly contributed to their getting the vote in 1919. When Churchill became Prime Minister in 1940, only one in twelve munitions workers was a woman, because the trade unions wanted to keep up men's jobs. But the shortage of munitions was so great that many more women had to be recruited.

ARISTOPHANES

from Lysistrata

Magistrate: You, I presume, could adroitly and gingerly
settle this intricate, tangled concern:
You in a trice could relieve our perplexities.
Lysistrata: Certainly.
Magistrate: How? Permit me to learn.
Lysistrata: Just as a woman, with nimble dexterity,
thus with her hands disentangles a skein,

Hither and thither her spindles unravel it,
  drawing it out, and pulling it plain.
So would this weary Hellenic entanglement
  soon be resolved by our womanly care,
So would our embassies neatly unravel it,
  drawing it here and pulling it there.
  Magistrate: Wonderful, marvellous feats, not a doubt of it,
  you with your skeins and your spindles can show:
Fools! do you really expect to unravel a
  terrible war like a bundle of tow?
  Lysistrata: Ah, if you only could manage your politics
  just in the way that we deal with a fleece!
  Magistrate: Tell us the recipe.
  Lysistrata: First, in the washing-tub
  plunge it, and scour it, and cleanse it from grease,
Purging away all the filth and the nastiness;
  then on the table expand it and lay,
Beating out all that is worthless and mischievous,
  picking the burrs and the thistles away.
Next, for the clubs, the cabals, and the coteries,
  banding unrighteously, office to win,
Treat them as clots in the wool, and dissever them,
  lopping the heads that are forming therein.
Then you should card it, and comb it, and mingle it,
  all in one basket of love and of unity,
Citizens, visitors, strangers, and sojourners,
  all the entire, undivided community.
Know you a fellow in debt to the Treasury?
  Mingle him merrily in with the rest.
Also remember the cities, our colonies,
  outlying states in the east and the west,
Scattered about to a distance surrounding us,
  these are our shreds and our fragments of wool;
These to one mighty political aggregate
  tenderly, carefully, gather and pull,
Twining them all in one thread of good fellowship;

thence a magnificent bobbin to spin,
Weaving a garment of comfort and dignity,
   worthily wrapping the People therein.
   Magistrate: Heard any ever the like of their impudence,
   those who have nothing to do with the war,
Preaching of bobbins, and beatings, and washing-tubs?
   Lysistrata: Nothing to do with it, wretch that you are!
We are the people who feel it the keenliest,
   doubly on us the affliction is cast;
Where are the sons that we sent to your battlefields?
   Magistrate: Silence! a truce to the ills that are past.
   Lysistrata: Then in the glory and grace of our woman-
     hood,
   all in the may and the morning of life,
Lo, we are sitting forlorn and disconsolate,
   what has a soldier to do with a wife?
We might endure it, but ah! for the younger ones,
   still in their maiden apartments they stay,
Waiting the husband that never approaches them,
   watching the years that are gliding away.
   Magistrate: Men, I suppose, have their youth everlast-
     ingly.
   Lysistrata: Nay, but it isn't the same with a man:
Grey though he be when he comes from the battlefield,
   still if he wishes to marry, he can.
Brief is the spring and the flower of our womanhood,
   once let it slip, and it comes not again;
Sit as we may with our spells and our auguries,
   never a husband will marry us then.

Translated from the Greek by B. B. Rogers

DOROTHY PARKER

Penelope

In the pathway of the sun,
  In the footsteps of the breeze,
Where the world and sky are one,
  He shall ride the silver seas,
    He shall cut the glittering wave.
I shall sit at home, and rock;
Rise, to heed a neighbour's knock;
Brew my tea, and snip my thread;
Bleach the linen for my bed.
    They will call him brave.

JOHN BETJEMAN

In Westminster Abbey

Let me take this other glove off
  As the *vox humana* swells,
And the beauteous fields of Eden
  Bask beneath the Abbey bells.
Here, where England's statesmen lie,
Listen to a lady's cry.

Gracious Lord, oh bomb the Germans.
  Spare their women for Thy Sake.
And if that is not too easy
  We will pardon Thy Mistake.
But, gracious Lord, whate'er shall be,
Don't let anyone bomb me.

Keep our Empire undismembered
  Guide our Forces by Thy Hand,

Gallant blacks from far Jamaica,
    Honduras and Togoland;
Protect them Lord in all their fights,
And, even more, protect the whites.

Think of what our Nation stands for,
    Books from Boots' and country lanes,
Free speech, free passes, class distinction,
    Democracy and proper drains.
Lord, put beneath Thy special care
One-eighty-nine Cadogan Square.

Although dear Lord I am a sinner,
    I have done no major crime;
Now I'll come to Evening Service
    Whensoever I have the time.
So, Lord, reserve for me a crown;
And do not let my shares go down.

I will labour for Thy Kingdom,
    Help our lads to win the war,
Send white feathers to the cowards
    Join the Women's Army Corps,
Then wash the Steps around Thy Throne
In the Eternal Safety Zone.

Now I feel a little better,
    What a treat to hear Thy Word,
Where the bones of leading statesmen,
    Have so often been interr'd.
And now, dear Lord, I cannot wait
Because I have a luncheon date.

MADELINE IDA BEDFORD

Munition Wages

Earning high wages? Yus,
　　Five quid a week.
A woman, too, mind you,
　　I calls it dim sweet.

Ye'are asking some questions –
　　But bless yer, here goes:
I spends the whole racket
　　On good times and clothes.

Me saving? Elijah!
　　Yer do think I'm mad.
I'm acting the lady,
　　But – I ain't living bad.

I'm having life's good times.
　　See 'ere, it's like this:
The 'oof come o' danger,
　　A touch-and-go bizz.

We're all here today, mate,
　　Tomorrow – perhaps dead,
If Fate tumbles on us
　　And blows up our shed.

Afraid! Are yer kidding?
　　With money to spend!
Years back I wore tatters,
　　Now – silk stockings, mi friend!

I've bracelets and jewellery,
　　Rings envied by friends;
A sergeant to swank with,
　　And something to lend.

I drive out in taxis,
  Do theatres in style,
And this is mi verdict –
  It is jolly worth while.

Worth while, for tomorrow
  If I'm blown to the sky,
I'll have repaid mi wages
  In death – and pass by.

ANONYMOUS

Far Away

Around her leg she wore a purple garter,
  She wore it in the springtime and in the month of May.
And if you asked her why the hell she wore it,
  She wore it for an airman who is far, far away.

Chorus: Far away, far away, far away, far away,
        She wore it for an airman who is far, far away.

Around the block she pushed a baby carriage,
  She pushed it in the springtime and in the month of May,
And if you asked her why the hell she pushed it,
  She pushed it for an airman who is far, far away.

        Far away, far away, far away, far away,
        She pushed it for an airman who is far, far away.

Behind the door her father kept a shotgun,
  He kept it in the springtime and in the month of May,
And if you asked him why the hell he kept it,
  He kept it for an airman who is far, far away.

        Far away, far away, far away, far away,
        He kept it for an airman who is far, far away.

Upon his grave she placed a bunch of flowers,
    She placed it in the springtime and in the month of May,
And if you asked her why the hell she placed it,
    She placed it for an airman who is *six feet down*.

        Six feet down, six feet down, six feet down, six feet
            down,
        She placed it for an airman who is six feet down.

KEITH DOUGLAS

Vergissmeinicht

Three weeks gone and the combatants gone,
returning over the nightmare ground
we found the place again, and found
the soldier sprawling in the sun.

The frowning barrel of his gun
overshadowing. As we came on
that day, he hit my tank with one
like the entry of a demon.

Look. Here in the gunpit spoil
the dishonoured picture of his girl
who has put: *Steffi. Vergissmeinicht*
in a copybook gothic script.

We see him almost with content
abased, and seeming to have paid
and mocked at by his own equipment
that's hard and good when he's decayed.

But she would weep to see today
how on his skin the swart flies move;
the dust upon the paper eye
and the burst stomach like a cave.

For here the lover and killer are mingled
who had one body and one heart.
And death who had the soldier singled
has done the lover mortal hurt.

Recruiting

Most wars start with armies of volunteers and end with armies of conscripts. In 1914 Kitchener's face and thrusting finger graced the most famous poster of the day, with its caption, 'Your country needs you'. By the end of 1914 1.1 million men had volunteered to join up, but just two years later conscription had to be introduced. Throughout history, the recruiting sergeant was never a popular visitor.

WILLIAM GIFFORD

from A Posie of Gilliflowers

Ye buds of Brutus' land, courageous youths, now play your
    parts!
Unto your tackle stand! Abide the brunt with valiant hearts!
For news is carried to and fro, that we must forth to warfare
    go:
Men muster now in every place, and soldiers are pressed forth
    apace.
Faint not, spend blood, to do your Queen and country good!
Fair words, good pay, will make men cast all care away.

The time of war is come: prepare your corslet, spear, and
    shield!
Methinks I hear the drum strike doleful marches to the field;
Tantarà! tantarà! the trumpets sound, which makes our hearts
    with joy abound.
The roaring guns are heard afar, and every thing denounceth
    war.
Serve God! Stand stout! Bold courage brings this gear about.
Fear not! Forth run! Faint heart fair lady never won.

Ye curious carpet knights, that spend the time in sport and
    play,
Abroad, and see new sights! your country's cause calls you
    away;
Do not, to make your ladies' game, bring blemish to your
    worthy name!
Away to field and win renown, with courage beat your
    enemies down!
Stout hearts gain praise, when dastards sail in Slander's seas.
Hap what hap shall, we sure shall die but once for all.

Alarm methinks they cry. Be packing, mates, be gone with
    speed!
Our foes are very nigh; shame have that man that shrinks at
    need!
Unto it boldly let us stand, God will give right the upper hand.
Our cause is good, we need not doubt. In sign of courage give a
    shout!
March forth! Be strong! Good hap will come ere it be long.
Shrink not! Fight well! For lusty lads must bear the bell.

All you that will shun evil, must dwell in warfare every day;
The world, the flesh, and devil, always do seek our souls'
    decay,
Strive with these foes with all your might, so shall you fight a
    worthy fight.
That conquest doth deserve most praise, where vice do yield to
    virtue's ways.
Beat down foul sin, a worthy crown then shall ye win:
If we live well, in heaven with Christ our souls shall dwell.

ANONYMOUS

Over the Hills and Far Away

Hark, now the drums beat up again,
For all true soldier gentlemen,
Then let us 'list and march, I say,
Over the hills and far away.
Over the hills and o'er the main,
To Flanders, Portugal and Spain,
Queen Anne commands and we'll obey,
Over the hills and far away.

R. H. ELLIS

from Ode to St Crispin's Day

Walk up, walk up, my bonny boys,
    Walk up and join the British Army!
O hear th' enlisting Sergeant's voice –
Admire the language he employs –
O make the manly, only choice
    (Keep out, unless you're barmy).

Walk up, you young gregarious fools
    With Territorial ambitions –
Black-coated owls from office stools –
Smart types from almost-Public Schools
Whose origin or accent rules
    You out for Regular commissions –

Young gents who in an OTC
    Learned to regard yourselves as leaders –
O let them all report to me,
And get fell in, in ranks of three.

I'll give them bloody morning tea,
  I'll train the little bleeders.

Walk up, old grizzled bloodshot men,
  Survivors of trench, wire and mud –
Never shall that occur again!
We've learnt a thing or two since then.
Town majors lie in bed till ten,
  No need to spill your cooling blood.

Each in his democratic way
  Must start as Subaltern or Private,
Yet e'er the last great Victory Day
Shall dawn in glory, who can say
(Provided you have cards to play)
  What dizzy rank you may arrive at?

Our Way of Life may be at stake,
  But Values still, thank God, are Stable.
On Higher Things our stand we take.
His father's gods who dare foresake?
Our Bough shall never, never break –
  To arms! Defend your cradle!

ANONYMOUS

Arthur McBride

I once knew a fellow named Arthur McBride,
And he and I rambled down by the sea-side,
A-looking for pleasure or what might betide,
And the weather was pleasant and charming.

So gaily and gallant we went on our tramp,
And we met Sergeant Harper and Corporal Cramp,
And the little wee fellow who roused up the camp
With his row-de-dow-dow in the morning.

Good morning, young fellows, the sergeant he cried.
And the same to you, sergeant, was all our reply.
There was nothing more spoken, we made to pass by,
And continue our walk in the morning.

Well now, my fine fellows, if you will enlist,
A guinea in gold I will slap in your fist,
And a crown in the bargain to kick up the dust
And drink the Queen's health in the morning.

Oh no, mister sergeant, we aren't for sale,
We'll make no such bargain, and your bribe won't avail.
We're not tired of our country, and don't care to sail,
Though your offer is pleasant and charming.

If we were such fools as to take your advance,
It's right bloody slender would be our poor chance,
For the Queen wouldn't scruple to send us to France
And get us all shot in the morning.

Ha now, you young blackguards, if you say one more word,
I swear by the herrins, I'll draw out my sword
And run through your bodies as my strength may afford.
So now, you young buggers, take warning.

Well, we beat that bold drummer as flat as a shoe,
And we make a football of his row-de-dow-do,
And as for the others we knocked out the two.
Oh, we were the boys in that morning.

We took the old weapons that hung by their side
And flung them as far as we could in the tide.
May the devil go with you, says Arthur McBride,
For delaying our walk this fine morning.

SYLVIA TOWNSEND WARNER

'Become as little children'

Become as little children,
Said the Recruiting Sergeant;
With every hope as frantic,
With every fear as urgent.
Be seen and not heard
While the cannon volley
As sleep when you are bid
By Death, your tall Nannie.

ANONYMOUS

I Don't Want to Be a Soldier

I don't want to be a soldier,
I don't want to go to war.
I'd sooner hang around
Piccadilly underground,
Living on the earnings of a high-born lady.

Don't want a bullet up me arsehole,
Don't want me bollocks shot away.
I'd rather live in England,
In merry, merry England,
And fornicate me fucking life away.

Impressment and Conscription

Press-gangs were disliked, feared and sometimes attacked. The *Journal of the Admiralty* recorded that, in January 1674, 'About one hundred seamen in a body did, in a mutinous manner, march with a black flag before through the City of London as far as Guildhall, assaulting all pressed mariners and rescuing oppressed men.' Press-gangs were not officially used in Britain after 1815.

Throughout the eighteenth century, the country was embroiled in wars on the continent. In the War of the Austrian Succession in the 1740s, Britain supported Maria-Theresa of Austria against France and Prussia. In this cause, and to defend his Hanoverian possessions in 'High Germany', George II assembled and led a largely conscript army of over 40,000 which won a great victory at Dettingen in 1743.

Elizabeth Barrett Browning's 'Forced Recruit' had to fight in the bitter war between Austria and the kingdom of Italy. The Battle of Solferino, in 1859, resulted in such appalling casualties that it prompted the foundation of the International Red Cross.

'Taking the King's shilling' was the phrase for joining up. When I was summoned, like Christopher Logue, to do National Service in 1953, I received a postal order for one week's pay, 28 shillings – 4 shillings a day – the first money I had ever 'earned'.

ANONYMOUS

High Germany

'Oh Polly love, Oh Polly, the rout has now begun,
And we must march along by the beating of the drum;
Go dress yourself all in your best, and come along with me,
I'll take you to the war that's in High Germany.'

'O Harry, O Harry, you mind what I do say,
My feet they are so tender I cannot march away;
And, besides, my dearest Harry, I am with child by thee,
I'm not fitted for the cruel wars in High Germany.'

'I'll buy a horse, my love, and on it you shall ride,
And all my delight shall be riding by your side;
We'll call at every ale-house, and drink when we are dry,
So quickly on the road, my boys, we'll marry by and by.'

'O curséd were the cruel wars that ever they should rise!
And out of merry England pressed many a lad likewise;
They pressed young Harry from me, likewise my brothers
    three,
And sent them to the cruel wars in High Germany.'

ANONYMOUS

'Oh cruel was the press-gang'

Oh cruel was the press-gang
  That took my love from me.
Oh cruel was the little ship
  That took him out to sea.

And cruel was the splinter-board
  That took away his leg.
Now he is forced to fiddle-scrape,
  And I am forced to beg.

ELIZABETH BARRETT BROWNING

The Forced Recruit

Solferino, 1859

In the ranks of the Austrian you found him,
  He died with his face to you all;
Yet bury him here where around him
  You honour your bravest that fall.

Venetian, fair-featured and slender,
  He lies shot to death in his youth,
With a smile on his lips over-tender
  For any mere soldier's dead mouth.

No stranger, and yet not a traitor,
  Though alien the cloth on his breast,
Underneath it how seldom a greater
  Young heart has a shot sent to rest!

By your enemy tortured and goaded
  To march with them, stand in their file,
His musket (see) never was loaded,
  He facing your guns with that smile!

As orphans yearn on to their mothers,
  He yearned to your patriot bands; —
Let me die for our Italy, brothers,
  If not in your ranks, by your hands!

'Aim straightly, fire steadily! spare me
  A ball in the body which may
Deliver my heart here, and tear me
  This badge of the Austrian away!'

So thought he, so died he this morning.
  What then? Many others have died.

Ay, but easy for men to die scorning
    The death-stroke, who fought side by side –

One tricolor floating above them;
    Struck down 'mid triumphant acclaims
Of an Italy rescued to love them
    And blazen the brass with their names.

But he, – without witness or honour,
    Mixed, shamed in his country's regard,
With the tyrants who march in upon her,
    Died faithful and passive: 'twas hard.

'Twas sublime. In a cruel restriction
    Cut off from the guerdon of sons,
With most filial obedience, conviction,
    His soul kissed the lips of her guns.

That moves you? Nay, grudge not to show it,
    While digging a grave for him here:
The others who died, says your poet,
    Have glory, – let *him* have a tear.

CHRISTOPHER LOGUE

The Song of the Dead Soldier

For seven years at school I named
    Our kings, their wars – if these were won –
A boy trained simple as we come,
    I read of an island in the sun,
    Where the Queen of Love was born.

At seventeen the postman brought,
    Into the room – my place of birth –
Some correspondence from the Crown,
    Demanding that with guns I earn,
    The modern shilling I was worth.

Lucky for me that I could read,
  Lucky for me our captain said,
You'll see the world for free my son,
  You're posted to an island John,
  Where the Queen of Love was born.

So twenty weeks went by and by,
  My back was straightened out my eye
Dead true as any button shone,
  And nine white-bellied porpoise led,
  Our ship of shillings through the sun.

We landed with our drums and clad
  In war suits worth ten well-taxed pounds –
The costliest I ever had –
  Our foreign shoulders crossed the town,
  The Queen of Love our coloured flag.

And three by three through our curfew,
  Mother we marched like black and tan,
Singing to match our captain's cheers,
  Then I drank my eyes out of my head
  And wet Her shilling with my fears.

When morning came our captain bold
  Said the island shaped like an ass' skin
Must be kept calm, must be patrolled,
  For outposts are the heart and soul
  Of empire, love, and lawful rule.

I did not know to serve meant kill,
  And I did not see the captain fall,
As my life went out through a bullet hole,
  Mother, I said, your womb is done,
  Did they spend your English shilling well?

And then I saw a hag whose eyes
  Were big as medals and grey as lead,
I called my rifle but it was dead,

Our captain roared but my ears went dud,
The hag kissed warm, we met in blood.

English shilling – Queen of Love.

Mercenaries

The trade of the mercenary soldier is a far cry from Horace's noble calling. For obvious reasons, mercenaries have tended to be either mocked or despised by poets. The only poem that I have found which attempts to put the case for them is the one by Housman, and this elicited a sharp riposte from Hugh MacDiarmid. But throughout history mercenaries have been needed and their business flourishes today.

As early as 341 BC, Demosthenes, in his third *Philippic*, urged the Greeks: 'Cease to hire your armies. Go yourself, every man of you, and stand in the ranks.'

BEN JONSON

To Captain Hungry

Do what you come for, Captain, with your news,
    That's sit and eat; do not my ears abuse.
I oft look on false coin, to know't from true:
    Not that I love it more than I will you.
Tell the gross Dutch those grosser tales of yours,
    How great you were with their two emperors,
And yet are with their princes; fill them full
    Of your Moravian horse, Venetian bull.
Tell them what parts you've ta'en, whence run away,
    What states you've gulled, and which yet keeps you in pay.
Give them your services and embassies
    In Ireland, Holland, Sweden (pompous lies),
In Hungary and Poland, Turkey too;
    What at Leghorn, Rome, Florence you did do;
And, in some year, all these together heaped,
    For which there must more sea and land be leaped

– If but to be believed you have the hap –
   Than can a flea at twice skip in the map.
Give your young statesmen (that first make you drunk
   And then lie with you, closer than a punk,
For news) your Villeroys and Silleries,
   Janins, your nuncios and your Tuileries,
Your archduke's agents and your Beringhams,
   That are your words of credit. Keep your names
Of Hannow, Shieter-huissen, Popenheim,
   Hans-spiegle, Rotteinberg and Boutersheim
For your next meal: this you are sure of. Why
   Will you part with them here, unthriftily?
Nay, now you puff, tusk, and draw up your chin,
   Twirl the poor chain you run a-feasting in.
Come, be not angry, you are Hungry: eat;
   Do what you come for, Captain: there's your meat.

ANONYMOUS

from The Mercenary Soldier

I

No money yet, why then let's pawn our swords,
And drink an health to their confusion
Who do instead of money send us words.
Let's not be subject to the vain delusion
   Of those would have us fight without our pay;
   While money chinks, my Captain I'll obey.

II

I'll not be slave to any servile Groom,
Let's to the Sutlers and there drink and sing.
My Captain for a while shall have my room,
Come hither, Tom, of Ale two dozen bring,

Plac'd Ranke and File, Tobacco bring us store,
And as the Pots do empty, fill us more.

III

Let the Drum cease, and never murmur more,
Until it beat, warning us to repair
Each man for to receive of Cash good store,
Let not the Trumpet shrill, or rend the air
    Until it cites us to the place where we
    May heaps of silver for our payment see.

IV

I come not forth to do my Country good,
I come to rob, and take my fill of pleasure,
Let fools repel their foes with angry mood,
Let those do service while I share the treasure:
    I do not mean my body e'er shall swing
    Between a pair of crutches, tottering.

V

Let thousands fall, it ne'er shall trouble me,
Those pulling fools deserve no better fate,
They mirth's Opposers were, and still would be,
Did they survive. Let me participate
    Of pleasures, gifts, while here I live, and I
    Care not, although I mourn eternally.

VI

I laugh to think how many times I have
Whiles others fighting were against the foe,
Within some Thicket croucht myself to save,
Yet taken for a valiant Soldier though,
    When I amongst them come, for I with words,
    Can terrify, as others can with swords.

A. E. HOUSMAN

Epitaph on an Army of Mercenaries

These, in the day when heaven was falling,
    The hour when earth's foundations fled,
Followed their mercenary calling
    And took their wages and are dead.

Their shoulders held the sky suspended;
    They stood, and earth's foundations stay;
What God abandoned, these defended,
    And saved the sum of things for pay.

HUGH MACDIARMID

Another Epitaph on an Army of Mercenaries

It is a God-damned lie to say that these
Saved, or knew, anything worth any man's pride,
They were professional murderers and they took
Their blood money and impious risks and died.
In spite of all their kind some elements of worth
With difficulty persist here and there on earth.

The Training of Conscripts

The thoroughness of the training given by non-commissioned officers is the foundation on which the success of the British Army rests. The Drill Sergeant yelling 'Get fell in, you dozy lot!' is something which every National Serviceman – myself included – will remember till his dying day. The endless square-bashing, presentation of arms, weapon-stripping and cleaning, and range practice, to which we were subjected, were all part of the routine of repetition which turned the most unpromising material into a fighting man.

Eventually, we all had to do bayonet training, to equip us for the modern style of hand-to-hand fighting. For this, you were expected to scream at the man you were about to kill and look him straight in the eyes as you plunged your bayonet in. Many myths have been created concerning the bayonet, but in actual warfare few casualties are inflicted by it. In the First World War, shells and mortar bombs accounted for 58.7 per cent of British casualties, bullets 39 per cent, grenades 2 per cent and bayonets 0.3 per cent.

VERNON SCANNELL

Bayonet Training

From far away, a mile or so,
The wooden scaffolds could be seen
    On which fat felons swung;
But closer view showed these to be
Sacks, corpulent with straw and tied
    To beams from which they hung.

The sergeant halted his platoon.
'Right lads,' he barked, 'you see them sacks?
    I want you to forget

That sacks is what they are and act
As if they was all Jerries – wait!
 Don't move a muscle yet!

'I'm going to show you how to use
The bayonet as it should be done.
 If any of you feel
Squeamish like, I'll tell you this:
There's one thing Jerry just can't face
 And that thing is cold steel.

'So if we're going to win this war
You've got to understand you must
 Be brutal, ruthless, tough.
I want to hear you scream for blood
As you rip out his guts and see
 The stuff he had for duff.

'Remember this. You're looking at
A bunch of Jerries over there
 They'd kill you if they could,
And fuck your sisters, mother too.
You've got to stop the bastards, see?
 I hope that's understood.

'All right? Platoon, in your own time,
Fix your bayonets; stand at ease
 Then watch my moves with care.
First, the High Port, done like this:
You cant the rifle straight across
 Your chest and hold it there.

'Note the angle: left hand firm
Around the barrel, half-way down.
 The right hand grasps the small.
Whatever happens never change
Your grip upon your weapon. No!
 I don't mean that at all!

'You dirty-minded little sods!
The next position – that's On Guard –
    You swing the bayonet out
In front of you like this, chest high,
Take one pace forward with your left
    Knee bent. Let's see you try.

'High Port! On Guard! High Port! On Guard!
All right. You've got the rough idea.
    Stand easy and keep still.
And now – Delivery of the Point –
In other words the moment when
    You go in for the kill.

'So watch me now and listen good.
I'll want to hear you yell like me,
    So take a good deep breath
Before you stick the bayonet in.
If you don't kill him with the blade
    You'll scare the sod to death!'

The young recruits stood there and watched
And listened as their tutor roared
    And stabbed his lifeless foe;
Their faces were expressionless,
Impassive as the winter skies
    Black with threats of snow.

HENRY REED

Naming of Parts

from Lessons of the War

To-day we have naming of parts. Yesterday,
We had daily cleaning. And to-morrow morning,
We shall have what to do after firing. But to-day,

To-day we have naming of parts. Japonica
Glistens like coral in all of the neighbouring gardens,
    And to-day we have naming of parts.

This is the lower sling swivel. And this
Is the upper sling swivel, whose use you will see,
    When you are given your slings. And this is the piling swivel,
Which in your case you have not got. The branches
Hold in the gardens their silent, eloquent gestures,
    Which in our case we have not got.

This is the safety-catch, which is always released
With an easy flick of the thumb. And please do not let me
See anyone using his finger. You can do it quite easy
If you have any strength in your thumb. The blossoms
Are fragile and motionless, never letting anyone see
    Any of them using their finger.

And this you can see is the bolt. The purpose of this
Is to open the breech, as you see. We can slide it
Rapidly backwards and forwards: we call this
Easing the spring. And rapidly backwards and forwards
The early bees are assaulting and fumbling the flowers:
    They call it easing the Spring.

They call it easing the Spring: it is perfectly easy
If you have any strength in your thumb: like the bolt,
And the breech, and the cocking-piece, and the point of
    balance,
Which in our case we have not got; and the almond-blossom
Silent in all the gardens and the bees going backwards and
    forwards,
    For to-day we have naming of parts.

TOM RAWLING

Gas Drill

The sergeant's been on a gas course
he cranks his rattle once more
we begin the drill but slip-knots jam
we're slow to be masked to be caped
tin-hats tumble eye-pieces mist
we rubber-gasp as we run
we're Fred Karno's Army
with a comical-tragical face
we can't hear commands can only guess
what we have to do can't see the dials
we're clumsy we're cluttered strange
creatures cheeks flensed of flesh
reduced to eye-sockets to skulls
with windpipes hanging loose
green shrouded spectres.

ANONYMOUS

Drill's the Thing

To the tune of 'The Red Flag'

While battles rage and cannons roar,
The foul Hun's spilling Russian gore.
The Free French die, Norwegians too.
Is that concern for me and you?
The foreigners don't understand
That drill's the thing that rules the land.
For wherever we are on land or sea
The time is always 'One, Two, Three'.

While Chinese dead lie stiff as boards,
The east's o'errun by Nippon's hordes.
The Philippinos lost the fight
Because they don't know left from right,
And although they're brave and fit and fleet,
They never used to stamp their feet.
For wherever we are on land or sea,
The time is always 'One, Two, Three'.

The Dutch who ruled on Java's isle
Had to leave for quite a while
The cause of this there is no doubt
Was their improper kit layout.
The OCTU lads, you must agree,
Are quite the smartest squad you'll see.
For wherever we are on land or sea
The time is always 'One, Two, Three'.

Australian troops, though most astute,
Are useless at the front salute,
And though New Zealand men can fight,
They never give a good eyes-right.
But drill's the thing, there is no doubt
To beat the Jap and Nazi lout.
For wherever we are on land or sea
The time is always 'One, Two, Three'.

ANONYMOUS

Tatton Parachute Training School

To the tune of 'The Mountains of Mourne'

Oh Mary, this Tatton's a wonderful sight,
With the paratroops jumping by day and by night.
They land on potatoes and barley and corn,
And there's gangs of them wishing they'd never been born.

At least, when I asked them, that's what I was told,
The jumping is easy, slow pairs leave them cold.
They said that they'd rather bale out of the moon,
Than jump any more from that fucking balloon.

ROBERT GARIOCH

1941

Stinking of chlorine and sweit, the sweirt recruits
    wi gaspreif battledress frottan at our skin,
feet duntan about in great boss buitts,
    bash our tackety ballet, out in the sun.

In sicht of us, some civvy amang the trees,
    wi deck-chair, sandals, bottles on the ice,
cooling his bubbly cyder, sits at ease,
    and kens that Man was meant for Paradise.

Military Justice and Punishment

Clemenceau said, after the exemplary executions of French deserters in 1916, 'Military justice stands in the same relationship to justice as military music does to music.' It has always been rough and ready, for no army can tolerate indiscipline or cowardice. In 1755, General Wolfe issued Regimental Orders which bluntly warned, 'A soldier who quits his rank, or offers to flag, is instantly to be put to death by the officer who commands that platoon. . . . A soldier does not deserve to live who will not fight for his King and country.'

On campaign, justice was usually exacted in the field before a drumhead Court Martial; there were few niceties of procedure or elaborate appeals. Hanging was the usual penalty for desertion and murder, and until the twentieth century the hangman was required to be a volunteer from the regiment. Poor old Bardolph was hanged for stealing a 'pax of little price'.

Flogging was widely used. A War Office report from the 1830s tells us that in one year there had been 588 floggings for mutiny, insubordination, drunkenness on duty, the selling of arms and stealing from comrades. A movement to stop flogging was started in 1846, after the death of Private John Wilkes at the Cavalry Barracks on Hounslow Heath, as the result of 150 lashes. Oliver Reynolds's poem shows how things were done in the Prussian army of Frederick the Great.

Desertion was the greatest military crime. In the Second World War, there were more than 100,000 deserters from the British Army and 300,000 from the German Army. In the Vietnam War, 73 American soldiers in every 1,000 deserted.

I have included here a poem by Harry ('Breaker') Morant, written on the night before his execution in the Boer War. He was an Australian freebooter who had been charged with, and found guilty of, killing Boer prisoners. His case was especially controversial, as he claimed that he had been acting under orders.

Although the Court recommended mercy, Kitchener refused to reprieve him. Just before his execution, Morant smoked a last cigarette, then gave his silver case to the officer commanding the firing-squad; he refused to be blindfolded and his last words were: 'Shoot straight, you bastards!'

WILLIAM SHAKESPEARE

from Henry V (Act 3, Scene vi)

Pistol: Fortune is Bardolph's foe, and frowns on him;
For he hath stol'n a pax, and hanged must a' be,
A damned death!
Let gallows gape for dog, let man go free
And let not hemp his wind-pipe suffocate.
But Exeter hath given the doom of death
For pax of little price.
Therefore, go speak; the duke will hear thy voice;
And let not Bardolph's vital thread be cut
With edge of penny cord and vile reproach:
Speak, captain, for his life, and I will thee requite.
Fluellen: Aunchient Pistol, I do partly understand your meaning.
Pistol: Why then, rejoice therefore.
Fluellen: Certainly, aunchient, it is not a thing to rejoice at; for, if, look you, he were my brother,
I would desire the duke to use his good pleasure
and put him to execution; for discipline ought
to be used.
Pistol: Die and be damn'd; and figo for thy friendship!
Fluellen: It is well.
Pistol: The fig of Spain!

OLIVER REYNOLDS

Hazel

Take two hundred soldiers.
Form into two ranks facing each other
at a distance of six to seven feet.

Each man has a rod of hazel,
soaked in water, a yard long
and about three-quarters of an inch thick.

The offender is stripped to the waist
and his hands tied in front of him.
He is made to walk between the ranks.

(A sergeant precedes him, walking backwards
with a pike levelled at his chest,
to dissuade him from trying to run.)

Pipes and drums play throughout.
Each soldier gives the offender
one blow on his bare back.

Corporals with staves should be ready
to beat any soldier
not exerting himself.

Depending on the severity of the offence,
the gauntlet is to be run
twelve, twenty-four or thirty-six times.

Those undergoing it thirty-six times
(spread over three days)
usually die.

Blood-loss may so exhaust the offender
(the back will be flayed and strips of skin
often hang down over the breeches)

that he collapses: he should receive
the remaining blows lying down,
the soldiers marching past him in file.

ANONYMOUS

The Lay of the Lash

Be tied to the halberds, or grating, and whipped,
WHY should the soldier, or sailor – back stripped –
While the 'officer' – acting, perhaps, very much worse –
Is secured from the Lash, by the strength of the purse?
By the strength of the purse! for to what, but to that,
Does he owe his commission, 'signed, sealed', and all that?
So raise the stern cry, not till death let it fall: –
'The Lash be for none – or the Lash be for all!'

ANONYMOUS

The Deserter

In fair London city I was born,
And for a soldier I was drawn;
A kidnapping-sergeant on me did prevail,
And he hoisted me down to the Savoy jail

When to the Savoy jail I did come;
The irons on both legs they clapt me on:
And backwards in the yard they did me put
With some more young fellows they had just got.

Then up and down the yard we do stray,
The county allows us but sixpence a day;
But sixpence a day will not our bellies stuff:
Of the Savoy Savoy jail I've had quite enough

When the turnkey comes to lock us all in
The bugs and the fleas cover all our skin,
Striving to see which could bite the best;
So we poor prisoners can get no rest.

O then a court martial they did call,
And I was brought before them all;
My sentence was past – I was to be shot,
But a thousand lashes was my lot

Now I have gain'd my sweet liberty,
My brother comrades I'll go to see,
Wishing that they may all get free,
That they may all know sweet liberty as well as me.

GILBERT FRANKAU

The Deserter

'I'm sorry I done it, Major.'
We bandaged the livid face;
And led him out, ere the wan sun rose,
To die his death of disgrace.

The bolt-heads locked to the cartridge;
The rifles steadied to rest,
As cold stock nestled at colder cheek
And foresight lined on the breast.

'*Fire!*' called the Sergeant-Major.
The muzzles flamed as he spoke:
And the shameless soul of a nameless man
Went up in the cordite-smoke.

RUDYARD KIPLING

Danny Deever

'What are the bugles blowin' for?' said Files-on-Parade.
'To turn you out, to turn you out,' the Colour-Sergeant said.
'What makes you look so white, so white?' said Files-on-
    Parade.
'I'm dreadin' what I've got to watch,' the Colour-Sergeant
    said.
    For they're hangin' Danny Deever, you can hear the Dead
        March play,
    The Regiment's in 'ollow square — they're hangin' him to-
        day;
    They've taken of his buttons off an' cut his stripes away.
    An' they're hangin' Danny Deever in the mornin'.

'What makes the rear-rank breathe so 'ard?' said Files-on-
    Parade.
'It's bitter cold, it's bitter cold,' the Colour-Sergeant said.
'What makes that front-rank man fall down?' said Files-on-
    Parade.
'A touch o' sun, a touch o' sun,' the Colour-Sergeant said.
    They are hangin' Danny Deever, they are marchin' of 'im
        round,
    They 'ave 'alted Danny Deever by 'is coffin on the ground;
    An' 'e'll swing in 'arf a minute for a sneakin' shootin'
        hound —
    O they're hangin' Danny Deever in the mornin'!

'Is cot was right-'and cot to mine,' said Files-on-Parade.
''E's sleepin' out an' far to-night,' the Colour-Sergeant said.
'I've drunk 'is beer a score o' times,' said Files-on-Parade.
''E's drinkin' bitter beer alone,' the Colour-Sergeant said.
    They are hangin' Danny Deever, you must mark 'im to 'is
        place,

For 'e shot a comrade sleepin' – you must look 'im in the
  face;
Nine 'undred of 'is county an' the Regiment's disgrace,
While they're hangin' Danny Deever in the mornin'.

'What's that so black again the sun?' said Files-on-Parade.
'It's Danny fightin' 'ard for life,' the Colour-Sergeant said.
'What's that that whimpers over'ead?' said Files-on-Parade.
'It's Danny's soul that's passin' now,' the Colour-Sergeant
  said.
  For they've done with Danny Deever, you can 'ear the
    quickstep play,
  The Regiment's in column, an' they're marchin' us away;
  Ho! the young recruits are shakin', an' they'll want their
    beer to-day,
  After hangin' Danny Deever in the mornin'!

HARRY MORANT

The Last Rhyme and Testament of Tony Lumpkin

In prison cell I sadly sit –
A d-d crestfallen chappy!
And own to you I feel a bit –
A little bit – unhappy!

It really ain't the place nor time
To reel off rhyming diction –
But yet we'll write a final rhyme
While waiting cru-ci-fixion!

No matter what 'end' they decide –
Quicklime? or 'b'iling ile?' sir!
We'll do our best when crucified
To finish off in style, sir!

But we bequeath a parting tip
For sound advice as such men
Who come across in transport ship
To polish off the Dutchmen!

If you encounter any Boers
You really must not loot 'em,
And if you wish to leave these shores
For pity's sake *don't shoot 'em*!

And if you'd earn a DSO –
Why every British sinner
Should know the proper way to go
Is: '*Ask the Boer to dinner*'!

Let's toss a bumper down our throat
Before we pass to Heaven,
And toast: 'the trim-set petticoat
We leave behind in Devon.'

RUDYARD KIPLING

from Cells

I've a head like a concertina, I've a tongue like a button-stick,
I've a mouth like an old potato, and I'm more than a little sick,
But I've had my fun o' the Corp'ral's Guard; I've made the
    cinders fly,
And I'm here in the Clink for a thundering drink and blacking
    the Corporal's eye.
        With a second-hand overcoat under my head,
        And a beautiful view of the yard,
    O it's pack-drill for me and a fortnight's CB
        For 'drunk and resisting the Guard!'
        Mad drunk and resisting the Guard –
        'Strewth, but I socked it them hard!

So it's pack-drill for me and a fortnight's CB
    For 'drunk and resisting the Guard.'

ROBERT GRAVES

Sergeant-Major Money

It wasn't our battalion, but we lay alongside it,
    So the story is as true as the telling is frank.
They hadn't one Line-officer left, after Arras,
    Except a batty major and the Colonel, who drank.

'B' Company Commander was fresh from the Depôt,
    An expert on shell-fish, otherwise a dud;
So Sergeant-Major Money carried on, as instructed,
    And that's where the swaddies began to sweat blood.

His Old Army humour was so well-spiced and hearty
    That one poor sod shot himself, and one lost his wits;
But discipline's maintained, and back in rest-billets
    The Colonel congratulates 'B' company on their kits.

The subalterns went easy, as was only natural
    With a terror like Money driving the machine,
Till finally two Welshmen, butties from the Rhondda,
    Bayoneted their bugbear in a field-canteen.

Well, we couldn't blame the officers, they relied on Money;
    And we couldn't blame those pitboys, their courage was
      grand;
Or, least of all, blame Money, an old stiff surviving
    In a New (bloody) Army he couldn't understand.

The Spirit of the Fighting Man

Soldiers have often been taken for granted and they have resented it. Peter Woodhouse, writing in 1605, foreshadows Kipling's 'Tommy Atkins', and the complaint of the British Other Rank is taken up, in 1945, by H. H. Tilley, brassed off in Burma.

A lot of soldiering is tedious: long periods are spent in a kind of exile, and a soldier is frequently hungry, thirsty, cold or otherwise uncomfortable – 'But it's "Thin red line of 'eroes" when the drums begin to roll.'

ANONYMOUS

'Because we're here'

Tune: 'Auld Lang Syne'

We're here because we're here,
Because we're here, because we're here.
We're here because we're here,
Because we're here, because we're here.
Oh, here we are, oh, here we are,
Oh, here we are again.
Oh, here we are, oh, here we are,
Oh, here we are again.

W. H. AUDEN

Roman Wall Blues

Over the heather the wet wind blows,
I've lice in my tunic and a cold in my nose.

The rain comes pattering out of the sky,
I'm a Wall soldier, I don't know why.

The mist creeps over the hard grey stone,
My girl's in Tungria; I sleep alone.

Aulus goes hanging around her place,
I don't like his manners, I don't like his face.

Piso's a Christian, he worships a fish;
There'd be no kissing if he had his wish.

She gave me a ring but I diced it away;
I want my girl and I want my pay.

When I'm a veteran with only one eye
I shall do nothing but look at the sky.

BUNNO

Song of the Bowmen of Shu

Here we are, picking the first fern-shoots
And saying: When shall we get back to our country?
Here we are because we have the Ken-nin for our foemen,
We have no comfort because of these Mongols.
We grub the soft fern-shoots,
When anyone says 'Return', the others are full of sorrow.
Sorrowful minds, sorrow is strong, we are hungry and thirsty.
Our defence is not yet made sure, no one can let his friend
    return.
We grub the old fern-stalks.
We say: Will we be let to go back in October?
There is no ease in royal affairs, we have no comfort.
Our sorrow is bitter, but we would not return to our country.
What flower has come into blossom?
Whose chariot? The General's.

Horses, his horses even, are tired. They were strong.
We have no rest, three battles a month.
By heaven, his horses are tired.
The generals are on them, the soldiers are by them.
The horses are well trained, the generals have ivory arrows and
    quivers ornamented with fish-skin.
The enemy is swift, we must be careful.
When we set out, the willows were drooping with spring,
We come back in the snow,
We go slowly, we are hungry and thirsty,
Our mind is full of sorrow, who will know of our grief?

      Translated from the Chinese by Ezra Pound

RUDYARD KIPLING

Tommy

I went into a public-'ouse to get a pint o' beer,
The publican 'e up an' sez, 'We serve no red-coats here.'
The girls be'ind the bar they laughed an' giggled fit to die,
I outs into the street again an' to myself sez I:
    O it's Tommy this, an' Tommy that, an' 'Tommy, go away';
    But it's 'Thank you, Mister Atkins,' when the band begins to
      play –
    The band begins to play, my boys, the band begins to play,
    O it's 'Thank you, Mister Atkins,' when the band begins to
      play.

I went into a theatre as sober as could be,
They gave a drunk civilian room, but 'adn't none for me;
They sent me to the gallery or round the music-'alls,
But when it comes to fightin', Lord! they'll shove me in the
    stalls!
    For it's Tommy this, an' Tommy that, an' 'Tommy, wait
      outside';

But it's 'Special train for Atkins' when the trooper's on the
  tide –
The troopship's on the tide, my boys, the troopship's on the
  tide,
O it's 'Special train for Atkins' when the trooper's on the
  tide.

Yes, makin' mock o' uniforms that guard you while you sleep
Is cheaper than them uniforms, an' they're starvation cheap;
An' hustlin' drunken soldiers when they're goin' large a bit
Is five times better business than paradin' in full kit.
  Then it's Tommy this, an' Tommy that, an' 'Tommy, 'ow's
    yer soul?'
  But it's 'Thin red line of 'eroes' when the drums begin to
    roll –
  The drums begin to roll, my boys, the drums begin to roll,
  O it's 'Thin red line of 'eroes' when the drums begin to roll.

We aren't no thin red 'eroes, nor we aren't no blackguards too,
But single men in barricks, most remarkable like you;
An' if sometimes our conduck isn't all your fancy paints,
Why, single men in barricks don't grow into plaster saints;
  While it's Tommy this, an' Tommy that, an' 'Tommy, fall
    be'hind,'
  But it's 'Please to walk in front, sir,' when there's trouble in
    the wind –
  There's trouble in the wind, my boys, there's trouble in the
    wind,
  O it's 'Please to walk in front, sir,' when there's trouble in
    the wind.

You talk o' better food for us, an' schools, an' fires, an' all:
We'll wait for extry rations if you treat us rational.
Don't mess about the cook-room slops, but prove it to our face
The Widow's Uniform is not the soldier-man's disgrace.
  For it's Tommy this, an' Tommy that, an' 'Chuck him out,
    the brute!'

But it's 'Saviour of 'is country' when the guns begin to
   shoot;
An' it's Tommy this, an' Tommy that, an' anything you
   please;
An' Tommy ain't a bloomin' fool – you bet that Tommy
   sees!

PETER WOODHOUSE

I see a Soldiers service is forgot,
In time of peace the world regards us not.

H. H. TILLEY

from Citizen BOR Speaking

Democracy, my grannie's foot!
I'm just another smell;
A lump o' dirt that's kicked around
This stinking, fly-blown hell.

I'm good enough to sweat an' stew,
And guard 'em from Japan;
I'm good enough, oh yes, to rot
In murderous Arakan.

I'm good enough to save the world
While they go out to play;
But if I ask 'em for a dance
They turn the other way.

Democracy! Don't make me laugh!
Don't trot out all that bunk!
I never even have the chance
To go an' get blind drunk.

The brightest jewel in the crown!
My God, it makes you weep!
Just listen here . . . but what's the use?
Let me get back to sleep.

ANONYMOUS

Soldiers

Soldiers who wish to be a hero
Are practically zero,
But those who wish to be civilians,
Jesus, they run into millions.

US Army, World War II

Unlikely Soldiers

There have been many unlikely soldiers, and a particular favourite of mine is the Chinese scholar who had to abandon his book and sash and put on a coat of rhinoceros-skin.

By far the most glorious representative of the type is Sir John Falstaff. There is no strictly poetic characterization of him, as Shakespeare gives him and his companions prose to speak, but I have included one of Falstaff's own speeches because it is close to poetry.

In Elizabeth I's reign, counties and shires were required to raise certain numbers of soldiers – Justices of the Peace and constables became the recruiting sergeants. A certain Captain Rich confirmed Falstaff's description of the sort of person who was recruited, when he cited drunkards, quarrellers and 'such a one that had some skill in stealing a goose'. This system raised over 80,000 men for Elizabeth's military expeditions overseas, most of which were disastrous failures. Drake and her other sea captains proved much more successful.

PAO CHAO

The Scholar Recruit

Now late
I follow Time's Necessity:
Mounting a barricade I pacify remote tribes.
Discarding my sash I don a coat of rhinoceros-skin:
Rolling up my skirts I shoulder a black bow.
Even at the very start my strength fails:
What will become of me before it's all over?

Translated from the Chinese by Arthur Waley

WILLIAM SHAKESPEARE

from Henry IV, Part I (Act 4, Scene ii)

Falstaff: Bardolph, get thee before to Coventry; fill me a bottle of sack: our soldiers shall march through: we'll to Sutton-Co'fil' to-night.

Bardolph: Will you give me money, captain?

Falstaff: Lay out, lay out.

Bardolph: This bottle makes an angel.

Falstaff: An if it do, take it for thy labour; and if it make twenty, take them all, I'll answer the coinage. Bid my Lieutenant Peto meet me at the town's end.

Bardolph: I will, captain: farewell.

Falstaff: If I be not ashamed of my soldiers, I am a soused gurnet. I have misused the king's press damnably. I have got, in exchange of a hundred and fifty soldiers, three hundred and odd pounds. I press me none but good householders, yeomen's sons; inquire me out contracted bachelors, such as had been asked twice on the banns; such a commodity of warm slaves, as had as lief hear the devil as a drum; such as fear the report of a caliver worse than a struck fowl or a hurt wild-duck. I pressed me none but such toasts-and-butter, with hearts in their bellies no bigger than pins' heads, and they have bought out their services; and now my whole charge consists of ancients, corporals, lieutenants, gentlemen of companies, slaves as ragged as Lazarus in the painted cloth, where the glutton's dogs licked his sores; and such as indeed were never soldiers, but discarded unjust serving-men, younger sons to younger brothers, revolted tapsters and ostlers trade-fallen, the cankers of a calm world and a long peace; ten times more dishonourable ragged than an old faced ancient: and such have I, to fill up the rooms of them that have bought out their services, that you would think that I had a hundred and fifty tattered prodigals, lately come from swine-keeping, from

eating draff and husks. A mad fellow met me on the way and
told me I had unloaded all the gibbets and pressed the dead
bodies. No eye hath seen such scarecrows. I'll not march
through Coventry with them, that's flat: nay, and the villains
march wide betwixt the legs, as if they had gyves on; for,
indeed I had the most of them out of prison. There's but a shirt
and a half in all my company; and the half shirt is two napkins
tacked together and thrown over the shoulders like a herald's
coat without sleeves; and the shirt, to say the truth, stolen from
my host at Saint Alban's, or the red-nose inn-keeper of
Daventry. But that's all one; they'll find linen enough on every
hedge.

HERMAN MELVILLE

The College Colonel

He rides at their head;
  A crutch by his saddle just slants in view,
One slung arm is in splints, you see,
  Yet he guides his strong steed – how coldly too.

He brings his regiment home –
  Not as they filed two years before,
But a remnant half-tattered, and battered, and worn,
Like castaway sailors, who – stunned
    By the surf's loud roar,
  Their mates dragged back and seen no more –
Again and again breast the surge,
  And at last crawl, spent, to shore.

A still rigidity and pale –
  An Indian aloofness lones his brow;
He has lived a thousand years
Compressed in battle's pains and prayers,
  Marches and watches slow.

There are welcoming shouts, and flags;
  Old men off hat to the Boy,
Wreaths from gay balconies fall at his feet,
  But to *him* – there comes alloy.

It is not that a leg is lost,
  It is not that an arm is maimed,
It is not that the fever has racked –
  Self he has long disclaimed.

But all through the Seven Days' Fight,
  And deep in the Wilderness grim,
And in the field-hospital tent,
  And Petersburg crater, and dim
Lean brooding in Libby, there came –
  Ah heaven! – what *truth* to him.

RUDYARD KIPLING

Gentlemen-Rankers

To the legion of the lost ones, to the cohort of the damned,
  To my brethren in their sorrow overseas,
Sings a gentleman of England cleanly bred, machinely
    crammed,
  And a trooper of the Empress, if you please.
Yes, a trooper of the forces who has run his own six horses,
  And faith he went the pace and went it blind,
And the world was more than kin while he held the ready tin,
  But to-day the Sergeant's something less than kind.
        We're poor little lambs who've lost our way,
            Baa! Baa! Baa!
        We're little black sheep who've gone astray,
            Baa – aa – aa!
        Gentlemen-rankers out on the spree,
        Damned from here to Eternity,

> God ha' mercy on such as we,
> Baa! Yah! Bah!

Oh, it's sweet to sweat through stables, sweet to empty kitchen
  slops,
  And it's sweet to hear the tales the troopers tell,
To dance with blowzy housemaids at the regimental hops
  And thrash the cad who says you waltz too well.
Yes, it makes you cock-a-hoop to be 'Rider' to your troop,
  And branded with a blasted worsted spur,
When you envy, O how keenly, one poor Tommy living
  cleanly
  Who blacks your boots and sometimes calls you 'Sir.'

If the home we never write to, and the oaths we never keep,
  And all we know most distant and most dear,
Across the snoring barrack-room return to break our sleep,
  Can you blame us if we soak ourselves in beer?
When the drunken comrade mutters and the great guard-
  lantern gutters
  And the horror of our fall is written plain,
Every secret, self-revealing on the aching whitewashed ceiling,
  Do you wonder that we drug ourselves from pain?

We have done with Hope and Honour, we are lost to Love and
  Truth,
  We are dropping down the ladder rung by rung,
And the measure of our torment is the measure of our youth.
  God help us, for we knew the worst too young!
Our shame is clean repentance for the crime that brought the
  sentence,
  Our pride it is to know no spur of pride,
And the Curse of Reuben holds us till an alien turf enfolds us
  And we die, and none can tell Them where we died.
> We're poor little lambs who've lost our way,
> Baa! Baa! Baa!
> We're little black sheep who've gone astray,
> Baa – aa – aa!

Gentlemen-rankers out on the spree,
Damned from here to Eternity,
God ha' mercy on such as we,
  Baa! Yah! Bah!

IVOR GURNEY

The Bohemians

Certain people would not clean their buttons,
Nor polish buckles after latest fashions,
Preferred their hair long, putties comfortable,
Barely escaping hanging, indeed hardly able,
In Bridge and smoking without army cautions
Spending hours that sped like evil for quickness,
(While others burnished brasses, earned promotions)
These were those ones who jested in the trench,

While others argued of army ways, and wrenched
What little soul they had still further from shape,
And died off one by one, or became officers
Without the first of dream, the ghost of notions
Of ever becoming soldiers, or smart and neat,
Surprised as ever to find the army capable
Of sounding 'Lights out' to break a game of Bridge,
As to fear candles would set a barn alight.
In Artois or Picardy they lie – free of useless fashions.

Women Warriors

Women have not, in the main, engaged in the actual business of fighting. I have not come across any notable nineteenth-century female warriors, and in the twentieth century women have tended to provide supporting services for the front-line troops. One of these was Joy Corfield, who joined the ATS in 1944 as a wireless operator and whose 'Morse Lesson' is included here.

Before that, though, there are a few women who did take up weapons and were as ferocious as any male warrior. Boadicea is a national heroine; Gildippe is not the only woman to have shown herself more than a match for her male adversaries in Tasso's epic of the Crusades; Margaret of Anjou was married to the weak and gentle Henry VI, and so at times during the Wars of the Roses had to lead and inspire his Lancastrian troops; and Polly Oliver is an example of the enterprising type whose exploits are the stuff of numerous songs and tales.

If there are poems about fighting women closer to our own time, I should be glad to know of them.

ALFRED, LORD TENNYSON

from Boädicea

'Hear Icenian, Catieuchlanian, hear Coritanian, Trinobant!
Me the wife of rich Prasutagus, me the lover of liberty,
Me they seized and me they tortured, me they lash'd and
    humiliated,
Me the sport of ribald Veterans, mine of ruffian violators!
See they sit, they hide their faces, miserable in ignominy!
Wherefore in me burns an anger, not by blood to be satiated.
Lo the palaces and the temple, lo the colony Cámulodúne!

There they ruled, and thence they wasted all the flourishing
    territory,
Thither at their will they haled the yellow-ringleted
    Britoness —
Bloodily, bloodily fall the battle-axe, unexhausted, inexorable.
Shout Icenian, Catieuchlanian, shout Coritanian, Trinobant,
Till the victim hear within and yearn to hurry precipitously
Like the leaf in a roaring whirlwind, like the smoke in a
    hurricane whirl'd.
Lo the colony, there they rioted in the city of Cúnobeline!
There they drank in cups of emerald, there at tables of ebony
    lay,
Rolling on their purple couches in their tender effeminacy.
There they dwelt and there they rioted; there — there — they
    dwell no more.
Burst the gates, and burn the palaces, break the works of the
    statuary,
Take the hoary Roman head and shatter it, hold it
    abominable,
Cut the Roman boy to pieces in his lust and voluptuousness,
Lash the maiden into swooning, me they lash'd and
    humiliated,
Chop the breasts from off the mother, dash the brains of the
    little one out,
Up my Britons, on my chariot, on my chargers, trample them
    under us.'

  So the Queen Boädicéa, standing loftily charioted,
Brandishing in her hand a dart and rolling glances lioness-like,
Yell'd and shrieked between her daughters in her fierce
    volubility.
Till her people all around the royal chariot agitated,
Madly dash'd the darts together, writhing barbarous
    lineäments,
Made the noise of frosty woodlands, when they shiver in
    January,

Roar'd as when the rolling breakers boom and blanch on the
  precipices,
Yell'd as when the winds of winter tear an oak on a
  promontory.
So the silent colony hearing her tumultuous adversaries
Clash the darts and on the buckler beat with rapid unanimous
  hand,
Thought on all her evil tyrannies, all her pitiless avarice,
Till she felt the heart within her fall and flutter tremulously,
Then her pulses at the clamouring of her enemy fainted away.
Out of evil evil flourishes, out of tyranny tyranny buds.
Ran the land with Roman slaughter, multitudinous agonies.
Perish'd many a maid and matron, many a valorous legionary.
Fell the colony, city, and citadel, London, Verulam,
  Cámulodúne.

TORQUATO TASSO

from Jerusalem Delivered, Canto XX

32

Who first of Christian warriors now did chance,
Of noble deeds the well-earn'd praise to claim?
Thou Gildippe first struck with foremost lance
The great Hyrcanian that from Ormuz came,
His realm. The heav'ns this glory grant thy name,
Thy woman's hand shall cleave his breast in two;
Divided and transpierced he falls. With shame
He hears and knows, e'en as he tumbles low,
The foeman's shout of praise, that greets the conquering
  blow.

33

With strong right hand the lady swiftly drew
(Since snapt the lance had been) her goodly blade,
And Persia's ranks as one long lane press'd through
And thinn'd the crowded legions there array'd.
Zopiro next she gathered in, and made
(Just where a man his girdle draws around)
Two halves of him, that swift apart were sway'd.
To young Alarco's throat she dealt a wound,
And cut the double path of food, and vocal sound.

34

She strikes down Artaxerxes next, and then
Attacking Argeo, with the point she fights,
One stunn'd and senseless lies, the other slain.
A pliant joint the hand and arm unites,
There cuts her sword when Ismael she smites.
The lopp'd hand falls, the rein unmanaged lies,
While the steed's ear the falling blow affrights,
When now no more his mouth the bridle tries,
He bounds athwart the ranks and breaks them as he flies.

35

These and far more whose names in silence lie
All hid by Time, she did from life assoil,
When closing up their ranks, the Persians try
Thus to surround and seize her as their spoil.
This mark'd her faithful mate amid his toil,
And rush'd to rescue his beloved again.
Conjoin'd once more the foe they best can foil
By fighting thus in concert; so the twain
From faithful union here a doubled strength maintain.

36

New arts of sure defence, now used no more
These lovers true, magnanimous did show.
Thus often one all guard of self forbore,
And diligent appears to stay each foe
Who threats the other's life with sudden woe.
Thus she the lady knight, is often freed
To pay his foemen with her unseen blow
For all his hurts, whilst he with shield in need
Or e'en bared head, or form, guards her and strikes with speed.

37

Defence of one, the other's duty grew,
And all their vengeance likewise they divide,
But now 'twas he that Artabano slew
Who ruled Boecan's isle in kingly pride,
And by the selfsame hand Alvanto died,
Who dared to wound her who was life's delight.
Then she cut Arimonto side to side
(Whose steel upon her lord had proved his might),
His face she shore in twain, where lashes shield the sight. [. . .]

41

While none now dares his fury to confront
(Nor to attack will lead the others on),
Him Gildippe will face as is her wont,
Nor fears to make such bold comparison.
Ne'er by Thermodon's stream did Amazon
Brace shield on arm the battle axe to wield
With nobler carriage than in her now shone,
Who fears not to surpass with sword and shield
The doughty Persian's might, but rushes to the field.

42

Where rich enamcl and thc massive gold
Of his barbaric crown in spendour gleam'd
Above the helm, she struck. The fragments roll'd
Wide scatter'd, while the head that erst had seem'd
Superb and high, bent lowly as it deem'd
A mighty hand indeed had dealt the blow,
To him a king, nor lightly he esteem'd
His shame, nor was in vindicating slow,
Shame and revenge inspired, to lay his foeman low.

43

Then in an instant, on that lady fell
His answ'ring blow, and so malign its force,
That sense and vigour fled, and in her selle
She reel'd, and prone had tumbled from her horse,
But that her faithful knight in last resource
Upheld her there – By luck or virtue, she
Was saved, for lo! the Persian held his course,
As with the lion's magnanimity
Who spares the stricken man, he look'd, and pass'd her by.

Translated from the Italian by G. Grinnell-Milne

WILLIAM SHAKESPEARE

from Henry VI, Part III (Act 5, Scene iv)

Queen: Great lords, wise men ne'er sit and wail their loss,
But cheerly seek how to redress their harms.
What though the mast be now blown overboard,
The cable broke, the holding-anchor lost,
And half our sailors swallowed in the flood?
Yet lives our pilot still. Is't meet that he

Should leave the helm and, like a fearful lad,
With tearful eyes add water to the sea,
And give more strength to that which hath too much,
Whiles, in his moan, the ship splits on the rock,
Which industry and courage might have saved?
Ah, what a shame! Ah, what a fault were this!
Say Warwick was our anchor; what of that?
And Montague our topmast; what of him?
Our slaughtered friends the tackles; what of these?
Why, is not Oxford here another anchor?
And Somerset another goodly mast?
The friends of France our shrouds and tacklings?
And, though unskilful, why not Ned and I
For once allowed the skilful pilot's charge?
We will not from the helm to sit and weep,
But keep our course, though the rough wind say no,
From shelves and rocks that threaten us with wrack.
As good to chide the waves as speak them fair.
And what is Edward but a ruthless sea?
What Clarence but a quicksand of deceit?
And Richard but a ragged fatal rock?
All these the enemies to our poor bark.
Say you can swim; alas, 'tis but a while!
Tread on the sand; why, there you quickly sink.
Bestride the rock; the tide will wash you off,
Or else you famish; that's a threefold death.
This speak I, lords, to let you understand,
If case some one of you would fly from us,
That there's no hoped-for mercy with the brothers
More than with ruthless waves, with sands and rocks.
Why, courage then! What cannot be avoided
'Twere childish weakness to lament or fear.
  Prince: Methinks a woman of this valiant spirit
Should, if a coward heard her speak these words,
Infuse his breast with magnanimity,
And make him, naked, foil a man at arms.

ANONYMOUS

Sweet Polly Oliver

As sweet Polly Oliver lay musing in bed,
A sudden strange fancy came into her head:
'Nor mother nor father shall make me false prove,
I'll 'list for a soldier and follow my love.'

So early next morning she softly arose
And dressed herself up in her dead brother's clothes.
She cut her hair close and she stained her face brown,
And went for a soldier to fair London town.

Then up spoke the sergeant one day at his drill:
'Now who's good for nursing? A captain, he's ill.'
'I'm ready,' said Polly. To nurse him she's gone,
And finds it's her true love, all wasted and wan.

The first week the doctor kept shaking his head.
'No nursing, young fellow, can save him,' he said;
But when Polly Oliver had nursed him back to life,
He cried, 'You have cherished him as if you were his wife.'

O then Polly Oliver, she burst into tears
And told the good doctor her hopes and her fears,
And very shortly after, for better or for worse,
The captain took joyfully his pretty soldier nurse.

ANONYMOUS

My Sodger Laddie

My yellow mou'd mistress, I bid you adieu,
For I've been too long in slavery with you,
With washing and scouring I'm seldom in bedy

And now I will go with my sodger laddie,
My sodger laddie, my sodger laddie,
The kisses are sweet of a sodger laddie.

With the crust of your loaf, and dregs of your tea,
You fed your lap doggie far better than me,
With rinning and spinning, my head was unsteady,
But now I will go with my sodger laddie.

For yarn, for yarn, you always did cry,
And look'd to my pirn, ay as ye went by;
Now the drums they do beat, and my bundle is ready,
And I'll go along with my sodger laddie.

I'll always be ready, with needle and soap,
For possing and patching to serve the whole troop,
I'll be loving and kind, and live like a lady,
When I go abroad with my sodger laddie.

In heat of battles, I'll keep on the flank,
With a stone in a stocking, and give them a clank,
If he be knocked down, though he be my daddy,
I'll bring all his clink to my sodger laddie.

For robbing the dead is no thievish trick,
I'll rifle his breeches, and then his knapsack,
But yet on a friend I'll not be so ready,
If he's been acquaint with my sodger laddie.

JOY CORFIELD

Morse Lesson

A cold, cold room with cold, cold girls
In buttoned greatcoats, scarves and mitts;
Frozen fingers try to write
The letters for the dah-dah-dits.

'Faster, faster,' says the sergeant;
Slower, slower work our brains.
Feet are numb, our blood is frozen,
Every movement causing pains.

Yet – four of us swam in the sea
Just last week, on Christmas Day,
Through frosty foam and fringe of ice,
Warmer than we are today.

Rest and Recreation

The soldiery has always been rude and licentious. As usual, Kipling
put it accurately and crisply: 'Single men in barricks don't grow
into plaster saints.' Furloughs, 48-hour passes, home leave –
anything is welcome if it means getting away from the monotony
of barrack life. Such freedom is inevitably short, however:
pleasures have to be seized and the business of soldiering forgotten
in drunkenness and debauchery. Peter Sanders, a Captain in the
Western Desert, describes what happened after the successful
capture of Tripoli, when the British Army was introduced to
unlimited quantities of wine, with the usual results.

As armies move, so camp followers move with them. On the
edge of every battle zone, private enterprise, in the person of the
pimp, flourishes. In Cairo, during the Second World War, the 8th
Army got its relief in the bars, brothels and night clubs of Pond
Street, which was officially out of bounds. In the course of the
Vietnam War, the Americans virtually destroyed Bangkok by
turning it into a vast market of sensual gratification, the whole
purpose of which was to soothe the stress of jungle warfare.

Some armies supplied their soldiers' needs. After Cromwell's
army had defeated Charles I at the Battle of Naseby in 1645, the
Parliamentarians took a large number of prisoners, including one
hundred English and Irish prostitutes. In 1918, the French Prime
Minister, Clemenceau, advised General Pershing, commander of
the US Forces, to establish official brothels – advice which was not
taken, for President Wilson would have been shocked. The British
Army, muddling along as ever, had to cope with over 400,000
cases of venereal disease in the First World War.

RUDYARD KIPLING

The Ladies

I've taken my fun where I've found it;
  I've rogued an' I've ranged in my time;
I've 'ad my pickin' o' sweethearts,
  An' four o' the lot was prime.
One was an 'arf-caste widow,
  One was a woman at Prome,
One was the wife of a *jemadar-sais*,
  An' one is a girl at 'ome.

Now I aren't no 'and with the ladies,
  For, takin' 'em all along,
You never can say till you've tried 'em,
  An' then you are like to be wrong.
There's times when you'll think that you mightn't,
  There's times when you'll know that you might;
But the things you will learn from the Yellow an' Brown,
  They'll 'elp you a lot with the White!

I was a young un at 'Oogli,
  Shy as a girl to begin;
Aggie de Castrer she made me,
  An' Aggie was clever as sin;
Older than me, but my first un —
  More like a mother she were —
Showed me the way to promotion an' pay,
  An' I learned about women from 'er!

Then I was ordered to Burma,
  Actin' in charge o' Bazar,
An' I got me a tiddy live 'eathen
  Through buyin' supplies off 'er pa.
Funny an' yellow an' faithful —
  Doll in a teacup she were —

But we lived on the square, like a true-married pair,
    An' I learned about women from 'er!

Then we was shifted to Neemuch
    (Or I might ha' been keepin' 'er now),
An' I took with a shiny she-devil,
    The wife of a nigger at Mhow;
'Taught me the gipsy-folks' *bolee*;
    Kind o' volcano she were,
For she knifed me one night 'cause I wished she was white,
    And I learned about women from 'er!

Then I come 'ome in a trooper,
    'Long of a kid o' sixteen –
'Girl from a convent at Meerut,
    The straightest I ever 'ave seen.
Love at first sight was 'er trouble,
    She didn't know what it were;
An' I wouldn't do such, 'cause I liked 'er too much,
    But – I learned about women from 'er!

I've taken my fun where I've found it,
    An' now I must pay for my fun,
For the more you 'ave known o' the others
    The less will you settle to one;
An' the end of it's sittin' and thinkin',
    An' dreamin' Hell-fires to see;
So be warned by my lot (which I know you will not),
    An' learn about women from me!

What did the Colonel's Lady think?
    Nobody never knew.
Somebody asked the Sergeant's Wife,
    An' she told 'em true!
When you get to a man in the case,
    They're like as a row of pins –
For the Colonel's Lady an' Judy O'Grady
    Are sisters under their skins!

EDMUND BLUNDEN

Concert Party: Busseboom

The stage was set, the house was packed,
    The famous troop began;
Our laughter thundered, act by act;
    Time light as sunbeams ran.

Dance sprang and spun and neared and fled,
    Jest chirped at gayest pitch,
Rhythm dazzled, action sped
    Most comically rich.

With generals and lame privates both
    Such charms worked wonders, till
The show was over – lagging loth
    We faced the sunset chill;

And standing on the sandy way,
    With the cracked church peering past,
We heard another matinée,
    We heard the maniac blast

Of barrage south by Saint Eloi,
    And the red lights flaming there
Called madness: Come, my bonny boy,
    And dance to the latest air.

To this new concert, white we stood;
    Cold certainty held our breath;
While men in the tunnels below Larch Wood
    Were kicking men to death.

ALAN ROSS

Messdeck

The bulkhead sweating, and under naked bulbs
Men writing letters, playing ludo. The light
Cuts their arms off at the wrist, only the dice
Lives. Hammocks swing, nuzzling in tight
Like foals into flanks of mares. Bare shoulders
Glisten with oil, tattoo-marks rippling their scales on
Mermaids or girls' thighs as dice are shaken, cards played.
We reach for sleep like a gas, randy for oblivion.
But, laid out on lockers, some get waylaid;
And lie stiff, running off films in the mind's dark-room.
The air soupy, yet still cold; a beam sea rattles
Cups smelling of stale tea, knocks over a broom.
The light is watery, like the light of the sea-bed.
Marooned in it, stealthy as fishes, we may even be dead.

PETER A. SANDERS

Tripoli

I've a mouth like a parrot's cage
And a roaring thirst inside,
My liver's a swollen, sullen rage –
Last night I was blind to the wide.

Canned as an owl, last night,
Drunk as a fiddler's bitch,
Oiled and stewed and pissed and tight,
Sewn-up, asleep in a ditch.

I can't remember much
And I wouldn't remember more

For vino gave me the golden touch
And a wit like Bernard Shaw's.

I'm rather weak at the knee
And not too strong in the head
But last night angels sang to me
And the world was a rosy red!

GAVIN EWART

Officers' Mess

It's going to be a thick night to-night (and the night before was
      a thick one);
I've just seen the Padre disappearing into 'The Cock and Bull'
      for a quick one.
I don't mind telling you this, old boy, we got the Major
      drinking –
You probably know the amount of gin he's in the habit of
      sinking –
And then that new MO came in, the Jewish one, awful fellow,
And his wife, a nice little bit of stuff, dressed in a flaming
      yellow.
Looked a pretty warmish piece, old boy – no, have this one
      with me –
They were both so blind (and so was the Major) that they
      could hardly see.
She had one of those amazing hats and a kind of silver fox fur
(I wouldn't mind betting several fellows have had a go at her).
She made a bee-line for the Major, bloody funny, old boy,
Asked him a lot about horses and India, you know, terribly
      coy –
And this MO fellow was mopping it up and at last he passed
      right out
(Some silly fool behind his back put a bottle of gin in his stout).

I've never seen a man go down so quick. Somebody drove him
    home.
His wife was almost as bad, old boy, said she felt all alone
And nestled up to the Major – it's a great pity you weren't
    there –
And the Padre was arguing about the order of morning and
    evening prayer.
Never laughed so much in all my life. We went on drinking till
    three.
And this woman was doing her best to sit on the Major's knee!
Let's have the blackout boards put up and turn on the other
    light.
Yes, I think you can count on that, old boy – to-night'll be a
    thick night.

PAUL WIDDOWS

Minutiae 3

I am not your lover and you will never know me.
We do not even speak the same language.
When you pass by with a pitcher on your hip
Your steps hurry, and you look purposefully ahead,
And I concentrate on my book.

But next time you come wear the same dress, the blue,
Fasten the same jasmine in your braided hair,
The same golden earrings and jingling anklets wear,
And the song you always stop singing when you near me –
Please let it continue.

ANONYMOUS

Shari Wag El Burka

To the tune of 'Onward, Christian Soldiers'

There is a street in Cairo, full of sin and shame.
Shari Wag El Burka is the bastard's name.

Chorus
Russian, Greek and French bints all around I see,
Shouting out: 'You stupid prick, abide with me.'

Two or three weeks later when I see my dick,
Swiftly pack my small kit and fall in with the sick.

Five or six months later, free from sin and shame,
Back to the El Burka, just for fun and games.

JOHN SHORT

Leave in Mid-Winter

I dig my teeth into the crust of this land
And feel pastry on my lips, in my mouth;
I suck the rhubarb juice of these rivers,
Slaking my drouth.

And winter is pouring white cream
Over this richness as I eat on,
Ravenous as a boy home from snowballing,
Leda with her Swan.

For a plenitude of loveliness
To the soldier starved of physical delight
Alone can fill the belly
And the womanless night.

And though it is his animal carcass
That sleeps and has access to visions of joy,
And has the capacity for repairing
What his nerves destroy,

In the moment of quietness or explosion
When the tree turns into rusty steel,
It is spirit knocks at his rib-bones
And on the tendon of his heel.

The Consolations of Obscenity

The British soldier goes into battle with one word on his lips. There is no imagination required, no variety, no ingenuity; simply the comfort that comes from repetition and the release of frustration. The Padre during my National Service basic training devoted one whole address to the subject of swearing and obscenity. He assured us that the word 'fuck' did not come from the Latin *facere*, 'to do' – he was right there – but stood for 'Felonious Use of Carnal Knowledge'.

ANONYMOUS

Oh! Fucking Halkirk

This fucking town's a fucking cuss.
No fucking trams, no fucking bus.
Nobody cares for fucking us,
In fucking Halkirk.

The fucking roads are fucking bad,
The fucking folk are fucking mad,
It makes the brightest fucking sad,
In fucking Halkirk.

All fucking clouds, all fucking rain,
No fucking kerbs, no fucking drains.
The council's got no fucking brains,
In fucking Halkirk.

No fucking sport, no fucking games,
No fucking fun. The fucking dames
Won't even give their fucking names,
In fucking Halkirk.

Everything's so fucking dear –
A fucking bob for fucking beer.
And is it good? No fucking fear,
In fucking Halkirk.

The fucking flicks are fucking old,
The fucking seats are always sold,
You can't get in for fucking gold,
In fucking Halkirk.

The fucking dances make you smile.
The fucking band is fucking vile.
It only cramps your fucking style,
In fucking Halkirk.

Best fucking place is fucking bed,
With fucking ice on your fucking head.
You might as well be fucking dead,
In fucking Halkirk.

No fucking grub, no fucking mail,
Just fucking snow and fucking hail.
In anguish deep, we fucking wail,
In fucking Halkirk.

The fucking pubs are fucking dry.
The fucking barmaid's fucking fly.
With fucking grief we fucking cry
OH! FUCK HALKIRK!

ANONYMOUS

Generals Ride in Cars

Under the fucking truck, chum,
Flat on me fucking back,
Right in the fucking muck, chum,

Stuck on the fucking track.
Generals ride in cars, chum,
Or go marching smartly by.
But I'm flat on my back on the fucking track,
With oil in me fucking eye.

ANONYMOUS

The Twats in the Ops Room

To the tune of 'John Brown's Body'

We had been flying all day long at one hundred fucking feet,
The weather fucking awful, fucking rain and fucking sleet,
The compass it was swinging fucking south and fucking north,
But we made a fucking landfall in the Firth of Fucking Forth.

Chorus: Ain't the Air Force fucking awful?
Ain't the Air Force fucking awful?
Ain't the Air Force fucking awful?
We made a fucking landing in the Firth of Fucking Forth.

We joined the Air Force 'cos we thought it fucking right,
But don't care if we fucking fly or fucking fight,
But what we do object to are those fucking Ops Room twats,
Who sit there sewing stripes on at the rate of fucking knots.

ANONYMOUS

No Balls at All

The night of the wedding she got into bed.
She sighed with lust, her cheeks were quite red.
She felt for his tool, and his tool was quite small.
She felt for his balls. He'd got no balls at all.

No balls, no balls at all,
She'd married a soldier with no balls at all.

She went to her mother. 'Oh mother,' she said,
'I'd rather be single. I'd rather be dead.
I don't mind a man whose got rather small balls
But balls to a soldier with no balls at all,
No balls, no balls at all,
But balls to a soldier with no balls at all.'

ANONYMOUS

The Army Dance

To the tune of 'Come Comrades, Fill the Flowing Bowl'

First there came the general's wife,
And she was dressed in grey, sir,
And in her quite enormous quim,
She had a brewer's dray, sir.

> *She had those dark and dreamy eyes*
> *And she sang a song of love, sir,*
> *She was one of those black-eyed bints,*
> *She was one of the brigade.*

Next there came the colonel's wife,
And she was dressed in red, sir,
And in her quite enormous quim,
She had a feather bed, sir.

> *Chorus*

Next there came the major's wife,
And she was dressed in pink, sir,
And in her quite enormous quim,
She had a kitchen sink, sir.

> *Chorus*

Next there came the captain's wife,
And she was dressed in blue, sir,
And in her quite enormous quim,
She had some four-by-two, sir.

Chorus

Next there came the sergeant's wife,
And she was dressed in black, sir,
And in her quite enormous quim,
She had a chimney stack, sir.

Chorus

Next there came the corporal's wife,
And she was dressed in brown, sir,
And in her quite enormous quim,
She had all Tidworth town, sir.

Chorus

Home Thoughts

All soldiers want to go home and many sustain themselves simply by virtue of the memories of their loved ones, their friends, and the places where they once lived. This common nostalgia can have one of two effects: the first is to make the soldier so homesick that he is almost prepared to desert; the second is to stiffen his resolve. F. H. Doyle's poem describes an incident in one of the Chinese Opium Wars of the mid-nineteenth century, when a British soldier by the name of Moyle refused to kowtow to his Chinese captors and was executed.

Evocations of home are the main ingredient in Henry Newbolt's two most influential poems of chivalrous exhortation; and even if the scope for individual gallantry was limited, in the First World War, by the very nature of trench warfare – the slogging, interminable misery – thoughts of home helped many to retain their sanity.

Even in death, Rupert Brooke's soldier and Hardy's Drummer Hodge carried their Englishness with them into their graves.

JOHN CLARE

The Soldier

Home furthest off grows dearer from the way;
And when the army in the Indias lay
Friends' letters coming from his native place
Were like old neighbours with their country face.
And every opportunity that came
Opened the sheet to gaze upon the name
Of that loved village where he left his sheep
For more contented peaceful folk to keep;
And friendly faces absent many a year

Would from such letters in his mind appear.
And when his pockets, chafing through the case,
Wore it quite out ere others took the place,
Right loath to be of company bereft
He kept the fragments while a bit was left.

HENRY NEWBOLT

Drake's Drum

Drake he's in his hammock an' a thousand mile away,
　(Capten, art tha sleepin' there below?),
Slung atween the round shot in Nombre Dios Bay,
　An' dreamin' arl the time o' Plymouth Hoe.
Yarnder lumes the Island, yarnder lie the ships,
　Wi' sailor lads a dancin' heel-an'-toe,
An' the shore-lights flashin', an' the night-tide dashin',
　He sees et arl so plainly as he saw et long ago.

Drake he was a Devon man, an' ruled the Devon seas,
　(Capten, art tha sleepin' there below?),
Rovin' tho' his death fell, he went wi' heart at ease,
　An' dreamin' arl the time o' Plymouth Hoe.
'Take my drum to England, hang et by the shore,
　Strike et when your powder's runnin' low;
If the Dons sight Devon, I'll quit the port o' Heaven,
　An' drum them up the Channel as we drummed them long
　　ago.'

Drake he's in his hammock till the great Armadas come,
　(Capten, art tha sleepin' there below?),
Slung atween the round shot, listenin' for the drum,
　An' dreamin' arl the time o' Plymouth Hoe.
Call him on the deep sea, call him up the Sound,
　Call him when ye sail to meet the foe;
Where the old trade's plyin' an' the old flag flyin'

They shall find him ware an' wakin', as they found him long
    ago!

F. H. DOYLE

The Private of the Buffs

Last night, among his fellow roughs,
    He jested, quaffed, and swore,
A drunken private of the Buffs,
    Who never looked before.
To-day, beneath the foeman's frown,
    He stands in Elgin's place,
Ambassador from Britain's crown,
    And type of all her race.

Poor, reckless, rude, low-born, untaught,
    Bewildered, and alone,
A heart, with English instinct fraught,
    He yet can call his own.
Aye, tear his body limb from limb,
    Bring cord, or axe, or flame:
He only knows, that not through *him*
    Shall England come to shame.

Far Kentish hop-fields round him seemed,
    Like dreams, to come and go;
Bright leagues of cherry-blossom gleamed,
    One sheet of living snow;
The smoke, above his father's door,
    In grey soft eddyings hung:
Must he then watch it rise no more,
    Doomed by himself so young?

Yes, honour calls! — with strength like steel
    He put the vision by.

Let dusky Indians whine and kneel;
    An English lad must die.
And thus, with eyes that would not shrink,
    With knee to man unbent,
Unfaltering on its dreadful brink,
    To his red grave he went.

Vain, mightiest fleets of iron framed;
    Vain, those all-shattering guns;
Unless proud England keep, untamed,
    The strong heart of her sons.
So, let his name through Europe ring –
    A man of mean estate,
Who died, as firm as Sparta's king,
    Because his soul was great.

HENRY NEWBOLT

Vitaï Lampada

There's a breathless hush in the Close tonight –
    Ten to make and the match to win –
A bumping pitch and a blinding light,
    An hour to play and the last man in.
And it's not for the sake of a ribboned coat,
    Or the selfish hope of a season's fame,
But his Captain's hand on his shoulder smote –
    'Play up! play up! and play the game!'

The sand of the desert is sodden red, –
    Red with the wreck of a square that broke; –
The Gatling's jammed and the Colonel dead,
    And the regiment blind with dust and smoke.
The river of death has brimmed his banks,
    And England's far, and Honour a name,

But the voice of a schoolboy rallies the ranks:
  'Play up! play up! and play the game!'

This is the word that year by year,
  While in her place the School is set,
Every one of her sons must hear,
  And none that hears it dare forget.
This they all with a joyful mind
  Bear through life like a torch in flame,
And falling fling to the host behind –
  'Play up! play up! and play the game!'

RUPERT BROOKE

The Soldier

If I should die, think only this of me:
  That there's some corner of a foreign field
That is for ever England. There shall be
  In that rich earth a richer dust concealed;
A dust whom England bore, shaped, made aware,
  Gave, once, her flowers to love, her ways to roam,
A body of England's, breathing English air,
  Washed by the rivers, blest by suns of home.

And think, this heart, all evil shed away,
  A pulse in the eternal mind, no less
    Gives somewhere back the thoughts by England given;
Her sights and sounds; dreams happy as her day;
  And laughter, learnt of friends; and gentleness,
    In hearts at peace, under an English heaven.

THOMAS HARDY

Drummer Hodge

I

They throw in Drummer Hodge, to rest
    Uncoffined – just as found:
His landmark is a kopje-crest
    That breaks the veldt around;
And foreign constellations west
    Each night above his mound.

II

Young Hodge the Drummer never knew –
    Fresh from his Wessex home –
The meaning of the broad Karoo,
    The Bush, the dusty loam,
And why uprose to nightly view
    Strange stars amid the gloam.

III

Yet portion of that unknown plain
    Will Hodge for ever be;
His homely Northern breast and brain
    Grow to some Southern tree,
And strange-eyed constellations reign
    His stars eternally.

Useful Tips

In the age before computer-directed missiles, victory in battle used to depend upon the spirit and fitness of the infantryman, who was the backbone of any army. He did not have to be particularly clever and it was a positive disadvantage, as Wilfred Owen points out, to be imaginative – 'Dullness best solves/ The tease and doubt of shelling'. But what he needed above all was steadfastness under fire, especially when his comrades were falling about him. Kipling's poem – 'And march to your front like a soldier' – may sound trite, but it is undeniably true. Sheer doggedness, built upon good training and the spirit of comradeship, has won more battles than any other aspect of personal behaviour.

In 1897, Cardinal Manning wrote an essay on courage which included this passage: 'The highest courage in a soldier is said to be standing still under fire. . . . It is the self-command of duty in obedience to authority . . . but to stand under fire, still and motionless, is a supreme act of the will.'

RUDYARD KIPLING

from The Young British Soldier

When first under fire an' you're wishful to duck
Don't look nor take 'eed at the man that is struck.
Be thankful you're livin', and trust to your luck
    And march to your front like a soldier.
        Front, front, front like a soldier.
        Front, front, front like a soldier,
        Front, front, front like a soldier,
          So-oldier *of* the Queen!

When 'arf of your bullets fly wide in the ditch,
Don't call your Martini a cross-eyed old bitch;
She's human as you are — you treat her as sich,
        An' she'll fight for the young British soldier.
            Fight, fight, fight for the soldier . . .

When shakin' their bustles like ladies so fine,
The guns o' the enemy wheel into line,
Shoot low at the limbers an' don't mind the shine,
        For noise never startles the soldier.
            Start-, start-, startles the soldier . . .

If your officer's dead and the sergeants look white,
Remember it's ruin to run from a fight:
So take open order, lie down, and sit tight,
        And wait for supports like a soldier.
            Wait, wait, wait like a soldier . . .

When you're wounded and left on Afghanistan's plains,
And the women come out to cut up what remains,
Jest roll to your rifle and blow out your brains
        An' go to your Gawd like a soldier.
            Go, go, go like a soldier,
            Go, go, go like a soldier,
            Go, go, go like a soldier,
                So-oldier *of* the Queen!

WILFRED OWEN

Insensibility

I

Happy are men who yet before they are killed
Can let their veins run cold.
Whom no compassion fleers
Or makes their feet

Sore on the alleys cobbled with their brothers.
The front line withers,
But they are troops who fade, not flowers
For poets' tearful fooling:
Men, gaps for filling:
Losses who might have fought
Longer; but no one bothers.

II

And some cease feeling
Even themselves or for themselves.
Dullness best solves
The tease and doubt of shelling,
And Chance's strange arithmetic
Comes simpler than the reckoning of their shilling.
They keep no check on armies' decimation.

III

Happy are those who lose imagination:
They have enough to carry with ammunition.
Their spirit drags no pack,
Their old wounds save with cold can not more ache.
Having seen all things red,
Their eyes are rid
Of the hurt of the colour of blood for ever.
And terror's first constriction over,
Their hearts remain small-drawn.
Their senses in some scorching cautery of battle
Now long since ironed,
Can laugh among the dying, unconcerned.

IV

Happy the soldier home, with not a notion
How somewhere, every dawn, some men attack,

And many sighs are drained.
Happy the lad whose mind was never trained:
His days are worth forgetting more than not.
He sings along the march
Which we march taciturn, because of dusk,
The long, forlorn, relentless trend
From larger day to huger night.

V

We wise, who with a thought besmirch
Blood over all our soul,
How should we see our task
But through his blunt and lashless eyes?
Alive, he is not vital overmuch;
Dying, not mortal overmuch;
Nor sad, nor proud,
Nor curious at all.
He cannot tell
Old men's placidity from his.

VI

But cursed are dullards whom no cannon stuns,
That they should be as stones;
Wretched are they, and mean
With paucity that never was simplicity.
By choice they made themselves immune
To pity and whatever moans in man
Before the last sea and the hapless stars;
Whatever mourns when many leave these shores;
Whatever shares
The eternal reciprocity of tears.

N. J. TRAPNELL

Lament of a Desert Rat

I've learnt to wash in petrol tins, and shave myself in tea
Whilst balancing the fragments of a mirror on my knee
I've learnt to dodge the eighty-eights, and flying lumps of lead
And to keep a foot of sand between a Stuka and my head
I've learnt to keep my ration bag crammed full of buckshee
    food
And to take my Army ration, and to pinch what else I could
I've learnt to cook my bully-beef with candle-ends and string
In an empty petrol can, or any other thing
I've learnt to use my jack-knife for anything I please
A bread-knife, or a chopper, or a prong for toasting cheese
I've learnt to gather souvenirs, that home I hoped to send
And hump them round for months and months, and dump
    them in the end
But one day when this blooming war is just a memory
I'll laugh at all these troubles, when I'm drifting o'er the sea
But until that longed-for day arrives, I'll have to be content
With bully-beef and rice and prunes, and sleeping in a tent.

Views of Death

These poems were all written by fighting men who were obliged to face the possibility of death every hour of the day. Its complete unpredictability fosters a certain fatalism, expressed in attitudes ranging from heroic confrontation to a simple shrug.

ALAN SEEGER

I Have a Rendezvous with Death

I have a rendezvous with Death
At some disputed barricade,
When Spring comes back with rustling shade
And apple-blossoms fill the air –
I have a rendezvous with Death
When Spring brings back blue days and fair.

It may be he shall take my hand
And lead me into his dark land
And close my eyes and quench my breath –
It may be I shall pass him still.
I have a rendezvous with Death
On some scarred slope of battered hill,
When Spring comes round again this year
And the first meadow-flowers appear.

God knows 'twere better to be deep
Pillowed in silk and scented down,
Where Love throbs out in blissful sleep,
Pulse nigh to pulse, and breath to breath,
Where hushed awakenings are dear . . .
But I've a rendezvous with Death
At midnight in some flaming town,

When Spring trips north again this year,
And I to my pledged word am true,
I shall not fail that rendezvous.

WILFRED OWEN

A Terre

Being the Philosophy of Many Soldiers

Sit on the bed. I'm blind, and three parts shell.
Be careful; can't shake hands now; never shall.
Both arms have mutinied against me, – brutes.
My fingers fidget like ten idle brats.

I tried to peg out soldierly, – no use!
One dies of war like any old disease.
This bandage feels like pennies on my eyes.
I have my medals? – Discs to make eyes close.
My glorious ribbons? – Ripped from my own back
In scarlet shreds. (That's for your poetry book.)

A short life and a merry one, my buck!
We used to say we'd hate to live dead-old, –
Yet now . . . I'd willingly be puffy, bald,
And patriotic. Buffers catch from boys
At least the jokes hurled at them. I suppose
Little I'd ever teach a son, but hitting,
Shooting, war, hunting, all the arts of hurting.
Well, that's what I learnt, – that, and making money.
Your fifty years ahead seem none too many?
Tell me how long I've got? God! For one year
To help myself to nothing more than air!
One Spring! Is one too good to spare, too long?
Spring wind would work its own way to my lung,
And grow me legs as quick as lilac-shoots.

My servant's lamed, but listen how he shouts!
When I'm lugged out, he'll still be good for that.
Here in this mummy-case, you know, I've thought
How well I might have swept his floors for ever.
I'd ask no nights off when the bustle's over,
Enjoying so the dirt. Who's prejudiced
Against a grimed hand when his own's quite dust,
Less live than specks that in the sun-shaft turn,
Less warm than dust that mixes with arms' tan?
I'd love to be a sweep, now, black as Town,
Yes; or a muckman. Must I be his load?

O Life, Life, let me breathe, – a dug-out rat!
Not worse than ours the existences rats lead –
Nosing along at night down some safe rut,
They find a shell-proof home before they rot.
Dead men may envy living mites in cheese,
Or good germs even. Microbes have their joys,
And subdivide, and never come to death.
Certainly flowers have the easiest time on earth.
'I shall be one with nature, herb, and stone,'
Shelley would tell me. Shelley would be stunned:
The dullest Tommy hugs that fancy now.
'Pushing up daisies' is their creed, you know.
To grain, then, go my fat, to buds my sap,
For all the usefulness there is in soap.
D'you think the Boche will ever stew man-soup?
Some day, no doubt, if . . .

                              Friend, be very sure
I shall be better off with plants that share
More peaceably the meadow and the shower.
Soft rains will touch me, – as they could touch once,
And nothing but the sun shall make me ware.
Your guns may crash around me. I'll not hear;
Or, if I wince, I shall not know I wince.
Don't take my soul's poor comfort for your jest.

Soldiers may grow a soul when turned to fronds,
But here the thing's best left at home with friends.
My soul's a little grief, grappling your chest,
To climb your throat on sobs; easily chased
On other sighs and wiped by fresher winds.

Carry my crying spirit till it's weaned
To do without what blood remained these wounds.

ROBERT GRAVES

The Leveller

Near Martinpuich that night of hell
Two men were struck by the same shell,
Together tumbling in one heap
Senseless and limp like slaughtered sheep.

One was a pale eighteen-year-old,
Blue-eyed and thin and not too bold,
Pressed for the war ten years too soon,
The shame and pity of his platoon.

The other came from far-off lands
With bristling chin and whiskered hands,
He had known death and hell before
In Mexico and Ecuador.

Yet in his death this cut-throat wild
Groaned 'Mother! Mother!' like a child,
While that poor innocent in man's clothes
Died cursing God with brutal oaths.

Old Sergeant Smith, kindest of men,
Wrote out two copies there and then
Of his accustomed funeral speech
To cheer the womenfolk of each: —

'He died a hero's death: and we
His comrades of "A" Company
Deeply regret his death: we shall
All deeply miss so true a pal.'

WILFRED GIBSON

Breakfast

We ate our breakfast lying on our backs
Because the shells were screeching overhead.
I bet a rasher to a loaf of bread
That Hull United would beat Halifax
When Jimmy Stainthorpe played full-back instead
Of Billy Bradford. Ginger raised his head
And cursed, and took the bet, and dropt back dead.
We ate our breakfast lying on our backs
Because the shells were screeching overhead.

J. G. MEDDEMMEN

L.R.D.G.

He threw his cigarette in silence, then he said:

You can't predict in war;
It's a matter of luck, nothing less, nothing more.
Now here's an instance. Darnley copped it in the head
His third day up the blue although he'd seen the lot
In Dunkerque, Greece and Crete –
The sort that went in tidy and came out neat;
He copped it when the going wasn't even hot.
And there was little Pansy Flowers,
Machine-gunned through the guts; he bled

(And not a murmur from him) for hours
Before he jagged it in.
                              And your remember Bowers?
Bowers got fragmentation in the lungs and thigh;
We couldn't do a thing: the moon was high
And a hell of a bright
On that particular night.
Poor sod, he won't kip in a civvy bed.

It's queer . . . I've even laughed
When blokes have chucked it in and gone daft.
I remember one that scarpered bollock-nude
One midnight, out across the dunes, calling for Mum;
You'd have thought him blewed.
He wasn't seen again – not this side of Kingdom Come.

One job that I really funked
Was when Fat Riley bunked
From a Jerry leaguer on a getaway.
We found him blind, with both hands gone.
When we got him back inside the lines
He'd only say,
Over and over, 'the mines, the mines, the mines'.
It's the lucky ones get dead:
He's still alive. I wonder if his wife understands
How you can't even shoot yourself without your hands.

Far East, 1940s

BARRY CONRAD AMIEL

'Death is a matter of mathematics'

Death is a matter of mathematics.

It screeches down at you from dirtywhite nothingness
And your life is a question of velocity and altitude,

With allowances for wind and the quick, relentless pull
Of gravity.

Or else it lies concealed
In that fleecy, peaceful puff of cloud ahead.
A streamlined, muttering vulture, waiting
To swoop upon you with a rush of steel.
And then your chances vary as the curves
Of your parabolas, your banks, your dives,
The scientific soundness of your choice
Of what to push or pull, and how, and when.

Or perhaps you walk oblivious in a wood,
Or crawl flat-bellied over pockmarked earth,
And Death awaits you in a field-gray tunic.
Sights upright and aligned. Range estimated
And set in. A lightning, subconscious calculation
Of trajectory and deflection. With you the focal point,
The centre of the problem. The A and B
Or Smith and Jones of schoolboy textbooks.

Ten out of ten means you are dead.

Gallantry and Heroism

The *Iliad* recounts numerous acts of valour carried out from a sense of overriding duty. Here, Sarpedon, King of Lycia and one of Troy's allies, tells Glaucus that, when the testing time of battle comes, kings, who have enjoyed hitherto all the good things in life, have a duty to lead from the front. Many a young First World War subaltern might have had that advice in mind as he led his men up and out of the trenches, straight into annihilating fire.

I have included the whole of Macaulay's 'Horatius', because, though long, it is impossible to cut without damage to the story. This tale of courage and self-sacrifice was one of the most popular poems in Victorian England.

But heroism has its capricious side, too. The passage from *The Song of Roland*, in a lively translation by Dorothy L. Sayers, describes Roland's refusal to blow his trumpet, the 'Oliphant', and thus summon Charlemagne and his army to help his much smaller band resist the invading Saracens. Roland's proud gesture was disastrous, since all his force was killed. As Dryden said, the minds of heroes 'stand exempted from the rules of war.'

Wellington's dry scepticism extended to acts of individual gallantry – 'There is nothing on earth', he observed, 'so stupid as a gallant officer.' But heroism is not just for the great, as Sorley Maclean generously recognises.

The last poem, a pastiche of Whitman, was published in 1903 by Ernest Crosby, who had no truck with late-Victorian evangelical patriotism.

HOMER

from The Iliad, Book XII

But Jove against the Greeks sent forth his son
Sarpedon, as a lion on a herd:
His shield's broad orb before his breast he bore,
Well-wrought, of beaten brass, which th' arm'rer's hand
Had beaten out, and lin'd with stout bull's-hide;
With golden rods, continuous, all around;
He thus equipp'd, two jav'lins brandishing,
Strode onward, as a lion, mountain-bred,
Whom, fasting long, his dauntless courage leads
To assail the flock, though in well-guarded fold;
And though the shepherds there he find, prepar'd
With dogs and lances to protect the sheep,
Not unattempted will he leave the fold;
But, springing to the midst, he bears his prey
In triumph thence; or in the onset falls,
Wounded by jav'lins hurl'd by stalwart hands:
So, prompted by his godlike courage, burn'd
Sarpedon to assail the lofty wall,
And storm the ramparts; and to Glaucus thus,
Son of Hippolochus, his speech address'd:
    'Whence is it, Glaucus, that in Lycian land
We two at feasts the foremost seats may claim,
The largest portions, and the fullest cups?
Why held as Gods in honour? why endow'd
With ample heritage, by Xanthus' banks,
Of vineyard, and of wheat-producing land?
Then by the Lycians should we not be seen
The foremost to affront the raging fight?
So may our well-arm'd Lycians make their boast;
"To no inglorious Kings we Lycians owe
Allegiance; they on richest viands feed;

Of luscious flavour drink the choicest wine;
But still their valour brightest shows; and they,
Where Lycians war, are foremost in the fight!"
O friend! if we, survivors of this war,
Could live, from age and death for ever free,
Thou shouldst not see me foremost in the fight,
Nor would I urge thee to the glorious field:
But since on man ten thousand forms of death
Attend, which none may 'scape, then on, that we
May glory on others gain, or they on us!'

Translated from the Greek by the Earl of Derby

THOMAS BABINGTON, LORD MACAULAY

Horatius

A Lay made about the Year of the City CCCLX

I

Lars Porsena of Clusium
   By the Nine Gods he swore
That the great house of Tarquin
   Should suffer wrong no more.
By the Nine Gods he swore it,
   And named a trysting day,
And bade his messengers ride forth,
East and west and south and north,
   To summon his array.

II

East and west and south and north
   The messengers ride fast,
And tower and town and cottage
   Have heard the trumpet's blast.

Shame on the false Etruscan
   Who lingers in his home,
When Porsena of Clusium
   Is on the march for Rome.

III

The horsemen and the footmen
   Are pouring in amain
From many a stately market-place;
   From many a fruitful plain;
From many a lonely hamlet,
   Which, hid by beech and pine,
Like an eagle's nest, hangs on the crest
   Of purple Apennine;

IV

From lordly Volaterræ,
   Where scowls the far-famed hold
Piled by the hands of giants
   For godlike kings of old;
From seagirt Populonia,
   Whose sentinels descry
Sardinia's snowy mountain-tops
   Fringing the southern sky;

V

From the proud mart of Pisæ,
   Queen of the western waves,
Where ride Massilia's triremes
   Heavy with fair-haired slaves;
From where sweet Clanis wanders
   Through corn and vines and flowers;
From where Cortona lifts to heaven
   Her diadem of towers.

VI

Tall are the oaks whose acorns
  Drop in dark Auser's rill:
Fat are the stags that champ the boughs
  Of the Ciminian hill;
Beyond all streams Clitumnus
  Is to the herdsman dear;
Best of all pools the fowler loves
  The great Volsinian mere.

VII

But now no stroke of woodman
  Is heard by Auser's rill;
No hunter tracks the stag's green path
  Up the Ciminian hill;
Unwatched along Clitumnus
  Grazes the milk-white steer;
Unharmed the water fowl may dip
  In the Volsinian mere.

VIII

The harvests of Arretium,
  This year, old men shall reap;
This year, young boys in Umbro
  Shall plunge the struggling sheep;
And in the vats of Luna,
  This year, the must shall foam
Round the white feet of laughing girls,
  Whose sires have marched to Rome.

IX

There be thirty chosen prophets,
  The wisest of the land,
Who alway by Lars Porsena

Both morn and evening stand:
Evening and morn the Thirty
  Have turned the verses o'er,
Traced from the right on linen white
  By mighty seers of yore.

X

And with one voice the Thirty
  Have their glad answer given:
'Go forth, go forth, Lars Porsena;
  Go forth, beloved of Heaven;
Go, and return in glory
  To Clusium's royal dome;
And hang round Nurscia's altars
  The golden shields of Rome.'

XI

And now hath every city
  Sent up her tale of men;
The foot are fourscore thousand,
  The horse are thousands ten.
Before the gates of Sutrium
  Is met the great array.
A proud man was Lars Porsena
  Upon the trysting day.

XII

For all the Etruscan armies
  Were ranged beneath his eye,
And many a banished Roman,
  And many a stout ally;
And with a mighty following
  To join the muster came
The Tusculan Mamilius,
  Prince of the Latian name.

XIII

But by the yellow Tiber
  Was tumult and affright:
From all the spacious champaign
  To Rome men took their flight.
A mile around the city,
  The throng stopped up the ways;
A fearful sight it was to see
  Through two long nights and days

XIV

For aged folks on crutches,
  And women great with child,
And mothers sobbing over babes
  That clung to them and smiled,
And sick men borne in litters
  High on the necks of slaves,
And troops of sun-burned husbandmen
  With reaping-hooks and staves,

XV

And droves of mules and asses
  Laden with skins of wine,
And endless flocks of goats and sheep,
  And endless herds of kine,
And endless trains of waggons
  That creaked beneath the weight
Of corn-sacks and of household goods,
  Choked every roaring gate.

XVI

Now, from the rock Tarpeian,
  Could the wan burghers spy
The line of blazing villages

Red in the midnight sky.
The Fathers of the City,
    They sat all night and day,
For every hour some horseman came
    With tidings of dismay.

XVII

To eastward and to westward
    Have spread the Tuscan bands;
Nor house, nor fence, nor dovecote
    In Crustumerium stands.
Verbenna down to Ostia
    Hath wasted all the plain;
Astur hath stormed Janiculum,
    And the stout guards are slain.

XVIII

I wish, in all the Senate,
    There was no heart so bold,
But sore it ached, and fast it beat,
    When that ill news was told.
Forthwith up rose the Consul,
    Up rose the Fathers all;
In haste they girded up their gowns,
    And hied them to the wall.

XIX

They held a council standing
    Before the River-Gate;
Short time was there, ye well may guess,
    For musing or debate.
Out spake the Consul roundly:
    'The bridge must straight go down;
For, since Janiculum is lost,
    Nought else can save the town.'

XX

Just then a scout came flying,
　All wild with haste and fear:
'To arms! to arms! Sir Consul;
　Lars Porsena is here.'
On the low hills to westward
　The Consul fixed his eye,
And saw the swarthy storm of dust
　Rise fast along the sky.

XXI

And nearer fast and nearer
　Doth the red whirlwind come;
And louder still and still more loud,
From underneath that rolling cloud,
Is heard the trumpet's war-note proud,
　The trampling, and the hum.
And plainly and more plainly
　Now through the gloom appears,
Far to left and far to right,
In broken gleams of dark-blue light,
The long array of helmets bright,
　The long array of spears.

XXII

And plainly and more plainly,
　Above that glimmering line,
Now might ye see the banners
　Of twelve fair cities shine;
But the banner of proud Clusium
　Was highest of them all,
The terror of the Umbrian,
　The terror of the Gaul.

XXIII

And plainly and more plainly
  Now might the burghers know,
By port and vest, by horse and crest,
  Each warlike Lucumo.
There Cilnius of Arretium
  On his fleet roan was seen;
And Astur of the four-fold shield,
Girt with the brand none else may wield,
Tolumnius with the belt of gold,
And dark Verbenna from the hold
  By reedy Thrasymene.

XXIV

Fast by the royal standard,
  O'erlooking all the war,
Lars Porsena of Clusium
  Sat in his ivory car.
By the right wheel rode Mamilius,
  Prince of the Latian name;
And by the left false Sextus,
  That wrought the deed of shame.

XXV

But when the face of Sextus
  Was seen among the foes,
A yell that rent the firmament
  From all the town arose.
On the house-tops was no woman
  But spat towards him and hissed
No child but screamed out curses,
  And shook its little fist.

XXVI

But the Consul's brow was sad,
    And the Consul's speech was low,
And darkly looked he at the wall,
    And darkly at the foe.
'Their van will be upon us
    Before the bridge goes down;
And if they once may win the bridge,
    What hope to save the town?'

XXVII

Then out spake brave Horatius,
    The Captain of the Gate:
'To every man upon this earth
    Death cometh soon or late.
And how can man die better
    Than facing fearful odds,
For the ashes of his fathers,
    And the temples of his Gods,

XXVIII

'And for the tender mother
    Who dandled him to rest,
And for the wife who nurses
    His baby at her breast,
And for the holy maidens
    Who feed the eternal flame,
To save them from false Sextus
    That wrought the deed of shame?

XXIX

'Hew down the bridge, Sir Consul,
    With all the speed ye may;
I, with two more to help me,

Will hold the foe in play.
In yon strait path a thousand
  May well be stopped by three.
Now who will stand on either hand,
  And keep the bridge with me?'

XXX

Then out spake Spurius Lartius;
  A Ramnian proud was he:
'Lo, I will stand at thy right hand,
  And keep the bridge with thee.'
And out spake strong Herminius;
  Of Titian blood was he:
'I will abide on thy left side,
  And keep the bridge with thee.'

XXXI

'Horatius,' quoth the Consul,
  'As thou sayest, so let it be.'
And straight against that great array
  Forth went the dauntless Three.
For Romans in Rome's quarrel
  Spared neither land nor gold,
Nor son nor wife, nor limb nor life,
  In the brave days of old.

XXXII

Then none was for a party;
  Then all were for the state;
Then the great man helped the poor,
  And the poor man loved the great:
Then lands were fairly portioned;
  Then spoils were fairly sold:
The Romans were like brothers
  In the brave days of old.

XXXIII

Now Roman is to Roman
  More hateful than a foe,
And the Tribunes beard the high,
  And the Fathers grind the low.
As we wax hot in faction,
  In battle we wax cold:
Wherefore men fight not as they fought
  In the brave days of old.

XXXIV

Now while the Three were tightening
  Their harness on their backs,
The Consul was the foremost man
  To take in hand an axe:
And Fathers mixed with Commons
  Seized hatchet, bar, and crow,
And smote upon the planks above,
  And loosed the props below.

XXXV

Meanwhile the Tuscan army,
  Right glorious to behold,
Came flashing back the noonday light,
Rank behind rank, like surges bright
  Of a broad sea of gold.
Four hundred trumpets sounded
  A peal of warlike glee,
As that great host, with measured tread,
And spears advanced, and ensigns spread,
Rolled slowly towards the bridge's head,
  Where stood the dauntless Three.

XXXVI

The Three stood calm and silent,
  And looked upon the foes,
And a great shout of laughter
  From all the vanguard rose:
And forth three chiefs came spurring
  Before that deep array;
To earth they sprang, their swords they drew,
And lifted high their shields, and flew
  To win the narrow way;

XXXVII

Aunus from green Tifernum,
  Lord of the Hill of Vines;
And Seius, whose eight hundred slaves
  Sicken in Ilva's mines;
And Picus, long to Clusium
  Vassal in peace and war,
Who led to fight his Umbrian powers
From that grey crag where, girt with towers,
The fortress of Nequinum lowers
  O'er the pale waves of Nar.

XXXVIII

Stout Lartius hurled down Aunus
  Into the stream beneath:
Herminius struck at Seius,
  And clove him to the teeth:
At Picus brave Horatius
  Darted one fiery thrust;
And the proud Umbrian's gilded arms
  Clashed in the bloody dust.

XXXIX

Then Ocnus of Falerii
　　Rushed on the Roman Three;
And Lausulus of Urgo,
　　The rover of the sea;
And Aruns of Volsinium,
　　Who slew the great wild boar,
The great wild boar that had his den
Amidst the reeds of Cosa's fen,
And wasted fields, and slaughtered men,
　　Along Albinia's shore.

XL

Herminius smote down Aruns:
　　Lartius laid Ocnus low:
Right to the heart of Lausulus
　　Horatius sent a blow.
'Lie there,' he cried, 'fell pirate!
　　No more, aghast and pale,
From Ostia's walls the crowd shall mark
The track of thy destroying bark.
No more Campania's hinds shall fly
To woods and caverns when they spy
　　Thy thrice accursed sail.'

XLI

But now no sound of laughter
　　Was heard among the foes.
A wild and wrathful clamour
　　From all the vanguard rose.
Six spears' lengths from the entrance
　　Halted that deep array,
And for a space no man came forth
　　To win the narrow way.

XLII

But hark! the cry is Astur:
　　And lo! the ranks divide;
And the great Lord of Luna
　　Comes with his stately stride.
Upon his ample shoulders
　　Clangs loud the four-fold shield,
And in his hand he shakes the brand
　　Which none but he can wield.

XLIII

He smiled on those bold Romans
　　A smile serene and high;
He eyed the flinching Tuscans,
　　And scorn was in his eye.
Quoth he, 'The she-wolf's litter
　　Stand savagely at bay:
But will ye dare to follow,
　　If Astur clears the way?'

XLIV

Then, whirling up his broadsword
　　With both hands to the height,
He rushed against Horatius,
　　And smote with all his might.
With shield and blade Horatius
　　Right deftly turned the blow.
The blow, though turned, came yet too nigh;
It missed his helm, but gashed his thigh:
The Tuscans raised a joyful cry
　　To see the red blood flow.

XLV

He reeled, and on Herminius
　　He leaned one breathing-space;
Then, like a wild cat mad with wounds,
　　Sprang right at Astur's face.
Through teeth, and skull, and helmet
　　So fierce a thrust he sped,
The good sword stood a hand-breadth out
　　Behind the Tuscan's head.

XLVI

And the great Lord of Luna
　　Fell at that deadly stroke,
As falls on Mount Alvernus
　　A thunder-smitten oak.
Far o'er the crashing forest
　　The giant arms lie spread;
And the pale augurs, muttering low,
　　Gaze on the blasted head.

XLVII

On Astur's throat Horatius
　　Right firmly pressed his heel,
And thrice and four times tugged amain,
　　Ere he wrenched out the steel.
'And see,' he cried, 'the welcome,
　　Fair guests, that waits you here!
What noble Lucumo comes next
　　To taste our Roman cheer?'

XLVIII

But at his haughty challenge
　　A sullen murmur ran,
Mingled of wrath, and shame, and dread,

Along that glittering van.
There lacked not men of prowess,
    Nor men of lordly race;
For all Etruria's noblest
    Were round the fatal place.

XLIX

But all Etruria's noblest
    Felt their hearts sink to see
On the earth the bloody corpses,
    In the path the dauntless Three:
And, from the ghastly entrance
    Where those bold Romans stood,
All shrank, like boys who unaware,
Ranging the woods to start a hare,
Come to the mouth of the dark lair
Where, growling low, a fierce old bear
    Lies amidst bones and blood.

L

Was none who would be foremost
    To lead such dire attack:
But those behind cried 'Forward!'
    And those before cried 'Back!'
And backward now and forward
    Wavers the deep array;
And on the tossing sea of steel,
To and fro the standards reel;
And the victorious trumpet-peal
    Dies fitfully away.

LI

Yet one man for one moment
    Strode out before the crowd;
Well known was he to all the Three,

And they gave him greeting loud.
'Now welcome, welcome, Sextus!
    Now welcome to thy home!
Why dost thou stay, and turn away?
    Here lies the road to Rome.'

LII

Thrice looked he at the city;
    Thrice looked he at the dead;
And thrice came on in fury,
    And thrice turned back in dread:
And, white with fear and hatred,
    Scowled at the narrow way
Where, wallowing in a pool of blood,
    The bravest Tuscans lay.

LIII

But meanwhile axe and lever
    Have manfully been plied;
And now the bridge hangs tottering
    Above the boiling tide.
'Come back, come back, Horatius!'
    Loud cried the Fathers all.
'Back, Lartius! back, Herminius!
    Back, ere the ruin fall!'

LIV

Back darted Spurius Lartius;
    Herminius darted back:
And, as they passed, beneath their feet
    They felt the timbers crack.
But when they turned their faces,
    And on the farther shore
Saw brave Horatius stand alone,
    They would have crossed once more.

LV

But with a crash like thunder
 Fell every loosened beam,
And, like a dam, the mighty wreck
 Lay right athwart the stream:
And a long shout of triumph
 Rose from the walls of Rome,
As to the highest turret-tops
 Was splashed the yellow foam.

LVI

And, like a horse unbroken
 When first he feels the rein,
The furious river struggled hard,
 And tossed his tawny mane,
And burst the curb, and bounded,
 Rejoicing to be free,
And whirling down, in fierce career,
Battlement, and plank, and pier,
 Rushed headlong to the sea.

LVII

Alone stood brave Horatius,
 But constant still in mind;
Thrice thirty thousand foes before,
 And the broad flood behind.
'Down with him!' cried false Sextus,
 With a smile on his pale face.
'Now yield thee,' cried Lars Porsena,
 'Now yield thee to our grace.'

LVIII

Round turned he, as not deigning
 Those craven ranks to see;

Nought spake he to Lars Porsena,
 To Sextus nought spake he;
But he saw on Palatinus
 The white porch of his home;
And he spake to the noble river
 That rolls by the towers of Rome.

LIX

'Oh, Tiber! father Tiber!
 To whom the Romans pray,
A Roman's life, a Roman's arms,
 Take thou in charge this day!'
So he spake, and speaking sheathed
 The good sword by his side,
And with his harness on his back,
 Plunged headlong in the tide.

LX

No sound of joy or sorrow
 Was heard from either bank;
But friends and foes in dumb surprise,
With parted lips and straining eyes,
 Stood gazing where he sank;
And when above the surges
 They saw his crest appear,
All Rome sent forth a rapturous cry,
And even the ranks of Tuscany
 Could scarce forbear to cheer.

LXI

But fiercely ran the current,
 Swollen high by months of rain:
And fast his blood was flowing;
 And he was sore in pain,
And heavy with his armour,

And spent with changing blows:
And oft they thought him sinking,
  But still again he rose.

LXII

Never, I ween, did swimmer,
  In such an evil case,
Struggle through such a raging flood
  Safe to the landing place:
But his limbs were borne up bravely
  By the brave heart within,
And our good father Tiber
  Bare bravely up his chin.

LXIII

'Curse on him!' quoth false Sextus;
  'Will not the villain drown?
But for this stay, ere close of day
  We should have sacked the town!'
'Heaven help him!' quoth Lars Porsena,
  'And bring him safe to shore;
For such a gallant feat of arms
  Was never seen before.'

LXIV

And now he feels the bottom;
  Now on dry earth he stands;
Now round him throng the Fathers
  To press his gory hands;
And now, with shouts and clapping,
  And noise of weeping loud,
He enters through the River-Gate,
  Borne by the joyous crowd.

LXV

They gave him of the corn-land,
  That was of public right,
As much as two strong oxen
  Could plough from morn till night;
And they made a molten image,
  And set it up on high,
And there it stands unto this day
  To witness if I lie.

LXVI

It stands in the Comitium,
  Plain for all folk to see;
Horatius in his harness,
  Halting upon one knee:
And underneath is written,
  In letters all of gold,
How valiantly he kept the bridge
  In the brave days of old.

LXVII

And still his name sounds stirring
  Unto the men of Rome,
As the trumpet-blast that cries to them
  To charge the Volscian home;
And wives still pray to Juno
  For boys with hearts as bold
As his who kept the bridge so well
  In the brave days of old.

LXVIII

And in the nights of winter,
  When the cold north winds blow,
And the long howling of the wolves

Is heard amidst the snow;
When round the lonely cottage
  Roars loud the tempest's din,
And the good logs of Algidus
  Roar louder yet within;

LXIX

When the oldest cask is opened,
  And the largest lamp is lit;
When the chestnuts glow in the embers,
  And the kid turns on the spit;
When young and old in circle
  Around the firebrands close;
When the girls are weaving baskets,
  And the lads are shaping bows;

LXX

When the goodman mends his armour,
  And trims his helmet's plume;
When the goodwife's shuttle merrily
  Goes flashing through the loom;
With weeping and with laughter
  Still is the story told,
How well Horatius kept the bridge
  In the brave days of old.

ANONYMOUS

from The Song of Roland

80

Oliver's climbed upon a hilly crest,
Looks to his right along a grassy cleft,
And sees the Paynims and how they ride addressed.

To his companion Roland he calls and says:
'I see from Spain a tumult and a press –
Many bright hauberks, and many a shining helm!
A day of wrath, they'll make it for our French.
Ganelon knew it, false heart and traitor fell;
When to the Emperor he named us for this stead!'
Quoth Roland: 'Silence, Count Oliver, my friend!
He is my stepsire, I will have no word said.'

81

Oliver's climbed a hill above the plain,
Whence he can look on all the land of Spain,
And see how vast the Saracen array;
All those bright helms with gold and jewels gay,
And all those shields, those coats of burnished mail;
And all those lances from which the pennons wave;
Even their squadrons defy all estimate,
He cannot count them, their numbers are so great;
Stout as he is, he's mightily dismayed.
He hastens down as swiftly as he may,
Comes to the French and tells them all his tale.

82

Quoth Oliver: 'The Paynim strength I've seen;
Never on earth has such a hosting been:
A hundred thousand in van ride under shield
Their helmets laced, their hauberks all agleam
Their spears upright, with heads of shining steel.
You'll have such battle as ne'er was fought on field.
My lords of France, God give you strength at need!
Save you stand fast, this field we cannot keep.'
The French all say: 'Foul shame it were to flee!
We're yours till death; no man of us will yield.'

83

Quoth Oliver: 'Huge are the Paynim hordes,
And of our French the numbers seem but small.
Companion Roland, I pray you sound your horn,
That Charles may hear and fetch back all his force.'
Roland replies: 'Madman were I and more,
And in fair France my fame would suffer scorn.
I'll smite great strokes with Durendal my sword,
I'll dye it red high as the hilt with gore.
This pass the Paynims reached on a luckless morn;
I swear to you death is their doom therefor.'

84

'Companion Roland, your Olifant now sound!
King Charles will hear and turn his armies round;
He'll succour us with all his kingly power.'
Roland replies: 'May never God allow
That I should cast dishonour on my house
Or on fair France bring any ill renown!
Rather will I with Durendal strike out,
With this good sword, here on my baldrick bound;
From point to hilt you'll see the blood run down.
Woe worth the Paynims that e'er they made this rout
I pledge my faith, we'll smite them dead on ground.'

85

'Companion Roland, your Olifant now blow;
Charles in the passes will hear it as he goes,
Trust me, the French will all return right so.'
'Now God forbid', Roland makes answer wroth,
'That living man should say he saw me go
Blowing of horns for any Paynim foe!
Ne'er shall my kindred be put to such reproach.
When I shall stand in this great clash of hosts

I'll strike a thousand and then sev'n hundred strokes,
Blood-red the steel of Durendal shall flow.
Stout are the French, they will do battle bold,
These men of Spain shall die and have no hope.'

86

Quoth Oliver: 'Herein I see no blame:
I have beheld the Saracens of Spain;
They cover all the mountains and the vales,
They spread across the hillsides and the plains;
Great is the might these foreigners display,
And ours appears a very small array.'
'I thirst the more', quoth Roland, 'for the fray.
God and His angels forbid it now, I pray,
That e'er by me fair France should be disfamed!
I'd rather die than thus be put to shame;
If the King loves us it's for our valour's sake.'

87

Roland is fierce and Oliver is wise
And both for valour may bear away the prize.
Once horsed and armed the quarrel to decide,
For dread of death the field they'll never fly.
The counts are brave, their words are stern and high.
Now the false Paynims with wondrous fury ride.
Quoth Oliver: 'Look, Roland, they're in sight.
Charles is far off, and these are very nigh;
You would not sound your Olifant for pride;
Had we the Emperor we should have been all right.
To Gate of Spain turn now and lift your eyes,
See for yourself the rear-guard's woeful plight.
Who fights this day will never more see fight.'
Roland relies: 'Speak no such foul despite!
Curst be the breast whose heart knows cowardise!

Here in our place we'll stand and here abide:
Buffets and blows be ours to take and strike!'

88

When Roland sees the battle there must be
Leopard nor lion ne'er grew so fierce as he.
He calls the French, bids Oliver give heed:
'Sir friend and comrade, such words you shall not speak!
When the King gave us the French to serve this need
These twenty thousand he chose to do the deed;
And well he knew not one would flinch or flee.
Men must endure much hardship for their liege,
And bear for him great cold and burning heat,
Suffer sharp wounds and let their bodies bleed.
Smite with your lance and I with my good steel,
My Durendal the Emperor gave to me:
And if I die, who gets it may agree
That he who bore it, a right good knight was he.'

Translated from the French by Dorothy L. Sayers

WILLIAM SHAKESPEARE

from Othello (Act I, Scene iii)

Othello: Her father lov'd me, oft invited me,
Still question'd me the story of my life,
From year to year; the battles, sieges, fortunes,
That I have pass'd:
I ran it through, even from my boyish days,
To the very moment that he bade me tell it.
Wherein I spake of most disastrous chances,
Of moving accidents by flood and field;
Of hair-breadth scapes i' th' imminent deadly breach;
Of being taken by the insolent foe;

And sold to slavery, and my redemption thence,
And with it all my travel's history;
Wherein of antres vast, and deserts idle,
Rough quarries, rocks and hills, whose heads touch heaven,
It was my hint to speak, such was the process:
And of the Cannibals, that each other eat;
The Anthropophagi, and men whose heads
Do grow beneath their shoulders: this to hear
Would Desdemona seriously incline;
But still the house-affairs would draw her thence,
And ever as she could with haste dispatch,
She'ld come again, and with a greedy ear
Devour up my discourse; which I observing,
Took once a pliant hour, and found good means
To draw from her a prayer of earnest heart,
That I would all my pilgrimage dilate,
Whereof by parcel she had something heard,
But not intentively: I did consent,
And often did beguile her of her tears,
When I did speak of some distressed stroke
That my youth suffer'd: my story being done,
She gave me for my pains a world of sighs;
She swore i' faith 'twas strange, 'twas passing strange;
'Twas pitiful, 'twas wondrous pitiful;
She wish'd she had not heard it, yet she wish'd
That heaven had made her such a man: she thank'd me,
And bade me, if I had a friend that lov'd her,
I should but teach him how to tell my story,
And that would woo her. Upon this hint I spake:
She lov'd me for the dangers I had pass'd,
And I lov'd her that she did pity them.
This only is the witchcraft I have us'd:
Here comes the lady, let her witness it.

JOHN DRYDEN

from The Conquest of Granada

 Almanzor: 'Tis war again, and I am glad 'tis so;
Success shall now by force and courage go.
Treaties are but the combat of the brain,
Where still the stronger lose, and weaker gain.
 Abdelmelech: On this assault, brave sir, which we prepare,
Depends the sum and fortune of the war.
Encamped without the fort the Spaniard lies,
And may, in spite of us, send in supplies.
Consider yet, ere we attack the place,
What 'tis to storm it in an army's face.
 Almanzor: The minds of heroes their own measures are,
They stand exempted from the rules of war.
One loose, one sally of the hero's soul,
Does all the military art control:
While timorous wit goes round, or fords the shore,
He shoots the gulf, and is already o'er;
And, when the enthusiastic fit is spent,
Looks back amazed at what he underwent.

THOMAS HARDY

from The Dynasts, Part I (Act 3, Scene iii)

 Decrès (to Napoléon): A certain sort of bravery
Some people have – to wit, this same Lord Nelson –
Which is but fatuous faith in one's own star
Swoln to the very verge of childishness,
(Smugly disguised as putting trust in God,
A habit with these English folk); whereby
A headstrong blindness to contingencies

Carries the actor on, and serves him well
In some nice issues clearer sight would mar.

W. B. YEATS

An Irish Airman Foresees His Death

I know that I shall meet my fate
Somewhere among the clouds above;
Those that I fight I do not hate,
Those that I guard I do not love;
My country is Kiltartan Cross,
My countrymen Kiltartan's poor,
No likely end could bring them loss
Or leave them happier than before.
Nor law, nor duty bade me fight,
Nor public men, nor cheering crowds,
A lonely impulse of delight
Drove to this tumult in the clouds;
I balanced all, brought all to mind,
The years to come seemed waste of breath,
A waste of breath the years behind
In balance with this life, this death.

HERBERT ASQUITH

The Volunteer

Here lies the clerk who half his life had spent
Toiling at ledgers in a city grey,
Thinking that so his days would drift away
With no lance broken in Life's tournament:
Yet ever 'twixt the books and his bright eyes
The gleaming eagles of the legions came,

And horsemen, charging under phantom skies,
Went thundering past beneath the oriflamme.
And now those waiting dreams are satisfied;
From twilight to the halls of dawn he went;
His lance is broken; but he lies content
With that high hour, in which he lived and died.
And falling thus, he wants no recompense,
Who found his battle in the last resort;
Nor needs he any hearse to bear him hence,
Who goes to join the men of Agincourt.

ROBERT GRAVES

David and Goliath

For D. C. T., killed at Fricourt, March 1916

Yet once an earlier David took
Smooth pebbles from the brook:
Out between the lines he went
To that one-sided tournament,
A shepherd boy who stood out fine
And young to fight a Philistine
Clad all in brazen mail. He swears
That he's killed lions, he's killed bears,
And those that scorn the God of Zion
Shall perish so like bear or lion.
But . . . the historian of that fight
Had not the heart to tell it right.

Striding within javelin range,
Goliath marvels at this strange
Goodly-faced boy so proud of strength.
David's clear eye measures the length;
With hand thrust back, he cramps one knee,
Poises a moment thoughtfully,
And hurls with a long vengeful swing.

The pebble, humming from the sling
Like a wild bee, flies a sure line
For the forehead of the Philistine;
Then . . . but there comes a brazen clink,
And quicker than a man can think
Goliath's shield parries each cast.
Clang! clang! and clang! was David's last.
Scorn blazes in the Giant's eye,
Towering unhurt six cubits high.
Says foolish David, 'Damn your shield!
And damn my sling! but I'll not yield.'
He takes his staff of Mamre oak,
A knotted shepherd-staff that's broke
The skull of many a wolf and fox
Come filching lambs from Jesse's flocks.
Loud laughs Goliath, and that laugh
Can scatter chariots like blown chaff
To rout; but David, calm and brave,
Holds his ground, for God will save.
Steel crosses wood, a flash, and oh!
Shame for beauty's overthrow!
(God's eyes are dim, His ears are shut.)
One cruel backhand sabre-cut –
'I'm hit! I'm killed!' young David cries,
Throws blindly forward, chokes . . . and dies.
And look, spike-helmeted, grey, grim,
Goliath straddles over him.

KEITH DOUGLAS

Aristocrats

'I think I am becoming a God'

The noble horse with courage in his eye
clean in the bone, looks up at a shellburst:

away fly the images of the shires
but he puts the pipe back in his mouth.

Peter was unfortunately killed by an 88:
it took his leg away, he died in the ambulance.
I saw him crawling on the sand; he said
It's most unfair, they've shot my foot off.

How can I live among this gentle
obsolescent breed of heroes, and not weep?
Unicorns, almost,
for they are falling into two legends
in which their stupidity and chivalry
are celebrated. Each, fool and hero, will be an immortal.

The plains were their cricket pitch
and in the mountains the tremendous drop fences
brought down some of the runners. Here then
under the stones and earth they dispose themselves,
I think with their famous unconcern.
It is not gunfire I hear but a hunting horn.

SORLEY MACLEAN

Heroes

I did not see Lannes at Ratisbon
nor MacLennan at Auldearn
nor Gillies MacBain at Culloden,
but I saw an Englishman in Egypt.

A poor little chap with chubby cheeks
and knees grinding each other,
pimply unattractive face –
garment of the bravest spirit.

He was not a hit 'in the pub
in the time of the fists being closed,'
but a lion against the breast of battle,
in the morose wounding showers.

His hour came with the shells,
with the notched iron splinters,
in the smoke and flame,
in the shaking and terror of the battlefield.

Word came to him in the bullet shower
that he should be a hero briskly,
and he was that while he lasted
but it wasn't much time he got.

He kept his guns to the tanks,
bucking with tearing crashing screech,
until he himself got, about the stomach,
that biff that put him to the ground,
mouth down in sand and gravel,
without a chirp from his ugly high-pitched voice.

No cross or medal was put to his
chest or to his name or to his family;
there were not many of his troop alive,
and if there were their word would not be strong.
And at any rate, if a battle post stands
many are knocked down because of him,
not expecting fame, not wanting a medal
or any froth from the mouth of the field of slaughter.

I saw a great warrior of England,
a poor manikin on whom no eye would rest;
no Alasdair of Glen Garry;
and he took a little weeping to my eyes.

ERNEST CROSBY

from War and Hell

Hail to the hero!
Decked out in blue, red, and gilt, as in war-paint –
Rejoicing like a savage in a long head-feather and gold
    shoulder fringes –
Proud to commit with these adornments all the crimes for
    which he would be disgraced and punished as a felon
    without them –
Modestly bearing on his breast a star and ribbon which say, 'I
    am a hero,' as plainly as the beggar's placard says 'I am
    blind' –
Followed by a brass band and brass drum, which screw up his
    courage at a pinch like the war dance and tom-tom of the
    Central African and redskin –
Vain of his manliness in the field while indulging in effeminate
    quarreling over the honors, at the rate of a month's
    quarreling to a half-hour's fighting –
Admitting that he obeys orders without thinking, and thus
    proclaiming his complete abdication of conscience and
    intellect –
Rushing home from the fray to advertise himself in the
    magazines at a hundred dollars a page –
Hail to the hero!

O shade of Cervantes!
Come back and draw for us another Don Quixote.
Prick this bubble of militarism as you pricked that other
    bubble of knight-errantry.
The world yearns for your reappearing.
Come and depict the hero!

Killing

Christopher Logue's treatment of the *Iliad* is very free, but it captures brilliantly the physical violence and sheer pace and heat of battle. The actual business of killing was much more brutal in the days of hand-to-hand fighting. Menelaus literally bites through the jugular vein of an opponent, and the spear of Patroclus, the handsome young companion of Achilles, does much the same work as the bayonet of Herbert Read's Happy Warrior. Kill or be killed is the lesson of war.

At the opposite dramatic extreme, Keith Douglas, in the Western Desert, coolly trains his sights on a German, whom he is about to turn into a ghost, and is amused to see how easy it is.

CHRISTOPHER LOGUE

from War Music: An Account of Books 16 to 19 of Homer's *Iliad*

Fate's sister, Fortune, favours those
Who keep their nerve.
Thestor was not like this.
He lost his head, first; then his life.
His chariot bucked too slow over the rutted corpses,
And as Patroclus drew abreast of him,
The terrified boy let the horses baulk,
Leaving the reins to flow beside the car,
And cowered in its varnished basket,
Weeping.
They passed so close that hub skinned hub.
Ahead, Patroclus braked a shade, and then,
And gracefully as men in oilskins cast
Fake insects over trout, he speared the boy,

And with his hip his pivot, prised Thestor up and out
As easily as later men detach
A sardine from an opened tin.

CHRISTOPHER LOGUE

from War Music: An Account of Books 16 to 19
of Homer's *Iliad*

   See how that Royal fights:
Flaking his blade on Python's hip,
He rakes its splintered edge down Cazca's back,
Tosses aside the stump,
And with his ever-vengeful, empty hands,
Grabs Midon, old King Raphno's eldest son
– Known as Count Suckle to his enemies –
Expert at dicing, good in bed, who once
(Just for a joke, of course) ate thirty vulture's eggs
At one of Helen's parties on the Wall.
And later men recalled how he was slain;
One swearing 'gutted,' one, 'that he was ripped
Up the front until his belly grinned,'
And some were quite convinced he ran away
And lived ten thousand days beside a cool
And amethystine lake in Phrygia;
But if you want the truth, well . . .
King Menalaos got him by the ears
Bowed back his chubby neck and bit
A lump out of his jugular –
'Sweet God, his dirty blood is in my eyes!
Some Trojan runt will stick me . . . ' but
She who admired him wiped the mess away.

HERBERT READ

The Happy Warrior

from The Scene of War

His wild heart beats with painful sobs
his strain'd hands clench an ice-cold rifle
his aching jaws grip a hot parch'd tongue
his wide eyes search unconsciously.

He cannot shriek.

Bloody saliva
dribbles down his shapeless jacket.

I saw him stab
and stab again
a well-killed Boche.

This is the happy warrior,
this is he . . .

F. W. D. BENDALL

Outposts

Sentry, sentry, what did you see
At gaze from your post beside Lone Tree?
A star-shell flared like a burning brand
But I saw no movement in No Man's Land.

Sentry, sentry, what did you hear
As the night-wind fluttered the grasses near?
I heard a rifle-shot on the flank,
And my mate slid down to the foot of the bank.

Sentry, sentry, what did you do,
And hadn't your mate a word for you?
I lifted his head and called his name.
His lips moved once, but no sound came.

Sentry, sentry, what did you say
As you watched alone till break of day?
I prayed the Lord that I'd fire straight
If I saw the man that killed my mate.

KEITH DOUGLAS

How to Kill

Under the parabola of a ball,
a child turning into a man,
I looked into the air too long.
The ball fell in my hand, it sang
in the closed fist: *Open Open
Behold a gift designed to kill.*

Now in my dial of glass appears
the soldier who is going to die.
He smiles, and moves about in ways
his mother knows, habits of his.
The wires touch his face: I cry
NOW. Death, like a familiar, hears

and look, has made a man of dust
of a man of flesh. This sorcery
I do. Being damned, I am amused
to see the centre of love diffused
and the waves of love travel into vacancy.
How easy it is to make a ghost.

The weightless mosquito touches
her tiny shadow on the stone,

and with how like, how infinite
a lightness, man and shadow meet.
They fuse. A shadow is a man
when the mosquito death approaches.

UYS KRIGE

The Taking of the Koppie

No, it was only a touch of dysentery, he said. He was doing
    fine now, thank you . . . What the hell were the chaps
    grousing about, anyhow?
He was sitting on the edge of his hospital cot clad only in a slip
    with both his feet on the floor,
his strong young body straight and graceful as a tree, golden as
    any pomegranate but only firmer,
its smooth surface uncracked, gashed with no fissure by the
    burning blazing sun of war;
and with his muscles rippling lightly
like a vlei's shallows by the reeds touched by the first breath of
    the wind of dawn,
as he swung his one leg over onto the other.

He was telling us about the death of the colonel and the major
whom all the men, especially the younger ones, worshipped.
'The colonel copped it from a stray bullet. It must have been a
    sniper . . .
just a neat little hole in the middle of his forehead, no bigger
    than a tickey, and he dropped dead in his tracks.
The major was leading us over some rough open ground
    between the gully and the far koppie
when a burst of machine gun bullets smacked from the kloof,
    tearing him open;
he was a long way ahead of us all and as he fell he shouted:
"Stop! Stay where you are! Don't come near me! Look out for
    those machine guns! There's one in the antheap and one

on the ledge. . . . Bring up the mortars! The rest take
　　cover!"
Then he rolled over on his back, blood streaming all over his
　　body,
and with a dabble of blood on his lips he died – Christ, what a
　　man he was!'
The boy reached for a match box, then lighting a cigarette, he
　　continued:
'We came on them about ten minutes later, three Ities curled
　　up on some straw in a sort of dugout
– as snug as a bug in a rug – and they were sleeping . . .
The two on the outside were young, I noticed. They were all
　　unshaven. The bloke in the middle had a dirty grey
　　stubble of beard – and that's all I noticed . . . '

As the boy stopped talking he moved, his hair falling in thick
　　yellow curls over his forehead, his eyes.
And as I caught the soft gleam of blue behind the strands of
　　gold
I was suddenly reminded of quiet pools of water after rain
among the golden gorse that mantle in early summer
the browning hills of Provence.

'Then I put my bayonet through each of them in turn, just in
　　the right place, and they did not even grunt or
　　murmur . . . '

There was no sadism in his voice, no savagery, no brutal pride
　　or perverse eagerness to impress,
no joy, no exultation.
He spoke as if he were telling of a Rugby match
in which he wasn't much interested
and in which he took no sides.

And as I looked at his eyes again
I was struck with wonderment
at their bigness, their blueness, their clarity
and how young they were, how innocent.

Leadership

All successful armies need a strong and visible leader – Alexander, Hannibal, Napoleon and Montgomery all fitted this role. So did Henry V. At Agincourt, the English were outnumbered by the French three to one, and Shakespeare describes how Henry, on the eve of battle, visits his troops to bolster up their spirits with 'A little touch of Harry in the night'. This finds an echo in John Brookes's poem about a natural leader in the Australian army.

History has generally been kind to charismatic military leaders. If they die at the moment of victory, as Wolfe and Nelson did, they are likely to attain instant immortality: their banners are hung in chapels, statues are erected and – if they happen to be British – the ultimate honour is that pubs are named after them. Byron, however, loathed the lot.

ARCHILOCHUS

The Ideal General

Not for me the general renowned nor the well-groomed dandy,
Nor he who is proud of his curls or is shaven in part;
But give me a man that is small and whose legs are bandy,
Provided he's firm on his feet and is valiant in heart.

Translated from the Greek (7th century BC) by A. Watson Bain

WILLIAM SHAKESPEARE

from Troilus and Cressida (Act 1, Scene iii)

Ulysses: They tax our policy and call it cowardice,
Count wisdom as no member of the war,

Forestall prescience, and esteem no act
But that of hand; the still and mental parts
That do contrive how many hands shall strike
When fitness calls them on, and know by measure
Of their observant toil the enemy's weight –
Why, this hath not a finger's dignity:
They call this bed-work, mappery, closet-war;
So that the ram that batters down the wall,
For the great swing and rudeness of his poise,
They place before his hand that made the engine
Or those that with the fineness of their souls
By reason guide his execution.

WILLIAM SHAKESPEARE

from Henry V (Act 4, Prologue)

Chorus: Now entertain conjecture of a time,
When creeping murmur, and the poring dark,
Fills the wide vessel of the universe.
From camp to camp, through the foul womb of night,
The hum of either army stilly sounds,
That the fixed sentinels almost receive
The secret whispers of each other's watch.
Fire answers fire; and through their paly flames
Each battle sees the other's umbered face.
Steed threatens steed in high and boastful neighs,
Piercing the night's dull ear: and from the tents,
The armorers, accomplishing the knights,
With busy hammers closing rivets up,
Give dreadful note of preparation.
The country cocks do crow, the clocks do toll,
And the third hour of drowsy morning name.
Proud of their numbers, and secure in soul,
The confident and over-lusty French

Do the low-rated English play at dice;
And chide the cripple, tardy-gaited night,
Who, like a foul and ugly witch, doth limp
So tediously away. The poor, condemned English,
Like sacrifices, by their watchful fires
Sit patiently, and inly ruminate
The morning's danger; and their gestures sad,
Investing lank-lean cheeks, and war-torn coats,
Presenteth them unto the gazing moon
So many horrid ghosts. O, now, who will behold
The royal captain of this ruined band,
Walking from watch to watch, from tent to tent,
Let him cry – Praise and glory on his head!
For forth he goes, and visits all his host;
Bids them good morrow, with a modest smile;
And calls them – brothers, friends, and countrymen.
Upon his royal face there is no note,
How dread an army hath enrounded him;
Nor doth he dedicate one jot of color
Unto the weary and all-watched night;
But freshly looks, and over-bears attaint,
With cheerful semblance and sweet majesty;
That every wretch, pining and pale before,
Beholding him, plucks comfort from his looks.
A largess universal, like the sun,
His liberal eye doth give to every one,
Thawing cold fear. Then, mean and gentle all,
Behold, as may unworthiness define,
A little touch of Harry in the night.
And so our scene must to the battle fly;
Where (O for pity!) we shall much disgrace –
With four or five most ragged foils,
Right ill-disposed, in brawl ridiculous –
The name of Agincourt. Yet, sit and see;
Minding true things, by what their mockeries be.

ROBERT GRAVES

1805

At Viscount Nelson's lavish funeral,
    While the mob milled and yelled about the Abbey,
A General chatted with an Admiral:

'One of your Colleagues, Sir, remarked today
    That Nelson's *exit*, though to be lamented,
Falls not inopportunely, in its way.'

'He was a thorn in our flesh,' came the reply –
    'The most bird-witted, unaccountable,
Odd little runt that ever I did spy.

'One arm, one peeper, vain as Pretty Poll,
    A meddler, too, in foreign politics
And gave his heart in pawn to a plain moll.

'He would dare lecture us Sea Lords, and then
    Would treat his ratings as though men of honour
And play at leap-frog with his midshipmen!

'We tried to box him down, but up he popped,
    And when he'd banged Napoleon at the Nile
Became too much the hero to be dropped.

'You've heard that Copenhagen "blind eye" story?
    We'd tied him to Nurse Parker's apron-strings –
By G–d, he snipped them through and snatched the glory!'

'Yet,' cried the General, 'six-and-twenty sail
    Captured or sunk by him off Trafalgar –
That writes a handsome *finis* to the tale.'

'Handsome enough. The seas are England's now.
    That fellow's foibles need no longer plague us.
He died most creditably, I'll allow.'

'And, Sir, the secret of his victories?'
   'By his unServicelike, familiar ways, Sir,
He made the whole Fleet love him, damn his eyes!'

GEORGE GORDON, LORD BYRON

from Don Juan, Canto IX

I

Oh, Wellington! (or 'Vilainton' – for Fame
   Sounds the heroic syllables both ways;
France could not even conquer your great name,
   But punn'd it down to this facetious phrase –
Beating or beaten she will laugh the same)
   You have obtain'd great pensions and much praise:
Glory like yours should any dare gainsay,
Humanity would rise, and thunder 'Nay!'

II

I don't think that you used Kinnaird quite well
   In Marinet's affair – in fact 'twas shabby,
And like some other things won't do to tell
   Upon your tomb in Westminster's old abbey.
Upon the rest 'tis not worth while to dwell,
   Such tales being for the tea-hours of some tabby;
But though your years as *man* tend fast to *zero*,
In fact your grace is still but a *young hero*.

III

Though Britain owes (and pays you too) so much
   Yet Europe doubtless owes you greatly more:
You have repair'd Legitimacy's crutch,
   A prop not quite so certain as before:
The Spanish, and the French, as well as Dutch,

Have seen, and felt, how strongly you *restore*;
And Waterloo has made the world your debtor
(I wish your bards would sing it rather better).

IV

You are 'the best of cut-throats': — do not start;
    The phrase is Shakespeare's, and not misapplied: —
War's a brain-spattering, windpipe-slitting art,
    Unless her cause by right be sanctified.
If you have acted *once* a generous part,
    The world, not the world's masters, will decide,
And I shall be delighted to learn who,
Save you and yours, have gain'd by Waterloo?

V

I am no flatterer — you've supp'd full of flattery:
    They say you like it too — 'tis no great wonder.
He whose whole life has been assault and battery,
    At last may get a little tired of thunder;
And swallowing eulogy much more than satire, he
    May like being praised for every lucky blunder,
Call'd 'Saviour of the Nations' — not yet saved,
And 'Europe's Liberator' — still enslaved.

JOHN BROOKES

Officers and Gentlemen Down Under

We had as our platoon commander one
Lieutenant Teague. Nobody knew for sure,
but someone spread the rumour he had done
a bit of wrestling as an amateur.
In fact he was a funny sort of bloke
we had not rumbled yet. When he read out

the leave arrangements no-one put their spoke
in straight away until this bit about
the red light district being out of bounds
to other ranks till further notice. Then
from all three sections came the muttered sounds
of unmistakable frustration. When,
to ease the situation, 'Sarge' stepped in
and like all bloody NCOs rebuffed
the whole platoon concerning discipline
etcetera, some joker said 'Get stuffed!'
The sergeant yelled 'That man is on a charge!'
(not being certain who the bastard was)
and when somebody said 'Good on yer, Sarge!'
this Teague bloke took command again because
the matter looked like getting out of hand.
He brought us to attention 'Shun!', ordered
the corporals to shoulder arms and stand
behind the sergeant which no doubt deferred
to principles wherein to undermine
the NCOs in front of other ranks
was infra-dig, walked up and down each line
like on inspection, then came round the flanks
and took up a position facing us.
You could have heard a pin drop. First he took
his bush hat off and with punctilious
exactitude according to the book,
he placed it carefully upon the ground,
removed his fancy jacket and Sam Browne
and folded them, and then with a profound
deliberation bent and put them down
beside the hat, stood up erect and faced
the lot of us, and anyone could see
that he was lean and muscular. He paced
once forward then with calm authority
he said 'Forget the regulations for
the moment, where if any soldier strikes

an officer he'll get three years or more;
if any one of you brave bastards likes
to put his courage where his mouth is, just
step forward now and try it on. No names,
no pack-drill either. Nothing. Shit or bust!'
An opportunity for fun and games?
My bloody oath! But silence. No-one moved.
So HE had rumbled US! There was no need
for further comment. Mr Teague had proved
his point. And afterwards we all agreed
he was the sort of bloke a man could fight
the war with AND call sir. Too bloody right!

Napoleon

Napoleon has a section of his own because he stands as the exemplary military genius. Within a space of fifteen years, he had conquered every country in Europe, apart from Britain. He came to grief only in trying to do the impossible, defeated by those two old Russian generals, January and February. When his Grande Armée crossed into Russia (1812), it boasted some 600,000 men, but by the time of the ignominious retreat from Moscow in the following year it had shrunk to a mere 10,000. Napoleon once said: 'A man such as I am is not much concerned with the lives of a million men.'

HEINRICH HEINE

The Grenadiers

Two of Napoleon's grenadiers
  Came from a Russian jail;
But as they passed through Germany
  They heard a dismal tale.

That France at last had lost the day,
  That fortune had forsaken
The army once, in proud array,
  And the Emperor was taken!

Then wept the two old grenadiers
  To conquered France returning;
Said one, when he had heard the news,
  'How my old wound is burning!'

'Our game is lost!' the other groaned;
  'I would that I were dead;

But I have wife and child in France,
    And they must still be fed!'

'Who cares for wife and children now?
    Our standards are forsaken!
Let wife and children go and beg;
    The Emperor is taken!

'But, comrade, grant me one request:
    If on the way I die,
Carry me home, and let my bones
    Beside French ashes lie!

'And let my cross of honour hang
    Just here, upon my breast;
And put the musket in my hand,
    Then leave me to my rest.

'And like a sentinel in the grave,
    I'll listen for the day,
Till I hear the galloping hoofs again,
    And the thundering cannons bray:

'When rides the Emperor o'er my head,
    Believe me, I'll be sure
To spring up, shouting from the grave
    With "Vive l'Empereur!" '

Translator from the German unknown

VICTOR HUGO

Russia 1812

The snow fell, and its power was multiplied.
For the first time the Eagle bowed its head –
dark days! Slowly the Emperor returned –
behind him Moscow! Its onion domes still burned.

The snow rained down in blizzards — rained and froze.
Past each white waste a further white waste rose.
None recognized the captains or the flags.
Yesterday the Grand Army, today its dregs!
No one could tell the vanguard from the flanks.
The snow! The hurt men struggled from the ranks,
hid in the bellies of dead horse, in stacks
of shattered caissons. By the bivouacs,
one saw the picket dying at his post,
still standing in his saddle, white with frost,
the stone lips frozen to the bugle's mouth!
Bullets and grapeshot mingled with the snow,
that hailed . . . The Guard, surprised at shivering, march
in a dream now; ice rimes the grey moustache.
The snow falls, always snow! The driving mire
submerges; men, trapped in that white empire,
have no more bread and march on barefoot — gaps!
They were no longer living men and troops,
but a dream drifting in a fog, a mystery,
mourners parading under the black sky.
The solitude, vast, terrible to the eye,
was like a mute avenger everywhere,
as snowfall, floating through the quiet air,
buried the huge army in a huge shroud.
Could anyone leave this kingdom? A crowd —
each man, obsessed with dying, was alone.
Men slept — and died! The beaten mob sludged on,
ditching the guns to burn their carriages.
Two foes. The North, the Czar. The North was worse.
In hollows where the snow was piling up,
one saw whole regiments fallen asleep.
Attila's dawn, Cannaes of Hannibal!
The army marching to its funeral!
Litters, wounded, the dead, deserters — swarm,
crushing the bridges down to cross a stream.
They went to sleep ten thousand, woke up four.

Ney, bringing up the former army's rear,
hacked his horse loose from three disputing Cossacks . . .
All night, the *qui vive?* The alert! Attacks;
retreats! White ghosts would wrench away our guns,
or we would see dim, terrible squadrons,
circles of steel, whirlpools of savages,
rush sabring through the camp like dervishes.
And in this way, whole armies died at night.

The Emperor was there, standing – he saw.
This oak already tembling from the axe,
watched his glories drop from him branch by branch:
chiefs, soldiers. Each one had his turn and chance –
they died! Some lived. These still believed his star,
and kept their watch. They loved the man of war,
this small man with his hands behind his back,
whose shadow, moving to and fro, was black
behind the lighted tent. Still believing, they
accused their destiny of *lèse-majesté.*
His misfortune had mounted on their back.
The man of glory shook. Cold stupefied
him, then suddenly he felt terrified.
Being without belief, he turned to God:
'God of armies, is this the end?' he cried.
And then at last the expiation came,
as he heard some one call him by his name,
some one half-lost in shadow, who said, 'No,
Napoleon.' Napoleon understood,
restless, bareheaded, leaden, as he stood
before his butchered legions in the snow.

Translated from the French by Robert Lowell

W. M. THACKERAY

Napoleon

He captured many thousand guns;
　He wrote 'The Great' before his name;
And dying, only left his sons
　The recollection of his shame.

Though more than half the world was his,
　He died without a rood his own;
And borrowed from his enemies
　Six foot of ground to lie upon.

He fought a thousand glorious wars,
　And more than half the world was his,
And somewhere, now, in yonder stars,
　Can tell, mayhap, what greatness is.

FORD MADOX FORD

from Antwerp

For the white-limbed heroes of Hellas ride by upon their
　　horses
For ever through our brains.
The heroes of Cressy ride by upon their stallions;
And battalions and battalions and battalions –
The Old Guard, the Young Guard, the men of Minden and of
　　Waterloo,
Pass, for ever staunch,
Stand for ever true;
And the small man with the large paunch,
And the grey coat, and the large hat, and the hands behind the
　　back,

Watches them pass
In our minds for ever . . .
But that clutter of sodden corses
On the sodden Belgian grass –
That is a strange new beauty.

RUDYARD KIPLING

A St Helena Lullaby

'How far is St Helena from a little child at play?'
What makes you want to wander there with all the world
    between?
Oh, Mother, call your son again or else he'll run away.
(*No one thinks of winter when the grass is green!*)

'How far is St Helena from a fight in Paris street?'
I haven't time to answer now – the men are falling fast.
The guns begin to thunder, and the drums begin to beat.
(*If you take the first step, you will take the last!*)

'How far is St Helena from the field of Austerlitz?'
You couldn't hear me if I told – so loud the cannon roar.
But not so far for people who are living by their wits.
(*'Gay go up' means 'Gay go down' the wide world o'er!*)

'How far is St Helena from an Emperor of France?'
I cannot see – I cannot tell – the crowns they dazzle so.
The Kings sit down to dinner, and the Queens stand up to
    dance.
(*After open weather you may look for snow!*)

'How far is St Helena from the Capes of Trafalgar?'
A longish way – a longish way – with ten year more to run.
It's South across the water underneath a falling star.
(*What you cannot finish you must leave undone!*)

'How far is St Helena from the Beresina ice?'
An ill way – a chill way – the ice begins to crack.
But not so far for gentlemen who never took advice.
(*When you can't go forward you must e'en come back!*)

'How far is St Helena from the field of Waterloo?'
A near way – a clear way – the ship will take you soon.
A pleasant place for gentlemen with little left to do.
(*Morning never tries you till the afternoon!*)

'How far from St Helena to the Gate of Heaven's Grace?'
That no one knows – that no one knows – and no one ever
          will.
But fold your hands across your heart and cover up your face,
And after all your trapesings, child, lie still!

Donkeys

From his bitter experience of the First World War, Clemenceau remarked, 'War is far too serious a business to be left to the generals'. The British Army in that war has been described as consisting of 'lions led by donkeys', which could just as well have been said of many another British force. In the Crimea, for example, the high command was virtually all geriatric: Lord Raglan, the Commander-in-Chief, was 67 years old at his appointment, and all his senior commanders were aged between 60 and 70.

Regimental officers, like Hotspur, who have to do the fighting, have always had contempt for the sort of comfortably-billeted and pampered staff officer whom Hotspur here describes as 'perfumed like a milliner'. When Romania declared war on the side of Russia and the Allies in 1916, an order was issued restricting the use of make-up to officers above the rank of Major.

The fine, contemptuous poem 'A Bas la Gloire!' is the work of Lieutenant Edward Tennant, who had enlisted at the age of seventeen. When he was killed by a sniper in 1916, a great poetic talent was lost, though he once wrote to his mother, 'I think of death with a light heart, and as a friend whom there is no need to fear.'

WILLIAM SHAKESPEARE

from Henry IV, Part I (Act 1, Scene iii)

Hotspur:
My liege, I did deny no prisoners.
But I remember, when the fight was done,
When I was dry with rage and extreme toil,
Breathless and faint, leaning upon my sword,
Came there a certain lord, neat, and trimly dress'd,

Fresh as a bridegroom; and his chin new reap'd
Show'd like a stubble-land at harvest-home;
He was perfumed like a milliner;
And twixt his finger and his thumb he held
A pouncet-box, which ever and anon
He gave his nose and took't away again;
Who therewith angry, when it next came there,
Took it in snuff; and still he smiled and talk'd,
And as the soldiers bore dead bodies by,
He call'd them untaught knaves, unmannerly,
To bring a slovenly unhandsome corse
Betwixt the wind and his nobility.
With many holiday and lady terms
He question'd me; amongst the rest, demanded
My prisoners in your majesty's behalf.
I then, all smarting with my wounds being cold,
To be pester'd with a popinjay,
Out of my grief and my impatience,
Answer'd neglectingly I know not what,
He should or he should not; for he made me mad
To see him shine so brisk and smell so sweet
And talk so like a waiting-gentlewoman
Of guns and drums and wounds, – God save the mark! –
And telling me the sovereign'st thing on earth
Was parmaceti for an inward bruise;
And that it was great pity, so it was,
This villanous salt-petre should be digg'd
Out of the bowels of the harmless earth,
Which many a good tall fellow had destroy'd
So cowardly; and but for these vile guns,
He would himself have been a soldier.
This bald unjointed chat of his, my lord,
I answer'd indirectly, as I said;
And I beseech you, let not his report
Come current for an accusation
Betwixt my love and your high majesty.

HO XUAN HONG

The General's Plaque

This much-praised general made such a cock of things
That thousands of men were slaughtered. All may view
The temple-plaque in his honour. No one sings
Praise of the wives, each left with the work of two.

Translated from the Chinese and Vietnamese by Graeme Wilson

W. S. LANDOR

The Crimean Heroes

Hail, ye indomitable heroes, hail!
Despite of all your generals, ye prevail.

SIEGFRIED SASSOON

The General (1917)

'Good morning – good morning!' the General said
When we met him last week on our way to the Line.
Now the soldiers he smiled at are most of 'em dead,
And we're cursing his staff for incompetent swine.
'He's a cheery old card' grunted Harry to Jack
As they slogged up to Arras with rifle and pack.
But he did for them both with his plan of attack.

RUDYARD KIPLING

Mesopotamia 1917

They shall not return to us, the resolute, the young,
  The eager and whole-hearted whom we gave:
But the men who left them thriftily to die in their own dung,
  Shall they come with years and honour to the grave?

They shall not return to us, the strong men coldly slain
  In sight of help denied from day to day:
But the men who edged their agonies and chid them in their
    pain,
  Are they too strong and wise to put away?

Our dead shall not return to us while Day and Night divide —
  Never while the bars of sunset hold.
But the idle-minded overlings who quibbled while they died,
  Shall they thrust for high employments as of old?

Shall we only threaten and be angry for an hour?
  When the storm is ended shall we find
How softly but how swiftly they have sidled back to power
  By the favour and contrivance of their kind?

Even while they soothe us, while they promise large amends,
  Even while they make a show of fear,
Do they call upon their debtors, and take counsel with their
    friends,
  To confirm and re-establish each career?

Their lives cannot repay us — their death could not undo —
  The shame that they have laid upon our race.
But the slothfulness that wasted and the arrogance that slew,
  Shall we leave it unabated in its place?

SIEGFRIED SASSOON

Base Details

If I were fierce, and bald, and short of breath,
   I'd live with scarlet Majors at the Base,
And speed glum heroes up the line to death.
   You'd see me with my puffy petulant face,
Guzzling and gulping in the best hotel,
   Reading the Roll of Honour. 'Poor young chap,'
I'd say – 'I used to know his father well;
   Yes, we've lost heavily in this last scrap.'
And when the war is done and youth stone dead,
I'd toddle safely home and die – in bed.

EDWARD TENNANT

A Bas la Gloire!

The powers that be in solemn conclave sat
And dealt out honour from a large tureen,
And those unhonour'd said 'twas rather flat,
Not half so sparkling as it should have been.
Those honour'd silently pass'd round the hat,
Then let themselves be freely heard and seen.

And all this time there were a lot of men
Who were in France and couldn't get away
To be awarded honours. Now and then
They died, so others came and had to stay
Till they died too, and every field and fen
Was heavy with the dead from day to day.

But there were other men who didn't die
Although they were in France – these sat in cars,

And whizzed about with red-band caps, awry,
Exuding brandy and the best cigars,
With bands and tabs of red, they could defy
The many missiles of explosive Mars.

But one there was who used to serve in bars
And for his pretty wit much fame had got;
Though really not so fit to serve in wars,
They made him a staff-colonel on the spot,
And threw a knighthood in as well, because
He really had done such an awful lot.

Up fluttered eyebrows (incomes fluttered down),
His erstwhile yeomanry stood all aghast,
This Juggernaut, devourer of renown,
Was he their fellow-mug in days long past?
In France he went by train from town to town,
Men thought his zenith had been reached at last.

To this the Powers That Be replied, 'Oh No!'
And they discovered (else my mem'ry fails)
That he had gone by train some months ago
From Paris with despatches to Marseilles!
'See here', they cried, 'a well-earned DSO
Because you did not drop them 'neath the rails.'

So now from spur to plume he is a star,
Of all an Englishman should strive to be,
His one-time patrons hail him from afar
As 'Peerless warrior,' 'battle-scarred KG'
And murmur as he passes in his car,
'For this and all thy mercies, glory be!'

But all this time the war goes on the same,
And good men go, we lose our friends and kith,
The men who sink knee-deep in boosted fame
Prove that 'rewarded courage' is a myth:
I could sum up by mentioning a name:
A pseudonym will do, we'll call him Smith.

ANONYMOUS

The Old Barbed Wire

If you want to find the sergeant,
I know where he is, I know where he is;
If you want to find the sergeant,
I know where he is,
He's lying on the canteen floor.
I've seen him, I've seen him,
Lying on the canteen floor,
I've seen him,
Lying on the canteen floor.

If you want to find the quarter-bloke,
I know where he is, I know where he is;
If you want to find the quarter-bloke,
I know where he is,
He's miles and miles behind the line.
I've seen him, *etc.*

If you want to find the sergeant-major,
I know where he is, I know where he is,
If you want to find the sergeant-major,
I know where he is,
He's boozing up the privates' rum.
I've seen him, *etc.*

If you want to find the CO,
I know where he is, I know where he is,
If you want to find the CO,
I know where he is,
He's down in the deep dug-outs.
I've seen him, *etc.*

If you want to find the whole battalion,
I know where they are, I know where they are,
If you want to find the whole battalion,
I know where they are,
They're hanging on the old barbed wire.
I've seen 'em, *etc.*

Statesmen, Politicians and Profiteers

After the donkeys, the politicians who start wars and the unscrupulous opportunists who do well out of them provide poets with their next targets. Significantly, while there were many bitter attacks upon the politicians who had led Europe into the First World War and kept it going for four long years, there were no such recriminations against Churchill in the Second World War, because it was accepted that the conflict was inevitable and justified by the evil nature of the Nazi regime.

Dr Johnson believed that war was so evil that the leaders of nations had a duty not to provoke it; all too often wars had started through slights that were exaggerated. He wrote, 'As war is one of the heaviest of national evils, a calamity, in which every species of misery is involved; as it sets the general safety to hazard, suspends commerce, and desolates the country; as it exposes great numbers to great hardships, dangers, captivity and death; no man, who desires the publick prosperity, will inflame general resentment by aggravating minute injuries, or enforcing disputable rights of little importance.'

By way of contrast, the poem by Richard Heller, published here for the first time, takes the British Foreign Secretary to task for appeasing the Serbs in Bosnia.

AESCHYLUS

from Agamemnon

  Choros:
For Ares, gold-exchanger for the dead,
And balance-holder in the fight o' the spear,
Due-weight from Ilion sends —
What moves the tear on tear —

A charred scrap to the friends:
Filling with well-packed ashes every urn,
For man that was the sole return.
And they groan – praising much, the while,
Now this man as experienced in the strife,
Now that, fallen nobly on a slaughtered pile,
Because of – not his own – another's wife.
But things there be, one barks,
When no man harks:
A surreptitious grief that's grudge
Against the Atreidai, who first sought the judge.
But some there, round the rampart, have
In Ilian earth, each one his grave:
All fair-formed as at birth,
It hid them – what they have and hold – the hostile earth.

   Translated from the Greek by Robert Browning

CHARLES CHURCHILL

from Night

Perplex'd with trifles thro' the vale of life,
Man strives 'gainst man, without a cause for strife;
Armies embattled meet, and thousands bleed,
For some vile spot, which cannot fifty feed.
Squirrels for nuts contend, and, wrong or right,
For the world's empire, kings ambitious fight,
What odds? – to us 'tis all the self-same thing,
A Nut, a World, a Squirrel, and a King.

WILLIAM COWPER

from The Task, Book V: 'The Winter Morning Walk'

Great princes have great playthings. Some have played
At hewing mountains into men, and some
At building human wonders mountain high.
Some have amassed the dull sad years of life
(Life spent in indolence, and therefore sad)
With schemes of monumental fame, and sought
By pyramids and mausolean pomp,
Short-lived themselves, t'immortalize their bones.
Some seek diversion in the tented field
And make the sorrows of mankind their sport.
But war's a game which, were their subjects wise,
Kings should not play at. Nations would do well
T'exhort their truncheons from the puny hands
Of heroes, whose infirm and baby minds
Are gratified with mischief, and who spoil,
Because men suffer it, their toy the world.

RUDYARD KIPLING

A Dead Statesman

I could not dig: I dared not rob:
Therefore I lied to please the mob.
Now all my lies are proved untrue
And I must face the men I slew.
What tale shall serve me here among
Mine angry and defrauded young?

G. K. CHESTERTON

Elegy in a Country Churchyard

The men that worked for England
They have their graves at home:
And bees and birds of England
About the cross can roam.

But they that fought for England,
Following a falling star,
Alas, alas for England
They have their graves afar.

And they that rule in England,
In stately conclave met,
Alas, alas for England
They have no graves as yet.

PABLO NERUDA

Almería

A bowl for the bishop, a crushed and bitter bowl,
a bowl with remnants of iron, with ashes, with tears,
a sunken bowl, with sobs and fallen walls,
a bowl for the bishop, a bowl of Almería
blood.

A bowl for the banker, a bowl with cheeks
of children from the happy South, a bowl
with explosions, with wild waters and ruins and fright,
a bowl with split axles and trampled heads,
a black bowl, a bowl of Almería blood.

Each morning, each turbid morning of your lives
you will have it steaming and burning at your tables:
you will push it aside a bit with your soft hands
so as not to see it, not to digest it so many times:
you will push it aside a bit between the bread and the grapes,
this bowl of silent blood
that will be there each morning, each
morning.

A bowl for the Colonel and the Colonel's wife
at a garrison party, at each party,
above the oaths and the spittle, with the wine light of early
    morning
so that you may see it trembling and cold upon the world.

Yes, a bowl for all of you, richmen here and there,
monstrous ambassadors, ministers, table companions,
ladies with cozy tea parties and chairs:
a bowl shattered, overflowing, dirty with the blood of the
    poor,
for each morning, for each week, forever and ever,
a bowl of Almería blood, facing you, forever.

Translated from the Spanish by Donald D. Walsh

DYLAN THOMAS

'The hand that signed the paper felled a city'

The hand that signed the paper felled a city;
Five sovereign fingers taxed the breath,
Doubled the globe of dead and halved a country;
These five kings did a king to death.

The mighty hand leads to a sloping shoulder,
The finger joints are cramped with chalk;
A goose's quill has put an end to murder
That put an end to talk.

The hand that signed the treaty bred a fever,
And famine grew, and locusts came;
Great is the hand that holds dominion over
Man by a scribbled name.

The five kings count the dead but do not soften
The crusted wound nor stroke the brow;
A hand rules pity as a hand rules heaven;
Hands have no tears to flow.

STEPHEN SPENDER

Ultima Ratio Regum

The guns spell money's ultimate reason
In letters of lead on the spring hillside.
But the boy lying dead under the olive trees
Was too young and too silly
To have been notable to their important eye.
He was a better target for a kiss.

When he lived, tall factory hooters never summoned him
Nor did restaurant plate-glass doors revolve to wave him in.
His name never appeared in the papers.
The world maintained its traditional wall
Round the dead with their gold sunk deep as a well,
Whilst his life, intangible as a Stock Exchange rumour, drifted
    outside.

O too lightly he threw down his cap
One day when the breeze threw petals from the trees.
The unflowering wall sprouted with guns,

Machine-gun anger quickly scythed the grasses;
Flags and leaves fell from hands and branches;
The tweed cap rotted in the nettles.

Consider his life which was valueless
In terms of employment, hotel ledgers, news files.
Consider. One bullet in ten thousand kills a man.
Ask. Was so much expenditure justified
On the death of one so young and so silly
Lying under the olive trees, O world, O death?

OSBERT SITWELL

Judas and the Profiteer

Judas descended to this lower Hell
    To meet his only friend – the profiteer –
Who, looking fat and rubicund and well,
    Regarded him, and then said with a sneer,
'Iscariot, they did you! Fool! to sell
    For silver pence the body of God's Son,
Whereas from maiming men with tank and shell
    I gain at least a golden million.'

    But Judas answered: 'You deserve your gold;
    It's not His body but His soul *you've* sold!'

RICHARD HELLER

'The Minister has all his notes in place'

The Minister has all his notes in place.
No line of truth has etched his handsome face.
The House is sparse; they've heard it all before.
His expert lies massage away the war.

While Serbian artillery take aim,
Decide which new civilians they should maim,
He fills the Chamber high with empty talk,
And here's another child will never walk.

The opposition make synthetic rant;
He answers with the Foreign Office cant.
Some random shrapnel takes a boy's right eye:
The other one is all he needs to cry.

'Next business', and the Minister displays
A lapdog urge to hear officials' praise.
A woman fetching water stops a shell.
He smiles: 'That all went over rather well.'

Armour

Armour is surrounded by myths and mystique. Even putting it on
became a form of ceremony, and the ultimate expression of status,
from the siege of Troy to the sixteenth century, was to commission
smiths and craftsmen to fashion the most elaborate suits of
armour.

The sheer weight of armour that a medieval knight had to bear
must have been tolerable only to the very strongest. Although it
gave protection from the sword, the arrow and the spear, it
severely restricted the flexibility and agility of those who wore it.

HOMER

from The Iliad, Book XI

Atrides summon'd all to arms, to arms himself dispos'd.
First on his legs he put bright greaves with silver buttons
    clos'd;
Then with rich curace arm'd his breast, which Cinyras
    bestow'd
To gratify his royal guest; for even to Cyprus flow'd
Th' unbounded fame of those designs the Greeks propos'd
    for Troy,
And therefore gave he him those arms, and wish'd his
    purpose joy.
Ten rows of azure mix'd with black, twelve golden like the
    sun,
Twice ten of tin, in beaten paths, did through this armour
    run.
Three serpents to the gorget crept, that like three rainbows
    shin'd

Such as by Jove are fix'd in clouds when wonders are
     divin'd.
About his shoulders hung his sword, whereof the hollow hilt
Was fashion'd all with shining bars, exceeding richly gilt;
The scabbard was of silver plate, with golden hangers
     grac'd.
Then took he up his weighty shield, that round about him
     cast
Defensive shadows; ten bright zones of gold-affecting brass
Were driven about it, and of tin, as full of gloss as glass,
Swell'd twenty bosses out of it; in centre of them all
One of black metal had engraven, full of extreme appall,
An ugly Gorgon, compassed with Terror and with Fear.
At it a silver bawdrick hung, with which he us'd to bear,
Wound on his arm, his ample shield, and in it there was
     woven
An azure dragon, curl'd in folds, from whose one neck was
     cloven
Three heads contorted in an orb. Then plac'd he on his head
His four-plum'd casque; and in his hands two darts he
     managed,
Arm'd with bright steel that blaz'd to heaven.

     Translated from the Greek by George Chapman

HOMER

from The Iliad, Book XIX

   The host set forth, and pour'd his steel waves far out of the
     fleet.
And as from air the frosty north wind blows a cold thick sleet,
That dazzles eyes, flakes after flakes incessantly descending;
So thick, helms, curets, ashen darts, and round shields, never
     ending,

Flow'd from the navy's hollow womb. Their splendours gave
    heav'n's eye
His beams again. Earth laugh'd to see her face so like the sky;
Arms shin'd so hot, and she such clouds made with the dust she
    cast,
She thunder'd, feet of men and horse importun'd her so fast.
In midst of all, divine Achilles his fair person arm'd,
His teeth gnash'd as he stood, his eyes so full of fire they
    warm'd,
Unsuffer'd grief and anger at the Trojans so combin'd.
His greaves first us'd, his goodly curets on his bosom shin'd,
His sword, his shield that cast a brightness from it like the
    moon.
And as from sea sailors discern a harmful fire let run
By herdsmen's faults, till all their stall flies up in wrastling
    flame;
Which being on hills is seen far off; but being alone, none came
To give it quench, at shore no neighbours, and at sea their
    friends
Driv'n off with tempests; such a fire, from his bright shield
    extends
His ominous radiance, and in heav'n impress'd his fervent
    blaze.

       Translated from the Greek by George Chapman

ANONYMOUS

from Sir Gawain and the Green Knight

He dwelt there all that day, and at dawn on the morrow
Asked for his armour. Every item was brought.

First a crimson carpet was cast over the floor
And the great pile of gilded war-gear glittered upon it.
The strong man stepped on it, took the steel in hand.

The doublet he dressed in was dear Turkestan stuff;
Then came the courtly cape, cut with skill,
Finely lined with fur, and fastened close.
Then they set the steel shoes on the strong man's feet,
Lapped his legs in steel with lovely greaves,
Complete with knee-pieces, polished bright
And connecting at the knee with gold-knobbed hinges.
Then came the cuisses, which cunningly enclosed
His thighs thick of thew, and which thongs secured.
Next the hauberk, interlinked with argent steel rings
Which rested on rich material, wrapped the warrior round.
He had polished armour on arms and elbows,
Glinting and gay, and gloves of metal,
And all the goodly gear to give help whatever
  Betide;
  With surcoat richly wrought,
  Gold spurs attached in pride,
  A silken sword-belt athwart,
  And steadfast blade at his side.

  Translated from the Middle English by Brian Stone

WALTER SCOTT

from Marmion, Canto I

 v

Along the bridge Lord Marmion rode,
Proudly his red-roan charger trode,
His helm hung at the saddlebow;
Well by his visage you might know
He was a stalworth knight, and keen,
And had in many a battle been;
The scar on his brown cheek revealed
A token true of Bosworth field;

His eyebrow dark, and eye of fire,
Showed spirit proud, and prompt to ire;
Yet lines of thought upon his cheek
Did deep design and counsel speak.
His forehead, by his casque worn bare,
His thick mustache, and curly hair,
Coal-black, and grizzled here and there,
    But more through toil than age;
His square-turned joints, and strength of limb,
Showed him no carpet knight so trim,
But in close fight a champion grim,
    In camps a leader sage.

VI

Well was he armed from head to heel,
In mail and plate of Milan steel;
But his strong helm, of mighty cost,
Was all with burnished gold embossed;
Amid the plumage of the crest,
A falcon hovered on her nest,
With wings outspread, and forward breast;
E'en such a falcon, on his shield,
Soared sable in an azure field:
The golden legend bore aright,
Who checks at me, to death is dight.
Blue was the charger's broidered rein;
Blue ribbons decked his arching mane;
The knightly housing's ample fold
Was velvet blue, and trapped with gold.

VII

Behind him rode two gallant squires,
Of noble name, and knightly sires;
They burned the gilded spurs to claim;
For well could each a war-horse tame,

Could draw the bow, the sword could sway,
And lightly bear the ring away;
Nor less with courteous precepts stored,
Could dance in hall, and carve at board,
And frame love-ditties passing rare,
And sing them to a lady fair.

VIII

Four men-at-arms came at their backs,
With halbert, bill, and battle-axe:
They bore Lord Marmion's lance so strong,
And led his sumpter-mules along,
And ambling palfrey, when at need
Him listed ease his battle-steed.
The last and trustiest of the four,
On high his forky pennon bore;
Like swallow's tail, in shape and hue,
Fluttered the streamer glossy blue,
Where, blazoned sable, as before,
The towering falcon seemed to soar.
Last, twenty yeomen, two and two,
In hosen black, and jerkins blue,
With falcons broidered on each breast,
Attended on their lord's behest.
Each, chosen for an archer good,
Knew hunting-craft by lake or wood;
Each one a six-foot bow could bend,
And far a cloth-yard shaft could send;
Each held a boar-spear tough and strong,
And at their belts their quivers rung.
Their dusty palfreys and array
Showed they had marched a weary way.

GEOFFREY ADKINS

Children in Armour

The trouble with home-made armour
wasn't wearing it but removing it
when the mock wars had ended.
Most of us have a few bluish
faint scars from those days, as mementoes
of incaution, because your surrogate tin face
(carved crudely from a 20lb marmalade can)
had to be lifted upwards
and to the side, subtly – otherwise
you'd tear the skin. These tender difficulties
always defeated somebody – one day Lancelot,
Sir Guy the next, Arthur himself,
often, forgetting
that masks can't just be cast aside
in unstately haste, not casually discarded.
You have to negotiate
their putting-off. A pause, a stance
of caution, a slow bow at the street dust,
as those chivalric edges
ease past your eyes and release you
from a shining world. For if you rush,
the past stings home. The riskiness
of grails and tournaments
bites deep,
and the very make-believe bleeds.

Weapons

The importance of a soldier's weapon – the instrument which he uses to kill or to prevent himself from being killed – is such that he treats it more or less as a living being, with a personality of its own. The names given to Arthur's sword, or Roland's, or that of any other legendary hero, are simply expressions of the relationship acknowledged by every fighting man.

So to keep his weapon close and to care for it properly are at the very front of a soldier's mind, and to lose it is a serious military crime. For the Gunners, the greatest disgrace that can befall a regiment is to lose a gun. It is no accident that Death himself is depicted as carrying a thrusting spear.

W. E. HENLEY

from The Song of the Sword

I am the feast-maker:
Hark, through a noise
Of the screaming of eagles,
Hark how the Trumpet,
The mistress of mistresses,
Calls, silver-throated
And stern, where the tables
Are spread, and the meal
Of the Lord is in hand!
Driving the darkness,
Even as the banners
And spears of the Morning;
Sifting the nations,
The slag from the metal,

The waste and the weak
From the fit and the strong;
Fighting the brute,
The abysmal Fecundity;
Checking the gross,
Multitudinous blunders,
The groping, the purblind
Excesses in service
Of the Womb universal,
The absolute drudge;
Firing the charactry
Carved on the World,
The miraculous gem
In the seal-ring that burns
On the hand of the Master –
Yea! and authority
Flames through the dim,
Unappeasable Grisliness
Prone down the nethermost
Chasms of the Void! –
Clear singing, clean slicing;
Sweet spoken, soft finishing;
Making death beautiful,
Life but a coin
To be staked in the pastime
Whose playing is more
Than the transfer of being;
Arch-anarch, chief builder,
Prince and evangelist,
I am the Will of God:
I am the Sword.

The Sword
Singing –
The voice of the Sword from the heart of the Sword
Clanging majestical,

As from the starry-staired
Courts of the primal Supremacy,
His high, irresistible song.

ANONYMOUS

Song of the English Bowmen

Agincourt, Agincourt!
Know ye not Agincourt,
Where English slew and hurt
       All their French foemen?
With their pikes and bills brown,
How the French were beat down,
       Shot by our Bowmen!

Agincourt, Agincourt!
Know ye not Agincourt,
Never to be forgot,
       Or known to no men?
Where English cloth-yard arrows,
Killed the French like tame sparrows,
       Slain by our Bowmen!

Agincourt, Agincourt!
Know ye not Agincourt?
English of every sort,
       High men and low men,
Fought that day wondrous well,
All our old stories tell,
       Thanks to our Bowmen!

Agincourt, Agincourt!
Know ye not Agincourt?
Where our fifth Harry taught
       Frenchmen to know men:

And, when the day was done,
Thousands there fell to one
     Good English Bowman!

Agincourt, Agincourt!
Know ye not Agincourt?
Dear was the vict'ry bought
     By fifty yeomen.
Ask any English wench,
They were worth all the French:
     Rare English Bowmen!

ERNEST BRYLL

A Ballad of the Bayonet

First they taught us earth. The Napoleonic death
was still: close the ranks, close the ranks . . . and they closed
as bleeding fingers – whoever had the harder
fist – would win. With shaggy bearskin caps
cannons' throats used to be extinguished . . .
The bayonet alone
did not burn out, always useful:
you can carve initials with it on a concrete wall,
open tin cans. Its flame
not touched by any wind, is purer than prayer,
faultless as pious thought. A nobleman
among those thuds, that gutting of the earth,
those clownish leaps.
               Then they taught us sky
– and again evolution turns back, a retreat
into the perfection of the reptiles, an armoured head,
a protective colour.
            It alone requires us
to fight, standing. It alone orders us

to look at the enemy's faces, to sniff drops of sweat,
to kill sensing the heartbeat up the hilt. To fall
tearing earth not yet corroded to the bone . . .
It alone did not burn out. More faithful than God,
it reminds us that under the larval earth
and its smooth skin – against the gases – there is
a bit of warmth to be reached by the blade.

Translated from the Polish by Czeslaw Milosz

RUDYARD KIPLING

'Brown Bess'

The Army Musket – 1700–1815

In the days of lace-ruffles, perukes and brocade
    Brown Bess was a partner whom none could despise –
An out-spoken, flinty-lipped, brazen-faced jade,
    With a habit of looking men straight in the eyes –
At Blenheim and Ramillies fops would confess
They were pierced to the heart by the charms of Brown Bess.

Though her sight was not long and her weight was not small,
    Yet her actions were winning, her language was clear;
And everyone bowed as she opened the ball
    On the arm of some high-gaitered, grim grenadier.
Half Europe admitted the striking success
Of the dances and routs that were given by Brown Bess.

When ruffles were turned into stiff leather stocks,
    And people wore pigtails instead of perukes,
Brown Bess never altered her iron-grey locks.
    She knew she was valued for more than her looks.
'Oh, powder and patches was always my dress,
And I think I am killing enough,' said Brown Bess.

So she followed her red-coats, whatever they did,
   From the heights of Quebec to the plains of Assaye,
From Gibraltar to Acre, Cape Town and Madrid,
   And nothing about her was changed on the way;
(But most of the Empire which now we possess
Was won through those years by old-fashioned Brown Bess.)

In stubborn retreat or in stately advance,
   From the Portugal coast to the cork-woods of Spain,
She had puzzled some excellent Marshals of France
   Till none of them wanted to meet her again:
But later, near Brussels, Napoleon – no less –
Arranged for a Waterloo ball with Brown Bess.

She had danced till the dawn of that terrible day –
   She danced till the dusk of more terrible night,
And before her linked squares his battalions gave way,
   And her long fierce quadrilles put his lancers to flight:
And when his gilt carriage drove off in the press,
'I have danced my last dance for the world!' said Brown Bess.

If you go to Museums – there's one in Whitehall –
   Where old weapons are shown with their names writ
     beneath,
You will find her, upstanding, her back to the wall,
   As stiff as a ramrod, the flint in her teeth.
And if ever we English had reason to bless
Any arm save our mothers', that arm is Brown Bess!

STANLEY KUNITZ

Careless Love

Who have been lonely once
Are comforted by their guns.
Affectionately they speak

To the dark beauty, whose cheek
Beside their own cheek glows.
They are calmed by such repose,
Such power held in hand;
Their young bones understand
The shudder in that frame.
Without nation, without name,
They give the load of love,
And it's returned, to prove
How much the husband heart
Can hold of it: for what
This nymphomaniac enjoys
Inexhaustibly is boys.

ANONYMOUS

Every Bullet Has Its Billet

I'm a tough true-hearted sailor,
    Careless and all that, d'ye see,
Never at the times a railer —
    What is time or tide to me?
All must die when fate shall will it,
    Providence ordains it so;
Every bullet has its billet,
    Man the boat, boys — Yeo, heave yeo,

'Life's at best a sea of trouble,
    He who fears it is a dunce;
Death to me's an empty bubble,
    I can never die but once.
Blood, if duty bids, I'll spill it:
    Yet I have a tear for woe;'
Every bullet has its billet,
    Man the boat, boys — Yeo, heave yeo.

Shrouded in a hammock, glory
  Celebrates the falling brave;
Oh! how many, famed in story,
  Sleep below in ocean's cave.
Bring the can, boys — let us fill it;
  Shall we shun the fight? O, no!
Every bullet has its billet,
  Man the boat, boys — Yeo, heave yeo.

FRANCIS SCARFE

Grenade

As a full fruit, ripe,
I hold you in my palm
As a child holds an apple,
The fingers curling,
Glad of the weight,
Till it grows warm
And ready for tasting.

May they who take you
Into their flesh,
Whose ears are split
By your mad laughter,
Not know how long
I weighed your evil
And flung for shame.

EUGENIUS VULGARIUS

Metrum Parhemiacum Tragicum

O sorrowful and ancient days,
   Where learned ye to make sepulchres?
Who taught you all the evil ways
   Wherein to wound men's souls in wars?

Woe to that sacrificial priest,
   First craftsman of the blacksmith's forge,
Who saw strange shapes within his fire,
   And hammered out illgotten swords.

Whoever fashioned first the bow,
   And flight of arrows, swift, secure,
Launched anger on the air and made
   The bitterness of death more sure.

Who tempered spearheads for their work,
   He breathed upon the anvil death;
He hammered out the slender blade,
   And from the body crushed the breath.

He gave to death a thrusting spear,
   Who first drew up his battle-hosts.
Long since hath fared his vaunting soul
   To dwell a ghost amid the ghosts.

Translated from the Medieval Latin by Helen Waddell

Artillery and Big Bombs

The invention of gunpowder transformed warfare. It redressed the balance in sieges by increasing the destructive power of the attacking forces, and castles, more vulnerable now, became redundant. It also spelt the end of hand-to-hand fighting, for death could thereafter be delivered from a distance. Edward III commanded a few primitive cannon at the Battle of Crécy in 1346, but the era in which the field gun dominated the battle-field started a century later and was to lead to the stalemate of trench warfare in the First World War. The development of artillery continues to accelerate: as a Gunner, I was trained on the 25-pounder and the large 4.2-inch mortar, both now obsolete – items for the military museum.

In tracing the history of the artillery, I begin with Milton, for whom the device must have been particularly frightening and whose imagination allowed him to see, in Satan's invention, something close to the actual event at Hiroshima described by the Japanese poet and eye-witness, Toge Sankichi. Artillery meant that success in war depended upon the industrial power of the combatants.

I have included, too, Kipling's poem, 'Screw-Guns', screw-guns being small and easily dismantled artillery pieces used by Indian mountain troops. The poem has become the regimental song of the Gunners and goes to the tune of the 'Eton Boating Song'.

JOHN MILTON

from Paradise Lost, Book VI

He sat; and in the assembly next upstood
Nisroc, of principalities the prime;
As one he stood escaped from cruel fight,

Sore toiled, his riven arms to havoc hewn,
And cloudy in aspect thus answering spake.
Deliverer from new lords, leader to free
Enjoyment of our right as gods; yet hard
For gods, and too unequal work we find
Against unequal arms to fight in pain,
Against unpained, impassive; from which evil
Ruin must needs ensue; for what avails
Valour or strength, though matchless, quelled with pain
Which all subdues, and makes remiss the hands
Of mightiest. Sense of pleasure we may well
Spare out of life perhaps, and not repine,
But live content, which is the calmest life:
But pain is perfect misery, the worst
Of evils, and excessive, overturns
All patience. He who therefore can invent
With what more forcible we may offend
Our yet unwounded enemies, or arm
Our selves with like defence, to me deserves
No less than for deliverance what we owe.
    Whereto with look composed Satan replied.
Not uninvented that, which thou aright
Believest so main to our success, I bring;
Which of us who beholds the bright surface
Of this ethereous mould whereon we stand,
This continent of spacious heaven, adorned
With plant, fruit, flower ambrosial, gems and gold,
Whose eye so superficially surveys
These things, as not to mind from whence they grow
Deep under ground, materials dark and crude,
Of spiritous and fiery spume, till touched
With heaven's ray, and tempered they shoot forth
So beauteous, opening to the ambient light.
These in their dark nativity the deep
Shall yield us pregnant with infernal flame,
Which into hollow engines long and round

Thick-rammed, at the other bore with touch of fire
Dilated and infuriate shall send forth
From far with thundering noise among our foes
Such implements of mischief as shall dash
To pieces, and o'erwhelm whatever stands
Adverse, that they shall fear we have disarmed
The thunderer of his only dreaded bolt.
Nor long shall be our labour, yet ere dawn,
Effect shall end our wish. Mean while revive;
Abandon fear; to strength and counsel joined
Think nothing hard, much less to be despaired.
He ended, and his words their drooping cheer
Enlightened, and their languished hope revived.
The invention all admired, and each, how he
To be the inventor missed, so easy it seemed
Once found, which yet unfound most would have thought
Impossible: yet haply of thy race
In future days, if malice should abound,
Some one intent on mischief, or inspired
With devilish machination might devise
Like instrument to plague the sons of men
For sin, on war and mutual slaughter bent.
Forthwith from council to the work they flew;
None arguing stood, innumerable hands
Were ready, in a moment up they turned
Wide the celestial soil, and saw beneath
The originals of nature in their crude
Conception; sulphurous and nitrous foam
They found, they mingled, and with subtle art,
Concocted and adusted they reduced
To blackest grain, and into store conveyed:
Part hidden veins digged up (nor hath this earth
Entrails unlike) of mineral and stone,
Whereof to found their engines and their balls
Of missive ruin; part incentive reed
Provide, pernicious with one touch to fire.

So all ere day-spring, under conscious night
Secret they finished, and in order set,
With silent circumspection unespied.
Now when fair morn orient in heaven appeared
Up rose the victor angels, and to arms
The matin trumpet sung: in arms they stood
Of golden panoply, refulgent host,
Soon banded; others from the dawning hills
Looked round, and scouts each coast light-armed scour,
Each quarter, to descry the distant foe,
Where lodged, or whither fled, or if for fight,
In motion or in halt: him soon they met
Under spread ensigns moving nigh, in slow
But firm battalion; back with speediest sail
Zophiel, of cherubim the swiftest wing,
Came flying, and in mid air aloud thus cried.
  Arm, warriors, arm for fight, the foe at hand,
Whom fled we thought, will save us long pursuit
This day, fear not his flight, so thick a cloud
He comes, and settled in his face I see
Sad resolution and secure: let each
His adamantine coat gird well, and each
Fit well his helm, gripe fast his orbed shield,
Borne even or high, for this day will pour down,
If I conjecture aught, no drizzling shower,
But rattling storm of arrows barbed with fire.
So warned he them aware themselves, and soon
In order, quit of all impediment;
Instant without disturb they took alarm,
And onward move embattled; when behold
Not distant far with heavy pace the foe
Approaching gross and huge; in hollow cube
Training his devilish enginery, impaled
On every side with shadowing squadrons deep,
To hide the fraud. At interview both stood
A while, but suddenly at head appeared

Satan: and thus was heard commanding loud.
　Vanguard, to right and left the front unfold;
That all may see who hate us, how we seek
Peace and composure, and with open breast
Stand ready to receive them, if they like
Our overture, and turn not back perverse;
But that I doubt, however witness heaven,
Heaven witness thou anon, while we discharge
Freely our part; ye who appointed stand
Do as you have in charge, and briefly touch
What we propound, and loud that all may hear.
　So scoffing in ambiguous words he scarce
Had ended; when to right and left the front
Divided, and to either flank retired.
Which to our eyes discovered new and strange,
A triple mounted row of pillars laid
On wheels (for like to pillars most they seemed
Or hollowed bodies made of oak or fir,
With branches lopped, in wood or mountain felled)
Brass, iron, stony mould, had not their mouths
With hideous orifice gaped on us wide,
Portending hollow truce; at each behind
A seraph stood, and in his hand a reed
Stood waving tipped with fire; while we suspense,
Collected stood within our thoughts amused,
Not long, for sudden all at once their reeds
Put forth, and to a narrow vent applied
With nicest touch. Immediate in a flame,
But soon obscured with smoke, all heaven appeared,
From those deep throated engines belched, whose roar
Embowelled with outrageous noise the air,
And all her entrails tore, disgorging foul
Their devilish glut, chained thunderbolts and hail
Or iron globes, which on the victor host
Levelled, with such impetuous fury smote,
That whom they hit, none on their feet might stand,

Though standing else as rocks, but down they fell
By thousands, angel on archangel rolled;
The sooner for their arms, unarmed they might
Have easily as spirits evaded swift
By quick contraction or remove; but now
Foul dissipation followed and forced rout;
Nor served it to relax their serried files.

THOMAS DIBDIN

The Origin of Naval Artillery

When Vulcan forged the bolts of Jove
  In Etna's roaring glow,
Neptune petition'd he might prove
  Their use and power below;
But finding in the boundless deep
Their thunders did but idly sleep,
He with them arm'd Britannia's hand,
To guard from foes her native land.

Long may she hold the glorious right,
  And when through circling flame
She darts her thunder in the fight,
  May justice guide her aim!
And when opposed in future wars,
Her soldiers brave and gallant tars
Shall launch her fires from every hand
On every foe to Britain's land.

RUDYARD KIPLING

Screw-Guns

Smokin' my pipe on the mountings, sniffin' the mornin' cool,
I walks in my old brown gaiters along o' my old brown mule,
With seventy gunners be'ind me, an' never a beggar forgets
It's only the pick of the Army that handles the dear little pets –
    'Tss! 'Tss!
      For you all love the screw-guns – the screw-guns they all
        love you!
      So when we call round with a few guns, o' course you will
        know what to do – hoo! hoo!
      Jest send in your Chief an' surrender – it's worse if you
        fights or you runs:
      You can go where you please, you can skid up the trees,
        but you don't get away from the guns!

They sends us along where the roads are, but mostly we goes
    where they ain't.
We'd climb up the side of a sign-board an' trust to the stick o'
    the paint:
We've chivied the Naga an' Looshai; we've give the Afreedee-
    man fits;
For we fancies ourselves at two thousand, we guns that are
      built in two bits – 'Tss! 'Tss!
      For you all love the screw-guns . . .

If a man doesn't work, why, we drills 'im an' teaches 'im 'ow to
    behave.
If a beggar can't march, why, we kills 'im an' rattles 'im into 'is
    grave.
You've got to stand up to our business an' spring without
    snatchin' or fuss.
D'you say that you sweat with the field-guns? By God, you

must lather with us – 'Tss! 'Tss!
For you all love the screw-guns . . .

The eagles is screamin' around us, the river's a-moanin' below,
We're clear o' the pine an' the oak-scrub, we're out on the
    rocks an' the snow,
An' the wind is as thin as a whip-lash what carries away to the
    plains
The rattle an' stamp o' the lead-mules – the jinglety-jink o' the
    chains – 'Tss! 'Tss!
For you all love the screw-guns . . .

There's a wheel on the Horns o' the Mornin', an' a wheel on
    the edge o' the Pit,
An' a drop into nothin' beneath you as straight as a beggar can
    spit:
With the sweat runnin' out o' your shirt-sleeves, an' the sun off
    the snow in your face,
An' 'arf o' the men on the drag-ropes to hold the old gun in 'er
    place – 'Tss! 'Tss!
For you all love the screw-guns . . .

Smokin' my pipe on the mountings, sniffin' the mornin'-cool,
I climbs in my old brown gaiters along o' my old brown mule.
The monkey can say what our road was – the wild-goat 'e
    knows where we passed.
Stand easy, you long-eared old darlin's! Out drag-ropes! With
    shrapnel! Hold fast – 'Tss! 'Tss!
    For you all love the screw-guns – the screw-guns they all
        love you!
    So when we take tea with a few guns, o' course you will
        know what to do – hoo! hoo!
    Jest send in your Chief an' surrender – it's worse if you
        fights or you runs:
    You may hide in the caves, they'll be only your graves, but
        you can't get away from the guns!

HILAIRE BELLOC

The Maxim Gun

We did the thing that he projected,
The Caravan grew disaffected,
      And Sin and I consulted;
Blood understood the Native mind.
He said: 'We must be firm but kind.'
      A Mutiny resulted.
I never shall forget the way
That Blood upon this awful day
Preserved us all from death.
He stood upon a little mound,
Cast his lethargic eyes around,
And said beneath his breath:

'Whatever happens we have got
The Maxim Gun, and they have not.'

ERNEST CROSBY

from War and Hell

I am a great inventor, did you but know it.
I have new weapons and explosives and devices to substitute
    for your obsolete tactics and tools.
Mine are the battle-ships of righteousness and integrity –
The armor-plates of quiet conscience and self-respect –
The impregnable conning-tower of divine manhood –
The Long Toms of persuasion –
The machine guns of influence and example –
The dum-dum bullets of pity and remorse –
The impervious cordon of sympathy –
The concentration camps of brotherhood –

The submarine craft of forgiveness –
The torpedo-boat-destroyer of love –
And behind them all the dynamite of truth!
I do not patent my inventions.
Take them. They are free to all the world.

Boer War, 1901

D. H. LAWRENCE

Bombardment

The Town has opened to the sun.
Like a flat red lily with a million petals
She unfolds, she comes undone.

A sharp sky brushes upon
The myriad glittering chimney-tips
As she gently exhales to the sun.

Hurrying creatures run
Down the labyrinth of the sinister flower.
What is it they shun?

A dark bird falls from the sun.
It curves in a rush to the heart of the vast
Flower: the day has begun.

GUILLAUME APOLLINAIRE

Post Card

Sent to André Rouveyre, 20 August 1915

I write to you beneath this tent
While summer day becomes a shade
And startling magnificent

Flowers of the cannonade
Stud the pale blue firmament
And before existing fade

Translated from the French by Oliver Bernard

HAMISH HENDERSON

Opening of an Offensive

(*a*) the waiting

Armour has foregathered, snuffling
through tourbillions of fine dust.
The crews don't speak much. They've had
last brew-up before battle. The tawny
deadland lies in a silence
not yet smashed by salvoes.
No sound reaches us
from the African constellations.
The low ridge too is quiet.
But no fear we're sleeping,
no need to remind us
that the nervous fingers of the searchlights
are nearly meeting and time is flickering
and this I think in a few minutes
while the whole power crouches for the spring.
X–20 in thirty seconds. Then begin

(*b*) the barrage

Let loose (rounds)
the exultant bounding hell-harrowing of sound.
Break the batteries. Confound
the damnable domination. Slake
the crashing breakers-húrled rúbble of the guns.
Dithering darkness, we'll wake you! Héll's bélls

blind you. Be broken, bleed
deathshead blackness!
        The thongs of the livid
firelights lick you
               jagg'd splinters rend you
                       underground
we'll bomb you, doom you, tomb you into grave's mound

Cyrenaica, 1941

LOUIS MACNEICE

The Streets of Laredo

O early one morning I walked out like Agag,
Early one morning to walk through the fire
Dodging the pythons that leaked on the pavements
With tinkle of glasses and tangle of wire;

When grimed to the eyebrows I met an old fireman
Who looked at me wryly and thus did he say:
'The streets of Laredo are closed to all traffic,
We won't never master this joker today.

'O hold the branch tightly and wield the axe brightly,
The bank is in powder, the banker's in hell,
But loot is still free on the streets of Laredo
And when we drive home we drive home on the bell.'

Then out from a doorway there sidled a cockney,
A rocking-chair rocking on top of his head:
'O fifty-five years I been feathering my love-nest
And look at it now – why, you'd sooner be dead.'

At which there arose from a wound in the asphalt,
His big wig a-smoulder, Sir Christopher Wren
Saying: 'Let them make hay of the streets of Laredo;
When your ground-rents expire I will build them again.'

Then twanging their bibles with wrath in their nostrils
From Bunhill Fields came Bunyan and Blake:
'Laredo the golden is fallen, is fallen;
Your flame shall not quench nor your thirst shall not slake.'

'I come to Laredo to find me asylum,'
Says Tom Dick and Harry the Wandering Jew;
'They tell me report at the first police station
But the station is pancaked – so what can I do?'

Thus eavesdropping sadly I strolled through Laredo
Perplexed by the dicta misfortunes inspire
Till one low last whisper inveigled my earhole –
The voice of the Angel, the voice of the fire:

O late, very late, have I come to Laredo
A whimsical bride in my new scarlet dress
But at last I took pity on those who were waiting
To see my regalia and feel my caress.

Now ring the bells gaily and play the hose daily,
Put splints on your legs, put a gag on your breath;
O you streets of Laredo, you streets of Laredo,
Lay down the red carpet – My dowry is death.

MERVYN PEAKE

from The Rhyme of the Flying Bomb

A babe was born in the reign of George
To a singular birth-bed song,
Its boisterous tune was off the beat
And all of its words were wrong;

But a singular song it was, for the house
As it rattled its ribs and danced,
Had a chorus of doors that slammed their jaws
And a chorus of chairs that pranced.

And the thud of the double-bass was shot
With the wail of the floating strings,
And the murderous notes of the ice-bright glass
Set sail with a clink of wings –

Set sail from the bursted window-frame
To stick in the wall like spears,
Or to slice off the heads of the birthday flowers
Or to nest on a chest-of-drawers.

And a hurdling siren wailed with love
And the windows bulged with red,
And the babe that was born in the reign of George
Wailed back from its raddled bed.

And its mother died when the roof ran in
And over the counterpane,
And the babe that was born in the reign of George
Was found in a golden drain

Was found in a fire-bright drain asleep
By a sailor dazed and lost
In a waterless world where the searchlights climbed
The sky with their fingers crossed.

Through streets where the little red monkey flames
Run over the roofs and hop
From beam to beam, and hang by their tails
Or pounce on a table-top –

Through streets where the monkey-flames run wild
And slide down the banisters.
The sailor strode with the new-born babe
To the hiss of the falling stars.

Through streets where over the window-sills
The loose wallpapers pour
And ripple their waters of nursery whales
By the light of a world at war;

And ripple their wastes of bulls and bears
And their meadows of corn and hay
In a harvest of love that was cut off short
By the scythe of an ape at play —

Through the scarlet streets and the yellow lanes
And the houses like shells of gold
With never a sign of a living soul
The sailor carried the child.

And a ton came down on a coloured road,
And a ton came down on a gaol,
And a ton came down on a freckled girl,
And a ton on the black canal,

And a ton came down on a hospital,
And a ton on a manuscript,
And a ton shot up through the dome of a church,
And a ton roared down to the crypt.

And a ton danced over the Thames and filled
A thousand panes with stars,
And the splinters leapt on the Surrey shore
To the tune of a thousand scars.

And the babe that was born in the reign of George
Lay asleep in the sailor's arm,
With the bombs for its birthday lullaby
And the flames for its birthday dream.

R. N. CURREY

Unseen Fire

This is a damned inhuman sort of war.
I have been fighting in a dressing-gown
Most of the night; I cannot see the guns,
The sweating gun-detachments or the planes;

I sweat down here before a symbol thrown
Upon a screen, sift facts, initiate
Swift calculations and swift orders; wait
For the precise split-second to order fire.

We chant our ritual words; beyond the phones
A ghost repeats the orders to the guns:
One Fire . . . Two Fire . . . ghosts answer: the guns roar
Abruptly; and an aircraft waging war
Inhumanly from nearly five miles height
Meets our bouquet of death – and turns sharp right.

*

This is a damned unnatural sort of war;
The pilot sits among the clouds, quite sure
About the values he is fighting for;
He cannot hear beyond his veil of sound,

He cannot see the people on the ground;
He only knows that on the sloping map
Of sea-fringed town and country people creep
Like ants – and who cares if ants laugh or weep?

To us he is no more than a machine
Shown on an instrument; what can he mean
In human terms? – a man, somebody's son,
Proud of his skill; compact of flesh and bone
Fragile as Icarus – and our desire
To see that damned machine come down on fire.

YEHUDA AMICHAI

from Time

The radius of the bomb was twelve inches
And the radius of its effective force seven yards
Containing four dead and eleven wounded.

And around those, in a wider circle
Of pain and time, are scattered two hospitals
And one graveyard. But the young woman,
Buried in the place she came from,
Over a hundred kilometers from here,
Widens the circle quite a bit,
And the lonely man mourning her death
In the provinces of a Mediterranean land,
Includes the whole world in the circle.
And I shall omit the scream of orphans
That reaches God's throne
And way beyond, and widens the circle
To no end and no God.

Translated from the Hebrew by Benjamin and Barbara Harshav

TOGE SANKICHI

Flames

Pushing up through smoke
from a world half-darkened
by overhanging cloud –
the shroud that mushroomed out
and struck the dome of the sky,
the angry flames –
black, red, blue –
dance into the air,
merge,
scatter glittering sparks,
already tower
over the whole city.

Quivering like seaweed,
the mass of flames spurts forward.
Cattle bound for the slaughterhouse

avalanche down the riverbank;
wings drawn in, a single ash-colored pigeon
lies on its side atop the bridge.
Popping up in the dense smoke,
crawling out
wreathed in fire:
countless human beings
on all fours.
In a heap of embers that erupt and subside,
hair rent,
rigid in death,
there smolders a curse.

After that concentrated moment
of the explosion,
pure incandescent hatred
spreads out, boundless.
Blank silence
piles up into the air.

The hot rays of uranium
that shouldered the sun aside
burn onto a girl's back
the flowered pattern of thin silk,
set instantaneously ablaze
the black garb of the priest –
August 6, 1945:
that midday midnight
man burned the gods
at the stake.
Hiroshima's
night of fire
casts its glow over sleeping humanity;
before long
history will set an ambush
for all who would play God.

Translated from the Japanese by Richard H. Minear

CONNIE BENSLEY

War Games

After the nuclear strike
The bowling green remained strangely intact –
Shielded, perhaps, by the high park wall and trees,
Or a quirk of the blast.

It carried resonances for a few moments –
White figures bending and beckoning,
And the faint cries of children
At play. Then silence.

Something, like rags,
Moved once in the rubbled pavilion:
But soon the dust settled over it.

Fortifications

Making effective fortifications was a high military art and
Tamburlaine gives an impressively technical lesson to his sons.
Wellington, centuries later, seems to have imposed his own
character on defence-works erected in the course of his Peninsular
campaign (1808–12).

CHRISTOPHER MARLOWE

from Tamburlaine the Great, Part II (Act 3, Scene ii)

Tamburlaine: But now my boys, leave off, and list to me,
That mean to teach you rudiments of war:
I'll have you learn to sleep upon the ground,
March in your armour through watery fens,
Sustain the scorching heat and freezing cold,
Hunger and thirst, right adjuncts of the war.
And after this, to scale a castle wall,
Besiege a fort, to undermine a town,
And make whole cities caper in the air.
Then next, the way to fortify your men,
In champion grounds, what figure serves you best,
For which the quinque-angle form is meet,
Because the corners there may fall more flat:
Whereas the fort may fittest be assailed,
And sharpest where th'assault is desperate.
The ditches must be deep, the counterscarps
Narrow and steep, the walls made high and broad,
The bulwarks and the rampires large and strong,
With cavalieros and thick counterforts,
And room within to lodge six thousand men.
It must have privy ditches, countermines,

And secret issuings to defend the ditch.
It must have high argins and covered ways
To keep the bulwark fronts from battery,
And parapets to hide the musketeers:
Casemates to place the great artillery,
And store of ordnance that from every flank
May scour the outward curtains of the fort,
Dismount the cannon of the adverse part,
Murder the foe and save the walls from breach.
When this is learned for service on the land,
By plain and easy demonstration,
I'll teach you how to make the water mount,
That you may dry-foot march through lakes and pools,
Deep rivers, havens, creeks and little seas,
And make a fortress in the raging waves,
Fenced with the concave of a monstrous rock,
Invincible by nature of the place.
When this is done, then are ye soldiers,
And worthy sons of Tamburlaine the Great.

THOMAS HARDY

from The Dynasts, Part II (Act 6, Scene ii)

Masséna, Foy, Loison and French officers confront Wellington's
ramparts in the dusk

  Masséna:
Something stands here to peril our advance,
Or even prevent it!

  Foy:
                    These are the English lines –
Their outer horns and tusks – whereof I spoke,

Constructed by Lord Wellington of late
To keep his foothold firm in Portugal.

  Masséna:
Thrusts he his burly, bossed disfigurements
So far to north as this? I had pictured me
They lay much nearer Lisbon. Little strange
Lord Wellington rode placid at Busaco
With this behind his back! Well, it is hard
But that we turn them somewhere, I assume?
They scarce can close up every southward gap
Between the Tagus and the Atlantic Sea.

  Foy:
I hold they can, and do; although, no doubt,
By searching we shall spy some raggedness
Which customed skill may force.

  Masséna:
                         Plain 'tis, no less,
We may heap corpses vainly hereabout,
And crack good bones in waste. By human power
This passes mounting! What say you's behind?

  Loison:
Another line exactly like the first,
But more matured. Behind its back a third.

  Masséna:
How long have these prim ponderosities
Been rearing up their foreheads to the moon?

  Loison:
Some months in all. I know not quite how long.
They are Lord Wellington's select device,
And, like him, heavy, slow, laborious, sure.

Masséna:
May he enjoy their sureness. He deserves to.
I had no inkling of such barriers here.
A good road runs along their front, it seems,
Which offers us advantage. . . . What a night!

Climate and Circumstances

The climatic conditions in which a soldier has to fight often
determine the outcome. Field-Marshal Wavell wrote to Sir Basil
Liddell Hart, 'If I had time and anything like your ability to study
war, I think I should concentrate almost entirely on the
"actualities" of war – the effects of tiredness, hunger, fear, lack of
sleep, weather. . . . The principles of strategy and tactics and the
logistics of war are really absurdly simple: it is the actualities that
make war so complicated and so difficult and are usually so
neglected by historians.'

In the First World War, rain, mud and the freezing cold totally
overwhelmed the strategy of the generals, snug and warm in their
châteaux behind the lines. The ordinary soldiers left memorable
descriptions of the appalling conditions which made not just
fighting, but existence too, unendurable. In 1917, Henri Barbusse
wrote, 'Dampness rusts men like rifles, more slowly but more
deeply.'

In the Second World War, soldiers had to adapt to campaigns in
the desert and the jungle. The Khamsin, a wind that blows from
the Sahara, so called because it lasts for 50 days, whips up stinging
sand-storms which make it impossible for men to fight and fouls
up vehicles and guns. In the Far East, troops had to cope with
insects and other creatures and the general swampy, eerie
uncertainty of the jungle, conditions which could have a
devastating effect upon morale.

WILLIAM SHAKESPEARE

from Henry V (Act 4, Scene iii)

King Henry:
We are but warriors for the working-day;
Our gayness and our gilt are all besmirch'd
With rainy marching in the painful field.

EDWARD THOMAS

Rain

Rain, midnight rain, nothing but the wild rain
On this bleak hut, and solitude, and me
Remembering again that I shall die
And neither hear the rain nor give it thanks
For washing me cleaner than I have been
Since I was born into this solitude.
Blessed are the dead that the rain rains upon:
But here I pray that none whom once I loved
Is dying tonight or lying still awake
Solitary, listening to the rain,
Either in pain or thus in sympathy
Helpless among the living and the dead,
Like a cold water among broken reeds,
Myriads of broken reeds all still and stiff,
Like me who have no love which this wild rain
Has not dissolved except the love of death,
If love it be towards what is perfect and
Cannot, the tempest tells me, disappoint.

WILFRED OWEN

from The Sentry

We'd found an old Boche dug-out, and he knew,
And gave us hell, for shell on frantic shell
Hammered on top, but never quite burst through.
Rain, guttering down in waterfalls of slime,
Kept slush waist-high and rising hour by hour,
And choked the steps too thick with clay to climb.
What murk of air remained stank old, and sour
With fumes of whizz-bangs, and the smell of men
Who'd lived there years, and left their curse in the den,
If not their corpses. . . .
                              There we herded from the blast
Of whizz-bangs, but one found our door at last, –
Buffeting eyes and breath, snuffing the candles,
And thud! flump! thud! down the steep steps came thumping
And sploshing in the flood, deluging muck –
The sentry's body; then, his rifle, handles
Of old Boche bombs, and mud in ruck on ruck.
We dredged him up, for killed, until he whined
'O sir, my eyes – I'm blind – I'm blind, I'm blind!'
Coaxing, I held a flame against his lids
And said if he could see the least blurred light
He was not blind; in time he'd get all right.
'I can't,' He sobbed. Eyeballs, huge-bulged like squids',
Watch my dreams still; but I forgot him there
In posting Next for duty, and sending a scout
To beg a stretcher somewhere, and flound'ring about
To other posts under the shrieking air.

JOHN JARMAIN

Sand

We have seen sand frothing like the sea
About our wheels, and in our wake
Clouds rolling yellow and opaque,
Thick-smoking from the ground;
Wrapped in the dust from sun and sky
Without a mark to guide them by
Men drove alone unseeing in the cloud,
Peering to find a track, to find a way,
With eyes stung red, clown-faces coated grey.
Then with sore lips we cursed the sand,
Cursed this sullen gritty land
— Cursed and dragged on our blind and clogging way.

We have felt the fevered Khamsin blow
Which whips the desert into sting and spite
Of dry-sand driving rain (the only rain
The parched and dusty sand-lands know,
The hot dry driven sand): the desert floor
Whipped by the wind drives needles in the air
Which pricked our eyelids blind; and in a night,
Sifting the drifted sandhills grain by grain,
Covers our shallow tracks, our laboured road,
Makes false the maps we made with such slow care.

And we have seen wonders, spinning towers of sand
— Moving pillars of cloud by day —
Which passed and twitched our tents away;
Lakes where no water was, and in the sky
Grey shimmering palms. We have learned the sun and stars
And new simplicities, living by our cars
In wastes without one tree or living thing,

Where the flat horizon's level ring
Is equal everywhere without a change.

Yet sand has been kind for us to lie at ease,
Its soft-dug walls have sheltered and made a shield
From fear and danger, and the chilly night.
And as we quit this bare unlovely land,
Strangely again see houses, hills, and trees,
We will remember older things than these,
Indigo skies pricked out with brilliant light,
The smooth unshadowed candour of the sand.

ROBERT GARIOCH

Property

A man should have no thought for property,
he said, and drank down his pint.
Mirage is found in the Desert and elsewhere.
Later, in Libya (sand & scrub,
the sun two weeks to midsummer)
he carried all his property over the sand:
socks, knife and spoon, a dixie,
toilet kit, the Works of Shakespeare,
blanket, groundsheet, greatcoat,
and a water-bottle holding no more water.
He walked with other scorched men
in the dryness of this littoral waste land,
a raised beach without even sea water
with a much damned escarpment
unchanged throughout a day's truck-bumping
or a lifetime of walking without water,
confirming our worst fears of eternity.
Two men only went on whistling,
skidding on a beat-frequency.

Tenderness to music's dissonances,
and much experience of distress in art
was distressed, this time, in life.
A hot dry wind rose, moving the sand,
the sand-shifting Khamsin, rustling over
the land, whistling through hardy sandy
scrub, where sand-snails' brittle
shells on the sand, things in themselves,
roll for ever. Suffusing the sand in the
air, the sun burned in darkness.
No man now whistled, only the sandy wind.
The greatcoat first, then blanket discarded
and the other property lay absurd on the Desert,
but he kept his water-bottle.
In February, in a cold wet climate,
he has permanent damp in his bones
for lack of that groundsheet.
He has a different notion of the values of things.

'K'

Jungle Night

The man with the green cigarette strolls down the path
Waving it in the air in conversation.
The man with the tiny anvil strikes it softly like a bell –
Tink-tink; tink-tink.
The man with the dark blue cloak goes quietly by.
There goes the man with the green cigarette again.

They are not really there. You know quite well
They are not there.
Then one of them whistles softly
You finger the trigger of your Bren.

Half-fearing, half-desiring the sudden hell
Pressure will loose.
You listen —
Nothing —
Then

The man with the green cigarette strolls by again
Waving it in the air.
Down comes the dew,
Drip-drip; drip-drip.
The man with the tiny silver anvil
Strikes twice; strikes twice
Softly passes the man with the cloak of blue.

> Fireflies.
> Bell birds
> Shadows
> Japanese.

Burma, 1940s

GEORGE SCURFIELD

The Bitter Mangoes

I'll only tell the story once
it doesn't do to tell it twice;
the sergeant and the family man
will tell you that it isn't nice.
O the bitter mangoes O.

There were bamboos to the left of us
and bamboos to the right
bamboos all the morning
and thorns of course at night.
O the bitter mangoes O.

How shall we ever get there?
We shan't the captain said,
he fell among the cane trees
and broke his stupid head.
O the bitter mangoes O.

Stuck in the mud for lunchtime
stuck in the mud for tea
with centipedes and leeches
crawling round your knee.
O the bitter mangoes O.

Breaking your nails for supper
climbing up a cliff
trembling like a jelly
not daring once to sniff
O the bitter mangoes O

Crawling round for breakfast
under bamboo bush and tree
the ants are biting nicely
they're getting in your tea.
O the bitter mangoes O.

The rain is falling gently
the rain it's tumbling down
every single thing is wet
wouldn't you like to drown.
O the bitter mangoes O.

They're shooting in the pine trees
grenades are crashing down
the little man behind the tree
is going to get you soon.
O the bitter mangoes O.

ALUN LEWIS

from The Jungle

Grey monkeys gibber, ignorant and wise.
We are the ghosts, and they the denizens;
We are like them anonymous, unknown,
Avoiding what is human, near,
Skirting the villages, the paddy fields
Where boys sit timelessly to scare the crows
On bamboo platforms raised above their lives.

A trackless wilderness divides
Joy from its cause, the motive from the act:
The killing arm uncurls, strokes the soft moss;
The distant world is an obituary,
We do not hear the tappings of its dread.
The act sustains; there is no consequence.
Only aloneness, swinging slowly
Down the cold orbit of an older world
Than any they predicted in the schools,
Stirs the cold forest with a starry wind,
And sudden as the flashing of a sword
The dream exalts the bowed and golden head
And time is swept with a great turbulence,
The old temptation to remould the world.

The bamboos creak like an uneasy house;
The night is shrill with crickets, cold with space.
And if the mute pads on the sand should lift
Annihilating paws and strike us down
Then would some unimportant death resound
With the imprisoned music of the soul?
And we become the world we could not change?

Or does the will's long struggle end
With the last kindness of a foe or friend?

EDGELL RICKWORD

Winter Warfare

Colonel Cold strode up the Line
  (tabs of rime and spurs of ice);
stiffened all that met his glare:
  horses, men, and lice.

Visited a forward post,
  left them burning, ear to foot;
fingers stuck to biting steel,
  toes to frozen boot.

Stalked on into No Man's Land,
  turned the wire to fleecy wool,
iron stakes to sugar sticks
  snapping at a pull.

Those who watched with hoary eyes
  saw two figures gleaming there;
Hauptmann Kälte, Colonel Cold,
  gaunt in the grey air.

Stiffly, tinkling spurs they moved,
  glassy-eyed, with glinting heel
stabbing those who lingered there
  torn by screaming steel.

ALAN ROSS

Destroyers in the Arctic

Camouflaged, they detach lengths of sea and sky
When they move; offset, speed and directions are a lie.

Everything is grey anyway; ships, water, snow, faces.
Flanking the convoy, we rarely go through our paces.

But sometimes on tightening waves at night they wheel
Drawing white moons on strings from dripping keel.

Cold cases them, like ships in glass; they are formal,
Not real, except in adversity. Such deception is normal.

At dusk they intensify dusk, strung out, non-committal:
Waves spill from our wake, crêpe paper magnetised by gun-
  metal.

They breathe silence, less solid than ghosts, ruminative
As the Arctic breaks up on their sides and they sieve

Moisture into mess-decks. Heat is cold-lined there,
Where we wait for a torpedo and lack air.

Repetitive of each other, imitating the sea's lift and fall,
On the wings of the convoy they indicate rehearsal.

Merchantmen move sideways, with the gait of crustaceans,
Round whom like eels escorts take up their stations.

Landfall, Murmansk; but starboard now a lead-coloured
Island, Jan Mayen. Days identical, hoisted like sails, blurred.

Counters moved on an Admiralty map, snow like confetti
Covers the real us. We dream we are counterfeits tied to our
  jetty.

But cannot dream long; the sea curdles and sprawls,
Liverishly real, horizon and water tilting in to walls.

AESCHYLUS

from Agamemnon

Herald:
If I were to tell of our labours, our hard lodging,
The sleeping on crowded decks, the scanty blankets,
Tossing and groaning, rations that never reached us –
And the land too gave matter for more disgust,
For our beds lay under the enemy's walls.
Continuous drizzle from the sky, dews from the marshes.
Rotting our clothes, filling our hair with lice.
And if one were to tell of the bird-destroying winter
Intolerable from the snows of Ida
Or of the heat when the sea slackens at noon
Waveless and dozing in a depressed calm –
But why make complaints? The weariness is over;
Over indeed for some who never again
Need even trouble to rise.
Why make a computation of the lost?
Why need the living sorrow for the spites of fortune?
I wish to say a long goodbye to disasters.
For us, the remnant of the troops of Argos,
The advantage remains, the pain can not outweigh it;
So we can make our boast to this sun's light,
Flying on words above the land and sea:
'Having taken Troy the Argive expedition
Has nailed up throughout Greece in every temple
These spoils, these ancient trophies.'
Those who hear such things must praise the city
And the generals. And the grace of God be honored
Which brought these things about. You have the whole story.

Translated from the Greek by Louis MacNeice

Fellow Creatures

Corpses left on a battlefield attract further armies – of devouring animals, insects and birds: crows, kites, buzzards, rats and the like. It is surprising how quickly soldiers grow accustomed to their carnivorous companions.

Fleas and lice become all too intimate in their companionship and have to be destroyed, as Isaac Rosenberg describes so graphically. George Orwell, from his experience of the Spanish Civil War, wrote, 'In war all soldiers are lousy, at least when it is warm enough. The men who fought at Verdun, at Waterloo, at Flodden, at Senlac, at Thermopylae – every one of them had lice crawling over his testicles.'

ARTHUR RIMBAUD

The Rooks

Lord, when the meadow has gone cold
And in the shell-torn villages
The angelus is no more tolled
And Nature shows her ravages,
Make them descend from the great heights,
The rooks, my darlings and delights!

Strange army with such austere cries,
The bitter winds attack your nests.
Along the river's yellow crests,
On roads with ancient Calvaries,
Over the trenched and pitted ground
Scatter and wheel and rally round!

By thousands over the French plain,
Where sleep the dead of two days back,
In winter won't you wheel and clack
To make each passer think again?
Be crier, then, of duty's word,
Our funeral and sable bird.

But, saints of heaven, at oak's high top,
Mast on which magic eve doth close,
Forsake May's warblers, turn to those
Who in the wood's deep places stop,
In grass from which there's no retreat,
Chained by a futureless defeat!

Translated from the French by Norman Cameron

ALEXANDER BLOK

The Kite

Over the empty fields a black kite hovers,
  And circle after circle smoothly weaves.
In the poor hut, over her son in the cradle
 A mother grieves:
'There, suck my breast: there, grow and take our bread,
And learn to bear your cross and bow your head.'

Time passes. War returns. Rebellion rages.
 The farms and villages go up in flame,
And Russia in her ancient tear-stained beauty,
 Is yet the same,
Unchanged through all the ages. How long will
The mother grieve and the kite circle still?

Translated from the Russian by Frances Cornford
and Esther Polinowsky Salaman

JOHN RIMINGTON

God of the Flies

Mundy, McCall, and Browne, and Saul,
Mulholland, Geer, and Snoddie,
Porton, Horton, and Heptonstall
Are dying in the wadi.

Charlie and Fred are already dead,
And Sergeant Crisp is sleeping
His final sleep beside the jeep . . .
His wife will soon be weeping.

But tell our wives that *Life* survives,
For God is mighty clever.
While He supplies eternal flies
The desert lives for ever.

Yes, tell our wives that *Life* survives.
A clever fellow, God is,
For He supplies eternal flies
To populate the wadis.

ISAAC ROSENBERG

Louse Hunting

Nudes – stark and glistening,
Yelling in lurid glee. Grinning faces
And raging limbs
Whirl over the floor one fire.
For a shirt verminously busy
Yon soldier tore from his throat, with oaths
Godhead might shrink at, but not the lice.

And soon the shirt was aflare
Over the candle he'd lit while we lay.

Then we all sprang up and stript
To hunt the verminous brood.
Soon like a demons' pantomime
The place was raging.
See the silhouettes agape,
See the gibbering shadows
Mixed with the battled arms on the wall.
See gargantuan hooked fingers
Pluck in supreme flesh
To smutch supreme littleness.
See the merry limbs in hot Highland fling
Because some wizard vermin
Charmed from the quiet this revel
When our ears were half lulled
By the dark music
Blown from Sleep's trumpet.

DAVID JONES

from In Parenthesis, Part 3

You can hear the silence of it:
you can hear the rat of no-man's-land
rut-out intricacies,
weasel-out his patient workings,
scrut, scrut, sscrut,
harrow-out earthly, trowel his cunning paw;
redeem the time of our uncharity, to sap his own amphibious
    paradise.
You can hear his carrying-parties rustle our corruptions
through the night-weeds — contest the choicest morsels in his
tiny conduits, bead-eyed feast on us; by a rule of his nature,
at night-feast on the broken of us.

Those broad-pinioned;
blue-burnished, or brinded-back;
whose proud eyes watched
                the broken emblems
droop and drag dust,
suffer with us this metamorphosis.
    These too have shed their fine feathers; these too have
slimed their dark-bright coats; these too have condescended
to dig in.
    The white-tailed eagle at the battle ebb,
                        where the sea wars against the river
the speckled kite of Maldon
and the crow
have naturally selected to be un-winged;
to go on the belly, to
sap   sap   sap
with festered spines, arched under the moon; furrit with
whiskered snouts the secret parts of us.
    When it's all quiet you can hear them:
scrut scrut scrut
when it's as quiet as this is.
    It's so very still.
    Your body fits the crevice of the bay in the most comfor-
        table fashion imaginable.
    It's cushy enough.

Night Scenes

Nightfall usually brings battles to an end or introduces a lull in the fighting. Night offers not only the chance of recuperation but time to reconnoitre and prepare for the next day's action. Soldiers must grab whatever sleep they can: Ivor Gurney reported that, off duty in the trenches, you were lucky to catch just three hours' sleep a night.

Graeme West's 'Night Patrol' gives a wonderfully vivid description of a night spent in No Man's Land. When West was rejected for a commission because of his poor eyesight, he enlisted as an ordinary soldier. He eventually rose to the rank of Captain, but was killed in 1917, by which time he was so sickened by what he had witnessed that he was on his way to becoming a conscientious objector.

ARTHUR GRAEME WEST

The Night Patrol

Over the top! The wire's thin here, unbarbed
Plain rusty coils, not staked, and low enough:
Full of old tins, though – 'When you're through, all three,
Aim quarter left for fifty yards or so,
Then straight for that new piece of German wire;
See if it's thick, and listen for a while
For sounds of working; don't run any risks;
About an hour; now, over!'
                        And we placed
Our hands on the topmost sand-bags, leapt, and stood
A second with curved backs, then crept to the wire,
Wormed ourselves tinkling through, glanced back, and
     dropped.

The sodden ground was splashed with shallow pools,
And tufts of crackling cornstalks, two years old,
No man had reaped, and patches of spring grass,
Half-seen, as rose and sank the flares, were strewn
With the wrecks of our attack: the bandoliers,
Packs, rifles, bayonets, belts, and haversacks,
Shell fragments, and the huge whole forms of shells
Shot fruitlessly — and everywhere the dead.
Only the dead were always present — present
As a vile sickly smell of rottenness;
The rustling stubble and the early grass,
The slimy pools — the dead men stank through all,
Pungent and sharp; as bodies loomed before,
And as we passed, they stank: then dulled away
To that vague fœtor, all encompassing,
Infecting earth and air. They lay, all clothed,
Each in some new and piteous attitude
That we well marked to guide us back: as he,
Outside our wire, that lay on his back and crossed
His legs Crusader-wise; I smiled at that,
And thought on Elia and his Temple Church.
From him, at quarter left, lay a small corpse,
Down in a hollow, huddled as in bed,
That one of us put his hand on unawares.
Next was a bunch of half a dozen men
All blown to bits, an archipelago
Of corrupt fragments, vexing to us three,
Who had no light to see by, save the flares.
On such a trail, so lit, for ninety yards
We crawled on belly and elbows, till we saw,
Instead of lumpish dead before our eyes,
The stakes and crosslines of the German wire.
We lay in shelter of the last dead man,
Ourselves as dead, and heard their shovels ring
Turning the earth, then talk and cough at times.
A sentry fired and a machine-gun spat;

They shot a flare above us; when it fell
And spluttered out in the pools of No Man's Land,
We turned and crawled past the remembered dead:
Past him and him, and them and him, until,
For he lay some way apart, we caught the scent
Of the Crusader and slid past his legs,
And through the wire and home, and got our rum.

GIUSEPPE UNGARETTI

Watch

Cima Quattro, 23 December 1915

A whole night through
thrown down beside
a butchered comrade
with his clenched teeth
turned to the full moon
and the clutching
of his hands
thrust
into my silence
I have written
letters full of love

Never have I
clung
so fast to life

Translated from the Italian by Patrick Creagh

CHARLES WOLFE

The Burial of Sir John Moore after Corunna

Not a drum was heard, not a funeral note,
　　As his corpse to the rampart we hurried;
Not a soldier discharged his farewell shot
　　O'er the grave where our hero we buried.

We buried him darkly at dead of night,
　　The sods with our bayonets turning,
By the struggling moonbeam's misty light
　　And the lanthorn dimly burning.

No useless coffin enclosed his breast,
　　Not in sheet or in shroud we wound him;
But he lay like a warrior taking his rest
　　With his martial cloak around him.

Few and short were the prayers we said,
　　And we spoke not a word of sorrow;
But we steadfastly gazed on the face that was dead,
　　And we bitterly thought of the morrow.

We thought, as we hollowed his narrow bed
　　And smoothed down his lonely pillow,
That the foe and the stranger would tread o'er his head,
　　And we far away on the billow!

Lightly they'll talk of the spirit that's gone,
　　And o'er his cold ashes upbraid him –
But little he'll reck, if they let him sleep on
　　In the grave where a Briton has laid him.

But half of our heavy task was done
　　When the clock struck the hour for retiring;
And we heard the distant and random gun
　　That the foe was sullenly firing.

Slowly and sadly we laid him down,
  From the field of his fame fresh and gory;
We carved not a line, and we raised not a stone,
  But we left him alone with his glory.

THOMAS HARDY

from The Dynasts, Part III (Act 6, Scene viii)

  Chorus of the Years:
The eyelids of eve fall together at last,
And the forms so foreign to field and tree
Lie down as though native, and slumber fast!

  Chorus of the Pities:
Sore are the thrills of misgiving we see
In the artless champaign at this harlequinade,
Distracting a vigil where calm should be!

The green seems opprest, and the Plain afraid
Of a Something to come, whereof these are the proofs, –
Neither earthquake, nor storm, nor eclipse's shade!

  Chorus of the Years:
Yea, the coneys are scared by the thud of hoofs,
And their white scuts flash at their vanishing heels,
And swallows abandon the hamlet-roofs.

The mole's tunnelled chambers are crushed by wheels,
The lark's eggs scattered, their owners fled;
And the hedgehog's household the sapper unseals.

The snail draws in at the terrible tread,
But in vain; he is crushed by the felloe-rim;
The worm asks what can be overhead,

And wriggles deep from a scene so grim,
And guesses him safe; for he does not know
What a foul red flood will be soaking him!

Beaten about by the heel and toe
Are butterflies, sick of the day's long rheum,
To die of a worse than the weather-foe.

Trodden and bruised to a miry tomb
Are ears that have greened but will never be gold,
And flowers in the bud that will never bloom.

   Chorus of the Pities:
So the season's intent, ere its fruit unfold,
Is frustrate, and mangled, and made succumb,
Like a youth of promise struck stark and cold! . . .

And what of these who to-night have come?

   Chorus of the Years:
The young sleep sound; but the weather awakes
In the veterans, pains from the past that numb;

Old stabs of Ind, old Peninsular aches,
Old Friedland chills, haunt their moist mud bed,
Cramps from Austerlitz; till their slumber breaks.

   Chorus of Sinister Spirits:
And each soul shivers as sinks his head
On the loam he's to lease with the other dead
From to-morrow's mist-fall till Time be sped!

GEORGE GORDON, LORD BYRON

from Childe Harold's Pilgrimage, Canto III

There was a sound of revelry by night,
And Belgium's capital had gather'd then
Her Beauty and her Chivalry, and bright
The lamps shone o'er fair women and brave men;
A thousand hearts beat happily; and when
Music arose with its voluptuous swell,
Soft eyes look'd love to eyes which spake again,
And all went merry as a marriage-bell;
But hush! hark! a deep sound strikes like a rising knell!

Did ye not hear it? – No; 'twas but the wind,
Or the car rattling o'er the stony street;
On with the dance! let joy be unconfined;
No sleep till morn, when Youth and Pleasure meet
To chase the glowing Hours with flying feet –
But, hark – that heavy sound breaks in once more,
As if the clouds its echo would repeat;
And nearer, clearer, deadlier than before!
Arm! Arm! it is – it is – the cannon's opening roar! . . .

Ah! then and there was hurrying to and fro,
And gathering tears, and tremblings of distress,
And cheeks all pale, which but an hour ago
Blush'd at the praise of their own loveliness;
And there were sudden partings, such as press
The life from out young hearts, and choking sighs
Which ne'er might be repeated; who could guess
If ever more should meet those mutual eyes,
Since upon night so sweet such awful morn could rise?

And there was mounting in hot haste: the steed,
The mustering squadron, and the clattering car,
Went pouring forward with impetuous speed,
And swiftly forming in the ranks of war;
And the deep thunder peal on peal afar;
And near, the beat of the alarming drum
Roused up the soldier ere the morning star;
While throng'd the citizens with terror dumb,
Or whispering, with white lips – 'The foe! They come! they
come!'

Spying

Spies are necessary in war and Kipling, ever a spokesman for the demeaned and uncelebrated, wrote their anthem: 'Slip through his lines and learn − / That is work for a spy!' Spies do not receive medals; they work on their own; and their deaths go unrecorded. The passage from the *Iliad* describes the fate of one Dolon, sent by Hector into the Greek lines. Discovered by Ulysses, he spills the beans about the disposition of the Trojan forces, hoping for a reward − literature's first double agent.

HOMER

from The Iliad, Book X

All silent stood; at last stood forth one Dolon, that did dare
This dangerous work, Eumedes' heir, a herald much
    renown'd.
This Dolon did in gold and brass exceedingly abound,
But in his form was quite deform'd, yet passing swift to run,
Amongst five sisters, he was left Eumedes' only son.
And he told Hector, his free heart would undertake t' explore
The Greeks' intentions, 'but,' said he, 'thou shalt be sworn
    before,
By this thy sceptre, that the horse of great Æacides,
And his strong chariot bound with brass, thou wilt (before all
    these)
Resign me as my valour's prise, and so I rest unmov'd
To be thy spy, and not return before I have approv'd
(By venturing to Atrides' ship, where their consults are held)
If they resolve still to resist, or fly as quite expell'd.'

He put his sceptre in his hand, and call'd the thunder's God,
Saturnia's husband, to his oath, those horse should not be rode
By any other man than he, but he for ever joy
(To his renown) their services, for his good done to Troy.
Thus swore he, and forswore himself, yet made base Dolon
        bold;
Who on his shoulders hung his bow, and did about him fold
A white wolf's hide, and with a helm of weasels' skins did arm
His weasel's head, then took his dart, and never turn'd to harm
The Greeks with their related drifts; but being past the troops
Of horse and foot, he promptly runs, and as he runs he stoops
To undermine Achilles' horse. Ulysses straight did see,
And said to Diomed: 'This man makes footing towards thee,
Out of the tents. I know not well, if he be us'd as spy
Bent to our fleet, or come to rob the slaughter'd enemy.
But let us suffer him to come a little further on,
And then pursue him. If it chance, that we be overgone
By his more swiftness, urge him still to run upon our fleet,
And (lest he 'scape us to the town) still let thy javelin meet
With all his offers of retreat.' Thus stepp'd they from the plain
Amongst the slaughter'd carcasses. Dolon came on amain,
Suspecting nothing; but once past, as far as mules outdraw
Oxen at plough, being both put on, neither admitted law,
To plough a deep-soil'd furrow forth, so far was Dolon past.
Then they pursu'd, which he perceiv'd, and stay'd his speedless
        haste,
Subtly supposing Hector sent to countermand his spy;
But, in a javelin's throw or less, he knew them enemy.
Then laid he on his nimble knees, and they pursu'd like wind.
As when a brace of greyhounds are laid in with hare or hind,
Close-mouth'd and skill'd to make the best of their industrious
        course,
Serve either's turn, and, set on hard, lose neither ground nor
        force;
So constantly did Tydeus' son, and his town-razing peer,
Pursue this spy, still turning him, as he was winding near

His covert, till he almost mix'd with their out-courts of guard.
   Then Pallas prompted Diomed, lest his due worth's reward
Should be impair'd if any man did vaunt he first did sheath
His sword in him, and he be call'd but second in his death.
Then spake he, threat'ning with his lance: 'Or stay, or this
     comes on,
And long thou canst not run before thou be by death outgone.'
   This said, he threw his javelin forth; which miss'd as
     Diomed would,
Above his right arm making way, the pile stuck in the mould.
He stay'd and trembled, and his teeth did chatter in his head.
They came in blowing, seiz'd him fast; he, weeping, offered
A wealthy ransom for his life, and told them he had brass,
Much gold, and iron, that fit for use in many labours was,
From whose rich heaps his father would a wondrous portion
     give,
If, at the great Achaian fleet, he heard his son did live.
   Ulysses bad him cheer his heart. 'Think not of death,' said
     he,
'But tell us true, why runn'st thou forth when others sleeping
     be?
Is it to spoil the carcasses? Or art thou choicely sent
T' explore our drifts? Or of thyself seek'st thou some wish'd
     event?'
   He trembling answer'd: 'Much reward did Hector's oath
     propose,
And urg'd me, much against my will, t' endeavour to disclose
If you determin'd still to stay, or bent your course for flight,
As all dismay'd with your late foil, and wearied with the fight.
For which exploit, Pelides' horse and chariot he did swear,
I only ever should enjoy.' Ulysses smil'd to hear
So base a swain have any hope so high a prise t' aspire,
And said, his labours did affect a great and precious hire,
And that the horse Pelides rein'd no mortal hand could use
But he himself, whose matchless life a Goddess did produce.
'But tell us, and report but truth, where left'st thou Hector
     now?

Where are his arms? His famous horse? On whom doth he
    bestow
The watch's charge? Where sleep the kings? Intend they still to
    lie
Thus near encamp'd, or turn suffic'd with their late victory?'
  'All this,' said he, 'I'll tell most true. At Ilus' monument
Hector with all our princes sits, t'advise of this event,
Who choose that place remov'd to shun the rude confused
    sounds
The common soldiers throw about. But, for our watch, and
    rounds,
Whereof, brave lord, thou mak'st demand, none orderly we
    keep.
The Trojans, that have roofs to save, only abandon sleep,
And privately without command each other they exhort
To make prevention of the worst; and in this slender sort
Is watch and guard maintain'd with us. Th' auxiliary bands
Sleep soundly, and commit their cares into the Trojans' hands,
For they have neither wives with them, nor children to protect;
The less they need to care, the more they succour dull neglect.'
  'But tell me,' said wise Ithacus, 'are all these foreign powers
Appointed quarters by themselves, or else commix'd with
    yours?'
  'And this,' said Dolon, 'too, my lords, I'll seriously unfold.
The Pæons with the crooked bows, and Cares, quarters hold
Next to the sea, the Leleges, and Caucons, join'd with them,
And brave Pelasgians. Thymber's mead, remov'd more from
    the stream,
Is quarter to the Lycians, the lofty Mysian force,
The Phrygians and Meonians, that fight with armed horse.
But what need these particulars? If ye intend surprise
Of any in our Trojan camps, the Thracian quarter lies
Utmost of all, and uncommix'd with Trojan regiments,
That keep the voluntary watch. New pitch'd are all their tents.
King Rhesus, Eioneus' son, commands them, who hath steeds

More white than snow, huge, and well-shap'd, their fiery pace
    exceeds
The winds in swiftness; these I saw; his chariot is with gold
And pallid silver richly fram'd, and wondrous to behold;
His great and golden armour is not fit a man should wear,
But for immortal shoulders fram'd. Come then, and quickly
    bear
Your happy prisoner to your fleet; or leave him here fast
    bound
Till your well-urg'd and rich return prove my relation sound.'
   Tydides dreadfully replied: 'Think not of passage thus,
Though of right acceptable news thou has advértis'd us,
Our hands are holds more strict than so; and should we set
    thee free
For offer'd ransom, for this 'scape thou still wouldst scouting
    be
About our ships, or do us scathe in plain opposed arms,
But, if I take thy life, no way can we repent thy harms.'
  With this, as Dolon reach'd his hand to use a suppliant's
    part
And stroke the beard of Diomed, he struck his neck athwart
With his forc'd sword, and both the nerves he did in sunder
    wound,
And suddenly his head, deceiv'd, fell speaking on the ground.
His weasel's helm they took, his bow, his wolf's skin, and his
    lance,
Which to Minerva Ithacus did zealously advance,
With lifted arm into the air; and to her thus he spake:
  'Goddess, triumph in thine own spoils; to thee we first will
    make
Our invocations, of all powers thron'd on th' Olympian hill;
Now to the Thracians, and their horse, and beds, conduct us
    still.'

Translated from the Greek by George Chapman

RUDYARD KIPLING

The Spies' March

'The outbreak is in full swing and our death-rate would sicken Napoleon.
... Dr M— died last week, and C— on Monday, but some more
medicines are coming. . . . We don't seem to be able to check it at all.
... Villages panicking badly. . . . In some places not a living soul.
... But at any rate the experience gained may come in useful, so I am
keeping my notes written up to date in case of accidents. . . . Death is a
queer chap to live with for steady company.' – *Extract from a private
letter from Manchuria.*

There are no leaders to lead us to honour, and yet without
    leaders we sally,
Each man reporting for duty alone, out of sight, out of reach,
    of his fellow.
There are no bugles to call the battalions, and yet without
    bugle we rally
From the ends of the earth to the ends of the earth, to follow
    the Standard of Yellow!
        Fall in ! O fall in! O fall in!

Not where the squadrons mass,
  Not where the bayonets shine,
Not where the big shell shout as they pass
  Over the firing-line;
Not where the wounded are,
  Not where the nations die,
Killed in the cleanly game of war –
  That is no place for a spy!
O Princes, Thrones and Powers, your work is less than ours –
  Here is no place for a spy!

Trained to another use,
  We march with colours furled,
Only concerned when Death breaks loose
  On a front of half a world.

Only for General Death
  The Yellow Flag may fly,
While we take post beneath —
  That is the place for a spy.
Where Plague has spread his pinions over Nations and
      Dominions —
Then will be work for a spy!

The dropping shots begin,
  The single funerals pass,
Our skirmishers run in,
  The corpses dot the grass!
The howling towns stampede,
  The tainted hamlets die.
Now it is war indeed —
  Now there is room for a spy!
O Peoples, Kings and Lands, we are waiting your commands —
What is the work for a spy?
          (Drums) — *Fear is upon us, spy!*

'Go where his pickets hide —
  Unmask the shape they take,
Whether a gnat from the waterside,
  Or a stinging fly in the brake,
Or filth of the crowded street,
  Or a sick rat limping by,
Or a smear of spittle dried in the heat —
  That is the work of a spy!
          (Drums) — *Death is upon us, spy!*

'What does he next prepare?
  Whence will he move to attack? –
By water, earth or air? –
  How can we head him back?
Shall we starve him out if we burn
  Or bury his food-supply?
Slip through his lines and learn –
  That is work for a spy!
          (Drums) – *Get to your business, spy!*

'Does he feint or strike in force?
  Will he charge or ambuscade?
What is it checks his course?
  Is he beaten or only delayed?
How long will the lull endure?
  Is he retreating? Why?
Crawl to his camp and make sure –
  That is the work for a spy!
          (Drums) – *Fetch us our answer, spy!*

'Ride with him girth to girth
  Wherever the Pale Horse wheels
Wait on his councils, ear to earth,
  And say what the dust reveals.
For the smoke of our torment rolls
  Where the burning thousands lie;
What do we care for men's bodies or souls?
  Bring us deliverance, spy!'

Victories

Wellington remarked that, 'Nothing except a battle lost can be half so melancholy as a battle won', but this is a view expressed in the tranquillity of the after-peace. At the time of fighting, victory is the sole aim, and so these poems celebrate unalloyed victories.

Jerusalem was saved from the Assyrians once and for all in 700 BC. At Agincourt, in 1415, English bowmen and pikemen unexpectedly defeated the impetuous and undisciplined French cavalry and gave Henry V the opportunity to govern half of France, which was to prove a bitter legacy for his son. The defeat of the Turkish fleet at Lepanto (1572) frustrated the expansion of Muslim power over the Eastern Mediterranean. At Naseby, in 1645, Cromwell's New Model Army decisively defeated Charles I, but the victors did have a two-to-one superiority of manpower. Borodino, in 1812, saw the end of Napoleon's invading army.

Nearly all victors claim that God is on their side. According to the biblical account of Sennacherib's defeat, an angel of the Lord intervened on behalf of the city – though in reality it is more probable that the Assyrians were simply weakened by pestilence. For Chesterton, Don John of Austria, the 'last knight of Europe', is engaged in a crusade against the Infidel. After Naseby, Cromwell observed, 'Sir, there is none other than the hand of God.'

GEORGE GORDON, LORD BYRON

The Destruction of Sennacherib

I

The Assyrian came down like the wolf on the fold,
And his cohorts were gleaming in purple and gold;
And the sheen of their spears was like stars on the sea,
When the blue wave rolls nightly on deep Galilee.

II

Like the leaves of the forest when Summer is green,
That host with their banners at sunset were seen:
Like the leaves of the forest when Autumn hath blown,
That host on the morrow lay withered and strown.

III

For the Angel of Death spread his wings on the blast,
And breathed in the face of the foe as he passed;
And the eyes of the sleepers waxed deadly and chill,
And their hearts but once heaved, and for ever grew still!

IV

And there lay the steed with his nostril all wide,
But through it there rolled not the breath of his pride:
And the foam of his gasping lay white on the turf,
And cold as the spray of the rock-beating surf.

V

And there lay the rider distorted and pale,
With the dew on his brow, and the rust on his mail;
And the tents were all silent, the banners alone,
The lances unlifted, the trumpet unblown.

VI

And the widows of Ashur are loud in their wail,
And the idols are broke in the temple of Baal;
And the might of the Gentile, unsmote by the sword,
Hath melted like snow in the glance of the Lord!

ALFRED, LORD TENNYSON

Battle of Brunanburh

I

Athelstan King,
Lord among Earls,
Bracelet-bestower and
Baron of Barons,
He with his brother,
Edmund Atheling,
Gaining a lifelong
Glory in battle,
Slew with the sword-edge
There by Brunanburh,
Brake the shield-wall,
Hewed the lindenwood,
Hacked the battleshield,
Sons of Edward with hammered brands.

II

Theirs was a greatness
Got from their Grandsires —
Theirs that so often in
Strife with their enemies
Struck for their hoards and their hearths and their homes.

III

Bowed the spoiler,
Bent the Scotsman,
Fell the shipcrews
Doomed to the death.

All the field with blood of the fighters
      Flowed, from when first the great
      Sun-star of morningtide,
      Lamp of the Lord God
      Lord everlasting,
Glode over earth till the glorious creature
      Sank to his setting.

  IV

      There lay many a man
      Marred by the javelin,
      Men of the Northland
      Shot over shield.
      There was the Scotsman
      Weary of war.

  V

      We the West-Saxons,
      Long as the daylight
      Lasted, in companies
Troubled the track of the host that we hated,
Grimly with swords that were sharp from the grindstone,
Fiercely we hacked at the flyers before us.

  VI

      Mighty the Mercian,
      Hard was his hand-play,
      Sparing not any of
      Those that with Anlaf,
      Warriors over the
      Weltering waters
      Borne in the bark's-bosom,
      Drew to this island:
      Doomed to the death.

VII

Five young kings put asleep by the sword-stroke,
Seven strong Earls of the army of Anlaf
Fell on the war-field, numberless numbers,
Shipmen and Scotsmen.

VIII

Then the Norse leader,
Dire was his need of it,
Few were his following,
Fled to his warship:
Fleeted his vessel to sea with the king in it,
Saving his life on the fallow flood.

IX

Also the crafty one,
Constantinus,
Crept to his North again,
Hoar-headed hero!

X

Slender warrant had
He to be proud of
The welcome of war-knives –
He that was reft of his
Folk and his friends that had
Fallen in conflict,
Leaving his son too
Lost in the carnage,
Mangled to morsels,
A youngster in war!

XI

Slender reason had
He to be glad of
The clash of the war-glaive –
Traitor and trickster
And spurner of treaties –
He nor had Anlaf
With armies so broken
A reason for bragging
That they had the better
In perils of battle
On places of slaughter –
The struggle of standards,
The rush of the javelins,
The crash of the charges,
The wielding of weapons –
The play that they played with
The children of Edward.

XII

Then with their nailed prows
Parted the Norsemen, a
Blood-reddened relic of
Javelins over
The jarring breaker, the deep-sea billow,
Shaping their way toward Dyflen again,
Shamed in their souls.

XIII

Also the brethren,
King and Atheling,
Each in his glory,
Went to his own in his own West-Saxonland,
Glad of the war.

XIV

Many a carcase they left to be carrion,
Many a livid one, many a sallow-skin –
Left for the white tailed eagle to tear it, and
Left for the horny-nibbed raven to rend it, and
Gave to the garbaging war-hawk to gorge it, and
That gray beast, the wolf of the weald.

XV

Never had huger
Slaughter of heroes
Slain by the sword-edge –
Such as old writers
Have writ of in histories –
Hapt in this isle, since
Up from the East hither
Saxon and Angle from
Over the broad billow
Broke into Britain with
Haughty war-workers who
Harried the Welshman, when
Earls that were lured by the
Hunger of glory gat
Hold of the land.

From the Anglo-Saxon

MICHAEL DRAYTON

A Ballad of Agincourt

Fair stood the wind for France,
When we our sails advance,
Nor now to prove our chance
  Longer will tarry;

But putting to the main,
At Kaux, the mouth of Seine,
With all his martial train,
　　Landed King Harry.

And taking many a fort,
Furnished in warlike sort,
Marcheth towards Agincourt
　　In happy hour;
Skirmishing day by day
With those that stopp'd his way,
Where the French General lay,
　　With all his power.

Which in his height of pride,
King Henry to deride,
His ransom to provide
　　To the king sending.
Which he neglects the while,
As from a nation vile,
Yet, with an angry smile,
　　Their fall portending.

And turning to his men,
Quoth our brave Henry then,
'Though they to one be ten,
　　Be not amazed.
Yet have we well begun,
Battles so bravely won
Have ever to the sun
　　By fame been raised.

'And for myself,' quoth he,
'This my full rest shall be,
England ne'er mourn for me,
　　Nor more esteem me!
Victor I will remain,
Or on this earth be slain,

Never shall she sustain
   Loss to redeem me.

'Poictiers and Cressy tell,
When most their pride did swell,
Under our swords they fell;
   No less our skill is,
Than when our grandsire great,
Claiming the regal seat,
By many a warlike feat
   Lopp'd the French lilies.'

The Duke of York so dread,
The eager vaward led;
With the main Henry sped
   Amongst his henchmen.
Excester had the rear,
A braver man not there;
O Lord, how hot they were
   On the false Frenchmen!

They now to fight are gone,
Armour on armour shone;
Drum now to drum did groan,
   To hear was wonder;
That with the cries they make
The very earth did shake,
Trumpet to trumpet spake
   Thunder to thunder.

Well it thine age became,
O noble Erpingham,
Which didst the signal aim
   To our hid forces;
When from a meadow by,
Like a storm suddenly,
The English archery
   Struck the French horses.

With Spanish yew so strong,
Arrows a cloth-yard long,
That like to serpents stung,
   Piercing the weather;
None from his fellow starts,
But playing manly parts,
And like true English hearts,
   Stuck close together.

When down their bows they threw,
And forth their bilbows drew,
And on the French they flew,
   Not one was tardy;
Arms were from shoulders sent,
Scalps to the teeth were rent,
Down the French peasants went –
   Our men were hardy.

This while our noble King,
His broad sword brandishing,
Down the French host did ding,
   As to o'erwhelm it;
And many a deep wound lent,
His arms with blood besprent,
And many a cruel dent
   Bruised his helmet.

Glos'ter, that Duke so good,
Next of the royal blood,
For famous England stood,
   With his brave brother;
Clarence, in steel so bright,
Though but a maiden knight,
Yet in that furious fight
   Scarce such another.

Warwick in blood did wade,
Oxford the foe invade,

And cruel slaughter made,
   Still as they ran up;
Suffolk his axe did ply,
Beaumont and Willoughby
Bare them right doughtily,
   Ferrers and Fanhope.

Upon St Crispin's day
Fought was this noble fray,
Which Fame did not delay
   To England to carry;
Oh, when shall English men
With such acts fill a pen,
Or England breed again
   Such a king Harry!

G. K. CHESTERON

Lepanto

White founts falling in the courts of the sun,
And the Soldan of Byzantium is smiling as they run;
There is laughter like the fountains in that face of all men
      feared,
It stirs the forest darkness, the darkness of his beard,
It curls the blood-red crescent, the crescent of his lips,
For the inmost sea of all the earth is shaken with his ships.
They have dared the white republics up the capes of Italy,
They have dashed the Adriatic round the Lion of the Sea,
And the Pope has cast his arms abroad for agony and loss,
And called the kings of Christendom for swords about the
      Cross,
The cold queen of England is looking in the glass;
The shadow of the Valois is yawning at the Mass;
From evening isles fantastical rings faint the Spanish gun,
And the Lord upon the Golden Horn is laughing in the sun.

Dim drums throbbing, in the hills half heard,
Where only on a nameless throne a crownless prince has
    stirred,
Where, risen from a doubtful seat and half attainted stall,
The last knight of Europe takes weapons from the wall,
The last and lingering troubadour to whom the bird has sung,
That once went singing southward when all the world was
    young,
In that enormous silence, tiny and unafraid,
Comes up along a winding road the noise of the Crusade.
Strong gongs groaning as the guns boom far,
Don John of Austria is going to the war,
Stiff flags straining in the night-blasts cold
In the gloom black-purple, in the glint old-gold,
Torchlight crimson on the copper kettle-drums,
Then the tuckets, then the trumpets, then the cannon, and he
    comes.
Don John laughing in the brave beard curled,
Spurning of his stirrups like the thrones of all the world,
Holding his head up for a flag of all the free.
Love-light of Spain – hurrah!
Death-light of Africa!
Don John of Austria
Is riding to the sea.

Mahound is in his paradise above the evening star,
(*Don John of Austria is going to the war.*)
He moves a mighty turban on the timeless houri's knees,
His turban that is woven of the sunset and the seas.
He shakes the peacock gardens as he rises from his ease,
And he strides among the tree-tops and is taller than the trees,
And his voice through all the garden is a thunder sent to bring
Black Azrael and Ariel and Ammon on the wing.
Giants and the Genii,
Multiplex of wing and eye,
Whose strong obedience broke the sky
When Solomon was king.

They rush in red and purple from the red clouds of the morn,
From temples where the yellow gods shut up their eyes in
    scorn;
They rise in green robes roaring from the green hells of the sea
Where fallen skies and evil hues and eyeless creatures be;
On them the sea-valves cluster and the grey sea-forests curl,
Splashed with a splendid sickness, the sickness of the pearl;
They swell in sapphire smoke out of the blue cracks of the
    ground, –
They gather and they wonder and give worship to Mahound.
And he saith, 'Break up the mountains where the hermit-folk
    can hide,
And sift the red and silver sands lest bone of saint abide,
And chase the Giaours flying night and day, not giving rest,
For that which was our trouble comes again out of the west.
We have set the seal of Solomon on all things under sun,
Of knowledge and of sorrow and endurance of things done,
But a noise is in the mountains, in the mountains, and I know
The voice that shook our palaces – four hundred years ago:
It is he that saith not 'Kismet'; it is he that knows not Fate;
It is Richard, it is Raymond, it is Godfrey in the gate!
It is he whose loss is laughter when he counts the wager worth,
Put down your feet upon him, that our peace be on the earth.'
For he heard drums groaning and he heard guns jar,
(*Don John of Austria is going to the war.*)

Sudden and still – hurrah!
Bolt from Iberia!
Don John of Austria
Is gone by Alcalar.

St Michael's on his mountain in the sea-roads of the north
(*Don John of Austria is girt and going forth.*)
Where the grey seas glitter and the sharp tides shift
And the sea folk labour and the red sails lift.
He shakes his lance of iron and he claps his wings of stone;

The noise is gone through Normandy; the noise is gone alone;
The North is full of tangled things and texts and aching eyes
And dead is all the innocence of anger and surprise,
And Christian killeth Christian in a narrow dusty room,
And Christian dreadeth Christ that hath a newer face of doom,
And Christian hateth Mary that God kissed in Galilee,
But Don John of Austria is riding to the sea.
Don John calling through the blast and the eclipse
Crying with the trumpet, with the trumpet of his lips.
Trumpet that sayeth ha!
        Domino gloria!
Don John of Austria
Is shouting to the ships.

King Philip's in his closet with the Fleece about his neck.
(*Don John of Austria is armed upon the deck.*)
The walls are hung with velvet that is black and soft as sin,
And little dwarfs creep out of it and little dwarfs creep in.
He holds a crystal phial that has colours like the moon,
He touches, and it tingles, and he trembles very soon,
And his face is as a fungus of a leprous white and grey
Like plants in the high houses that are shuttered from the day,
And death is in the phial, and the end of noble work,
But Don John of Austria has fired upon the Turk.
Don John's hunting, and his hounds have bayed –
Booms away past Italy the rumour of his raid
Gun upon gun, ha! ha!
Gun upon gun, hurrah!
Don John of Austria
Has loosed the cannonade.

The Pope was in his chapel before day or battle broke,
(*Don John of Austria is hidden in the smoke.*)
The hidden room in man's house where God sits all the year,
The secret window whence the world looks small and very
        dear.

He sees as in a mirror on the monstrous twilight sea
The crescent of his cruel ships whose name is mystery;
They fling great shadows foe-wards, making Cross and Castle
    dark,
They veil the plumèd lions on the galleys of St Mark;
And above the ships are palaces of brown, black-bearded
    chiefs,
And below the ships are prisons, where with multitudinous
    griefs,
Christian captives sick and sunless, all a labouring race repines
Like a race in sunken cities, like a nation in the mines.
They are lost like slaves that swat, and in the skies of morning
    hung
The stair-way of the tallest gods when tyranny was young.
They are countless, voiceless, hopeless as those fallen or fleeing
    on
Before the high Kings' horses in the granite of Babylon.
And many a one grows witless in his quiet room in hell
Where a yellow face looks inward through the lattice of his
    cell,
And he finds his God forgotten, and he seeks no more a sign –
(*But Don John of Austria has burst the battle-line!*)
Don John pounding from the slaughter-painted poop,
Purpling all the ocean like a bloody pirate's sloop,
Scarlet running over on the silvers and the golds,
Breaking of the hatches up and bursting of the holds,
Thronging of the thousands up that labour under sea
White for bliss and blind for sun and stunned for liberty.
Vivat Hispania!
Domino Gloria!
Don John of Austria
Has set his people free!

Cervantes on his galley sets the sword back in the sheath
(*Don John of Austria rides homeward with a wreath.*)
And he sees across a weary land a straggling road in Spain,

Up which a lean and foolish knight forever rides in vain,
And he smiles, but not as Sultans smile, and settles back the
    blade. . . .
(*But Don John of Austria rides home from the Crusade.*)

THOMAS BABINGTON, LORD MACAULAY

The Battle of Naseby

Oh! wherefore come ye forth, in triumph from the North,
    With your hands, and your feet, and your raiment all red?
And wherefore doth your rout send forth a joyous shout?
    And whence be the grapes of the wine-press which ye tread?

Oh evil was the root, and bitter was the fruit,
    And crimson was the juice of the vintage that we trod;
For we trampled on the throng of the haughty and the strong,
    Who sate in the high places, and slew the saints of God.

It was about the noon of a glorious day in June,
    That we saw their banners dance, and their cuirasses shine,
And the Man of Blood was there, with his long essenced hair,
    And Astley, and Sir Marmaduke, and Rupert of the Rhine.

Like a servant of the Lord, with his Bible and his sword,
    The General rode along us to form us to the fight,
When a murmuring sound broke out, and swell'd into a shout,
    Among the godless horsemen upon the tyrant's right.

And hark! like the roar of the billows on the shore,
    The cry of battle rises along their charging line!
For God! for the Cause! for the Church, for the Laws!
    For Charles King of England, and Rupert of the Rhine!

The furious German comes, with his clarions and his drums,
    His bravoes of Alsatia, and pages of Whitehall;

They are bursting on our flanks. Grasp your pikes, close your
    ranks;
  For Rupert never comes but to conquer or to fall.

They are here! They rush on! We are broken! We are gone!
  Our left is borne before them like stubble on the blast.
O Lord, put forth thy might! O Lord, defend the right!
  Stand back to back, in God's name, and fight it to the last.

Stout Skippon hath a wound; the centre hath given ground:
  Hark! hark! – What means the trampling of horsemen on
    our rear?
Whose banner do I see, boys? 'Tis he, thank God! 'tis he, boys,
  Bear up another minute: brave Oliver is here.

Their heads all stooping low, their points all in a row,
  Like a whirlwind on the trees, like a deluge on the dikes,
Our cuirassiers have burst on the ranks of the accurst,
  And at a shock have scattered the forest of his pikes.

Fast, fast, the gallants ride, in some safe nook to hide
  Their coward heads, predestined to rot on Temple Bar:
And he – he turns, he flies: – shame on those cruel eyes
  That bore to look on torture, and dare not look on war.

Ho! comrades, scour the plain; and, ere ye strip the slain,
  First give another stab to make your search secure,
Then shake from sleeves and pockets their broadpieces and
    lockets,
  The tokens of the wanton, the plunder of the poor.

Fools, your doublets shone with gold, and your hearts were
    gay and bold,
  When you kissed your lily hands to your lemans today;
And tomorrow shall the fox, from her chambers in the rocks,
  Lead forth her tawny cubs to howl above the prey.

Where be your tongues that late mocked at heaven and hell
    and fate,
  And the fingers that once were so busy with your blades,

Your perfumed satin clothes, your catches and your oaths,
  Your stage-plays and your sonnets, your diamonds and your
    spades?

Down, down, for ever down with the mitre and the crown,
  With the Belial of the Court, and the Mammon of the Pope;
There is woe in Oxford Halls; there is wail in Durham's Stalls:
  The Jesuit smites his bosom; the Bishop rends his cope.

And She of the seven hills shall mourn her children's ills,
  And tremble when she thinks of the edge of England's
    sword;
And the Kings of earth in fear shall shudder when they hear.
  What the hand of God hath wrought for the Houses and the
    Word.

MIKHAIL LERMONTOV

Borodino

'Come tell me, was it all for nought
That Moscow burned, although we fought
  And would not yield?
Come, Uncle, tell the tale again
Of how we fought with might and main,
And men remember, not in vain,
  Our Borodino's field.'

'Yes, in our times the men were men,
And from the heat of battle then
  How few returned,
How few returned their fields to till!
Heroes – not lads like you – they still
Fought on, but could not stay God's will,
  That Moscow burned.

'We beat retreat by day and night,
We fumed and waited for the fight;
   The old men jeered:
"We'd better winter in the bogs,
And build up huts and bring in logs,
But never turn to face the Frogs,
   And singe their beard."

'But then a noble stretch of ground
To build a great redoubt we found,
   And there entrench.
All night we listened. Nought astir!
But when the dawn touched fir by fir
And lit the guns – why then, good sir,
   We saw the French.

'I had my powder tightly rammed.
I'll serve you now and you be damned,
   My fine Mounseer!
No hope for you to lurk and crawl;
We'll stand against you like a wall;
And if needs must, we'll give our all
   For Moscow, here.

'For three whole days without a change
We only shot at distant range;
   No use at all!
You heard men saying left and right,
It's time to buckle to and fight –
Until across the fields the night
   Began to fall.

'I lay to sleep beside my gun,
But heard the cheer, till night was done,
   The Frenchmen made.

Our men were quiet. One would sit
And mend his coat where it was slit,
Or bite his long moustache and spit
   And clean his blade.

'The very hour night was fled
Our guns began to move ahead:
   My God, the rattle!
Our officers were gallant then;
They served their Tsar and loved their men,
They lie asleep in field or fen,
   Who led the battle.

'The Colonel set our hearts astir:
"Moscow's behind. My lads, for her,
   As all have heard,
Our fathers fought with might and main.
Let's swear to die for her again."
And there on Borodino's plain
   We kept our word.

'That was a day. Towards our redoubt
We saw the Frenchmen gallop out
   Through smoky air,
Dragoons as bright as on parade,
And blue hussars with golden braid,
And Uhlans – what a show they made!
   They all were there.

'That was a day will never die:
The flags like spirits streaming by –
   A fire ahead –
The clash of steel – the cannon's blast –
Our arms too weak to slay at last:
But few the bullets were that passed
   Our wall of dead.

'That day the foeman learned aright
The way we Russian soldiers fight –
   Fierce hand to hand,
Horses and men together laid,
And still the thundering cannonade;
Our breasts were trembling, as it made
   Tremble the land.

'Then darkness fell on hill and plain;
Yet we were game to fight again
   When dawn was red,
Till all at once the drums began,
And as they rolled the Frenchmen ran;
And we must reckon, man by man,
   Our friends, the dead.

'Yes, in our time the men were men;
Soldiers – not lads like you – were then
   Heroes indeed!
Hard was the fate their courage earned;
Not many from the field returned,
And never had our Moscow burned –
   But God decreed.'

Translated from the Russian by Frances Cornford
and Esther Polinowsky Salaman

Disasters

The Charge of the Light Brigade at Balaclava (1854) was the epitome of military disasters: of the 600 who galloped into the Valley of Death, 113 were killed and 134 wounded, while 500 horses were lost. In his poem, Tennyson coined the classic justification for obeying orders, however bad: 'Their's not to reason why,/Their's but to do and die.'

Isandula (Isandhlwana, 1879) was the most devastating defeat sustained by a British army in Victoria's reign. 1,750 British and native troops were wiped out by a force of 20,000 Zulus. Queen Victoria recorded in her journal: 'How this can happen, we cannot yet imagine.' The last command given to the soldiers appears in the first line of Nisbet's poem. The defeat, though, was redeemed on the following day by the valiant defence of Rorke's Drift, when fewer than one hundred men held off a force of 4,000 Zulus. The victories of the Zulus were short-lived, for the British prime minister, Disraeli, sent out a much larger army to re-establish the authority of the rifle over the African assegai.

George Gascoigne saw military service in Holland, from 1572 to 1575, and in 'The Fruits of War', he gives his account of the ignominious surrender of an English force to the Spaniards. The incident itself is little known and of small military importance, but Gascoigne's narrative is frank, fresh, and full of direct observation and personal feeling.

ALFRED, LORD TENNYSON

The Charge of the Light Brigade

Half a league, half a league,
  Half a league onward,
All in the valley of Death

Rode the six hundred.
'Forward, the Light Brigade!
Charge for the guns!' he said:
Into the valley of Death
   Rode the six hundred.

'Forward, the Light Brigade!'
Was there a man dismayed?
Not though the soldier knew
   Someone had blundered:
Their's not to make reply,
Their's not to reason why,
Their's but to do and die:
Into the valley of Death
   Rode the six hundred.

Cannon to right of them,
Cannon to left of them,
Cannon in front of them
   Volleyed and thundered;
Stormed at with shot and shell,
Boldly they rode and well,
Into the jaws of Death,
Into the mouth of Hell
   Rode the six hundred.

Flashed all their sabres bare,
Flashed as they turned in air
Sabring the gunners there,
Charging an army, while
   All the world wondered:

Plunged in the battery-smoke
Right through the line they broke;
Cossack and Russian
Reeled from the sabre-stroke
   Shattered and sundered.

Then they rode back, but not
   Not the six hundred.

Cannon to right of them,
Cannon to left of them,
Cannon behind them
   Volleyed and thundered;
Stormed at with shot and shell,
While horse and hero fell,
They that had fought so well
Came through the jaws of Death,
Back from the mouth of Hell,
All that was left of them,
   Left of six hundred.

When can their glory fade?
O the wild charge they made!
   All the world wondered.
Honour the charge they made!
Honour the Light Brigade,
   Noble six hundred!

HUME NISBET

Isandula

'Fix bayonets, and die, as English soldiers do, –
   Shoulder to shoulder, the enemy around;
Shut out hope of mercy, but keep your colours true,
   Raise a pile of death, as evidence when found.'

This the terse, stern order that last rang in their ears:
   Blind with the fury, the fear, or what you will,
Dazed all they glared in front, yelled their English cheers;
   Saw heaving waves of night; knew they had to kill;

Knew that their hour was come, knew that they had to fall,
    Ground close their chatt'ring teeth, took each vacant place;
Thirty to one the foe, each rushed a giant tall,
    Swinging his grisly corpse – frightful shields to face!

But still they faced it, raw young schoolboys mostly there.
    Stabbed when the bullets failed, took as well as gave;
Sold every drop of blood, piled up in the air
    Sable monuments around each English grave.

Devils desecrate the slain, raging through the camp,
    Black foe and white mingle in the trampled mud;
Down sinks a sickened sun; Night lifts up her pale lamp,
    Trailing silver threads 'tween mounds of dead in blood:

Lighting up two dauntless boys who had glory gained –
    Coghill and Melville – the colours twisted round,
Who rode through hell that day bearing them only stained
    With their red hearts' blood, now sinking in the ground.

So were they all met next morn when their comrades came:
    No tongues to spoil it, but marks of deeds that told
How they had worked that day. Oh, deathless tongue of fame!
    Temper our grief with pride for those heroes bold.

Honour Isandula! bury their bodies there;
    Thanks, Chard and Bromhead, who held Rorke's Drift so
        long;
Give as a winding-sheet the colours to that pair,
    Tell posterity their mighty acts in song.

LOUIS ARAGON

Night at Dunkirk

France underfoot like a worn-out carpet spread
Has shrunk away beneath our constant tread

We bivouac, a hundred thousand where
The beach of Malo bridges sea and air

And dead men drift like seaweed. Yachts and lighters
Are overturned to look like bishops' mitres

Into the air where rotting horseflesh reeks
Rises a sound as of stampeding beasts

The crossing gate lifts crooked arms to the sky
Within our breasts we feel the hearts awry

A hundred thousand hearts of landless men
When will they utter cries of love again?

O Saint Sebastians pierced, in agony
How much you are like me, how much like me

Alone will understand me the ill-starred
Who value more the heart's wound than the heart

But I shall cry this anguish, this desire
As night makes visible the flowers of fire

Shall cry aloud till sleepwalkers tumble down
From burning roofs all over the burning town

Shall cry my love like the man who used to screech
Knives, knives to grind, in the early-morning streets

Shall cry and cry, Where are you, eyes I love
Where have you flown, my lark, my mourning dove?

Louder than all the shells above me crying
Louder than drunkards, louder than the dying

Shall cry, Your lips are flagons where I find
The long draught of love that is like red wine

Your arms around me build a parapet
I cannot die. To die would be to forget

Seeing the eyes of the soldiers who embark
Who could forget his longing at Dunkirk?

Lying awake while star-shells flared and sank
Who could forget the potion that he drank?

Each soldier, having dug a life-size cave
Now sleeps as in the shadow of the grave

Faces like flint, demented attitudes
Over their slumber grim foreboding broods

Spring and its fragrance never haunt this land
Here May lies dying in the drifted sand.

Translated from the French by Rolf Humphries and Malcolm Cowley

GEORGE GASCOIGNE

from The Fruits of War

Soldiers, behold, and captains, mark it well,
How hope is harbinger of all mishap.
Some hope in honour for to bear the bell;
Some hope for gain and venture many a clap;
Some hope for trust and light in treason's lap.
Hope leads the way, our lodging to prepare,
Where high mishap oft keeps an inn of care.

I hoped to show such force against our foes
That those of Delft might see how true I was.
I hoped, indeed, for to be one of those
Whom fame should follow, where my feet should pass.
I hoped for gains, and found great loss, alas!
I hoped to win a worthy soldier's name,
And lit on luck which brought me still to blame.

In Valkenburgh (a fort but new begun)
With others more I was ordained to be,
And far before the work was half-way done,
Our foes set forth our sorry seat to see.
They came in time, but cursed time for me;
They came before the curtain raised were
One only foot above the trenches there.

What should we do? Four ensigns lately pressed,
Five hundred men were all the bulk we bare —
Our enemies three thousand at the least,
And so much more they might always prepare.
But what most was, the truth for to declare,
We had no store of powder nor of pence,
Nor meat to eat, nor means to make defence.

Here some may say that we were much to blame,
Which should presume in such a place to bide
And not foresee, however went the game,
Of meat and shot our soldiers to provide.
Who do so say have reason on their side,
Yet proves it still, though ours may be the blot,
That war seems sweet to such as know it not.

For had our fort been fully fortified,
Two thousand men had been but few enow
To man it once, and had the truth been tried.
We could not see by any reason how
The Prince should send us any succour now,
Which was constrained in towns himself to shield
And had no power to show his force in field.

Herewith we had nor powder packed in store,
Nor flesh nor fish in powdering tubs y-put,
Nor meat, nor malt, nor means (what would you more?)
To get such gear, if once we should be shut.
And God, He knows, the English soldier's gut

Must have his fill of victuals once a day,
Or else he will but homely earn his pay.

To scuse ourselves and Coronel withal,
We did foretell the Prince of all these needs,
Who promised always to be our wall
And bade us trust as truly as our creeds
That all good words should be performed with deeds,
And that, before our foes should come so near,
He would both send us men and merry cheer.

Yea, Robin Hood! our foes came down apace
And first they charged another fort likewise —
Alphen, I mean, which was a stronger place,
And yet too weak to keep in warlike wise.
Five other bands of English Fanteries
Were therein set for to defend the same,
And them they charged, for to begin the game.

This fort from ours was distant ten good miles,
I mean such miles as English measure makes.
Between us both stood Leyden town therewhiles,
Which every day with fair words undertakes
To feed us fat and cram us up with cakes.
It made us hope it would supply our need,
For we to it two bulwarks were indeed.

But, when it came unto the very pinch,
Leyden, farewell! We might for Leyden starve!
I like him well that promiseth an inch
And pays an ell; but what may he deserve,
That flatters much and can no faith observe?
An old-said saw, that fair words make fools fain,
Which proverb true we proved to our pain.

A conference among ourselves we called
Of officers and captains all yfere,
For, truth to tell, the soldiers were appalled

And, when we asked, 'Now, mates, what merry cheer?'
Their answer was, 'It is no biding here!'
So that perforce we must from thence be gone,
Unless we meant to keep the place alone.

Herewith we thought that, if in time we went
Before all straits were stopped and taken up,
We might perhaps our enemies prevent
And teach them eke to taste of sorrow's cup.
At Maesland Sluys we hoped for to sup,
A place whereat we might good service do
To keep them out which took it after too.

Whiles thus we talk, a messenger, behold,
From Alphen came and told us heavy news:
'Captains,' quoth he, 'hereof you may be bold,
Not one poor soul of all your fellow's crew
Can scape alive; they have no choice to choose.
They sent me thus, to bid you shift in time,
Else look, like them, to stick in Spanish lime.'

This tale once told, none other speech prevailed,
But, pack and trudge, our leisure was too long.
To mend the mart, our watch, which never failed,
Descried our foes which marched all along
And towards us began in haste to throng,
So that, before our last could pass the port,
The foremost foes were now within the fort.

I promised once, and did perform it too,
To bide therein as long as any would.
What booted that, or what could captains do,
When common sort would tarry for no gold?
To speak a truth, the good did what they could
To keep the bad in ranks and good array,
But labour's lost to hold that will away.

It needless were to tell what deeds were done,
Nor who did best, nor who did worst that day,

Nor who made head, nor who began to run,
Nor in retreat what chief was last alway;
But, soldierlike, we held our enemy's play,
And every captain strave to do his best
To stay his own, and so to stay the rest.

In this retire, three English miles we trod,
With face to foes and shot as thick as hail,
Of whose choice men full fifty souls and odd
We laid to ground, this is withouten fail.
Yet of our own we lost but three by tale.
Our foes themselves confessed they bought full dear
The hot pursuit which they attempted there.

Thus came we late at last to Leyden walls,
Too late, too soon – for so may we well say,
For notwithstanding all our cries and calls,
They shut their gates and turned their ears away.
In fine, they did forsake us every way
And bade us shift to save ourselves apace,
For unto them were fond to trust for grace.

They neither gave us meat to feed upon,
Nor drink, nor powder, pick-axe, tool, nor spade;
So might we starve, like misers woebegone,
And fend our foes with blows of English blade.
For shot was shrunk and shift could none be made –
Yea, more than this, we stood in open field
Without defence from shot ourselves to shield.

This thus well weighed, when weary night was past
And day gan peep, we heard the Spanish drums
Which struck a march about us round to cast,
And forth withal their ensigns quickly comes,
At sight whereof our soldiers bit their thumbs;
For well they wist it was no boot to fly,
And, biding there, there was no boot but die.

So that we sent a drum to summon talk
And came to parley middle way between.
Monsieur de Loques and Mario did walk
From foemen's side, and from our side were seen
Myself, that match for Mario might been,
And Captain Sheffield, born of noble race,
To match de Loques which there was chief in place.

Thus met, we talked, and stood upon our toes
With great demands, whom little might content!
We craved not only freedom from our foes,
But shipping eke with sails and all full bent
To come again from whence we first were went –
I mean, to come into our English coast,
Which soil was sure and might content us most.

An old-said saw, and often seen, that whereas
Thou comest to crave and doubtst for to obtain,
Inique pete, then, *ut aequum feras.*
This had I heard and sure I was full fain
To prove what profit we might thereby gain;
But at the last, when time was stolen away,
We were full glad to play another play.

We rendered then with safety for our lives,
Our ensigns splayed, and managing our arms,
With further faith that from all kinds of gyves
Our soldiers should remain withouten harms;
And, sooth to say, these were no false alarms.
For why they were within twelve days discharged
And sent away from prison quite enlarged.

They were sent home, and we remained still
In prison pent, but yet right gently used.
To take our lives it was not Loques' will –
That noble blood which never man abused,
Nor ever yet was for his faith accused.

Would God I had the skill to write his praise,
Which lent me comfort in my doleful days!

We bode behind four months or little less,
But whereupon that God he knows, not I;
Yet if I might be bold to give a guess,
Then would I say it was for to espy
What ransom we would pay contentedly,
Or else to know how much we were esteemed
In England here, and for what men y-deemed.

How so it were, at last we were despatched
And home we came, as children come from school,
As glad as fish which were but lately catched
And straight again were cast into the pool,
For, by my fay, I count him but a fool,
Which would not rather poorly live at large
Than rest in prison, fed with costly charge.

Hard Fighting

The actual business of fighting has always been hard, brutal and unglamorous, and it provides poets with some of their greatest challenges. Here are some excerpts from the *Iliad*, alongside the scene from *Macbeth* in which the hero's valour and decisive action in the thick of battle are reported by a wounded messenger. Sir Walter Scott's version of 'The Charge at Waterloo' reminds us that nearly all cavalry charges ended up in a ghastly mess.

The Portuguese poet, Luis de Camoens, had been a soldier and had lost an eye fighting the Moors. His epic poem, *The Lusiads*, tells of the exploits of the legendary heroes of Portugal as they fought their way along the coast of Africa. The translation here was made by Sir Richard Burton, the Victorian soldier, explorer and man of letters.

To provide a contrast with all this heroic clamour, I have included a passage from Thomas Bridges's burlesque treatment of the *Iliad*. The whole thing is full of eighteenth-century scepticism and humour, and should be better known.

HOMER

from The Iliad, Book XI

Then to th' extremest heat of fight he did his valour turn,
And led a multitude of Greeks, where foot did foot subdue,
Horse slaughter'd horse, Need feather'd flight, the batter'd
    centre flew
In clouds of dust about their ears, rais'd from the horses'
    hooves,
That beat a thunder out of earth as horrible as Jove's.
The king, persuading speedy chace, gave his persuasions way
With his own valour, slaught'ring still, as in a stormy day

In thick-set woods a ravenous fire wraps in his fierce repair
The shaken trees, and by the roots doth toss them into air;
Even so beneath Atrides' sword flew up Troy's flying heels,
Their horse drew empty chariots, and sought their thund'ring
    wheels
Some fresh directors through the field, where least the pursuit
    drives.
Thick fell the Trojans, much more sweet to vultures than their
    wives.

Translated from the Greek by George Chapman

HOMER

from The Iliad, Book XIII

                    Thus Neptune rous'd these men.
And round about th' Ajaces did their phalanxes maintain
Their station firm; whom Mars himself, had he amongst them
    gone,
Could not disparage, nor Jove's Maid that sets men fiercer on;
For now the best were chosen out, and they receiv'd th'
    advance
Of Hector and his men so full, that lance was lin'd with lance,
Shields thicken'd with opposéd shields, targets to targets
    nail'd,
Helms stuck to helms, and man to man grew, they so close
    assail'd,
Plum'd casques were hang'd in either's plumes, all join'd so
    close their stands,
Their lances stood, thrust out so thick by such all-daring
    hands.

Translated from the Greek by George Chapman

CHRISTOPHER LOGUE

from War Music: An Account of Books 16 to 19 of Homer's *Iliad*

 The battle swayed.
Half-naked men hacked slowly at each other
As the Greeks eased back the Trojans.
 They stood close;
Closer; thigh in thigh; mask twisted over iron mask
Like kissing.
 One moment fifty chariots break out; head for the ditch;
Three cross; the rest wheel back; vanish in ochre dust.
For an instant the Greeks falter. One is killed. And then
The Trojans are eased back a little more;
The ship is cleared, the fire smothered, and who cares
That Hector's chariot opens a new way,
Now moving, pausing now, now moving on again,
And his spear's tip flickers in the smoky light
Like the head of a crested adder over fern? –
Always the Trojans shift towards the ditch.

THOMAS BRIDGES

from Homer Travestie, Book VI (1764)

The squabbling gods the fight forsake,
And leave mankind to brew and bake
Just as they please, then broomsticks flew,
And smoking hot the squabble grew,
Which made Scamandria's streams look muddy,
But Simois seem'd a little bloody.
 First Ajax, like a Greenland whale,
Broke through the croud and turn'd the scale.

The Thracian Acamas he found,
And fell'd him headlong to the ground;
He hit him such a thund'ring rap,
The broomstick broke his brazen cap.
Axylus next, an honest foul,
Got a great knock o' th' jobbernoul:
At home he always kept good chear,
And made folks welcome far and near;
Close by the road his house did lie,
Where men and horses passing by
Might get a drink, if they were dry;
But now no friend to guard his side is,
So got demolish'd by Tydides.
His skip Calesius, by and by,
Tumbl'd to bear him company.
Euryalus knock'd Dresus down,
And next he crack'd Opheltius' crown;
Not so content with pairs begins,
And smash'd two young and tender twins,
Sons of Bucolion, who had made
A mistress of a woodland Naiad.
As on the ground the younkers lay
His rogueship stole their coats away.
Just after that one Polypætes
Dispatch'd Astyalus to greet his
Old friends in hell. Ulysses next,
Because the rogues his soul had vext,
Murder'd Pidytes; then comes Teucer,
And made poor Aretaon spew sir,
When in a rage ran Nestor's lad,
Chatt'ring just like his queer old dad,
I'll make these Trojan rascals fear us,
And straight demolish'd brave Ablerus;
Which when great Agamemnon saw,
He gave Elatus such a blow,
As fell'd him down upon his crupper,

And spoil'd the luckless Trojan's supper.
Such a damn'd knock the Grecian gave him,
That all his riches could not save him.
Eurypylus Melanthius slew,
And Phylacus from Leitus flew,
But could not 'scape him any how;
Adrastus by ill luck came bump
Upon a cursed crab-tree stump;
It smash'd his wheels both nave and spoke,
And all the cart to pieces broke.
The horses flew where none could find 'em,
And left their luckless load behind 'em.
As he lay kicking on the sands
The cuckold o'er him threat'ning stands;
Pilgarlick lifts his hands on high,
And begs for life most lustily:
May't please your honour let me live,
My father will great ransom give
When he shall hear I am not slain,
But, stow'd in your ship's hold, remain.
Of steel, and brass, and golden ore,
He has the Lord knows what in store.

WILLIAM SHAKESPEARE

from Macbeth (Act 1, Scene ii)

   Duncan: What bloody man is that? He can report,
As seemeth by his plight, of the revolt
The newest state.
   Malcolm: This is the Sergeant,
Who, like a good and hardy soldier, fought
'Gainst my captivity. – Hail, brave friend!
Say to the King the knowledge of the broil,
As thou didst leave it.

Captain: Doubtful it stood;
As two spent swimmers, that do cling together
And choke their art. The merciless Macdonwald
(Worthy to be a rebel, for to that
The multiplying villainies of nature
Do swarm upon him) from the western isles
Of Kernes and Gallowglasses is supplied;
And Fortune, on his damned quarrel smiling,
Show'd like a rebel's whore: but all's too weak;
For brave Macbeth (well he deserves that name),
Disdaining Fortune, with his brandish'd steel,
Which smok'd with bloody execution,
Like Valour's minion, carv'd out his passage,
Till he fac'd the slave;
Which ne'er shook hands, nor bade farewell to him,
Till he unseam'd him from the nave to th' chops,
And fix'd his head upon our battlements.
    Duncan: O valiant cousin! worthy gentleman!
    Captain: As whence the sun 'gins his reflection,
Shipwracking storms and direful thunders break,
So from that spring, whence comfort seem'd to come,
Discomfort swells. Mark, King of Scotland, mark:
No sooner justice had, with valour arm'd,
Compell'd these skipping Kernes to trust their heels,
But the Norweyan Lord, surveying vantage,
With furbish'd arms, and new supplies of men,
Began a fresh assault.
    Duncan: Dismay'd not this
Our captains, Macbeth and Banquo?
    Captain: Yes;
As sparrows eagles, or the hare the lion.
If I say sooth, I must report they were
As cannons overcharg'd with double cracks;
So they
Doubly redoubled strokes upon the foe:
Except they meant to bathe in reeking wounds,

Or memorize another Golgotha,
I cannot tell —
But I am faint, my gashes cry for help.
    Duncan: So well thy words become thee, as thy wounds:
They smack of honour both. — Go, get him surgeons.
Who comes here?
    Malcolm: The worthy Thane of Rosse.
    Lenox: What a haste looks through his eyes! So should he
      look
That seems to speak things strange.
    Rosse: God save the King!
    Duncan: Whence cam'st thou, worthy Thane?
    Rosse: From Fife, great King,
Where the Norweyan banners flout the sky,
And fan our people cold. Norway himself,
With terrible numbers,
Assisted by that most disloyal traitor,
The Thane of Cawdor, began a dismal conflict;
Till that Bellona's bridegroom, lapp'd in proof,
Confronted him with self-comparisons,
Point against point, rebellious arm 'gainst arm,
Curbing his lavish spirit: and, to conclude,
The victory fell on us; —
    Duncan: Great happiness!

ANONYMOUS

from The Battle of Otterbourne (1388)

At last these two stout erles did meet,
   Like captains of great might:
Like lions would, they laid on lode,
   And made a cruel fight:

They fought until they both did sweat,
  With swords of tempered steel;
Until the blood, like drops of rain,
  They trickling down did feel.

Yield thee, Lord Percy, Douglas said,
  In faith I will thee bring,
Where thou shalt high advancèd be
  By James our Scottish king:

Thy ransom I will freely give,
  And this report of thee,
Thou art the most courageous knight,
  That ever I did see.

No, Douglas, quoth Erle Percy then,
  Thy proffer I do scorn;
I will not yield to any Scot,
  That ever yet was born.

With that, there came an arrow keen
  Out of an English bow,
Which struck Erle Douglas to the heart,
  A deep and deadly blow:

Who never spake more words than these,
  Fight on, my merry men all;
For why, my life is at an end;
  Lord Percy sees my fall.

Then leaving life, Erle Percy took
  The dead man by the hand;
And said, Erle Douglas, for thy life
  Would I had lost my land.

O God! my very heart doth bleed
  With sorrow for thy sake;
For sure, more redoubted knight
  Mischance could never take.

A knight amongst the Scots there was
   Which saw Erle Douglas die,
Who straight in wrath did vow revenge
   Upon the Lord Percye:

Sir Hugh Mountgomery was he call'd,
   Who, with a spear most bright,
Well mounted on a gallant steed,
   Ran fiercely through the fight;

And past the English archers all,
   Without all dread or fear;
And through Erle Percy's body then
   He thrust his hateful spear;

With such a vehement force and might
   He did his body gore,
The staff ran through the other side
   A large cloth-yard, and more.

LUIS CAMOENS

from The Lusiads, Canto IV

'Battle's uncertain work begins; and move
   right wings on either part to take the plain;
   these fighting to defend the land they love,
   those eggèd on by hope that land to gain:
   Soon great Pereira, who would foremost prove
   the knightly valour of his noble strain;
charges and shocks, and strews the field till sown
with those who covet what is not their own.

'Now in the dust-blurred air with strident sound
   bolts, arrows, darts and man'ifold missiles fly;
   beneath the destrier's horny hoof the ground
   quaketh in terror, and the dales reply;

shiver the lances; thundereth around
    the frequent crash of fellèd armoury;
foes on the little force redoubling fall
of Nuno fierce, who makes great numbers small.

'See! there his brethren meet him in the fray:
    (Fierce chance and cruel case!) But dreads he nought;
    right little were it brother-foe to slay,
    who against King and Country trait'orous fought:
    Amid these ren'egades not a few that day
    war in the foremost squadrons fury-fraught
against their brethren and their kin (sad Fate!)
as in great Julius' warfare with the great.

'O thou, Sertorius! O great Coriolane!
    Catiline! all ye hosts of bygone age,
    who 'gainst your Fatherland with hearts profane
    ragèd with rav'ening parricidal rage;
    if where Sumánus holds his dismal reign
    most dreadful torments must your sin assuage,
tell him, that e'en our Portugal sometimes
suckled some traitors guilty of your crimes.

'Here doth the foremost of our lines give way,
    so many foemen have its force opprest:
    There standeth Nuno, brave as Ly'on at bay,
    where Africk Ceita rears her hilly crest;
    who sees th 'circling troop of cavalry,
    over the Tetu'an plain to chace addrest;
And raging as they couch the deadly spear
seems somewhat stirred, but hides all craven fear:

'With sidelong glance he sights them, but his spleen
    ferine forbids the King of Beasts to show
    a craven back; nay, rather on the screen
    of plumping lances leaps he as they grow.
    So stands our Knight, who stains and soils the green
    with alien gore-streams: On that field lie low

some of his own; howe'er with valour dowerèd
hearts lose their virtue by such odds o'erpowerèd.

'John felt the danger and the dure affront
of Nuno; straight like Captain wise and ware,
he rushed afield, viewed all, and in the brunt
with words and works taught men fresh deeds to dare.
As nursing Ly'oness, fere and fierce of front,
who, left for chase her whelps secure in lair,
findeth while for'aging for their wonted food
Massylian hind hath dared to rob her brood:

'Runs, frantick raging, while her roar and moan
make the Seven-Brother Mountains shake and rave.
So John with other chosen troop hath flown
foeward his dexter wing t' enforce and save:
"Oh strong Companions! Souls of high renown!
Cavaliers braver than what men hold brave,
strike for your country! now all earthly chance,
all hope of Liberty is on your lance!"

' "Behold me here, your Comrade and your King,
who 'mid the spear and harness, bolt and bow,
foremost I charge and first myself I fling;
smite, ye true Portughuese, deal yet one blow!"
Thus spake that great-soul'd Warrior, brandishing
four times his lance before the final throw;
and, thrusting forceful, by that single thrust
lanceth such wounds that many bite the dust.

'For, see, his soldiers brent with ardour new,
honoured repentance, honourable fire,
who shall display most courage staid and true,
and dare the dangers dealt by Mars his ire
contend: The steel that catcheth flamey hue,
aims first at plate, then at the breast aims higher;
thus, wounds they give and wounds they take again;
and, dealing Death, in Death they feel no pain.

'Many are sent to sight the Stygian wave,
  into whose bodies entered iron Death:
  Here dieth Sanct' Iágo's Master brave,
  who fought with fiercest sprite till latest breath;
  another Master dire of Calatrave,
  horrid in cruel havock, perisheth:
Eke the Pereiras foully renegate
die God denying and denouncing Fate.

'Of the vile, nameless Vulgar many bleed;
  flitting with Gentles to the Gulf profound;
  where hungers, rav'ening with eternal greed,
  for passing human Shades the three-head Hound:
  And humbling more that haughty, arr'ogant breed,
  and better taming enemies furibund,
Castilia's Gonfanon sublime must fall
beneath the forceful foot of Portugall.

'Here wildest Battle hath its cruel'est will,
  with deaths and shouts, and slash and gory shower;
  the multitud'inous Braves, who 're killed and kill,
  rob of their proper hues the bloom and flower:
  At length they fly! they die! now waxeth still
  War's note, while lance and spear have lost their power:
Castilia's King the fate of pride must own,
seeing his purpose changed, his host o'erthrown.

'The field he leaveth to the Conqueror,
  too glad his life had not been left in fight:
  Follow him all who can; and panick sore
  lends them not feet, but feather'd wings for flight:
  Their breasts are fillèd with a wild doloùr,
  for Deaths, for Treasure waste in wanton plight;
for woe, disgust, and foul dishonour's soil
to see the Victor rev'elling in their spoil.

'Some fly with furious curses, and blaspheme
    him who the World with Warfare made accurst;
    others that cov'etous breast all culp'able deem
    for Greed enquicken'd by his selfish thirst.
    That, alien wealth to win, with sore extreme
    he plunged his hapless folk in woes the worst;
leaving so many wives and mothers, lorn
of sons and spouses, evermore to mourn.'

Translated from the Portuguese by Richard Burton

WALTER SCOTT

The Charge at Waterloo

On came the whirlwind – like the last
But fiercest sweep of tempest blast:
On came the whirlwind – steel-gleams broke
Like lightning through the rolling smoke;
    The war was waked anew.
Three hundred cannon-mouths roar'd loud,
And from their throats, with flash and cloud,
    Their showers of iron threw.
Beneath their fire, in full career,
Rush'd on the ponderous cuirassier,
The lancer couched his ruthless spear.
And, hurrying as to havoc near,
    The cohorts' eagles flew.
In one dark torrent, broad and strong.
Th' advancing onset roll'd along,
Forth harbinger'd by fierce acclaim,
That from the shroud of smoke and flame,
Peal'd wildly the imperial name.
But on the British heart were lost
The terrors of the charging host;

For not an eye the storm that view'd
Changed its proud glance of fortitude;
Nor was one forward footstep stay'd,
As dropped the dying and the dead.
Fast as their ranks the thunders tear,
Fast they renew'd each serried square:
And on the wounded and the slain
Closed their diminish'd files again:
Till from their lines scarce spears' lengths three,
Emerging from the smoke they see
Helmet, and plume, and panoply –
   Then waked their fire at once!
Each musketeer's revolving knell
As fast, as regularly fell,
As when they practise to display
Their discipline on festal day.
   Then down went helm and lance,
Down rent the eagle-banners sent,
Down reeling steeds and riders went,
Corslets were pierced, and pennons rent:
   And to augment the fray,
Wheel'd full against their staggering flanks,
The English horsemen's foaming ranks
   Forced their resistless way:
Then to the musket knell succeeds
The clash of swords – the neigh of steeds:
As plies the smith his clanging trade,
Against the cuirass rang the blade;
And while amid their close array
The well-served cannon rent their way,
And while amid their scatter'd band
Raged the fierce rider's bloody brand,
Recoil'd in common rout and fear
Lancer, and guard, and cuirassier,
Horsemen and foot, – a mingled host,
Their leaders fallen, their standards lost.

Death in Action

The deaths of leaders and heroes have been well recorded, and I have included here Homer's account – in Pope's translation – of the death of Patroclus, boon companion of Achilles, together with other death-scenes from later centuries. It seems to have been left to our own time to show a poetic interest in the deaths of humbler fighting men.

HOMER

from The Iliad, Book XVI

Then rash Patroclus with new fury glows,
And breathing slaughter, pours amid the foes.
Thrice on the press like Mars himself he flew,
And thrice three heroes at each onset slew.
There ends thy glory! there the fates untwine
The last, black remnant of so bright a line:
Apollo dreadful stops thy middle way;
Death calls, and heaven allows no longer day!
　For lo! the god in dusky clouds enshrined,
Approaching dealt a staggering blow behind.
The weighty shock his neck and shoulders feel;
His eyes flash sparkles, his stunn'd senses reel
In giddy darkness; far to distance flung,
His bounding helmet on the champaign rung.
Achilles' plume is stain'd with dust and gore;
That plume which never stoop'd to earth before;
Long used, untouch'd, in fighting fields to shine,
And shade the temples of the mad divine.
Jove dooms it now on Hector's helm to nod;
Not long – for fate pursues him, and the god.

His spear in shivers falls; his ample shield
Drops from his arm; his baldric strows the field:
The corslet his astonish'd breast forsakes:
Loose is each joint; each nerve with horror shakes;
Stupid he stares, and all-assistless stands:
Such is the force of more than mortal hands!
   A Dardan youth there was, well known to fame,
From Panthus sprung, Euphorbus was his name;
Famed for the manage of the foaming horse,
Skill'd in the dart, and matchless in the course:
Full twenty knights he tumbled from the car,
While yet he learn'd his rudiments of war.
His venturous spear first drew the hero's gore;
He struck, he wounded, but he durst no more.
Nor, though disarm'd, Patroclus' fury stood:
But swift withdrew the long-protended wood.
Thus, by an arm divine, and mortal spear,
Wounded, at once, Patroclus yields to fear,
Retires for succour to his social train,
And flies the fate, which heaven decreed, in vain.
Stern Hector, as the bleeding chief he views,
Breaks through the ranks, and his retreat pursues:
The lance arrests him with a mortal wound;
He falls, earth thunders, and his arms resound.
With him all Greece was sunk; that moment all
Her yet-surviving heroes seem'd to fall.

   Translated from the Greek by Alexander Pope

ANONYMOUS

from The Song of Roland

168

Now Roland feels that he is at death's door;
Out of his ears the brain is running forth.
Now for his peers he prays God call them all,
And for himself St Gabriel's aid implores;
Then in each hand he takes, lest shame befal,
His Olifant and Durendal his sword.
Far as a quarrel flies from a cross-bow drawn,
Toward land of Spain he goes, to a wide lawn,
And climbs a mound where grows a fair tree tall,
And marble stones beneath it stand by four.
Face downward there on the green grass he falls,
And swoons away, for he is at death's door.

169

High are the hills and very high the trees are;
Four stones there are set there, of marble gleaming.
The County Roland lies senseless on the greensward.
A Saracen is there, watching him keenly;
He has feigned death, and lies among his people,
And has smeared blood upon his breast and features.
Now he gets up and runs towards him fleetly;
Strong was he, comely and of valour exceeding.
Now in his rage and in his overweening
He falls on Roland, his arms and body seizing;
He saith one word: 'Now Carlon's nephew's beaten.
I'll take his sword, to Araby I'll reive it.'
But as he draws it Roland comes to, and feels him.

170

Roland has felt his good sword being stol'n;
Opens his eyes and speaks this word alone:
'Thou'rt none of ours, in so far as I know.'
He takes his horn, of which he kept fast hold,
And smites the helm, which was all gemmed with gold;
He breaks the steel and the scalp and the bone,
And from his head batters his eyes out both,
And dead on ground he lays the villain low;
Then saith: 'False Paynim, and how wast thou so bold,
Foully or fairly, to seize upon me so?
A fool he'll think thee who hears this story told.
Lo, now! the mouth of my Olifant's broke;
Fallen is all the crystal and the gold.'

171

Now Roland feels his sight grow dim and weak;
With his last strength he struggles to his feet;
All the red blood has faded from his cheeks.
A grey stone stands before him at his knee:
Ten strokes thereon he strikes, with rage and grief;
It grides, but yet nor breaks nor chips the steel.
'Ah!' cries the Count, 'St Mary succour me!
Alack the day, Durendal, good and keen!
Now I am dying, I cannot fend for thee.
How many battles I've won with you in field!
With you I've conquered so many goodly fiefs
That Carlon holds, the lord with the white beard!
Let none e'er wield you that from the foe would flee –
You that were wielded so long by a good liege!
The like of you blest France shall never see.'

172

Count Roland smites the sardin stone amain.
The steel grides loud, but neither breaks nor bates.
Now when he sees that it will nowise break
Thus to himself he maketh his complaint:
'Ah, Durendal! so bright, so brave, so gay!
How dost thou glitter and shine in the sun's rays!
When Charles was keeping the vales of Moriane,
God by an angel sent to him and ordained
He should bestow thee on some count-capitayne.
On me he girt thee, the noble Charlemayn.
With this I won him Anjou and all Bretayn,
With this I won him Poitou, and conquered Maine;
With this I won him Normandy's fair terrain,
And with it won Provence and Acquitaine,
And Lombardy and all the land Romayne,
Bavaria too, and the whole Flemish state,
And Burgundy and all Apulia gained;
Constantinople in the King's hand I laid;
In Saxony he speaks and is obeyed;
With this I won Scotland, [Ireland and Wales,]
And England, where he set up his domain;
What lands and countries I've conquered by its aid,
For Charles to keep whose beard is white as may!
Now am I grieved and troubled for my blade;
Should Paynims get it, 'twere worse than all death's pains.
Dear God forbid it should put France to shame!'

173

Count Roland smites upon the marble stone;
I cannot tell you how he hewed it and smote;
Yet the blade breaks not nor splinters, though it groans;
Upward to heaven it rebounds from the blow.
When the Count sees it never will be broke,
Then to himself right softly he makes moan:

'Ah, Durendal, fair, hallowed, and devote,
What store of relics lie in thy hilt of gold!
St Peter's tooth, St Basil's blood, it holds,
Hair of my lord St Denis, there enclosed,
Likewise a piece of Blessed Mary's robe;
To Paynim hands 'twere sin to let you go;
You should be served by Christian men alone,
Ne'er may you fall to any coward soul!
Many wide lands I conquered by your strokes
For Charles to keep whose beard is white as snow,
Whereby right rich and mighty is his throne.'

174

Now Roland feels death press upon him hard;
It's creeping down from his head to his heart.
Under a pine-tree he hastens him apart,
There stretches him face down on the green grass,
And lays beneath him his sword and Olifant.
He's turned his head to where the Paynims are,
And this he doth for the French and for Charles,
Since fain is he that they should say, brave heart,
That he has died a conquerer at the last.
He beats his breast full many a time and fast,
Gives, with his glove, his sins into God's charge.

175

Now Roland feels his time is at an end;
On the steep hill-side, toward Spain he's turned his head,
And with one hand he beats upon his breast;
Saith: '*Mea culpa*; Thy mercy, Lord, I beg
For all the sins, both the great and the less,
That e'er I did since first I drew my breath
Unto this day when I'm struck down by death.'
His right-hand glove he unto God extends;
Angels from Heaven now to his side descend.

176

The County Roland lay down beneath a pine;
To land of Spain he's turned him as he lies,
And many things begins to call to mind:
All the broad lands he conquered in his time,
And fairest France, and the men of his line,
And Charles his lord, who bred him from a child;
He cannot help but weep for them and sigh.
Yet of himself he is mindful betimes;
He beats his breast and on God's mercy cries:
'Father most true, in whom there is no lie,
Who didst from death St Lazarus make to rise,
And bring out Daniel safe from the lions' might,
Save Thou my soul from danger and despite
Of all the sins I did in all my life.'
His right-hand glove he's tendered unto Christ,
And from his hand Gabriel accepts the sign.
Straightway his head upon his arm declines;
With folded hands he makes an end and dies.
God sent to him His Angel Cherubine,
And great St Michael of Peril-by-the-Tide;
St Gabriel too was with them at his side;
The County's soul they bear to Paradise.

Translated from the French by Dorothy L. Sayers

THOMAS HARDY

from The Dynasts, Part I (Act 5, Scene iv)

Nelson: What are you thinking, that you speak no word?
Hardy: Thoughts all confused, my lord: – their needs on
    deck,
Your own sad state, and your unrivalled past;
Mixed up with flashes of old things afar –

Old childish things at home, down Wessex way,
In the snug village under Blackdon Hill
Where I was born. The tumbling stream, the garden,
The placid look of the grey dial there,
Marking unconsciously this bloody hour,
And the red apples on my father's trees,
Just now ripe.
   Nelson: Ay, thus do little things
Steal into my mind, too. But ah, my heart
Knows not your calm philosophy! – There's one –
Come nearer to me, Hardy. – One of all,
As you well guess, pervades my memory now;
She, and my daughter – I speak freely to you.
'Twas good I made that codicil this morning
That you and Blackwood witnessed. Now she rests
Safe on the nation's honour. . . . Let her have
My hair, and the small treasured things I owned,
And take care of her, as you care for me! . . .
Does love die with our frame's decease, I wonder, .
Or does it live on ever? . . .
   Hardy: Now I'll leave,
See if your order's gone, and then return.
   Nelson: Yes, Hardy; yes; I know it. You must go. –
Here we shall meet no more; since Heaven forfend
That care for me should keep you idle now,
When all the ship demands you. Beatty, too,
Go to the others who lie bleeding there;
Them you can aid. Me you can render none!
My time here is the briefest. – If I live
But long enough I'll anchor . . . But – too late –
My anchoring's elsewhere ordered! . . . Kiss me, Hardy:
I'm satisfied. Thank God, I have done my duty!

CHARLES CAUSLEY

Song of the Dying Gunner AA1

Oh mother my mouth is full of stars
As cartridges in the tray
My blood is a twin-branched scarlet tree
And it runs all runs away.

Oh *Cooks to the Galley* is sounded off
And the lads are down in the mess
But I lie done by the forrard gun
With a bullet in my breast.

Don't send me a parcel at Christmas time
Of socks and nutty and wine
And don't depend on a long weekend
By the Great Western Railway line.

Farewell, Aggie Weston, the Barracks at Guz,
Hang my tiddley suit on the door
I'm sewn up neat in a canvas sheet
And I shan't be home no more.

W. S. GRAHAM

The Conscript Goes

I

Having fallen not knowing,
By what force put down or for
What reason, the young fellow raises
His dreaming bloody head. The fox
Glove towers and the whiskered rye
He sees between just. He sees

His mother wading through the field
In a uniform of the other side.
Urine and blood speak through
The warmth of his comfortable pain.

His fingers open towards her but
He is alone, only a high
International lark sings
'Hark Hark my boy among the rye.'

II

Far at home, the home he always
Was impatient of, his mother
Is making jam in a copper pan.
His mongrel he knows well lies down
To whine and knock his tail on once
The card-table's leg. Upstairs
His young sister Jean takes
A long time to get ready
To meet her boy she isn't sure
She loves or even likes or whether
To let him do everything today.

III

It is my mother wading through
The broken rye and I can see
Her plain, entering my good eye.

The approaching mother bush shocks
His fading guilt. The pain has gone.
As his parochial head nestles
Into the springing field he quite
Accurately sees a high sky-trail
Dispersing slowly to the west.

IV

Father and Mother I am not here.
They stir me with a wooden spoon.
I fell. I seemed to fall. I thought
You wanted to speak to me and I turned
For a second away from what I was doing.
I am frightened of flies. Surely
You must maybe want to speak to me.

Do you think I have done something bad?
Who is right and who is wrong?
The stalks of rye rustle and
A terrible fly is on my cheek.
You know you know I am calling you.
I'll wink my good eye once for yes
And twice for no, although the lid
Is weighing a ton and not even
My pinky moves when I want it to.

V

Lark, my high bright whistler
And friend, are you still exploring
Your blue place where you see me from?
Where I am lying is any where
Near you all. Pencil and slate
Has a funny smell I can smell now
In Kelvin's School just up the road.
The girl who sat in front of me,
Her name was Janet. She liked me.

VI

Dad O Mum, I know I'm cheeky.
I will be a better boy. I'll try
Better this time. You'll see you'll see.
My new suit out of Pointers?

Is it ready safe, hanging there?
Mother I didn't like it I mean
I'll be glad to get back away.
Mum, will you put me into the kitchen
To see your bright mantel-brasses
And keep the dog from licking my neck
And keep the flies off my face.
Mother, I am not well.

HUGH MACDIARMID

Under the Greenwood Tree

A sodger laddie's socht a hoose,
A hoose and toon to bide in.
He's fund a road but never a hoose
Or toon the haill warld wide in.

And syne he's come to an auld green tree
– Then wae for a sodger loon
Wha's tint his way frae the battlefield
And here maun lay him doon.

There's brainches here for his graith o' war,
A root to tether his horse,
And a shaddaw for a windin' sheet
To row aboot his corse.

Naval Engagements

Many of the most celebrated poems about sea battles are fanciful recreations, composed long after the event, but the three from which I have chosen excerpts in this group are vivid contemporary accounts. Naval battles are often more absolute than land battles, because when a ship goes down, most, if not all, lives are lost, as happened with the *Jervis Bay* in 1940. This ex-passenger liner was converted into a merchant cruiser to protect convoys in the North Atlantic. When attacked by the German pocket battleship *Admiral Scheer*, she gallantly drew fire on to herself, allowing thirty-two of the thirty-seven ships in the convoy to escape under cover of darkness.

Andrew Marvell describes the decisive engagement in the war between England and Spain of 1657, when Blake destroyed six Spanish treasure ships and ten escorts in the harbour of Santa Cruz in the Canary Islands. Blake, one of England's greatest admirals, died on the return voyage. In that war, England was defending its trading interests, and nine years later she had to do the same again, only on that occasion her enemies were Holland and France; the episode reported by Dryden is from that conflict. When it is said that trade 'followed the flag', the flag was usually on the bow of a ship and not that carried at the head of a regiment.

JOHN DONNE

A Burnt Ship

Out of a fired ship, which, by no way
But drowning, could be rescued from the flame,
Some men leap'd forth, and ever as they came
Near the foe's ships, did by their shot decay;
So all were lost, which in the ship were found,
    They in the sea being burnt, they in the burnt ship drowned.

ANDREW MARVELL

from The Victory Obtained by Blake over the Spaniards, in the Bay of Santa Cruz in the Island of Teneriffe, 1657

. . . For Sanctacruze the glad fleet takes her way,
And safely there casts anchor in the bay.
Never so many with one joyful cry,
That place saluted; where they all must dye.
Deluded men! Fate with you did but sport,
You scap't the sea, to perish in your port.
'Twas more for Englands fame you should dye there,
Where you had most of strength, and least of fear.
  The Peek's proud height, the Spaniards all admire,
Yet in their brests, carry a pride much higher.
Onely to this vast hill a power is given,
At once both to inhabit earth and heaven.
But this stupendious prospect did not neer,
Make them admire, so much as they did fear.

  For here they met with news, which did produce,
A grief, above the cure of grapes best juice.
They learn'd with terrour, that nor summers heat,
Nor winters storms, had made your fleet retreat.
To fight against such foes, was vain they knew,
Which did the rage of elements subdue.
Who on the ocean that does horror give.
To all besides, triumphantly do live.

  With hast they therefore all their gallions moar,
And flank with cannon from the neighbouring shore.
Forts, lines, and sconces all the bay along,
They build and act all that can make them strong.

Fond men who know not whilst such works they raise,
They only labour to exalt your praise.
Yet they by restless toyl, became at length,
So proud and confident of their made strength,
That they with joy their boasting general heard,
Wish then for that assault he lately fear'd.
His wish he has, for now undaunted Blake,
With winged speed, for Sanctacruze does make.
For your renown, the conquering fleet does ride,
Ore seas as vast as is the Spaniards pride.
Whose fleet and trenches view'd, you soon did say,
We to their strength are more oblig'd then they.
Wer't not for that, they from their fate would run,
And a third world seek out our armes to shun.
Those forts, which there, so high and strong appear,
Do not so much suppress, as shew their fear.
Of speedy victory let no man doubt,
Our worst works past, now we have found them out.
Behold their navy does at anchor lye,
And they are ours, for now they cannot fly.

This said, the whole fleet gave it their applause,
And all assumes your courage, in your cause.
That bay they enter, which unto them owes,
The noblest wreaths, that victory bestows.
Bold Stainer leads, this fleets design'd by fate,
To give him lawrel, as the last did plate.

The thund'ring cannon now begins the fight,
And though it be at noon, creates a night.
The air was soon after the fight begun,
Far more enflam'd by it, then by the sun.
Never so burning was that climate known,
War turn'd the temperate, to the torrid zone.

Fate these two fleets between both worlds had brought.
Who fight, as if for both those worlds they sought.
Thousands of wayes, thousands of men there dye,
Some ships are sunk, some blown up in the skie.
Nature never made cedars so high aspire,
As oakes did then, urg'd by the active fire.
Which by quick powders force, so high was sent,
That it return'd to its own element.
Torn limbs some leagues into the island fly,
Whilst others lower, in the sea do lye.
Scarce souls from bodies sever'd are so far,
By death, as bodies there were by the war.
Th' all-seeing sun, ne'er gaz'd on such a sight,
Two dreadful navies there at anchor fight.
And neither have, or power, or will to fly,
There one must conquer, or there both must dye.
Far different motives yet, engag'd them thus,
Necessity did them, but choice did us.

A choice which did the highest worth express,
And was attended by as high success.
For your resistless genius there did raign,
By which we laurels reapt ev'n on the mayn.
So prosperous stars, though absent to the sence,
Bless those they shine for, by their influence.

Our cannon now tears every ship and sconce,
And o're two elements triumphs at once.
Their gallions sunk, their wealth the sea does fill,
The only place where it can cause no ill.

Ah would those treasures which both Indies have,
Were buryed in as large, and deep a grave,
Wars chief support with them would buried be,
And the land owe her peace unto the sea . . .

JOHN DRYDEN

from Annus Mirabilis

LIV

Our fleet divides, and straight the Dutch appear,
  In number, and a famed commander, bold;
The narrow seas can scarce their navy bear,
  Or crowded vessels can their soldiers hold.

LV

The Duke, less numerous, but in courage more,
  On wings of all the winds to combat flies;
His murdering guns a loud defiance roar,
  And bloody crosses on his flag-staffs rise.

LVI

Both furl their sails, and strip them for the fight;
  Their folded sheets dismiss the useless air;
The Elean plains could boast no nobler sight,
  When struggling champions did their bodies bare.

LVII

Borne each by other in a distant line,
  The sea-built forts in dreadful order move;
So vast the noise, as if not fleets did join,
  But lands unfixed, and floating nations strove.

LVIII

Now passed, on either side they nimbly tack;
  Both strive to intercept and guide the wind;
And, in its eye, more closely they come back,
  To finish all the deaths they left behind.

LIX

On high-raised decks the haughty Belgians ride,
  Beneath whose shade our humble frigates go;
Such port the elephant bears, and so defied
  By the rhinoceros, her unequal foe.

LX

And as the built, so different is the fight,
  Their mounting shot is on our sails designed;
Deep in their hulls our deadly bullets light,
  And through the yielding planks a passage find.

LXI

Our dreaded admiral from far they threat,
  Whose battered rigging their whole war receives;
All bare, like some old oak which tempests beat,
  He stands, and sees below his scattered leaves.

LXII

Heroes of old, when wounded, shelter sought;
  But he, who meets all danger with disdain,
Even in their face his ship to anchor brought,
  And steeple-high stood propt upon the main.

LXIII

At this excess of courage, all amazed,
  The foremost of his foes a while withdraw;
With such respect in entered Rome they gazed,
  Who on high chairs the godlike Fathers saw.

LXIV

And now, as where Patroclus' body lay,
  Here Trojan chiefs advanced, and there the Greek;

Ours o'er the Duke their pious wings display,
  And theirs the noblest spoils of Britain seek.

LXV

Meantime his busy mariners he hastes,
  His shattered sails with rigging to restore;
And willing pines ascend his broken masts,
  Whose lofty heads rise higher than before.

LXVI

Straight to the Dutch he turns his dreadful prow,
  More fierce the important quarrel to decide;
Like swans, in long array, his vessels show,
  Whose crests advancing do the waves divide.

LXVII

They charge, recharge, and all along the sea
  They drive, and squander the huge Belgian fleet;
Berkley alone, who nearest danger lay,
  Did a like fate with lost Creusa meet.

LXVIII

The night comes on, we eager to pursue
  The combat still, and they ashamed to leave;
Till the last streaks of dying day withdrew,
  And doubtful moonlight did our rage deceive.

LXIX

In the English fleet each ship resounds with joy,
  And loud applause of their great leader's fame;
In fiery dreams the Dutch they still destroy,
  And, slumbering, smile at the imagined flame.

LXX

Not so the Holland fleet, who tired and done,
  Streched on their decks, like weary oxen, lie;
Faint sweats all down their mighty members run,
  Vast bulks, which little souls but ill supply.

LXXI

In dreams they fearful precipices tread;
  Or, shipwrecked, labour to some distant shore;
Or in dark churches walk among the dead;
  They wake with horror, and dare sleep no more.

MICHAEL THWAITES

from The *Jervis Bay*

. . . On either side the *Jervis Bay* the convoy was dipping,
And the Captain as he paced the bridge paused, one hand
    gripping
A stanchion, to study them against the amber rim
Of sky – the ships whose safety was entrusted to him.
They spread, a broad battalion, massed in columns nine
    abreast,
There *Trewellard, Cornish City, San Demetrio* – North-by-
West
Was it smoke or cloud? – *Castillian, Rangitiki,* and the rest.
Satisfied, he turned to go below; when a sudden gleam
Flickered in the north, and a shout from the lookout, 'Ship on
    the port beam.'
Two seconds, and Captain Fegen's glasses rake the horizon to
    norrard,
Two more, and the bells ring Action Stations. Aft, amidships,
    forrard,

The guns are manned, loaded and trained – the crews were
    standing by –
And the men below are running to their stations, and every
    pulse beats high.
And Fegen's pulse is racing hard, but his eye is steady and
    clear,
And the smudge on the horizon shimmers into shape, and is
    the *Admiral Scheer*.

The telegraph clangs to 'Full Ahead'. Her great heart pounding
The *Jervis Bay* trembles and surges forward, sounding
The alarm on her siren. From her bridge the Aldis chatters
To an answering flicker from where the Commodore scatters
The foaming seas, awaiting his orders for the convoy.
'Warship, thought hostile, my port beam.' An envoy
Of wrath, a white column spouts sudden and high
Topping the mast. A detonation shakes the sea and sky.

'Scatter under smoke.' – Fluttering flags and sirens blowing
Down the columns of the convoy. – But the *Jervis Bay* is going
Steady onward as they turn. From the smoke floats are flowing
Streams of velvet solid smoke drifting over the ocean swell,
But the enemy gunners know their job. A salvo of shell
Roars in the sea – one, two, three – by the *Rangitiki*'s bow
As she twists in flight. Already they have found for line. And
    now
A salvo spouts alongside – the iron jaws closing
On the vulnerable spine. Now the convoy are nosing
East, south, west, away fanwise are scattering,
But the shells fall like drops in thunder ominously pattering,
And Captain Fegen had that day a second, or maybe two,
As he stood on the bridge of the *Jervis Bay*, to choose what he
    would do.
Astern of him the convoy, labouring heavily in flight,
And one long hour till they could win to cover of the night.
To port the Nazi battleship, with six eleven-inch guns
Secure in triple turrets ranged to hurl their angry tons

Of blasting steel across the miles his guns could never span,
With twice his speed, with a Naval crew, trained, expert to a
    man,
With armour-plated sides and a deck, a warship through and
    through,
The pride of the German builders' craft. All this Fegen knew,
Knew his foeman as he came in overmastering might,
Knew well there was no hope at all in such unequal fight,
Knew his own unarmoured sides, his few old six-inch guns,
His fourteen meagre knots, his men, their country's sturdy
    sons,
But hasty-trained and still untried in the shock and din of
    action.
To starboard were the merchantmen, and he was their
    protection . . .

Now the *Jervis Bay* is ablaze. The fo'c'sle is blown away.
Splinters rive her decks to ribbons and bury her under spray,
And her burning hull as she plunged on was a bright torch that
    day.
She shudders. With the clearing smoke her main bridge is
    gone,
And Fegen's arm is a shredded stump, and he fights on.
He staggers aft to the docking bridge. Another blinding blast.
The Ensign down. 'Another Ensign! Nail it to the mast.'
A seaman climbs and nails it there, where the House Flag used
    to fly.
And there it speaks defiance to the shaker of the sky.
He strives to climb to the after bridge, but it is unavailing,
One arm and half the shoulder gone, and strength fast failing.
But there is still the after gun that he can bring to bear.
'Independent fire!' he cries, as heaves into the air
The after bridge. He lives, and staggers forrard again, before
The rolling smoke envelops him, and he is seen no more.
Now her engines had ceased to turn, but still the shells came
    pouring,

Till with a roar her boilers burst, and the white steam went
    soaring
Away to the sky. Her back was broken, and she was settling
    fast,
And the fire blazed, and the smoke-pall brooded like a banyan
    vast,
But still the torn Ensign flew from the black stump mast,
And the after gun was firing still and asking no quarter
When the hot barrel hissed into the wild grey water.

So ended the fight of the *Scheer* and the *Jervis Bay*
That for twenty vital minutes drew the raider's fire that day,
When of the convoy's thirty-seven, thirty-two went safe away
And home at last to England came, without the *Jervis Bay*.

But now thick night was over the sea, and a wind from the west
    blew keen,
And the hopeless waters tossed their heads where the *Jervis
    Bay* had been,
And the raider was lost in the rain and the night, and low
    clouds hid the seas,
But high above sea and storm and cloud appeared the galaxies,
The Bear, Orion, myriad stars that timeless vigil keep,
A glimmering host the stars came out across the heaving deep,
And they shone bright over the good shepherd of sheep.

Old Ships

As the regiment is to the soldier, so the ship is to the sailor. All ships become in time victims of technological progress, whether it be a case of sail giving way to steam, or ironclads to aircraft carriers. Like old soldiers, though, the old ships never die – they simply fade away.

HENRY WADSWORTH LONGFELLOW

from The Building of the Ship

And as he laboured, his mind ran o'er
The various ships that were built of yore,
And above them all, and strangest of all,
Towered the Great Harry, crank and tall,
Whose picture was hanging on the wall,
With bows and stern raised high in air,
And balconies hanging here and there,
And signal lanterns and flags afloat,
And eight round towers, like those that frown
From some old castle, looking down
Upon the drawbridge and the moat.

HERMAN MELVILLE

The *Temeraire*

The gloomy hulls, in armour grim,
  Like clouds o'er moors have met,
And prove that oak, and iron, and man
  Are tough in fibre yet.

But Splendours wane. The sea-fight yields
  No front of old display;
The garniture, emblazonment,
  And heraldry all decay.

Towering afar in parting light,
  The fleets like Albion's forelands shine –
The full-sailed fleets, the shrouded show
  Of Ships-of-the-Line.
The fighting *Temeraire*,
  Built of a thousand trees,
Lunging out her lightnings,
  And beetling o'er the seas –
O Ship, how brave and fair,
  That fought so oft and well,
On open decks you manned the gun Armorial.
What cheerings did you share,
  Impulsive in the van,
When down upon leagued France and Spain
  We English ran –
The freshet at your bowsprit
  Like the foam upon the can.
Bickering, your colours
  Licked up the Spanish air,
You flapped with flames of battle-flags –
  Your challenge, *Temeraire*!
The rear ones of our fleet
  They yearned to share your place,
Still vying with the *Victory*
  Throughout that earnest race –
The *Victory*, whose Admiral,
  With orders nobly won,
Shone in the globe of the battle glow –
  The angel in that sun.
Parallel in story,
  Lo, the stately pair,

As late in grapple ranging,
    The foe between them there –
When four great hulls lay tiered,
And the fiery tempest cleared,
And your prizes twain appeared,/*Temeraire*!

But Trafalgar is over now,
    The quarter-deck undone;
The carved and castled navies fire
    Their evening-gun
O, Titan *Temeraire*,
    Your stern-lights fade away;
Your bulwarks to the years must yield,
    And heart-of-oak decay.
A pigmy steam-tug tows you,
    Gigantic, to the shore –
Dismantled of your guns and spars,
    And sweeping wings of war.

The rivets clinch the ironclads,
    Men learn a deadlier lore;
But Fame has nailed your battle-flags –
    Your ghost it sails before:
O, the navies old and oaken,
    O, the *Temeraire* no more!

CHARLES CAUSLEY

HMS *Glory*

I was born on an Irish sea of eggs and porter,
I was born in Belfast, in the MacNeice country,
A child of Harland & Wolff in the iron forest,
My childbed a steel cradle slung from a gantry.

I remember the Queen's Road trams swarming with workers,
The lovely northern voices, the faces of the women,
The plane trees by the City Hall: an *Alexanderplatz*,
And the sailors coming off shore with silk stockings and linen.

I remember the jokes about sabotage and Dublin,
The noisy jungle of cranes and sheerlegs, the clangour,
The draft in February of a thousand matelots from Devonport,
Surveying anxiously my enormous flight-deck and hangar.

I remember the long vista of ships under the quiet mountain,
The signals from Belfast Castle, the usual panic and sea-fever
Before I slid superbly out on the green lough
Leaving the tiny cheering figures on the jetty for ever:

Turning my face from home to the Southern Cross,
A map of crackling stars, and the albatross.

Sieges

The poetic archetype of all sieges is, inevitably, that of Troy, which lasted for ten years. Dryden's translation, from Virgil, of Aeneas' account of the Greeks' gift of the Wooden Horse is followed by C. H. Sisson's treatment of what followed its acceptance. I have also included a paraphrase, adapted for dramatic purposes, by Marlowe, because for centuries every educated person was steeped in the details of the fall of Troy and its tale was told over and over again.

Thomas Deloney, the Elizabethan writer of verse narratives, itemizes the horrors faced by the beleaguered inhabitants of Jerusalem, as famine begins to take a grip. He probably does not exaggerate. Usually, those under siege lived in fear of the rapine, plunder and killing that would follow a surrender. At Harfleur in 1415, the Burghers surrendered to Henry V on the understanding that his English troops, 'the flesh'd soldier, rough and hard of heart', should not be allowed to pillage their town.

When the Germans laid siege to Leningrad for over two years (1942–4), 600,000 Russians died in defence of the city. Morale there was lifted by the playing, over loud-speakers, of Shostakovich's Seventh Symphony, composed in honour of the people of Leningrad.

At Lucknow, during the Indian Mutiny (1857), the 300 Europeans pinned down there believed that, if they surrendered, they would be massacred, as had happened to the British garrison at Cawnpore; so they hung on for six months and were eventually rewarded by hearing the skirl of the pipes from Havelock's relief column.

The most famous instance of the Boer War was that of Mafeking, which, under Baden-Powell, withstood a siege for eight months. When it was relieved in May 1899, the entire country rejoiced. I remember my grandfather telling me that, when the news reached his town of Newport, people poured out from their

houses into the streets, shouting, singing and dancing. A new word
was coined: to 'maffick'.

VIRGIL

from The Aeneid, Book II

By destiny compell'd, and in despair,
The Greeks grew weary of the tedious war,
And, by Minerva's aid, a fabric rear'd,
Which like a steed of monstrous height appear'd:
The sides were plank'd with pine: they feign'd it made
For their return, and this the vow they paid.
Thus they pretend, but in the hollow side,
Selected numbers of their soldiers hide:
With inward arms the dire machine they load;
And iron bowels stuff the dark abode.

The Trojans, coop'd within their walls so long,
Unbar their gates, and issue in a throng,
Like swarming bees, and with delight survey
The camp deserted, where the Grecians lay:
The quarters of the sev'ral chiefs they show'd –
Here Phœnix, here Achilles, made abode;
Here join'd the battles; there the navy rode.
Part on the pile their wond'ring eyes employ –
The pile by Pallas rais'd to ruin Troy.
Thymœtes first ('tis doubtful whether hir'd,
Or so the Trojan destiny requir'd)
Mov'd that the ramparts might be broken down,
To lodge the monster fabric in the town.
But Capys, and the rest of sounder mind,
The fatal present to the flames design'd,
Or to the wat'ry deep; at least to bore
The hollow sides, and hidden frauds explore.
The giddy vulgar, as their fancies guide,

With noise say nothing, and in parts divide.
Laocoön follow'd by a num'rous crowd,
Ran from the fort, and cry'd, from far, aloud:
'O wretched countrymen! what fury reigns?
What more than madness has possess'd your brains?
Think you the Grecians from your coasts are gone?
And are Ulysses' arts no better known?

This hollow fabric either must inclose,
Within its blind recess, our secret foes;
Or 'tis an engine rais'd above the town,
T' o'erlook the walls, and then to batter down.
Somewhat is sure design'd by fraud or force –
Trust not their presents, nor admit the horse.'
Thus having said, against the steed he threw
His forceful spear, which, hissing as it flew,
Pierc'd through the yielding planks of jointed wood,
And trembling in the hollow belly stood.
The sides, transpierc'd, return a rattling sound;
And groans of Greeks inclos'd come issuing through the
    wound.
And, had not heav'n the fall of Troy design'd,
Or had not men been fated to be blind,
Enough was said and done, t' inspire a better mind.
Then had our lances pierc'd the treach'rous wood,
And Ilian tow'rs and Priam's empire stood.

Translated from the Latin by John Dryden

VIRGIL

from The Aeneid, Book II

Then indeed into all our fluttering hearts
There comes another terror: Laocoon,
Everyone says, deserved what he got;

He violated that sacred tree
When he threw his spear at the horse's flanks.
The image must be put where it belongs,
They shout, the goddess must be paid with prayers.
We cut through the city walls and throw them open.
Everyone gets to work and they put rollers
Under the horse and tug at its neck with ropes.
Up goes the fatal engine, through the walls,
Full of arms as it is. Around, the boys
And the unmarried girls sing hymns, they cannot
Keep their hands off the ropes, they are so pleased.
Up she comes, there she is with all her menace
Inside the city. So much for our country.
Home of the gods, Ilium, Dardan walls
Famous in war! The horse stuck four times
At the very gates, and four times from within
There was a sound of weapons shaken up:
We press on all the same without a thought,
Blind and mad, and set the monster firm
Inside our consecrated citadel.
And Sinon, favoured by an unjust fate,
Undoes the door of pine-wood secretly
Where the Greeks crouch inside. The opened horse
Gives them back to the outer air. Well pleased
They issue forth, Thessandrus, Sthenelus,
Both captains, and the merciless Ulysses;
A rope is lowered and they all slide down,
With Thoas, Acamas, Neoptolemus
The sons of Peleus, and Machaon,
With Menelaus and with Epeus
Who was the rascal who designed the horse.
They creep into the city, which is buried
In wine and sleep, and fall upon the sentries,
Then open wide the gates, let in their friends:
The plot has worked, the forces have joined up.

   Translated from the Latin by C. H. Sisson

CHRISTOPHER MARLOWE

from Dido, Queen of Carthage

Æneas: The Grecian soldiers, tired with ten years' war,
Began to cry, 'Let us unto our ships,
Troy is invincible, why stay we here?'
With whose outcries Atrides being appalled,
Summoned the Captains to his princely tent;
Who, looking on the scars we Trojans gave,
Seeing the number of their men decreased,
And the remainder weak and out of heart,
Gave up their voices to dislodge the camp,
And so in troops all marched to Tenedos:
Where when they came, Ulysses on the sand
Assayed with honey words to turn them back;
And as he spoke to further his intent,
The winds did drive huge billows to the shore,
And heaven was darkened with tempestuous clouds:
Then he alleged the Gods would have them stay,
And prophesied Troy should be overcome:
And therewithal he called false Sinon forth,
A man compact of craft and perjurie,
Whose ticing tongue was made of Hermes' pipe,
To force an hundred watchful eyes to sleep;
And him, Epeus having made the horse,
With sacrificing wreaths upon his head,
Ulysses sent to our unhappy town:
Who, grovelling in the mire of Xanthus' banks,
His hands bound at his back, and both his eyes
Turned up to heaven, as one resolved to die,
Our Phrygian shepherds hailed within the gates,
And brought unto the Court of Priamus:
To whom he used action so pitiful,
Looks so remorseful, vows so forcible,

As therewithal the old man, overcome,
Kissed him, embraced him, and unloosed his bands:
And then – O Dido, pardon me.
   Dido: Nay, leave not here; resolve me of the rest.
   Æneas: O th' enchanting words of that base slave
Made him to think Epeus' pine-tree Horse
A sacrifice t' appease Minerva's wrath:
The rather, for that one Laocoon
Breaking a spear upon his hollow breast,
Was with two winged Serpents stung to death.
Whereat aghast, we were commanded straight
With reverence to draw it into Troy.
In which unhappy worke was I employed.
These hands did help to hail it to the gates,
Through which it could not enter, 'twas so huge.
O had it never entered, Troy had stood.
But Priamus impatient of delay,
Enforced a wide breach in that rampiered wall,
Which thousand battering rams could never pierce,
And so came in this fatal instrument:
At whose accursed feet as overjoyed,
We banquetted till, overcome with wine,
Some surfeited, and others soundly slept.
Which Sinon viewing, caused the Greekish spies
To haste to Tenedos and tell the Camp.
Then he unlocked the Horse, and suddenly
From out his entrails, Neoptolemus
Setting his spear upon the ground, lept forth,
And after him a thousand Grecians more,
In whose stern faces shined the quenchless fire
That after burnt the pride of Asia.
By this, the Camp was come unto the walls,
And through the breach did march into the streets,
Where, meeting with the rest, 'Kill, kill!' they cried.
Frighted with this confused noise, I rose,
And, looking from a turret, might behold

Young infants swimming in their parents' blood,
Headless carcasses piled up in heaps,
Virgins half-dead, dragged by their golden hair,
And with main force flung on a ring of pikes,
Old men with swords thrust through their aged sides,
Kneeling for mercy to a Greekish lad,
Who with steel pole-axes dashed out their brains.
Then buckled I mine armour, drew my sword
And thinking to go down, came Hector's ghost,
With ashy visage, blueish sulphur eyes,
His arms torn from his shoulders, and his breast
Furrow'd with wounds, and, that which made me weep,
Thongs at his heels, by which Achilles' horse
Drew him in triumph through the Greekish camp,
Burst from the earth, crying 'Æneas, fly!
Troy is a-fire, the Grecians have the town!'

THOMAS DELONEY

from The Destruction of Jerusalem

For true report rung in his royall eares,
That bitter Famine did afflict them sore,
Which was the cause of many bitter teares,
And he to make their miserie the more,
  Depriv'd them quit of all their water cleere,
  Which in their want they did esteeme so deere.

Alack, what pen is able to expresse?
The extreame miserie of this people then?
Which were with Famine brought to great distresse,
For cruell hunger vext the welthiest men:
  When night approacht, well might they lye & winke,
  But cold not sleepe for want of meat and drinke.

For by this time full Fourteene monthes and more,
Had warlike *Titus* sieg'd that famous towne,
What time the Jewes had quite consum'd their store,
And being starv'd, like Ghosts went up and downe:
    For in the markets were no victuals found,
    Though for a *Lambe*, they might have twenty pound.

When bread was gone, then was he counted blest,
That in his hand had either cat or dogge,
To fill his emptie maw: and thus distrest,
A dozen men would fight for one poore frogge.
    The fairest Lady lighting on a mouce,
    Would keepe it from her best friend in the house.

A weazell was accounted daynty meate,
A hissing snake esteem'd a Princes dish,
A Queene upon a moule might seeme to eate,
A veanom neawt was thought a wholesome fish:
    Wormes from the earth were dig'd up great & small,
    And poysoned spiders eaten from the wall.

A hundred men under this grievous crosse,
With hunger-starved bodies wanting food,
Have for a morsell of a stinking horse,
In deadly strife, shed one an others blood:
    Like famisht Ravens, that in a shole doe pitch,
    To seaze a caryon in a noysome ditch.

But when these things were all consumed quite,
(For famines greedy mawe destroyeth all,)
Then did they bend their study day and night,
To see what next unto their share might fall:
    Necessitie doth seeke an hundred wayes,
    Famines fell torment from the heart to rayse.

Then did they take their horses leather raignes,
And broyling them suppos'd them wonderous sweete,
A hungry stomack naught at all refraines,

Nor did they spare their shooes upon their feete:
   But shooes, and bootes, and buskins, all they eate,
   And would not spare one morsell of their meate.

But out alas my heart doth shake to show,
When these things fail'd, what shift these wretches made,
Without salt teares how should I write their woe,
Sith sorrowes ground-worke in the same is layd:
   All English hearts which Christ in armes doe hem,
   Marke well the woes of fayre *Jerusalem*.

When all was spent, and nothing left to eate,
Whereby they might maintaine their feeble life,
Then doth the wife her husband deere intreat,
To end her misery by his wounding knife:
   Maides weepe for foode, & children make their moane,
   Their parents sigh when they can give them none.

Some men with hunger falleth raging mad,
Gnawing the stones and timber where they walke,
Some other staggering, weake and wonderous sad,
Dyes in the streetes, as with their friends they talke?
   And other some licks up the vomit fast,
   Which their sick neighbours in their houses cast.

Nay more then this, though this be all to much,
Josephus writes, that men and maidens young
The which of late did scorne brown-bread to touch,
Sustain'd themselves with one an others doong.
   Remember this you that so dainty bee,
   And praise Gods name for all things sent to thee.

All things were brought by famine out of frame,
For modest Chastitie to it gave place,
High honoured Virgins that for very shame,
Would hardly looke on men with open face,
   One bit of bread never so course and browne,
   Would winne them to the foulest knave in towne.

WILLIAM SHAKESPEARE

from Henry V (Act 3, Scene iii)

Before the gates of Harfleur

   King Henry:
How yet resolves the Governor of the town?
This is the latest parle we will admit;
Therefore to our best mercy give yourselves
Or, like to men proud of destruction,
Defy us to our worst; for, as I am a soldier,
A name that in my thoughts becomes me best,
If I begin the batt'ry once again.
I will not leave the half-achieved Harfleur
Till in her ashes she lie buried.
The gates of mercy shall be all shut up,
And the flesh'd soldier, rough and hard of heart,
In liberty of bloody hand shall range
With conscience wide as hell, mowing like grass
Your fresh fair virgins and your flow'ring infants.
What is it then to me if impious war,
Array'd in flames, like to the prince of fiends,
Do, with his smirch'd complexion, all fell feats
Enlink'd to waste and desolation?
What is't to me when you yourselves are cause,
If your pure maidens fall into the hand
Of hot and forcing violation?
What rein can hold licentious wickedness
When down the hill he holds his fierce career?
We may as bootless spend our vain command
Upon th' enraged soldiers in their spoil,
As send precepts to the Leviathan
To come ashore. Therefore, you men of Harfleur,
Take pity of your town and of your people

Whiles yet my soldiers are in my command;
Whiles yet the cool and temperate wind of grace
O'erblows the filthy and contagious clouds
Of heady murder, spoil, and villainy.
If not – why, in a moment look to see
The blind and bloody soldier with foul hand
Defile the locks of your shrill-shrieking daughters;
Your fathers taken by the silver beards,
And their most reverend heads dash'd to the walls;
Your naked infants spitted upon pikes,
Whiles the mad mothers with their howls confus'd
Do break the clouds, as did the wives of Jewry
At Herod's bloody-hunting slaughtermen.
What say you? Will you yield, and this avoid?
Or, guilty in defence, be thus destroy'd?

   Governor of Harfleur:
Our expectation hath this day an end:
The Dauphin, whom of succours we entreated,
Returns us that his powers are yet not ready
To raise so great a siege. Therefore, great King,
We yield our town and lives to thy soft mercy.
Enter our gates; dispose of us and ours;
For we no longer are defensible.

J. G. WHITTIER

The Pipes at Lucknow

An Incident of the Sepoy Mutiny

Pipes of the misty moorlands,
   Voice of the glens and hills;
The droning of the torrents,
   The treble of the rills;
Not the braes of bloom and heather,

Nor the mountains dark with rain,
Nor maiden bower, nor border tower,
  Have heard your sweetest strain!

Dear to the Lowland reaper,
  And plaided mountaineer, –
To the cottage and the castle
  The Scottish pipes are dear; –
Sweet sounds the ancient pibroch
  O'er mountain, loch, and glade;
But the sweetest of all music
  The pipes at Lucknow played.

Day by day the Indian tiger
  Louder yelled, and nearer crept;
Round and round the jungle-serpent
  Near and nearer circles swept.
'Pray for rescue, wives and mothers, –
  Pray to-day!' the soldier said;
'To-morrow, death's between us
  And the wrong and shame we dread.'

Oh, they listened, looked and waited,
  Till their hope became despair;
And the sobs of low bewailing
  Filled the pauses of their prayer.
Then up spake a Scottish maiden,
  With her ear unto the ground:
'Dinna ye hear it? – dinna ye hear it?
  The pipes o' Havelock sound!'

Hushed the wounded man his groaning:
  Hushed the wife her little ones;
Alone they heard the drum-roll
  And the roar of Sepoy guns.
But to sounds of home and childhood
  The Highland ear was true; –

As her mother's cradle-crooning
   The mountain pipes she knew.

Oh, they listened, dumb and breathless,
   And they caught the sound at last;
Faint and far beyond the Goomtee
   Rose and fell the piper's blast!
Then a burst of wild thanksgiving
   Mingled woman's voice and man's;
'God be praised! – the march of Havelock!
   The piping of the clans!'

Louder, nearer, fierce as vengeance,
   Sharp and shrill as swords at strife,
Came the wild MacGregor's clan-call,
   Stinging all the air to life.
But when the far-off dust-cloud
   To plaided legions grew,
Full tenderly and blithesomely
   The pipes of rescue blew!

Round the silver domes of Lucknow,
   Moslem mosque and Pagan shrine.
Breathed the air to Britons dearest,
   The air of Auld Lang Syne.
O'er the cruel roll of war-drums
   Rose that sweet and homelike strain;
And the tartan clove the turban,
   As the Goomtee cleaves the plain

Dear to the corn-land reaper
   And plaided mountaineer, –
To the cottage and the castle
   The piper's song is dear.
Sweet sounds the Gaelic pibroch
   O'er mountain, glen, and glade;
But the sweetest of all music
   The pipes at Lucknow played!

VERA INBER

from The Pulkovo Meridian

Leningrad, 1943

The teeth are bared, the mouth drawn tight, the face
Is waxen and the beard like a cadaver's
(A beard the razor hardly can displace).
The walk, without a balance center, wavers.
The pulse beneath the ashen-colored skin
Is weak. The albumin is gone. The end sets in.

Among the women many have a swelling.
They shiver constantly (though not from frost).
Their bosoms shrink to nothingness, compelling
The once-white kerchiefs to be tighter crossed.
Who would believe that once at such a breast
A child had ever sucked himself to rest?

Like melted candles in their apathy.
All the dry summaries and indications
Are here of what by learned designations
Doctors call 'alimental dystrophy.'
Non-Latinists, non-philologues will name
It simply hunger, but it means the same.

And after that the end is very near.
The body, rolled up in a dust-gray cover
Fastened with safety pins, and wound all over
With rope, upon a child's sled will appear,
So neatly laid out that it's plain to see
It's not the first one in the family.

Translated from the Russian by Dorothea Prall Radin
and Alexander Kaun

Nursing and Medicine

Until the twentieth century, soldiers were lucky to survive military medicine. Basic treatments included the cauterizing of wounds and the cutting-off of arms or legs to stop gangrene setting in. There was nothing to relieve pain or kill infection. The greatest advance in military medicine was made when doctors took to washing their hands. Florence Nightingale transformed the military hospitals of the Crimea simply by scrubbing them out and letting fresh air in. At times, though, it was more humane to put soldiers out of their misery. Ambroise Paré, one of the founders of military medicine, reported an incident at the siege of Turin in 1536: 'There came an old soldier who asked me if there was any means of curing them [certain wounded soldiers]. I told him no. At once he approached them and cut their throats gently.'

Up to the First World War, most deaths in war were caused by epidemic diseases like dysentery, enteric fever, cholera, typhus and plague. The French army sent to overthrow Toussaint L'Ouverture in Haiti in 1801 was reduced by yellow fever from 25,000 to 3,000. Even in the Boer War, more men were killed by disease than by bullets or shells.

The vivid poem by Walt Whitman is drawn from his own experience in the American Civil War when, in 1862, he went to a battlefield in Virginia to find his wounded brother. Appalled by what he saw, he stayed in Washington to help the wounded. Edgar Wallace, too, wrote from his experience of being a medical orderly. I have included a poem written from the war in Vietnam, where medical staff were well acquainted with the horrors of dealing with casualties brought about by a guerrilla war in which grenades and land-mines caused hideous personal injuries.

HOMER

from The Iliad, Book IV

This said, divine Talthybius he call'd, and bad him haste
Machaon, Æsculapius' son, who most of men was grac'd
With physic's sovereign remedies, to come and lend his hand
To Menelaus shot by one well-skill'd in the command
Of bow and arrows, one of Troy, or of the Lycian aid,
Who much hath glorified our foe, and us as much dismay'd.
   He heard, and hasted instantly, and cast his eyes about
The thickest squadrons of the Greeks, to find Machaon out.
He found him standing guarded well with well-arm'd men of
      Thrace;
With whom he quickly join'd, and said: 'Man of Apollo's race,
Haste, for the king of men commands, to see a wound
      impress'd
In Menelaus, great in arms, by one instructed best
In th' art of archery, of Troy, or of the Lycian bands,
That them with much renown adorns, us with dishonour
      brands.'
   Machaon much was mov'd with this, who with the herald
      flew
From troop to troop alongst the host, and soon they came in
      view
Of hurt Atrides circled round with all the Grecian kings,
Who all gave way, and straight he draws the shaft, which forth
      he brings
Without the forks; the girdle then, plate, curets, off he plucks,
And views the wound; when first from it the clotter'd blood he
      sucks,
Then medicines, wondrously compos'd, the skilful leech
      applied,

Which loving Chiron taught his sire, he from his sire had tried.
   While these were thus employ'd to ease the Atrean
     martialist,
The Trojans arm'd, and charg'd the Greeks . . .

   Translated from the Greek by George Chapman

HENRY WADSWORTH LONGFELLOW

Santa Filomena

Whene'er a noble deed is wrought,
Whene'er is spoken a noble thought,
   Our hearts, in glad surprise,
   To higher levels rise.

The tidal wave of deeper souls
Into our inmost being rolls,
   And lifts us unawares
   Out of all meaner cares.

Honour to those whose words or deeds
Thus help us in our daily needs,
   And by their overflow
   Raise us from what is low!

Thus thought I, as by night I read
Of the great army of the dead,
   The trenches cold and damp,
   The starved and frozen camp, –

The wounded from the battle-plain,
In dreary hospitals of pain,
   The cheerless corridors,
   The cold and stony floors.

Lo! in that house of misery
A lady with a lamp I see

Pass through the glimmering gloom,
And flit from room to room.

And slow, as in a dream of bliss,
The speechless sufferer turns to kiss
    Her shadow, as it falls
    Upon the darkening walls.

As if a door in heaven should be
Opened and then closed suddenly,
    The vision came and went,
    The light shone and was spent.

On England's annals, through the long
Hereafter of her speech and song,
    That light its rays shall cast
    From portals of the past.

A Lady with a Lamp shall stand
In the great history of the land,
    A noble type of good,
    Heroic womanhood.

Nor even shall be wanting here
The palm, the lily, and the spear,
    The symbols that of yore
    Saint Filomena bore.

WALT WHITMAN

from The Wound-Dresser

2

. . . Bearing the bandages, water and sponge,
Straight and swift to my wounded I go,
Where they lie on the ground after the battle brought in,
Where their priceless blood reddens the grass the ground,

Or to the rows of the hospital tent, or under the roof'd
    hospital,
To the long rows of cots up and down each side I return,
To each and all one after another I draw near, not one do I
    miss,
An attendant follows holding a tray, he carries a refuse pail,
Soon to be fill'd with clotted rags and blood, emptied, and
    fill'd again.

I onward go, I stop,
With hinged knees and steady hand to dress wounds,
I am firm with each, the pangs are sharp yet unavoidable,
One turns to me his appealing eyes – poor boy! I never knew
    you,
Yet I think I could not refuse this moment to die for you, if that
    would save you.

   3

On, on I go, (open doors of time! open hospital doors!)
The crush'd head I dress, (poor crazed hand tear not the
    bandage away,)
The neck of the cavalry-man with the bullet through and
    through I examine,
Hard the breathing rattles, quite glazed already the eye, yet life
    struggles hard,
(Come sweet death! be persuaded O beautiful death!
In mercy come quickly.)

From the stump of the arm, the amputated hand,
I undo the clotted lint, remove the slough, wash off the matter
    and blood,
Back on his pillow the soldier bends with curv'd neck and side-
    falling head,
His eyes are closed, his face is pale, he dares not look on the
    bloody stump,
And has not yet look'd on it.

I dress a wound in the side, deep, deep,
But a day or two more, for see the frame all wasted and
    sinking,
And the yellow-blue countenance see.

I dress the perforated shoulder, the foot with the bullet-
    wound,
Cleanse the one with a gnawing and putrid gangrene, so
    sickening, so offensive,
While the attendant stands behind aside me holding the tray
    and pail.

I am faithful, I do not give out,
The fractur'd thigh, the knee, the wound in the abdomen,
These and more I dress with impassive hand, (yet deep in my
    breast a fire, a burning flame.)

        4

Thus in silence in dreams' projections,
Returning, resuming, I thread my way through the hospitals,
The hurt and wounded I pacify with soothing hand,
I sit by the restless all the dark night, some are so young,
Some suffer so much, I recall the experience sweet and sad,
(Many a soldier's loving arms about this neck have cross'd and
    rested,
Many a soldier's kiss dwells on these bearded lips.)

EDGAR WALLACE

War

    I

A tent that is pitched at the base:
    A wagon that comes from the night:

A stretcher – and on it a Case:
  A surgeon, who's holding a light.
The Infantry's bearing the brunt –
  O hark to the wind-carried cheer!
A mutter of guns at the front:
  A whimper of sobs at the rear.
And it's *War*! 'Orderly, hold the light.
  You can lay him down on the table: so.
Easily – gently! Thanks – you may go.'
  And it's *War*! but the part that is not for show.

II

A tent, with a table athwart,
  A table that's laid out for one;
A waterproof cover – and nought
  But the limp, mangled work of a gun.
A bottle that's stuck by the pole,
  A guttering dip in its neck;
The flickering light of a soul
  On the wondering eyes of The Wreck,
And it's *War*! 'Orderly, hold his hand.
  I'm not going to hurt you, so don't be afraid.
A richochet! God! what a mess it has made!'
  And it's *War*! and a very unhealthy trade.

III

The clink of a stopper and glass:
  A sigh as the chloroform drips:
A trickle of – what? on the grass,
  And bluer and bluer the lips.
The lashes have hidden the stare . . .
  A rent, and the clothes fall away . . .
A touch, and the wound is laid bare . . .
  A cut, and the face has turned grey . . .

And it's *War*! 'Orderly, take It out.
   It's hard for his child, and it's rough on his wife,
There might have been — sooner — a chance for his life.
   But it's *War*! And — Orderly, clean this knife!'

RUDYARD KIPLING

Cholera Camp

Infantry in India

We've got the cholerer in camp — it's worse than forty fights;
We're dyin' in the wilderness the same as Isrulites.
It's before us, an' be'ind us, an' we cannot get away,
An' the doctor's just reported we've ten more to-day!

> *Oh, strike your camp an' go the bugle's callin',*
> *The Rains are fallin' —*
> *The dead are bushed an' stoned to keep 'em safe below.*
> *The Band's a-doin' all she knows to cheer us;*
> *The Chaplain's gone and prayed to Gawd to 'ear us —*
> *To 'ear us —*
> *O Lord, for it's a-killin' of us so!*

Since August, when it started, it's been stickin' to our tail,
Though they've 'ad us out by marches an' they've 'ad us back
      by rail;
But it runs as fast as troop trains, and we cannot get away,
An' the sick-list to the Colonel makes ten more to-day.

There ain't no fun in women nor there ain't no bite to drink;
It's much too wet for shootin'; we can only march and think;
An' at evenin', down the *nullahs*, we can 'ear the jackals say,
'Get up, you rotten beggers, you've ten more to-day!'

'Twould make a moneky cough to see our way o' doin'
      things —
Lieutenants takin' companies an' Captains takin' wings,

An' Lances actin' Sergeants – eight file to obey –
For we've lots o' quick promotion on ten deaths a day!

Our Colonel's white an' twitterly – 'e gets no sleep nor food,
But mucks about in 'orspital where nothing does no good.
'E sends us 'eaps o' comforts, all bought from 'is pay –
But there aren't much comfort 'andy on ten deaths a day.

Our Chaplain's got a banjo, an' a skinny mule 'e rides,
An' the stuff he says an' sings us, Lord, it makes us split our
    sides!
With 'is black coat-tails a-bobbin' to *Ta-ra-ra Boom-der-ay*!
'E's the proper kind o' *padre* for ten deaths a day.

An' Father Victor 'elps 'im with our Roman Catholicks –
He knows an 'eap of Irish songs an' rummy conjurin'-tricks;
An' the two they works together when it comes to play or pray.
So we keep the ball a-rollin' on ten deaths a day.

We've got the cholerer in camp – we've got it 'ot an' sweet.
It ain't no Christmas dinner, but it's 'elped an' we must eat.
We've gone beyond the funkin', 'cause we've found it doesn't
    pay,
An' we're rockin' round the Districk on ten deaths a day!

> Then strike your camp an' go, the Rains are fallin',
>   The Bugle's callin!
> The dead are bushed an' stoned to keep 'em safe below!
> An' them that do not like it they can lump it,
> An' them that cannot stand it they can jump it;
> We've got to die somewhere – some way – some'ow –
> We might as well begin to do it now!
> Then, Number One, let down the tent-pole slow,
> Knock out the pegs an' 'old the corners – so!
> Fold in the flies, furl up the ropes, an' stow!
> Oh, strike – oh, strike your camp an' go!
>   (Gawd 'elp us!)

STAN PLATKE

Gut Catcher

Have you ever seen
A gut catcher?
Perhaps not
If you never had to use one

There is no patent on them
They're makeshift
Depending upon time
And place

I've seen ponchos used
And a pack
And a canteen cover
Or your hands

You catch the guts of your buddy
As they spill out of his body
And try to stuff them back in
But they keep sliding out

For a face blown in
For an eye blown out
For an arm blown off
For a body blown open
          . . . A gut catcher.

DANA SHUSTER

Mellow on Morphine

Mellow on morphine, he smiles and floats
above the stretcher over which I hover.

I snip an annular ligament
and his foot plops unnoticed into the pail,
superfluous as a placenta after labor has ended.
His day was just starting when his hootch disappeared,
along with the foot and at least one friend.
Absently I brush his face,
inspecting, investigating,
validating data gathered by sight and intuition,
willing physical contact to fetter soul to earth.

'You the first white woman ever touch me.'

Too late my heart dodges and weaves, evades the inevitable.
Ambushed again.
Damn, I'm in love.
Bonded forever by professional intimacies,
unwitting disclosures offered and accepted,
fulfilling a covenant sealed in our chromosomes,
an encounter ephemeral as fireflies on a hot Georgia night
in a place and time too terrible to be real.
But it will shoot flaming tracers through all my dreams
until the time my soul, too, floats unfettered.

When daylight waxes and morphine wanes,
when pain crowds his brain
and phantasms of his footless future bleach the bones of
        present
our moment together will fade as a fever dream
misty, gossamer, melting from make-believe
through might-have-been

past probably-didn't
all the way into never happen, man –
as I move on to the next stretcher
and the next fleeting lover –
silken memories mounting, treasures in my soul.

Psychological Wounds

Psychological wounds can be just as damaging as physical ones.
The most poignant poems about soldiers losing their wits and even
committing suicide were written in the First World War. The
constant daily barrage from both sides created tension and anxiety,
and many soldiers were diagnosed as suffering from 'shell-shock' —
effects of which stayed with them for the rest of their lives.

SIEGFRIED SASSOON

Suicide in the Trenches

I knew a simple soldier boy
Who grinned at life in empty joy,
Slept soundly through the lonesome dark,
And whistled early with the lark.

In winter trenches, cowed and glum,
With crumps and lice and lack of rum,
He put a bullet through his brain.
No one spoke of him again.

You smug-faced crowds with kindling eye
Who cheer when soldier lads march by,
Sneak home and pray you'll never know
The hell where youth and laughter go.

WILFRED GIBSON

In the Ambulance

Two rows of cabbages,
Two of curly-greens,
Two rows of early peas,
Two of kidney-beans.

That's what he keeps muttering,
Making such a song,
Keeping other chaps awake
The whole night long.

Both his legs are shot away,
And his head is light,
So he keeps on muttering
All the blessed night:

Two rows of cabbages,
Two of curly-greens,
Two rows of early peas,
Two of kidney-beans.

EDWARD TENNANT

The Mad Soldier

I dropp'd here three weeks ago, yes – I know,
And it's bitter cold at night, since the fight –
I could tell you if I chose – no one knows
Excep' me and four or five, what ain't alive.
I can see them all asleep, three men deep,
And they're nowhere near a fire – but our wire
Has 'em fast as fast can be. Can't you see

When the flare goes up? Ssh! boys; what's that noise?
Do you know what these rats eat? Body-meat!
After you've been down a week, an' your cheek
Gets as pale as life, and night seems as white
As the day, only the rats and their brats
Seem more hungry when the day's gone away –
An' they look as big as bulls, an' they pulls
Till you almost sort o' shout – but the drought
What you hadn't felt before makes you sore.
And at times you even think of a drink . . .
There's a leg acrost my thighs – if my eyes
Weren't too sore, I'd like to see who it be,
Wonder if I'd know the bloke if I woke? –
Woke? By damn, I'm not asleep – there's a heap
Of us wond'ring why the hell we're not well . . .
Leastways I am – since I came it's the same
With the others – they don't know what I do,
Or they wouldn't gape and grin. – It's a sin
To say that Hell is hot – 'cause it's not:
Mind you, I know very well we're in hell.
– In a twisted hump we lie – heaping high
Yes! an' higher every day. – Oh, I say,
This chap's heavy on my thighs – damn his eyes.

Prisoners

Prisoners have always had a raw deal. The Romans killed their prisoners or made them slaves. In the Middle Ages, prisoners were taken as part of the booty of war. In 1864, following the appalling conditions in which Union prisoners were found to have been kept in the Andersonville Prison Camp, the Geneva Convention was established, laying down international rules for the confinement of prisoners. Only some countries observe them. Of the five million Russian prisoners taken by the Germans in the Second World War, four million died of disease or starvation. The Japanese, who believe that surrender is contemptible, during the same war worked their prisoners to death. The brutal incident described by the American poet James Dickey was characteristic.

WILLIAM MORRIS

In Prison

Wearily, drearily,
Half the day long,
Flap the great banners
High over the stone;
Strangely and eerily
Sounds the wind's song,
Bending the banner-poles.

While, all alone,
Watching the loophole's spark,
Lie I, with life all dark,
Feet tethered, hands fetter'd
Fast to the stone,
The grim walls square letter'd
With prison'd men's groan.

Still strain the banner-poles
Through the wind's song,
Westward the banner rolls
Over my wrong.

JOHN JARMAIN

Prisoners of War

Like shabby ghosts down dried-up river beds
The tired procession slowly leaves the field;
Dazed and abandoned, just a count of heads,
They file away, these who have done their last,
To that grey safety where the days are sealed,
Where no word enters, and the urgent past
Is relieved day by day against the clock
Whose hours are meaningless, whose measured rate
Brings nearer nothing, only serves to mock.

It is ended now. There's no more need to choose,
To fend and think and act: no need to hate.
Now all their will is worthless, none will lose
And none will suffer though their courage fail.
The tension in the brain is loosened now,
Its taut decisions slack: no more alone
– How I and each of us has been alone
Like lone trees which the lightnings all assail –
They are herded now and have no more to give.
Even fear is past. And death, so long so near,
Has suddenly receded to its station
In the misty end of life. For these will live,
They are quit of killing and sudden mutilation;
They no longer cower at the sound of a shell in the air,
They are safe. And in the glimmer at time's end
They will return – old, worn maybe, but sure –
And gather their bits of broken lives to mend.

RUDYARD KIPLING

Half-Ballad of Waterval

Non-commissioned Officers in Charge of Prisoners

When by the labour of my 'ands
  I've 'elped to pack a transport tight
With prisoners for foreign lands,
  I ain't transported with delight.
  I know it's only just an' right,
    But yet it somehow sickens me,
For I 'ave learned at Waterval
    The meanin' of captivity.

Be'ind the pegged barb-wire strands,
  Beneath the tall electric light,
We used to walk in bare-'ead bands,
  Explainin' 'ow we lost our fight;
  An' that is what they'll do to-night
    Upon the steamer out at sea,
If I 'ave learned at Waterval
    The meanin' of captivity.

They'll never know the shame that brands –
  Black shame no livin' down makes white –
The mockin' from the sentry-stands,
  The women's laugh, the gaoler's spite.
  We are too bloomin'-much polite,
    But that is 'ow I'd 'ave us be . . .
Since I 'ave learned at Waterval
    The meanin' of captivity.

They'll get those draggin' days all right,
  Spent as a foreigner commands,
An' 'orrors of the locked-up night,
  With 'Ell's own thinkin' on their 'ands.

I'd give the gold o' twenty Rands
   (If it was mine) to set 'em free
For I 'ave learned at Waterval
   The meanin' of captivity!

JAMES DICKEY

The Performance

The last time I saw Donald Armstrong
He was staggering oddly off into the sun,
Going down, of the Philippine Islands.
I let my shovel fall, and put that hand
Above my eyes, and moved some way to one side
That his body might pass through the sun,

And I saw how well he was not
Standing there on his hands,
On his spindle-shanked forearms balanced,
Unbalanced, with his big feet looming and waving
In the great, untrustworthy air
He flew in each night, when it darkened.

Dust fanned in scraped puffs from the earth
Between his arms, and blood turned his face inside out,
To demonstrate its suppleness
Of veins, as he perfected his role.
Next day, he toppled his head off
On an island beach to the south,

And the enemy's two-handed sword
Did not fall from anyone's hands
At that miraculous sight,
As the head rolled over upon
Its wide-eyed face, and fell
Into the inadequate grave

He had dug for himself, under pressure.
Yet I put my flat hand to my eyebrows
Months later, to see him again
In the sun, when I learned how he died,
And imagined him, there,
Come, judged, before his small captors,

Doing all his lean tricks to amaze them –
The back somersault, the kip-up –
And at last, the stand on his hands,
Perfect, with his feet together,
His head down, evenly breathing,
As the sun poured up from the sea

And the headsman broke down
In a blaze of tears, in that light
Of the thin, long human frame
Upside down in its own strange joy,
And, if some other one had not told him,
Would have cut off the feet

Instead of the head,
And if Armstrong had not presently risen
In kingly, round-shouldered attendance,
And then knelt down himself
Beside his hacked, glittering grave, having done
All things in this life that he could.

Civilian Victims

Goya devoted a suite of etchings to *The Disasters of War* to show
how quite innocent people are sucked into its violence and
brutality. Some are casual victims, like the wretched woman who is
raped in Bosnia, while others are sacrificed in the name of reprisal
or revenge.

In 1942, in retaliation for the murder of Heydrich 'the
Hangman', Deputy Head of the SS, the German Army to its
everlasting shame levelled Lidice, a mining village in
Czechoslovakia, shot 180 men and women and sent another 150 to
a concentration camp. The slaughter of entire village populations
has become all too typical of the civil wars that have broken out
around the world in the 1990s.

ERNST WALDINGER

Lidice

Lidice sounds like marriage bells in June,
A word that tinkles like a polka tune.

In the evening, while bright kerchiefs whirl,
The first kiss burns upon your mouth, young girl.

Dawn and sunset made one quiet flame
Of golden peace. And then the soldiers came;

Three years of slavery; yet all the while
The gallant head and the unbeaten smile,

And though the cock crowed thrice for treachery,
There were no traitors found in Lidice.

All the men were shot; as for the town
It is a town of ashes, it is gone.

All the women were driven away to places
Where they will never see their children's faces.

Lidice, ruins beneath the moon,
No longer tinkles like a polka tune;

It thunders with our planes across the sky.
The trumpet of its name will never die.

Translated from the German

DYLAN THOMAS

A Refusal to Mourn the Death, by Fire, of a Child in London

Never until the mankind making
Bird beast and flower
Fathering and all humbling darkness
Tells with silence the last light breaking
And the still hour
Is come of the sea tumbling in harness

And I must enter again the round
Zion of the water bead
And the synagogue of the ear of corn
Shall I let pray the shadow of a sound
Or sow my salt seed
In the last valley of sackcloth to mourn
The majesty and burning of the child's death.
I shall not murder
The mankind of her going with a grave truth
Nor blaspheme down the stations of the breath
With any further
Elegy of innocence and youth.

Deep with the first dead lies London's daughter,
Robed in the long friends,
The grains beyond age, the dark veins of her mother,
Secret by the unmourning water
Of the riding Thames.
After the first death, there is no other.

BORIS SLUTSKY

How Did They Kill My Grandmother?

How did they kill my grandmother?
I'll tell you how they killed her.
One morning a tank rolled up to
a building where
the hundred and fifty Jews of our town who,
weightless
             from a year's starvation,
and white
             with the knowledge of death,
were gathered holding their bundles.
And the German polizei were
herding the old people briskly;
and their tin mugs clanked as
the young men led them away
                              far away.

But my small grandmother
my seventy-year-old grandmother
began to curse and
scream at the Germans;
shouting that I was a soldier.
She yelled at them: My grandson
is off at the front fighting!

Don't you dare
touch me!
Listen, you
            can hear our guns!

Even as she went off, my grandmother
cried abuse,
            starting all over again
with her curses.
From every window then
Ivanovnas and Andreyevnas
Sidorovnas and Petrovnas
sobbed: You tell them, Polina
Matveyevna, keep it up!
They all yelled together:
            'What can we do against
this enemy, the Hun?'
Which was why the Germans chose
to kill her inside the town.

A bullet struck her hair
and kicked her grey plait down.
My grandmother fell to the ground.
That is how she died there.

    Translated from the Russian by Elaine Feinstein

HO THIEN

Green Beret

He was twelve years old,
and I do not know his name.
The mercenaries took him and his father,
whose name I do not know,
one morning upon the High Plateau.

Green Beret looked down on the frail boy
with the eyes of a hurt animal and thought,
a good fright will make him talk.
He commanded, and the father was taken away
behind the forest's green wall.
'Right kid tell us where they are,
tell us where or your father – dead.'
With eyes now bright and filled with terror
the slight boy said nothing.
'You've got one minute kid', said Green Beret,
'tell us where or we kill father'
and thrust his wrist-watch against a face all eyes,
the second-hand turning, jerking on its way.
'OK boy ten seconds to tell us where they are.'
In the last instant the silver hand shattered the
sky and the forest of trees.
'Kill the old guy' roared Green Beret
and shots hammered out
behind the forest's green wall
and sky and trees and soldiers stood
in silence, and the boy cried out.
Green Beret stood
in silence, as the boy crouched down
and shook with tears,
as children do when their father dies.

'Christ,' said one mercenary to Green Beret,
'he didn't know a damn thing
we killed the old guy for nothing.'
So they all went away,
Green Beret and his mercenaries.

And the boy knew everything.
He knew everything about them, the caves,
the trails, the hidden places and the names,
and in the moment that he cried out,
in that same instant,

protected by frail tears
far stronger than any wall of steel,
they passed everywhere
like tigers
across the High Plateau.

Translated from the Vietnamese

GRACE PALEY

Two Villages

In Duc Ninh a village of 1,654 households
Over 100 tons of rice and cassava were burned
18,138 cubic meters of dike were destroyed
There were 1077 air attacks
There is a bomb crater that measures 150 feet across
It is 50 feet deep

Mr Tat said: The land is more exhausted than the people
                I mean to say that the poor earth
                is tossed about
                thrown into the air again and again
                it knows no rest

                whereas the people have dug tunnels
                and trenches   they are able in this way
                to lead normal family lives

    In Trung Trach
a village of 850 households
a chart is hung in the House of Tradition

rockets	522
attacks	1201
big bombs	6998
napalm	1383

        time bombs   267
        shells   12291
        pellet bombs   2213

Mr Tuong of the Fatherland Front
has a little book
in it he keeps the facts
carefully added

YEHUDA AMICHAI

from Time

What is it? An airplane at dawn. No,
They're digging a sewer in the sky. No, it's
A deep rift along the wonderful nightingale. No,
It's the raucous screwing of a he-bulldozer and a she-
      bulldozer.
No, it's a peacock shrieking: this beautiful bird
Shrieks so bitterly. But it's a quiet hymn.
No, it's the consolation of mourners humming like a teapot
On a low flame. And now an explosion!
No, it was a nightingale, heavy and hollow.
It seems like night. No,
It's a lark heralding the rising sun.
It's the dawn of nations.
No, it's my friend the quiet artillery man whistling
And feeding home cannons with shells at dawn.

What is it? It's the misunderstanding of love:
Don't be scared, child, the dog loves you,
He just wants to play with you. Just
A misunderstanding of love, like our tears
At the ancient window overlooking the valley.

    Translated from the Hebrew by Benjamin and Barbara Harshav

HOLGER TESCHKE

The Minutes of Hasiba

from an interview on 6 November 1992

They came at night with their flashlights
Through PARTISANS' HALL
They took me with them and we drove
To a bridge over the Drina
On the bridge stood
Ten older women Tied up
And fifteen soldiers They yelled
Here comes one of yours See how we love her
Then they did everything with me All fifteen of them
Afterwards they smoked and put out their cigarettes
In my hair Then one soldier took
His knife and slit a farmer's throat
Not quite through So that his head stayed on his shoulders
It didn't bother me anymore I had
Seen so much already I didn't care
Then he tore his head off entirely and they played
Soccer with it and laughed and laughed
I knew the farmers They were
Neighbours colleagues relatives
Just a few weeks ago I knew most
Of the soldiers too They were
Neighbours colleagues relatives They were
Men like you

   Translated from the German by Margitt Lehbert

The Holocaust

I have included this section because the elimination of the Jewish race became one of Nazi Germany's war aims in the Second World War. The systematic and ruthless slaugher of millions of Jews must be the greatest crime against humanity the world has ever seen.

W. H. AUDEN

from Ten Songs

Say this city has ten million souls,
Some are living in mansions, some are living in holes:
Yet there's no place for us, my dear, yet there's no place for us.

Once we had a country and we thought it fair,
Look in the atlas and you'll find it there:
We cannot go there now, my dear, we cannot go there now.

In the village churchyard there grows an old yew,
Every spring it blossoms anew:
Old passports can't do that, my dear, old passports can't do
    that.

The consul banged the table and said;
'If you've got no passport you're officially dead';
But we are still alive, my dear, but we are still alive.

Went to a committee; they offered me a chair;
Asked me politely to return next year:
But where shall we go today, my dear, but where shall we go
    today?

Came to a public meeting; the speaker got up and said:
'If we let them in, they will steal our daily bread';

He was talking of you and me, my dear, he was talking of you
    and me.

Thought I heard the thunder rumbling in the sky;
It was Hitler over Europe, saying: 'They must die';
O we were in his mind, my dear, O we were in his mind.

Saw a poodle in a jacket fastened with a pin,
Saw a door opened and a cat let in:
But they weren't German Jews, my dear, but they weren't
    German Jews.

Went down the harbour and stood upon the quay,
Saw the fish swimming as if they were free:
Only ten feet away, my dear, only ten feet away.

Walked through a wood, saw the birds in the trees;
They had no politicians and sang at their ease:
They weren't the human race, my dear, they weren't the
    human race.

Dreamed I saw a building with a thousand floors,
A thousand windows and a thousand doors;
Not one of them was ours, my dear, not one of them was ours.

Stood on a great plain in the falling snow;
Ten thousand soldiers marched to and fro:
Looking for you and me, my dear, looking for you and me.

RANDALL JARRELL

A Camp in the Prussian Forest

I walk beside the prisoners to the road.
Load on puffed load,
Their corpses, stacked like sodden wood,
Lie barred or galled with blood

By the charred warehouse. No one comes today
In the old way
To knock the fillings from their teeth;
The dark, coned, common wreath

Is planted for their grave — a kind of grief.
The living leaf
Clings to the planted profitable
Pine if it is able;

The boughs sigh, mile on green, calm, breathing mile,
From this dead file
The planners ruled for them . . . One year
They sent a million here:

Here men were drunk like water, burnt like wood.
The fat of good
And evil, the breast's star of hope
Were rendered into soap.

I paint the star I sawed from yellow pine —
And plant the sign
In soil that does not yet refuse
Its usual Jews

Their first asylum. But the white, dwarfed star —
This dead white star —
Hides nothing, pays for nothing; smoke
Fouls it, a yellow joke,

The needles of the wreath are chalked with ash,
A filmy trash
Litters the black woods with the death
Of men; and one last breath

Curls from the monstrous chimney . . . I laugh aloud
Again and again;
The star laughs from its rotting shroud
Of flesh. O star of men!

PRIMO LEVI

Shemà

You who live secure
In your warm houses,
Who return at evening to find
Hot food and friendly faces:

> Consider whether this is a man,
> Who labors in the mud
> Who knows no peace
> Who fights for a crust of bread
> Who dies at a yes or a no.
> Consider whether this is a woman,
> Without hair or name
> With no more strength to remember
> Eyes empty and womb cold
> As a frog in winter.

Consider that this has been:
I commend these words to you.
Engrave them on your hearts
When you are in your house, when you walk on your way,
When you go to bed, when you rise.
Repeat them to your children.
Or may your house crumble,
Disease render you powerless,
Your offspring avert their faces from you.

10 January, 1946
Translated from the Italian by Ruth Feldman and Brian Stone

GEOFFREY HILL

September Song

born 19.6.32. – deported 24.9.42

Undesirable you may have been, untouchable
you were not. Not forgotten
or passed over at the proper time.

As estimated, you died. Things marched,
sufficient, to that end.
Just so much Zyklon and leather, patented
terror, so many routine cries.

(I have made
an elegy for myself it
is true)

September fattens on vines. Roses
flake from the wall. The smoke
of harmless fires drifts to my eyes.

This is plenty. This is more than enough.

The Distant View

These poems reflect either the feelings of non-combatants, vicariously thrilled or horrified as they follow events through news reports, or the stylized and possibly distorted impressions given to later generations by the film camera.

S. T. COLERIDGE

from Fears in Solitude

Thankless too for peace,

(Peace long preserved by fleets and perilous seas)
Secure from actual warfare, we have loved
To swell the war-whoop, passionate for war!
Alas! for ages ignorant of all
Its ghastlier workings (famine or blue plague,
Battle, or siege, or flight through wintry-snows),
We, this whole people, have been clamorous
For war and bloodshed: animating sports,
The which we pay for as a thing to talk of,
Spectators and not combatants! No guess
Anticipative of a wrong unfelt,
No speculation or contingency,
However dim and vague, too vague and dim
To yield a justifying cause; and forth,
(Stuffed out with big preamble, holy names,
And adjurations of the God in heaven,)
We sent our mandates for the certain death
Of thousands and ten thousands! Boys and girls,
And women, that would groan to see a child
Pull off an insect's leg, all read of war,
The best amusement for our morning-meal!

The poor wretch, who has learnt his only prayers
From curses, who knows scarcely words enough
To ask a blessing from his Heavenly Father.
Becomes a fluent phraseman, absolute
And technical in victories and defeats,
And all our dainty terms for fratricide;
Terms which we trundle smoothly o'er our tongues
Like mere abstractions, empty sounds to which
We join no feeling and attach no form!
As if the soldier died without a wound;
As if the fibres of this godlike frame
Were gored without a pang; as if the wretch,
Who fell in battle, doing bloody deeds,
Passed off to heaven, translated and not killed;
As though he had no wife to pine for him,
No God to judge him! Therefore, evil days
Are coming on us. O my countrymen!
And what if all-avenging Providence,
Strong and retributive, should make us know
The meaning of our words, force us to feel
The desolation and the agony
Of our fierce doings!

BERNARD SPENCER

A Thousand Killed

I read of a thousand killed.
And am glad because the scrounging imperial paw
Was there so bitten:
As a man at elections is thrilled
When the results pour in, and the North goes with him
And the West breaks in the thaw.

(That fighting was a long way off.)

Forgetting therefore an election
Being fought with votes and lies and catch-cries
And orator's frowns and flowers and posters' noise,
Is paid for with cheques and toys:
Wars the most glorious
Victory-winged and steeple-uproarious
. . . With the lives, burned-off,
Of young men and boys.

ADRIAN MITCHELL

To Whom It May Concern

I was run over by the truth one day.
Ever since the accident I've walked this way
    So stick my legs in plaster
    Tell me lies about Vietnam.

Heard the alarm clock screaming with pain,
Couldn't find myself so I went back to sleep again
    So fill my ears with silver
    Stick my legs in plaster
    Tell me lies about Vietnam.

Every time I shut my eyes all I see is flames.
Made a marble phone book and I carved all the names
    So coat my eyes with butter
    Fill my ears with silver
    Stick my legs in plaster
    Tell me lies about Vietnam.

I smell something burning, hope it's just my brains.
They're only dropping peppermints and daisy-chains
    So stuff my nose with garlic
    Coat my eyes with butter
    Fill my ears with silver

Stick my legs in plaster
Tell me lies about Vietnam.

Where were you at the time of the crime?
Down by the Cenotaph drinking slime
So chain my tongue with whisky
Stuff my nose with garlic
Coat my eyes with butter
Fill my ears with silver
Stick my legs in plaster
Tell me lies about Vietnam.

You put your bombers in, you put your conscience out,
You take the human being and you twist it all about
So scrub my skin with women
Chain my tongue with whisky
Stuff my nose with garlic
Coat my eyes with butter
Fill my ears with silver
Stick my legs in plaster
Tell me lies about Vietnam.

JOSEPH BRODSKY

Bosnia Tune

As you sip your brand of scotch,
crush a roach or scratch your crotch,
as your hand adjusts your tie,
people die.

In the towns with funny names,
hit by bullets, caught in flames,
by and large, not knowing why,
people die.

In small places you don't know
of, yet big for having no
chance to scream or say goodbye,
people die.

People die as you elect
new apostles of neglect,
self-restraint, etc. – whereby
people die.

Too far off to practise love
for thy neighbour/brother Slav,
where our cherubs dread to fly,
people die.

As you watch the athletes score,
check your latest statement, or
kissing your child a lullaby,
people die.

Time, whose sharp, blood-thirsty quill
parts the killed from those who kill,
will pronounce the latter tribe
as your type.

IAN HAMILTON

The Newscast

The Vietnam war drags on
In one corner of our living-room.
The conversation turns
To take it in.
Our smoking heads
Drift back to us
From the grey fires of South-east Asia.

GEOFFREY HILL

from The Mystery of the Charity of Charles Péguy

Violent contrariety of men and days; calm
juddery bombardment of a silent film
showing such things: its canvas slashed with rain
and St Elmo's fire. Victory of the machine!

The brisk celluloid clatters through the gate;
the cortège of the century dances in the street;
and over and over the jolly cartoon
armies of France go reeling towards Verdun.

ROBERT GARIOCH

Phooie!

With my girl,
watching an old movie,
I says,
'That's all wrong,'
I says.
'Those shells on the picture,'
I says,
'go Phooie-bang,'
I says,
'whereas, at the receiving-end,'
I says,
'they go Bang-phooie,'
I says,
'if you're still there to hear them coming,'
I says,
'after they've arrived, if you know what I mean,'
I says.

'Phooie!'
she says,
'I don't want to be told all that,
I just want to enjoy the movie,'
she says.

Eye-Witness

These non-combatants get a bit closer to the action.

A. H. CLOUGH

from Amours de Voyage, Canto II

Yes, we are fighting at last, it appears. This morning, as usual,
Murray, as usual, in hand, I enter the Caffè Nuovo;
Seating myself with a sense as it were of a change in the
    weather,
Not understanding, however, but thinking mostly of Murray,
And, for to-day is their day, of the Campidoglio Marbles;
Caffè-latte! I call to the waiter, – and *Non c' è latte*,
This is the answer he makes me, and this is the sign of a battle.
So I sit; and truly they seem to think anyone else more
Worthy than me of attention. I wait for my milkless *nero*,
Free to observe undistracted all sorts and sizes of persons,
Blending civilian and soldier in strangest costume, coming in,
    and
Gulping in hottest haste, still standing, their coffee, – with-
    drawing
Eagerly, jangling a sword on the steps, or jogging a musket
Slung to the shoulder behind. They are fewer, moreover, than
    usual,
Much and silenter far; and so I begin to imagine
Something is really afloat. Ere I leave, the Caffè is empty,
Empty too the streets, in all its length the Corso
Empty, and empty I see to my right and left the Condotti.
    Twelve o'clock, on the Pincian Hill, with lots of English,
Germans, Americans, French, – the Frenchmen, too, are
    protected, –

So we stand in the sun, but afraid of a probable shower;
So we stand and stare, and see, to the left of St Peter's,
Smoke, from the cannon, white, – but that is at intervals
      only, –
Black, from a burning house, we suppose, by the Cavalleggieri;
And we believe we discern some lines of men descending
Down through the vineyard-slopes, and catch a bayonet
      gleaming.
Every ten minutes, however, – in this there is no
      misconception, –
Comes a great white puff from behind Michel Angelo's dome,
      and
After a space the report of a real big gun, – not the
      Frenchman's –
That must be doing some work. And so we watch and
      conjecture.
   Shortly, an Englishman comes, who says he has been to St
      Peter's,
Seen the Piazza and troops, but that is all he can tell us;
So we watch and sit, and, indeed, it begins to be tiresome. –
All this smoke is outside; when it has come to the inside,
It will be time, perhaps, to descend and retreat to our houses.
   Half-past one, or two. The report of small arms frequent,
Sharp and savage indeed; that cannot all be for nothing:
So we watch and wonder; but guessing is tiresome, very.
Weary of wondering, watching, and guessing, and gossiping
      idly,
Down I go, and pass through the quiet streets with the knots of
National Guards patrolling, and flags hanging out at the
      windows,
English, American, Danish, – and, after offering to help an
Irish family moving *en masse* to the Maison Serny,
After endeavouring idly to minister balm to the trembling
Quinquagenarian fears of two lone British spinsters,
Go to make sure of my dinner before the enemy enter.
But by this there are signs of stragglers returning; and voices
Talk, though you don't believe it, of guns and prisoners taken;

And on the walls you read the first bulletin of the morning. –
This is all that I saw, and all I know of the battle.

JAMES FENTON

Dead Soldiers

When His Excellency Prince Norodom Chantaraingsey
Invited me to lunch on the battlefield
I was glad of my white suit for the first time that day.
They lived well, the mad Norodoms, they had style.
The brandy and the soda arrived in crates.
Bricks of ice, tied around with raffia,
Dripped from the orderlies' handlebars.

And I remember the dazzling tablecloth
As the APCs fanned out along the road,
The dishes piled high with frogs' legs,
Pregnant turtles, their eggs boiled in the carapace,
Marsh irises in fish sauce
And inflorescence of a banana salad.

On every bottle, Napoleon Bonaparte
Pleaded for the authenticity of the spirit.
They called the empties Dead Soldiers
And rejoiced to see them pile up at our feet.

Each diner was attended by one of the other ranks
Whirling a table-napkin to keep off the flies.
It was like eating between rows of morris dancers –
Only they didn't kick.

In a diary, I refer to Pol Pot's brother as the Jockey Cap.
A few weeks later, I find him 'in good form
And very skeptical about Chantaraingsey.'
'But one eats well there,' I remark.
'So one should,' says the Jockey Cap:

'The tiger always eats well,
It eats the raw flesh of the deer,
And Chantaraingsey was born in the year of the tiger.
So, did they show you the things they do
With the young refugee girls?'

And he tells me how he will one day give me the gen.
He will tell me how the prince financed the casino
And how the casino brought Lon Nol to power.
He will tell me this.
He will tell me all these things.
All I must do is drink and listen.

In those days, I thought that when the game was up
The prince would be far, far away –
In a limestone faubourg, on the promenade at Nice,
Reduced in circumstances but well enough provided for.
In Paris, he would hardly require his private army.
The Jockey Cap might suffice for café warfare,
And matchboxes for APCs.

But we were always wrong in these predictions.
It was a family war. Whatever happened,
The principals were obliged to attend its issue.
A few were cajoled into leaving, a few were expelled,
And there were villains enough, but none of them
Slipped away with the swag.

For the prince was fighting Sihanouk, his nephew,
And the Jockey Cap was ranged against his brother
Of whom I remember nothing more
Than an obscure reputation for virtue.
I have been told that the prince is still fighting
Somewhere in the Cardamoms or the Elephant Mountains.
But I doubt that the Jockey Cap would have survived his good
        connections.
I think the lunches would have done for him –
Either the lunches or the dead soldiers.

Whims and Fates of the Conquerors

The greater the conqueror, the wilder the whim. Alexander ordered that the city of Thebes be burnt to the ground (335 BC), but that the house of the poet, Pindar, who had died 150 years earlier, should be saved. In the extract from Nathaniel Lee's play of 1677, Alexander seizes a spear and kills an old friend who has dared to question his greatness.

If Tamburlaine's ambition was to 'ride in triumph through Persepolis', he more than succeeded. From 1350 to 1405, he led his horsemen from Tartary to overrun Persia and much of the Middle East, practising the most outlandish cruelties on the way. His calling-card was a pyramid of skulls.

The passage from Juvenal's *Satires*, translated by William Gifford in 1802, shows how Hannibal, whom some considered to be the greatest general in the whole history of warfare, failed to achieve his ambition to conquer Rome. In 'The Vanity of Human Wishes', Dr Johnson takes the same passage and replaces Hannibal with Charles XII of Sweden. Charles had invaded Russia, then ruled by Peter the Great, and after initial successes was defeated at the Battle of Poltava in 1709.

ANNA AKHMATOVA

Alexander at Thebes

The young king must have been terrible to behold
commanding his captain: 'You will destroy Thebes,'
while the city loomed in the old soldier's sight,
storied and proud, as he remembered it.

Put it all to the torch! And the king named one by one
the towers, the gates, the temples – this marvel of the world;

then brightened, as the thought leaped into words:
'Only be sure the Poet's House is spared.'

Translated from the Russian by Stanley Kunitz and Max Hayward

NATHANIEL LEE

from The Rival Queens; or, Alexander the Great (Act 4, Scene ii)

Lysimachus: Nay, *Clytus*, you that cou'd advise –
Alexander: Forbear;
Let him persist, be positive, and proud,
Sullen and dazzled, 'mongst the nobler Souls.
Like an infernal Spirit that had stole
From Hell, and mingled with the laughing Gods.
Clytus: When Gods grow hot, where's the Difference
'Twixt them and Devils? – Fill me *Greek* Wine, yet fuller,
For I want Spirits.
Alexander: Ha! let me hear a Song.
Clytus: Musick for Boys – *Clytus* would hear the Groans
Of dying Persons, and the Horses Neighings;
Or if I must be tortur'd with shrill Voices,
Give me the Cries of Matrons in sack'd Towns.
Hephestion: *Lysimachus*, the King looks sad, let us awake
    him:
Health to the son of *Jupiter Ammon*;
Ev'ry Man take his Goblet in his Hand,
Kneel all, and kiss the Earth with Adoration.
Alexander: Sound, sound, that all the Universe may hear,
That I could Speak like *Jove*, to tell abroad
The Kindness of my People – Rise, O rise,
My Hands, my Arms, my Heart is ever yours.
Clytus: I did not kiss the Earth, nor must your Hand,
I am unworthy, Sir.

Alexander: I know thou art.
Thou enviest my great Honour – Sir, my Friends,
Nay, I must have room – Now let us talk
Of War, for what more fits a Soldier's Mouth?
And speak, speak freely, or ye do not love me,
Who, think you, was the bravest General
That ever led an Army to the Field?
   Hephestion: I think the Sun Himself ne'er Saw a Chief
So truly great, so fortunately brave,
As *Alexander*; not the fam'd *Alcides*,
Nor fierce *Achilles*, who did twice destroy,
With their all-conqu'ring Arms, the famous *Troy*.
   Lysimachus: Such was not *Cyrus*.
   Alexander: O you flatter me.
   Clytus: They do inded, and yet ye love 'em for it,
But hate old *Clytus* for his hardy Virtue.
Come, shall I speak a Man more brave than you,
A better General, and more expert Soldier?
   Alexander: I should be glad to learn; instruct me, Sir.
   Clytus: Your Father *Philip* – I have seen him march,
And fought beneath his dreadful Banner, where
The stoutest at the Table wou'd ha' trembled:
Nay, frown not, Sir; you cannot look me dead.
When *Greeks* join'd *Greeks*, then was the Tug of War,
The labour'd Battel sweat, and Conquest bled.
Why should I fear to speak a Truth more noble
Then e'er your Father *Jupiter Ammon* told you?
Philip fought Men, but *Alexander* Women.
   Alexander: Spite! by the Gods, proud Spite! and burning
      Envy!
Is then my Glory come to this at last.
To vanquish Women? Nay, he said the stoutest here
Wou'd tremble at the Dangers he has seen.
In all the Sickness and Wounds I bore,
When from my Reins the Javelin Head was cut,
Lysimachus, *Hephestion*, speak, *Perdiccas*,

Did I e'er tremble? O the cursed Lyar!
Did I once shake or groan? or bear my self
Beneath my Majesty, my dauntless Courage?
   Hephestion: Wine has transported him.
   Alexander: No, 'tis plain mere Malice:
I was a Woman too at *Oxydrace*,
When planting at the Walls a scaling Ladder,
I mounted, spite of Showers of Stones, Bars, Arrows,
And all the Lumber which they thunder'd down,
When you beneath cried out, and spread your Arms,
That I should leap among you, did I so?
   Lysimachus: Turn the Discourse, my Lord, the old Man
     rav'd.
   Alexander: Was I a Woman, when, like *Mercury*,
I left the Walls to fly amongst my Foes,
And, like a baited Lion, dy'd my self
All over with the Blood of these bold Hunters?
Till spent with Toil, I battel'd on my knees,
Pluck'd forth the Darts that made my Shield a Forest,
And hurl'd 'm back with most unconquer'd Fury.
   Clytus: 'Twas all Bravado, for before you leap'd,
You saw that I had burst the Gates asunder.
   Alexander: Did I then turn me, like a Coward, round,
To seek for Succour? Age cannot be so base;
That thou wert young again, I would put off
My Majesty, to be more terrible,
That, like an Eagle, I might strike this Hare
Trembling to Earth; shake thee to Dust, and tear
Thy Heart for this bold Lye, thou feeble Dotard.
   Clytus: What, do you pelt me like a Boy with Apples?
Kill me, and bury the Disgrace I feel,
I know the reason that you use me so,
Because I sav'd your Life at *Granicus*;
And when your Back was turn'd, oppos'd my Breast
To bold *Rhesaces*' Sword; you hate me for't,
You do, proud Prince.

Alexander: Away, your Breath's too hot.

Clytus: You hate the Benefactor, tho' you took
The Gift, your Life, from this dishonour'd *Clytus*;
Which is the blackest, worst Ingratitude.

Alexander: Go, leave the Banquet: Thus far I forgive thee.

Clytus: Forgive yourself for all your Blasphemies,
The Riots of a most debauch'd and blotted Life;
Philotas' Murder –

Alexander: Ha! what said the Traitor?

Lysimachus: *Eumenes*, let us force him hence.

Clytus: Away.

Hephestion: You shall not tarry: Drag him to the Door.

Clytus: No, let him send me, if I must be gone
To *Philip*, *Attalus*, *Calisthenes*,
To great *Parmenio*, to his slaughter'd Sons;
Parmenio, who did many brave Exploits
Without the King – the King without him nothing.

Alexander: Give me a Javelin.

Hephestion: Hold, Sir.

Alexander: Off, Sirrah, lest
At once I strike it thro' his Heart and thine.

Lysimachus: O sacred Sir, have but a Moment's
Patience.

Alexander: Preach Patience to another Lion – What,
Hold my Arms? I shall be murder'd here,
Like poor *Darius*, by my own barb'rous Subjects.
Perdiccas, sound my Trumpets to the Camp,
Call my Soldiers to the Court; nay haste,
For there is Treason plotting 'gainst my Life;
And I shall perish e'er they come to rescue.

Lysimachus and *Hephestion*: Let us all die, e'er think so
damn'd a Deed.

Alexander: Where is the Traitor?

Clytus: Sure there's none about you;
But here stands honest *Clytus*, whom the King
Invited to his Banquet.

Alexander: Be gone and sup with *Philip*, (*Strikes him
    through*.)
Parmenio, Attalus, Calisthenes;
And let bold Subjects learn by thy sad Fate,
To tempt the Patience of a Man much above 'em.
    Clytus: The Rage of Wine is drown'd in gushing Blood:
O *Alexander*, I have been to blame;
Hate me not after Death, for I repent,
That so I urg'd your noblest, sweetest Nature.
    Alexander: What's this I hear? say on, my dying Soldier.
    Clytus: I shou'd ha' kill'd my self, had I but liv'd
To be once sober – Now I fall with Honour,
My own Hand wou'd ha' brought foul Death. O Pardon.
    (*Dies.*)
    Alexander: Then I am lost; what has my Vengeance done?
Who is it thou hast slain? *Clytus*; what was he?
The faithfullest Subject, worthiest Counsellor,
Who for saving thy Life, when
Thou foughtst bare-headed at the River *Granike*,
Has now a noble Recompence for speaking rashly;
For a Forgetfulness which Wine did work.

CHRISTOPHER MARLOWE

from Tamburlaine the Great, Part I (Act 2, Scene v)

Menaphon:
Your majesty shall shortly have your wish,
And ride in triumph through Persepolis.

Tamburlaine:
And ride in triumph through Persepolis?
Is it not brave to be a king, Techelles?
Usumcasane and Theridamas,

Is it not passing brave to be a king,
And ride in triumph through Persepolis?

CHRISTOPHER MARLOWE

from Tamburlaine the Great, Part II
(Act 1, Scene iii)

Turburlaine:
Bastardly boy, sprung from some coward's loins,
And not the issue of great Tamburlaine,
Of all the provinces I have subdued
Thou shalt not have a foot, unless thou bear
A mind courageous and invincible:
For he shall wear the crown of Persia,
Whose head hath deepest scars, whose breast most wounds,
Which being wroth, sends lightning from his eyes,
And in the furrows of his frowning brows,
Harbours revenge, war, death and cruelty:
For in a field whose superficies
Is covered with a liquid purple veil,
And sprinkled with the brains of slaughtered men,
My royal chair of state shall be advanced:
And he that means to place himself therein
Must armed wade up to his chin in blood.

ANONYMOUS

from The Poem of the Cid

The Franks come down the hill with a random course.
Just where the mountain ended, at the valley's source,
The Cid gave orders to his men to charge with all their force:

That order they perform'd with all their soul and heart,
With pennons and with lances so well they play'd their part,
Some are pierced and wounded, others beaten down,
The Count is taken captive, his host is overthrown,
His sword that was worth a thousand marks, the Cid has made
        his own,
The noble sword Colada that through the world was known.
He has adorn'd that mighty beard with honour and renown,
His beard, that as a banish'd man was left all overgrown –
The Count is taken with the Cid in close and steady ward
A surety for his creditors for them to watch and guard –
The Cid came from his tent, and at the door he stood,
His knights are crowding round him, all in a merry mood,
Right merry was the Cid, the spoil was rich and good. –
    For the service of the Cid a banquet was prepared,
Count Ramon would not eat of it, or pay the least regard:
They served the meat before him. He laugh'd at them again –
'I would not eat a morsel for all the wealth of Spain;
I would rather lose my life, and perish here outright,
Since such a set of ragged knaves have conquer'd me in fight.'
The good Cid Ruy Diaz, these were the words he said:
'Eat and drink, Sir Count, of the wine and of the bread,
If you do as I advise you shortly may be free,
Else you can never hope a Christian land to see –
Be merry, Don Rodrigo – feast and make good cheer.'
'I shall not eat a morsel; I mean to perish here.' –
They shared and pack'd the booty; till the third day was past,
The Count continued still to famish and to fast.
They could not make him eat a morsel nor a crumb:
At length the worthy Cid said, 'Come, Sir Ramon, come!
If ever you design to return to Christendom,
You needs must break your fast; therefore if you'll agree
To eat a goodly dinner fairly and lustily,
With two companions of your choice, I promise all the three
To quit you from your prison, and leave you ransom-free.'
The Count was joyful at the word, and answer'd cheerfully:

'Cid, if you mean it as you say, this way to ransom me,
As long as I shall live a marvel it will be.' –
'Then come to dinner, Count, and when you've eat your fill,
You with your two companions may go whene'er you will;
But for the booty that I gain'd, I mean to keep it still:
No not a farthing will I give of all the wealth you lost,
Your plea was overthrown in fight, and you must pay the cost;
Besides, I want the goods myself, for the service of my host,
My ragged hearty followers, my safeguard and my boast;
Thus we must live, till Heaven above has otherwise disposed,
Standing in anger of the king, with all the best and most
Of our inheritance and lands sequester'd and foreclosed;
As is the wont of banish'd men, we needs must think it fair
To keep our troop together, with plundering here and there.'
The Count was pleased, and call'd for water for his hands,
A bason with the banquet was brought at his commands:
Two knights were with him, that the Cid released him
        ransomless;
I warrant all the three were joyous at the mess.
Then spoke the noble Cid – 'Sir Count, before we part,
You must perform your promise, and eat with all your heart,
Else I must keep you with me to whet your appetite.'
The Count replied – 'The contract shall be fulfill'd aright;
I promise you to do my part, and dine with delight.'
The noble-minded Cid stood smiling there beside
To see the Count at meat, so fast his hands he plied.
And if it be your pleasure, Cid, now that our dinner's
        done,
Give order for our horses, and let us hence be gone:
Of all the meals I ever made this is the heartiest one. –
Three palfreys were brought up to them, with saddles rich and
        fair,
With mantles and with housings of cloth and peltry rare.
The Count was in the midst, his knights on either side,
The Cid for half a stage would escort him on his ride; –
'Farewell, Sir Count! you leave me ransomless and frank;

I quit you with all courtesies; and furthermore I thank
Your bounty for the booty you left with me behind;
And if you should repent of it, or chance to change your mind,
And wish to mend your luck, whenever you're inclined,
Myself and my companions are easy folks to find: –
But if you leave me quiet, (as well, methinks, you may)
Your lands will fare the better; and on a future day
With your own goods or others perhaps I may repay.' –
'Cid, you may fairly boast, you're safe upon that head;
For this year and the next my score is fully paid;
And as for coming after you let nothing more be said.'
   The Count went crowding on his pace, and looking fast
     behind
Pressing and urging onward, he doubted in his mind
The Cid might change his purpose. He little knew the Cid;
That would have been a treason, – a thing he never did;
He never would have done so base an act – not even
To purchase all the gold and treasure under heaven.

Translated from the Spanish by John Hookham Frere

JUVENAL

from Satires

Produce the urn that Hannibal contains,
And weigh the mighty dust which yet remains:
And is this all! Yet THIS was once the bold,
The aspiring chief, whom Afric could not hold,
Afric, outstretch'd from where the Atlantic roars,
To Nilus; from the Line, to Lybia's shores!
Spain conquer'd, o'er the Pyrenees he bounds;
Nature oppos'd her everlasting mounds,
Her Alps, and snows: through these he bursts his way,
And Italy already owns his sway –

Still thundering on, – 'think nothing done,' he cries,
'Till low in dust our haughty rival lies;
Till through her smoking streets I lead my powers,
And plant my standard on her hated towers.'
Big words! but view his figure, view his face:
O, for some master-hand the chief to trace,
As through the Etrurian swamps, by rains increas'd,
Spoil'd of an eye he flounc'd, on his Getulian beast!
    But what ensued, illusive glory! say?
Subdued on Zama's memorable day,
He flies in exile to a foreign state,
With headlong haste; and, at a despot's gate
Sits, wond'rous suppliant! of his fate in doubt,
'Till the Bithynian's morning nap be out.
    Just to his fame, what death has Heaven assign'd
The great controller of all human kind?
Did hostile armies give the fatal wound,
Or mountains press him, struggling, to the ground?
No; three small drops, within a ring conceal'd,
Aveng'd the blood he pour'd on Cannæ's field!
Go madman, go! the paths of fame pursue,
Climb other Alps, and other realms subdue,
To please the rhetoricians, and become,
A DECLAMATION for the boys of Rome!

    Translated from the Latin by William Gifford

SAMUEL JOHNSON

from The Vanity of Human Wishes

On what foundation stands the warrior's pride,
How just his hopes, let Swedish Charles decide;
A frame of adamant, a soul of fire,
No dangers fright him, and no labours tire;

O'er love, o'er fear, extends his wide domain,
Unconquered lord of pleasure and of pain;
No joys to him pacific sceptres yield,
War sounds the trump, he rushes to the field;
Behold surrounding kings their powers combine,
And one captitulate, and one resign;
Peace courts his hand, but spreads her charms in vain;
'Think nothing gained,' he cries, 'till naught remain,
On Moscow's walls till Gothic standards fly,
And all be mine beneath the polar sky.'
The march begins in military state,
And nations on his eye suspended wait;
Stern Famine guards the solitary coast,
And Winter barricades the realms of Frost;
He comes, nor want nor cold his course delay –
Hide, blushing Glory, hide Pultowa's day:
The vanquished hero leaves his broken bands,
And shows his miseries in distant lands;
Condemned a needy supplicant to wait,
While ladies interpose, and slaves debate.
But did not Chance at length her error mend?
Did no subverted empire mark his end?
Did rival monarchs give the fatal wound?
Or hostile millions press him to the ground?
His fall was destined to a barren strand,
A petty fortress, and a dubious hand;
He left the name at which the world grew pale,
To point a moral, or adorn a tale.

ANONYMOUS

'The world laid low, and the wind blew like a dust'

The world laid low, and the wind blew like a dust
Alexander, Caesar, and all their followers.
Tara is grass; and look how it stands with Troy.
And even the English – maybe they might die.

Translated from the Irish by Thomas Kinsella

Plunder and Spoils

For much of history, the spoils of war have been essential, supplying the very means by which armies were paid. Tamburlaine gives his troops Turkish concubines, but the Earl of Essex – as one might expect from an English patriotic ballad – announces that the women and children must be spared when Cadiz is taken; he has his eye on the Spanish treasure of gold and jewels.

In modern warfare, the tables have been turned. The demand for reparations is no longer made by the victorious side, and the losers are quite likely to receive international aid to help them rebuild their ravaged country.

CHRISTOPHER MARLOWE

from Tamburlaine the Great, Part II (Act 4, Scene iv)

Tamburlaine:
Now fetch me out the Turkish concubines,
I will prefer them for the funeral
They have bestowed on my abortive son.
Where are my common soldiers now, that fought
So lion-like upon Asphaltis' plains?

Soldiers:
Here my lord.

Tamburlaine:
Hold ye tall soldiers, take ye queens apiece –
I mean such queens as were kings' concubines.
Take them, divide them and their jewels too,
And let them equally serve all your turns.

Soldiers:
We thank your majesty.

Tamburlaine:
Brawl not, I warn you, for your lechery,
For every man that so offends shall die.

Orcanes:
Injurious tyrant, wilt thou so defame
The hateful fortunes of thy victory,
To exercise upon such guiltless dames
The violence of thy common soldiers' lust?

Tamburlaine:
Live continent then, ye slaves, and meet not me
With troops of harlots at your slothful heels.

Concubines:
O pity us my lord, and save our honours.

Tamburlaine:
Are ye not gone ye villains with your spoils?

GAVIN EWART

A Personal Footnote

'In additon, he will give you seven women, skilled in the
fine crafts, Lesbians whom he chose for their exceptional
beauty . . .'

The Iliad, Book IX

Nobody has ever offered
to give me seven Lesbians –
though I was once a warrior
for six long years,
slept in a tent too
on a sparse camp bed.

Somehow I missed the
spoils of the cities.
I was not important.
A silly Lieutenant
can't sulk and get
away with it

like grandiose Achilles.

ANONYMOUS

The Winning of Cales

Long the proud Spaniards had vaunted to conquer us,
    Threatening our country with fyer and sword;
Often preparing their navy most sumptuous
    With as great plenty as Spain could afford.
        Dub a dub, dub a dub, thus strike their drums:
        Tantara, tantara, the Englishman comes.

To the seas presently went our lord admiral,
  With knights courageous and captains full good;
The brave Earl of Essex, a prosperous general,
  With him prepared to pass the salt flood.
    Dub a dub, etc.

At Plymouth speedilye, took they ship valiantlye,
  Braver ships never were seen under sayle,
With their fair colours spread, and streamers ore their head,
  Now bragging Spaniards, take heed of your tayle.
    Dub a dub, etc.

Unto Cales cunninglye, came we most speedilye,
  Where the kinges navy securelye did ryde;
Being upon their backs, piercing their butts of sacks,
  Ere any Spaniards our coming descryde.
    Dub a dub, etc.

Great was the crying, the running and ryding,
  Which at that season was made in that place;
The beacons were fyred, as need then required;
  To hyde their great treasure they had little space.
    Dub a dub, etc.

There you might see their ships, how they were fyred fast,
  And how their men drowned themselves in the sea;
There might you hear them cry, wayle and weep piteously,
  When they saw no shift to scape thence away.
    Dub a dub, etc.

The great *St Phillip*, the pryde of the Spaniards,
  Was burnt to the bottom, and sunk in the sea;
But the *St Andrew*, and eke the *St Matthew*,
  Wee took in fight manfullye and brought away.
    Dub a dub, etc.

The Earl of Essex, most valiant and hardye,
  With horsemen and footmen marched up to the town;

The Spaniards, which saw them, were greatly alarmed,
   Did fly for their savegard, and durst not come down.
      Dub a dub, etc.

'Now,' quoth the noble Earl, 'courage my soldiers all,
   Fight and be valiant, the spoil you shall have;
And be well rewarded all from the great to the small;
   But looke that the women and children you save.'
      Dub a dub, etc.

The Spaniards at that sight, thinking it vain to fight,
   Hung upp flags of truce and yielded the towne;
Wee marched in presentlye, decking the walls on hye,
   With English colours which purchase renowne.
      Dub a dub, etc.

Entering the houses then, of the most richest men,
   For gold and treasure we searched eche day;
In some places we did find, pyes baking left behind,
   Meate at fire rosting, and folkes run away.
      Dub a dub, etc.

Full of rich merchandize, every top catched our eyes,
   Damasks and sattens and velvets full fayre;
Which soldiers measur'd out by the length of their swords;
   Of all commodities eche had a share.
      Dub a dub, etc.

Thus Cales was taken, and our brave general
   March'd to the market-place, where he did stand:
There many prisoners fell to our several shares,
   Many crav'd mercye, and mercye they fannd.
      Dub a dub, etc.

When our brave General saw they delayed all,
   And wold not ransome their towne as they said,
With their fair wanscots, their presses and bed-steads,
   Their joint-stools and tables a fire we made;

And when the town burned all in flame,
With tara, tantara, away we all came.

THOMAS LOVE PEACOCK

The War Song of Dinas Vawr

The mountain sheep are sweeter,
But the valley sheep are fatter;
We therefore deemed it meeter
To carry off the latter.
We made an expedition;
We met an host, and quelled it;
We forced a strong position,
And killed the men who held it.

On Dyfed's richest valley,
Where herds of kine were browsing,
We made a mighty sally,
To furnish our carousing.
Fierce warriors rushed to meet us;
We met them, and o'erthrew them:
They struggled hard to beat us;
But we conquered them, and slew them.

As we drove our prize at leisure,
The King marched forth to catch us:
His rage surpassed all measure,
But his people could not match us.
He fled to his hall-pillars;
And, ere our force we led off,
Some sacked his house and cellars,
While others cut his head off.

We there, in strife bewildering,
Spilt blood enough to swim in:

We orphaned many children,
And widowed many women.
The eagles and the ravens
We glutted with our foemen;
The heroes and the cravens,
The spearmen and the bowmen.

We brought away from battle,
And much their land bemoaned them,
Two thousand head of cattle,
And the head of him who owned them:
Ednyfed, King of Dyfed,
His head was borne before us;
His wine and beasts supplied our feasts,
And his overthrow, our chorus.

TONY HARRISON

The Cycles of Donji Vakuf

We take emerald to Bugojno, then the opal route
to Donji Vakuf, where Kalashnikovs still shoot
at retreating Serbs or at the sky
to drum up the leaden beat of victory.
Once more, though this time Serbian, homes
get pounded to facades like honeycombs.
This time it's the Bosnian Muslims' turn
to cleanse a taken town, to loot, and burn.
Donji Vakuf fell last night at 11.
Victoria is signalled by firing rounds to heaven
and for the god to whom their victory's owed.
We see some victors cycling down the road
on bikes that they're too big for. They feel so tall
as victors, all conveyances seem small,
but one, whose knees keep bumping on his chin,

rides a kid's cycle, with a mandolin,
also childish size, strapped to the saddle,
jogging against him as he tries to pedal.
His machine-gun and the mandolin impede
his furious pedalling, and slow down the speed
appropriate to victors, huge-limbed and big-booted,
and he's defeated by the small bike that he's looted.
The luckiest looters come down dragging cattle,
two and three apiece, they've won in battle.
A goat whose udder seems about to burst
squirts out her milk to quench a victor's thirst
which others quench with shared beer, as a cow,
who's no idea she's a Muslim's now,
sprays a triumphal arch of piss across
the path of her new happy Bosnian boss.
Another struggles with stuffed rucksack, gun, and bike,
small and red, he knows his kid will like,
and he hands me his Kalashnikov to hold
to free his hands. Rain makes it wet and cold.
When he's balanced his booty, he makes off,
for a moment forgetting his Kalashnikov,
which he slings with all his looted load
on to his shoulder and trudges down the road,
where a solitary reaper passes by,
scythe on his shoulder, wanting fields to dry,
hoping, listening to the thunder, that the day
will brighten up enough to cut his hay.
And tonight some small boy will be glad
he's got the present of a bike from soldier dad,
who braved the Serb artillery and fire
to bring back a scuffed red bike with one flat tyre.
And, among the thousands fleeing north, another,
with all his gladness gutted, with his mother,
knowing the nightmare they are cycling in,
will miss the music of his mandolin.

The Defeated

Some face defeat stubbornly, like Cleopatra who would not
succumb to Caesar, but most resign themselves to humiliation and
find some means of securing their survival. It is only the very few
who start immediately to plan their recovery and revenge.

Cavafy's poem is a profound analysis of the will to be defeated.

ANNA AKHMATOVA

Cleopatra

I am air and fire . . .
> – Shakespeare

She had already kissed Antony's dead lips,
she had already wept on her knees before Caesar . . .
and her servants have betrayed her. Darkness falls.
The trumpets of the Roman eagle scream.

And in comes the last man to be ravished by her beauty –
such a tall gallant! – with a shamefaced whisper:
'You must walk before him, as a slave, in the triumph.'
But the slope of her swan's neck is tranquil as ever.

Tomorrow they'll put her children in chains. Nothing
remains except to tease this fellow out of mind
and put the black snake, like a parting act of pity,
on her dark breast with indifferent hand.

Translated from the Russian by Stanley Kunitz and Max Hayward

NICCOLO DEGLI ALBIZZI

When the Troops Were Returning from Milan

If you could see, fair brother, how dead beat
  The fellows look who come through Rome today, –
  Black yellow smoke-dried visages, – you'd say
They thought their haste at going all too fleet.
Their empty victual-wagons up the street
  Over the bridge dreadfully sound and sway;
  Their eyes, as hanged men's, turning the wrong way;
And nothing on their backs, or heads, or feet.
One sees the ribs and all the skeletons
  Of their gaunt horses; and a sorry sight
Are the torn saddles, crammed with straw and stones.
  They are ashamed, and march throughout the night;
Stumbling, for hunger, on their marrowbones;
  Like barrels rolling, jolting, in this plight.
Their arms all gone, not even their swords are saved;
And each as silent as a man being shaved.

Translated from the Italian by D. G. Rossetti

SIDNEY KEYES

Dunbar, 1650

They came down from the ridge.
Scarped hills swallowed them.
Under the walls grew spiked
Iceweed and bleeding men.

The preachers cried. Their gowns
Flapped among the wrack.

The lame general rode
Ashamed, with a bent back.

Crossing the little river
Their pikes jostled and rang.
The ditches were full of dead.
A blackbird sang.

The southern terrible squire
Rode them down in the marsh.
The preachers scattered like crows –
The name of the day was WRATH.

EMILY DICKINSON

'My Portion is Defeat – today – '

My Portion is Defeat – today –
A paler luck than Victory –
Less Paeans – fewer Bells –
The Drums don't follow Me – with tunes –
Defeat – a somewhat slower – means –
More Arduous than Balls –

'Tis populous with Bone and stain –
And Men too straight to stoop again,
And Piles of solid Moan –
And Chips of Blank – in Boyish Eyes –
And scraps of Prayer –
And Death's surprise,
Stamped visible – in Stone –

There's somewhat prouder, over there –
The Trumpets tell it to the Air –
How different Victory

To Him who has it – and the One
Who to have had it, would have been
Contenteder – to die –

ALFRED HAYES

The City of Beggars

The wops came down to the port
When we docked
Dressed in the most fantastic rags,
Infantry caps on their heads
And feet tied in flour bags,
A garibaldian cape and throat scarved
With a dirty towel,
Half wild and half starved.
We threw them bread and cigarettes
Crowding over the starboard rail
To see what Italy was like.
They ducked their heads in an awful thanks,
Cramming the bread in a tin pail.
And we who had come on the foreign ship
Risking shark and submarine
Looked at the city the troops had won.
She lay in the Mediterranean sun
Under her moored balloons
With great holes knocked in her
As though with a wild hammer.
Fallen masonry and dust
Hanging balconies and stairs
Iron and iron rust
Abasso Il Duce on warehouse walls
And no glass anywheres.
Ruined and in ruins.
And American and Britisher

Who'd shelled her vias
And mined her waters
Hung on the pitted walls of their quarters
Their bulging aphrodites,
Rinsing their loneliness with cheap wine.
Morte del fascismo! Too late, too late.
The operatic dream and the reclaimed Caesar
Dredged from the swamp
Had climaxed in this:
Typhus and the walls down,
The gas escaping with a slow hiss.
And the adored jaw, the blared news,
To heat the mild Italian blood,
The second empire
From Tunis to the Nile
Had triumphed so:
The kids flopping in soldier shoes,
A cigarette picked out of the mud,
The bread depots and the water doles
In the tin cup,
The garibaldian cape shot full of bullet holes.

BERNARD SPENCER

The Invaders

They would bar your way in the street
to grab your astounding watch;
that unknown thing, a handkerchief,
they would threaten you for, and snatch
to enrich a village wife
a hemisphere far off;
a firearm gave them right.

Girls wore soiled, frumpy clothes,
scrubbed make-up away, looked rough
when they hurried down to the shops;
that was the epoch's vogue.

Through a longing to look older
one woman put powder on her hair
– well-worn Occupation stories;
there is this which a few prefer:

The child asking for a tame rabbit;
some kindly foreigners who heard;
and her cry and her flight from the soldier bringing
seven dead rabbits with blood
on their fur, and their necks swinging.

C. P. CAVAFY

Waiting for the Barbarians

What are we waiting for, gathered in the market-place?

  The barbarians are to arrive today.

Why so little activity in the senate?
Why do the senators sit there without legislating?

  Because the barbarians will arrive today.
  What laws should the senators make now?
  The barbarians, when they come, will do the legislating.

Why has our emperor risen so early,
and why does he sit at the largest gate of the city
on the throne, in state, wearing the crown?

Because the barbarians will arrive today.
And the emperor is waiting to receive
their leader. He has even prepared
a parchment for him. There
he has given him many titles and names.

Why did our two consuls and our praetors go out
today in the scarlet, the embroidered, togas?
Why did they wear bracelets with so many amethysts,
and rings with brilliant sparkling emeralds?
Why today do they carry precious staves
splendidly inlaid with silver and gold?

Because the barbarians will arrive today;
and such things dazzle barbarians.

And why don't the worthy orators come as always
to make their speeches, say what they have to say?

Because the barbarians will arrive today,
and they are bored by eloquence and public speaking.

What does this sudden uneasiness mean,
and this confusion? (How grave the faces have become!)
Why are the streets and squares rapidly emptying,
and why is everyone going back home so lost in thought?

Because it is night and the barbarians have not come.
And some men have arrived from the frontiers
and they say that barbarians don't exist any longer.

And now, what will become of us without barbarians?
They were a kind of solution.

Translated from the Greek by Edmund Keeley and Philip Sherrard

Returning from War

Both Clare and Housman describe the happiness of soldiers
returning to their homes and villages. But they were not the same
men who went out and many came back hideously disfigured and
disabled.

JOHN CLARE

The Returned Soldier

The soldier, full of battles and renown,
And gaping wonder of each quiet lown,
And strange to every face he knew so well,
Comes once again in this old town to dwell.
But man alone is changed; the very tree
He sees again where once he used to swee;
And the old fields where once he tented sheep,
And the old mole-hills where he used to leap,
And the old bush where once he found a nest
Are just the same, and pleasure fills his breast.
He sees the old path where he used to play
At chock and marbles many a summer day,
And loves to wander where he went a boy,
And fills his heart with pleasure and with joy.

ANONYMOUS

Johnny, I Hardly Knew Ye

While going the road to sweet Athy,
    Hurroo! Hurroo!
While going the road to sweet Athy,
    Hurroo! Hurroo!
While going the road to sweet Athy,
A stick in my hand and a drop in my eye,
A doleful damsel I heard cry: —
    'Och, Johnny, I hardly knew ye!
With drums and guns, and guns and drums
    The enemy nearly slew ye,
    My darling dear, you look so queer,
    Och, Johnny, I hardly knew ye!

'Where are your eyes that looked so mild?
    Hurroo! Hurroo!
Where are your eyes that looked so mild?
    Hurroo! Hurroo!
Where are your eyes that looked so mild
When my poor heart you first beguiled?
Why did you run from me and the child?
    Och, Johnny, I hardly knew ye!
With drums, &c.

'Where are the legs with which you run?
    Hurroo! Hurroo!
Where are the legs with which you run?
    Hurroo! Hurroo!
Where are the legs with which you run
When you went to carry a gun? —
Indeed your dancing days are done!
    Och, Johnny, I hardly knew ye!
With drums, &c.

'It grieved my heart to see you sail,
   Hurroo! Hurroo!
It grieved my heart to see you sail,
   Hurroo! Hurroo!
It grieved my heart to see you sail
Though from my heart you took leg bail, –
Like a cod you're doubled up head and tail.
   Och, Johnny, I hardly knew ye!
With drums, &c.

'You haven't an arm and you haven't a leg,
   Hurroo! Hurroo!
You haven't an arm and you haven't a leg,
   Hurroo! Hurroo!
You haven't an arm and you haven't a leg,
You're an eyeless, noseless, chickenless egg;
You'll have to be put in a bowl to beg;
   Och, Johnny, I hardly knew ye!
With drums, &c.

'I'm happy for to see you home,
   Hurroo! Hurroo!
I'm happy for to see you home,
   Hurroo! Hurroo!
I'm happy for to see you home,
All from the island of Sulloon,
So low in flesh, so high in bone,
   Och, Johnny, I hardly knew ye!
With drums, &c.

'But sad as it is to see you so,
   Hurroo! Hurroo!
But sad as it is to see you so,
   Hurroo! Hurroo!
But sad as it is to see you so,
And to think of you now as an object of woe,
Your Peggy'll still keep ye on as her beau;
   Och, Johnny, I hardly knew ye!

With drums and guns, and guns and drums
    The enemy nearly slew ye,
    My darling dear, you look so queer,
    Och, Johnny, I hardly knew ye!'

W. S. GRAHAM

What's the News?

What's the news, my bold
Retreater from the wars?
Play it on your fife
And rest your stump a bit.
You are the fork and knife
That ate the storm and strife.

Play your fife and I
Will bring you chitterlins.
He comes under the lamp
And I will make the words.
Settle your tender stump
Out of the night's damp.

Elizabeth, move the pot
Over nearer the fire.
Rob Kerr (at least a part
of him) has come back.
He's back to his own airt.
Bring that flannel shirt.

Hurry, Elizabeth, and bring
Maggie and Sheila out.
Old Maggie knows him well.
Tell Shaun and make him bring
His father's varnished fiddle.
Rob Kerr's come over the hill.

I'll pull the little cork.
And Shaun, fiddle easy.
Young Sheila, swing him gently
As the night goes, the night
Humming from the sea.
Rob Kerr's come home to stay.

SAMIH AL-QASIM

Sons of War

On his wedding night
They took him to war.

Five years of hardship.

One day he returned
On a red stretcher
And his three sons
Met him at the port.

   Translated from the Arabic by Abdullah al-Udhari

JESSIE POPE

The Beau Ideal

Since Rose a classic taste possessed,
   It naturally follows
Her girlish fancy was obsessed
   By Belvedere Apollos.
And when she dreamed about a mate,
   If any hoped to suit, he
Must in his person illustrate
   A type of manly beauty.

He must be physically fit,
  A graceful, stalwart figure,
Of iron and elastic knit
  And full of verve and vigour.
Enough! I've made the bias plain
  That warped her heart and thrilled it.
It was a maggot of her brain,
  And Germany has killed it.

To-day, the sound in wind and limb
  Don't flutter Rose one tittle.
Her maiden ardour cleaves to him
  Who's proved that he is brittle,
Whose healing cicatrices show
  The colours of a prism,
Whose back is bent into a bow
  By Flanders rheumatism.

The lad who troth with Rose would plight,
  Nor apprehend rejection
Must be in shabby khaki dight
  To compass her affection.
Who buys her an engagement ring
  And finds her kind and kissing,
Must have one member in a sling
  Or, preferably, missing.

BASIL T. PACQUET

Basket Case

I waited eighteen years to become a man.
My first woman was a whore off Tu Do street,
But I wish I never felt the first wild
Gliding lust, because the rage and thrust
Of a mine caught me hip high.

I felt the rip at the walls of my thighs,
A thousand metal scythes cut me open,
My little fish shot twenty yards
Into a swamp canal.
I fathered only this – the genderless bitterness
Of two stumps, and an unwanted pity
That births the faces of all
Who will see me till I die deliriously
From the spreading sepsis that was once my balls.

A. E. HOUSMAN

'On the idle hill of summer'

On the idle hill of summer,
  Sleepy with the flow of streams,
Far I hear the steady drummer
  Drumming like a noise in dreams.

Far and near and low and louder
  On the roads of earth go by,
Dear to friends and food for powder,
  Soldiers marching, all to die.

East and west on fields forgotten
  Bleach the bones of comrades slain,
Lovely lads and dead and rotten;
  None that go return again.

Far the calling bugles hollo,
  High the screaming fife replies,
Gay the files of scarlet follow:
  Woman bore me, I will rise.

Soldier from the wars returning,
　　Spoiler of the taken town,
Here is ease that asks not earning;
　　Turn you in and sit you down.

Peace is come and wars are over,
　　Welcome you and welcome all,
While the charger crops the clover
　　And his bridle hangs in stall.

Now no more of winters biting,
　　Filth in trench from fall to spring,
Summers full of sweat and fighting
　　For the Kesar or the King.

Rest you, charger, rust you, bridle;
　　Kings and kesars, keep your pay;
Soldier, sit you down and idle
　　At the inn of night for aye.

WILLIAM SHAKESPEARE

from Henry V (Act 5, Scene i)

Pistol: Doth Fortune play the huswife with me now?
News have I that my Nell is dead i' the spital
Of malady of France:
And there my rendezvous is quite cut off.
Old I do wax, and from my weary limbs
Honour is cudgelled. Well, bawd I'll turn,
And something lean to cutpurse of quick hand.
To England will I steal, and there I'll steal:
And patches will I get unto these cudgell'd scars,
And swear I got them in the Gallia wars.

Survivors

Until the British Legion was founded, old soldiers, with the exception of those taken care of by the royal establishment at the Hospital in Chelsea, were not well looked after. A Sergeant Brown, who had served twenty-one years in the 11th Hussars and had been at the Charge of the Light Brigade, duly received a pittance pension and ended up, via the workhouse, in a pauper's grave. Kipling's 'The Absent-Minded Beggar' was published by the *Daily Mail* in an effort to raise money for the wives and children of reservists who had been called up to serve in the Boer War. To dignify their begging, veterans of the First World War were given cards like the one carried by Frederick Butterfield, which carried the injunction, 'If you can directly or indirectly help this man to find work, you would be doing him a good turn.'

WILFRED OWEN

Disabled

He sat in a wheeled chair, waiting for dark,
And shivered in his ghastly suit of grey,
Legless, sewn short at elbow. Through the park
Voices of boys rang saddening like a hymn,
Voices of play and pleasure after day,
Till gathering sleep had mothered them from him.

*

About this time Town used to swing so gay
When glow-lamps budded in the light blue trees,
And girls glanced lovelier as the air grew dim, –
In the old times, before he threw away his knees.
Now he will never feel again how slim

Girls' waists are, or how warm their subtle hands;
All of them touch him like some queer disease.

*

There was an artist silly for his face,
For it was younger than his youth, last year.
Now, he is old; his back will never brace;
He's lost his colour very far from here,
Poured it down shell-holes till the veins ran dry,
And half his lifetime lapsed in the hot race,
And leap of purple spurted from his thigh.

*

One time he liked a blood-smear down his leg,
After the matches, carried shoulder-high.
It was after football, when he'd drunk a peg,
He thought he'd better join. – He wonders why.
Someone had said he'd look a god in kilts,
That's why; and may be, too, to please his Meg;
Aye, that was it, to please the giddy jilts
He asked to join. He didn't have to beg;
Smiling they wrote his lie; aged nineteen years.
Germans he scarcely thought of; all their guilt,
And Austria's, did not move him. And no fears
Of Fear came yet. He thought of jewelled hilts
For daggers in plaid socks; of smart salutes;
And care of arms; and leave; and pay arrears;
Esprit de corps; and hints for young recruits.
And soon, he was drafted out with drums and cheers.

*

Some cheered him home, but not as crowds cheer Goal.
Only a solemn man who brought him fruits
Thanked him; and then inquired about his soul.

*

Now, he will spend a few sick years in Institutes,
And do what things the rules consider wise,
And take whatever pity they may dole.
To-night he noticed how the women's eyes
Passed from him to the strong men that were whole.
How cold and late it is! Why don't they come
And put him into bed? Why don't they come?

IVOR GURNEY

Strange Hells

There are strange hells within the minds war made
Not so often, not so humiliatingly afraid
As one would have expected – the racket and fear guns made.
One hell the Gloucester soldiers they quite put out:
Their first bombardment, when in combined black shout

Of fury, guns aligned, they ducked lower their heads
And sang with diaphragms fixed beyond all dreads,
That tin and stretched-wire tinkle, that blither of tune:
'Après la guerre fini', till hell all had come down,
Twelve-inch, six-inch, and eighteen pounders hammering
      hell's thunders.

Where are they now, on state-doles, or showing shop-patterns
Or walking town to town sore in borrowed tatterns
Or begged. Some civic routine one never learns.
The heart burns – but has to keep out of face how heart burns.

TED HUGHES

Out

I The Dream Time

My father sat in his chair recovering
From the four-year mastication by gunfire and mud,
Body buffeted wordless, estranged by long soaking
In the colours of mutilation.
                              His outer perforations
Were valiantly healed, but he and the hearth-fire, its blood-
     flicker
On biscuit-bowl and piano and table-leg,
Moved into strong and stronger possession
Of minute after minute, as the clock's tiny cog
Laboured and on the thread of his listening
Dragged him bodily from under
The mortised four-year strata of dead Englishmen
He belonged with. He felt his limbs clearing
With every slight, gingerish movement. While I, small and
     four,
Lay on the carpet as his luckless double,
His memory's buried, immovable anchor,
Among jawbones and blown-off boots, tree-stumps, shell-
     cases and craters,
Under rain that goes on drumming its rods and thickening
Its kingdom, which the sun has abandoned, and where nobody
Can ever again move from shelter.

II

The dead man in his cave beginning to sweat;
The melting bronze visor of flesh
Of the mother in the baby-furnace —

Nobody believes, it
Could be nothing, all
Undergo smiling at
The lulling of blood in
Their ears, their ears, their ears, their eyes
Are only drops of water and even the dead man suddenly
Sits up and sneezes – Atishoo!
Then the nurse wraps him up, smiling,
And, though faintly, the mother is smiling,
And it's just another baby.

As after being blasted to bits
The reassembled infantryman
Tentatively totters out, gazing around with the eyes
Of an exhausted clerk.

III Remembrance Day

The poppy is a wound, the poppy is the mouth
Of the grave, maybe of the womb searching –

A canvas-beauty puppet on a wire
Today whoring everywhere. It is years since I wore one.

It is more years
The shrapnel that shattered my father's paybook

Gripped me, and all his dead
Gripped him to a time

He no more than they could outgrow, but, cast into one, like
    iron,
Hung deeper than refreshing of ploughs

In the woe-dark under my mother's eye –
One anchor

Holding my juvenile neck bowed to the dunkings of the
    Atlantic.
So goodbye to that bloody-minded flower.

You dead bury your dead.
Goodbye to the cenotaphs on my mother's breasts.

Goodbye to all the remaindered charms of my father's
        survival.
Let England close. Let the green sea-anemone close.

GEOFFREY ADKINS

Arthur

Lop-sided from a shrapnel wound,
he got a job as warehouseman at Twyfords,
and packed lavatory cisterns in straw.

His son Eric was pallid and fragile.
Nervous with love,
his father followed him everywhere.
Their voices matched. On Sundays,
at our house, the treble blended
with Arthur's cracked bass
which had won him, in Rome with the sixth army,
a NAAFI singing competition.

He was my famous soldier-uncle,
with real medals to show.
One-handed, he taught me to box,
easy left-hand feints and evasions
that never landed a real blow.
The new bureaucrats –
planners, managers, health officials –
schemed and struggled, as I did,
to get under that affectionate defence
and never managed it.

He is a survivor, as soft and steady
as his own slurred Longton accent.

He lives in Mawby Street,
a smoky terrace that tilts
over the hill's brow like a raisin-cake tiara.

They say a quiet victory
has stolen over this city.
New suit, crepe shoes, slow voice,
Arthur sidles through his sixties.
He is the gentlest of the heroes.
He goes dancing now, at the Locarno,
is handsome
in his new grey toupee.

ALAN ROSS

En Route

You've come a long way (they said).
I had a long way to come.

You are fortunate not to be dead.
My home was no longer home.

This has happened to others before.
The door is still ajar.

You could have been killed in the war.
I thank my lucky star.

The music is beginning to flame –
It comes from afar.

But you are –
Yes, I am.

F. G. BUTTERFIELD

For Services Rendered

Were you ever down, not a cent in your pockets?
  Apologies for boots on your feet.
The last square meal almost forgotten,
  How many such men do you meet?

There are thousands to-day in this plight;
  Through just one fault of their own.
They went out and 'strafed' the Germans,
  That safety might reign at home.

The jobs they left, now they're back again,
  Have in most cases been given away.
And many who went in the prime of their youth,
  Are physical wrecks to-day.

Where are those home-fires of welcome?
  Have they all burnt away?
Have Tommy and Jack, now they've come back,
  In the unemployment ranks to stay?

The price of this card will help this man
  A little bit on his way,
So don't send him away empty-handed
  But purchase a card to-day.

RUDYARD KIPLING

The Absent-Minded Beggar

When you've shouted 'Rule Britannia,' when you've sung
    'God save the Queen,'
  When you've finished killing Kruger with your mouth,

Will you kindly drop a shilling in my little tambourine
    For a gentleman in *kharki* ordered South?
He's an absent-minded beggar, and his weaknesses are great —
    But we and Paul must take him as we find him —
He is out on active service, wiping something off a slate —
    And he's left a lot of little things behind him!
    Duke's son — cook's son — son of a hundred kings —
    (Fifty thousand horse and foot going to Table Bay!)
Each of 'em doing his country's work
    (and who's to look after their things?)
Pass the hat for your credit's sake,
                        and pay — pay — pay!

There are girls he married secret, asking no permission to,
    For he knew he wouldn't get it if he did.
There is gas and coals and vittles, and the house-rent falling
        due,
    And it's more than rather likely there's a kid.
There are girls he walked with casual. They'll be sorry now
        he's gone,
    For an absent-minded beggar they will find him,
But it ain't the time for sermons with the winter coming on.
    We must help the girl that Tommy's left behind him!
Cook's son — duke's son — son of a belted earl —
    Son of a Lambeth publican — it's all the same to-day!
Each of 'em doing his country's work
    (and who's to look after the girl?)
Pass the hat for your credit's sake,
                        and pay — pay — pay!

There are families by thousands, far too proud to beg or speak,
    And they'll put their sticks and bedding up the spout,
And they'll live on half o' nothing, paid 'em punctual once a
        week
    'Cause the man that earns the wage is ordered out.
He's an absent-minded beggar, but he heard his country call,
    And his reg'ment didn't need to send to find him!

He chucked his job and joined it – so the job before us all
  Is to help the home that Tommy's left behind him!
Duke's job – cook's job – gardener, baronet, groom
  Mews or palace or paper-shop, there's someone gone away!
Each of 'em doing his country's work
  (and who's to look after the room?)
Pass the hat for your credit's sake,
                    and pay – pay – pay!

Let us manage so as, later, we can look him in the face,
  And tell him – what he'd very much prefer –
That, while he saved the Empire, his employer saved his place
  And his mates (that's you and me) looked out for *her*.
He's an absent-minded beggar and he may forget it all,
  But we do not want his kiddies to remind him
That we sent 'em to the workhouse while their daddy
    hammered Paul,
  So we'll help the homes that Tommy left behind him!
Cook's home – Duke's home – home of a millionaire,
  (Fifty thousand horse and foot going to Table Bay!)
Each of 'em doing his country's work
  (and what have you got to spare?)
Pass the hat for your credit's sake,
                    and pay – pay – pay!

MARTIN PARKER

The Maunding Soldier

Good, your worship, cast your eyes
Upon a souldier's miseries!
Let not my leane cheekes, I pray,
Your bounty from a souldier stay,
    But, like a noble friend,
    Some silver lend,

And Jove shall pay you in the end:
    And I will pray that Fate
    May make your fortunate
In heavenly, and in earth's estate.

They in Olympicke games have beene,
Whereas brave battels I have seene;
And where the cannons used to roare
My proper spheare was evermore;
    The danger I have past,
    Both first and last,
Would make your worship's selfe agast;
    A thousand times I have
    Been ready for the grave;
Three times I have been made a slave.

Twice through the bulke I have been shot;
My brains have boyl'd like a pot:
I have at lest these doozen times
Been blowne up by those roguish mines
    Under a barracado,
    In a bravado,
Throwing of a hand-granado;
    Oh! death was very neere,
    For it took away my eare,
And yet, thanke God! ch'am here, ch'am here.

I have upon the seas been tane
By th' Dunkerks, for the King of Spaine,
And stript out of my garments quite,
Exchanging all for canvis white;
    And in that pore aray
    For many a day
I have been kept, till friends did pay
    A ransome for release;
    And having bought my peace,
My woes againe did fresh increase.

There's no land-service as you can name
But I have been actor in the same;
In th' Palatinate and Bohemia
I served many a wofull day;
    At Frankendale I have,
    Like a souldier brave
Receiv'd what welcomes canons gave;
    For the honour of England
    Most stoutly did I stand
Gainst the Emperour's and Spinolae's band.

At push of pike I lost mine eye;
At Bergen siege I broke my thigh;
At Ostend, though I were a lad,
I laid about me as I were mad.
    Oh, you would little ween
    That I had been
An old, old souldier to the Queene;
    But if Sir Francis Vere
    Were living now and here,
Hee'd tell you how I slasht it there.

Since that, I have been in Breda
Besieg'd by Marquese Spinola;
And, since that, made a warlike dance
Both into Spaine and into France;
    And there I lost a flood
    Of noble blood,
And did but very little good:
    And now I home am come,
    With ragges about my bumme,
God bless you, Sir, from this poore summe!

And now my case you understand,
Good Sir, will you lend your helping hand?
A little thing will pleasure me,
And keepe in use your charity:

It is not bread nor cheese,
    Nor barrell lees,
Nor any scraps of meat, like these;
    But I doe beg of you
    A shilling or two,
Sweet Sir, your purse's strings undoe.

I pray your worship, thinke on me,
That am what I doe seeme to be –
No rooking rascall, nor no cheat,
But a souldier every way compleat;
    I have wounds to show
    That prove 'tis so;
Then courteous good Sir, ease my woe;
    And I for you will pray
    Both night and day
That your substance never may decay.

KATHERINE MANSFIELD

The Man with the Wooden Leg

There was a man lived quite near us;
He had a wooden leg and a goldfinch in a green cage.
His name was Farkey Anderson,
And he'd been in a war to get his leg.
We were very sad about him,
Because he had such a beautiful smile
And was such a big man to live in a very small house.
When he walked on the road his leg did not matter so much;
But when he walked in his little house
It made an ugly noise.
Little Brother said his goldfinch sang the loudest of all birds,
So that he should not hear his poor leg
And feel too sorry about it.

Enemies as Brothers

During the first Christmas night of the First World War, in 1914,
German, French, and English soldiers met, quite spontaneously, in
No Man's Land, where they shook hands, sang carols, and
exchanged cigarettes. When Lord French, the British Commander-
in-Chief, heard of this, he ordered that it should never happen
again. The classic expression of comradeship across the lines is
Wilfred Owen's 'I am the enemy you killed, my friend'. The blind
Argentinian poet, Jorge Luis Borges, eloquently rehearses the same
sentiment in his poem on the Falklands War (1982). This poem
appeared in *The Times* and Borges said, 'I was hoping that this
little poem would be read in England. *The Times* is one of the
world's great newspapers, and one of the most illustrious, and it
seems to me an excellent opportunity to say in England that not all
of us Argentines are demented. We are not accomplices.'

Most of the poems I have selected here were written by soldiers:
Owen survived most of the First World War before being killed in
1918; Heinrich Lersch was one of the 'Worker Poets' who served
in the German Army from 1914 to 1918; René Arcos was born in
1881 and published a collection of poems, *The Blood of Others*, in
1918; Joseph Lee enlisted in 1914, was commissioned in 1917, and
was taken prisoner the same year.

Fellow-feeling of this sort, the confession of a shared humanity,
does not characterise all wars. I could find no poems by Allied
soldiers expressing fraternal sentiments towards the Japanese in the
Second World War. Civil wars, too, are marked by mutual and
implacable hatred.

WILFRED OWEN

Strange Meeting

It seemed that out of battle I escaped
Down some profound dull tunnel, long since scooped
Through granites which titanic wars had groined.
Yet also there encumbered sleepers groaned,
Too fast in thought or death to be bestirred.
Then, as I probed them, one sprang up, and stared
With piteous recognition in fixed eyes,
Lifting distressful hands as if to bless.
And by his smile, I knew that sullen hall,
By his dead smile I knew we stood in Hell.
With a thousand pains that vision's face was grained;
Yet no blood reached there from the upper ground,
And no guns thumped, or down the flues made moan.
'Strange friend,' I said, 'here is no cause to mourn.'
'None,' said that other, 'save the undone years,
The hopelessness. Whatever hope is yours,
Was my life also; I went hunting wild
After the wildest beauty in the world,
Which lies not calm in eyes, or braided hair,
But mocks the steady running of the hour,
And if it grieves, grieves richlier than here.
For of my glee might many men have laughed,
And of my weeping something had been left,
Which must die now. I mean the truth untold,
The pity of war, the pity war distilled.
Now men will go content with what we spoiled,
Or, discontent, boil bloody, and be spilled.
They will be swift with swiftness of the tigress.
None will break ranks, though nations trek from progress.
Courage was mine, and I had mystery,
Wisdom was mine, and I had mastery:

To miss the march of this retreating world
Into vain citadels that are not walled.
Then, when much blood had clogged their chariot-wheels,
I would go up and wash them from sweet wells,
Even with truths that lie too deep for taint.
I would have poured my spirit without stint
But not through wounds; not on the cess of war.
Foreheads of men have bled where no wounds were.
I am the enemy you killed, my friend.
I knew you in this dark: for so you frowned
Yesterday through me as you jabbed and killed.
I parried; but my hands were loath and cold.
Let us sleep now. . . .'

THOMAS HARDY

The Man He Killed

'Had he and I but met
   By some old ancient inn,
We should have sat us down to wet
   Right many a nipperkin!

'But ranged as infantry,
   And staring face to face,
I shot at him as he at me,
   And killed him in his place.

'I shot him dead because –
   Because he was my foe
Just so: my foe of course he was;
   That's clear enough; although

'He thought he'd 'list, perhaps,
   Off-hand like – just as I –
Was out of work – had sold his traps –
   No other reason why.

'Yes; quaint and curious war is!
 You shoot a fellow down
You'd treat if met where any bar is,
 Or help to half-a-crown.'

PAUL MULDOON

Truce

It begins with one or two soldiers
And one or two following
With hampers over their shoulders.
They might be off wildfowling

As they would another Christmas Day,
So gingerly they pick their steps.
No one seems sure of what to do.
All stop when one stops.

A fire gets lit. Some spread
Their greatcoats on the frozen ground.
Polish vodka, fruit and bread
Are broken out and passed round.

The air of an old German song,
The rules of Patience, are the secrets
They'll share before long.
They draw on their last cigarettes

As Friday-night lovers, when it's over,
Might get up from their mattresses
To congratulate each other
And exchange names and addresses.

DONALD THOMPSON

On the Relative Merit of Friend and Foe, Being Dead

Young skull which the wind scrapes, which the sand
Makes smooth, within your echoing grin
Where the breeze, breathing through the orbit's sound-
Vent, idly keens, once curled a curious brain
Whose convolutions intricately wrought
Diversity of pleasure, pain, fear, thought.

Here, when the flesh was firm, there stood the ear
Fashioned to hoist disturbances of air,
To differentiate the shriek and crack
Of bombs, the formal counterpoint, the low
Whisper and scuffle under the haystack.

These shattered teeth once sheltered under pride
Of lips that pressed to kiss, pursed to deride.
At the wind's mouthpiece, here the eager eye
Assessed the sun's light, the hills' stride,
Dance of sea and leaf, whiteness of thigh.

I found you, half-buried in the sand, and bare,
Hollow, dull as stone; beside you lay
Two helmets, peeled by the scavenging sun;
One theirs, one ours. But as to which you wore,
No indication.

BERNARD GUTTERIDGE

The Enemy Dead

The dead are always searched.
It's not a man, the blood-soaked
Mess of rice and flesh and bones
Whose pockets you flip open;
And these belongings are only
The counterpart to scattered ball
Or the abandoned rifle.

Yet later the man lives.
His postcard of a light blue
Donkey and sandy minarets
Reveals a man at last.
'Object – the panther mountains!
Two – a tired soldier of Kiku!
Three – my sister the bamboo sigh!'

Then again the man dies.
And only what he has seen
And felt, loved and feared
Stays as a hill, a soldier, a girl:
Are printed in the skeleton
Whose white bones divide and float away
Like nervous birds in the sky.

DOUGLAS STREET

Love Letters of the Dead

A Commando Intelligence Briefing

'Go through the pockets of the enemy wounded,
Go through the pockets of the enemy dead –

There's a lot of good stuff to be found there –
That's of course if you've time', I said.
'Love letters are specially useful,
It's amazing what couples let slip –
Effects of our bombs for example,
The size and type of a ship.
These'll all give us bits of our jigsaw.
Any questions?' I asked as per rule-book;
A close-cropped sergeant from Glasgow,
With an obstinate jut to his jaw,
Got up, and at me he pointed;
Then very slowly he said:
'Do you think it right, well I don't,
For any bloody stranger to snitch
What's special and sacred and secret,
Love letters of the dead?'

HEINRICH LERSCH

Brothers

For long between the trenches a dead man lay in view,
The sun shone hot upon him, wind cooled him and the dew.

And every day I saw him across the empty space,
And thought, the more I saw him: that is my brother's face.

I saw him every moment, before me as he lay,
And heard his voice that called me each happy peaceful day.

Often at night a sobbing that woke me full of fear:
You love me then no longer, O brother, brother dear?

Until by night I went across, though round me bullets flew,
And brought him in. And buried him. A man I never knew.

My eyes alone deceived me. – My heart you're not misled:
My brother's features look from all the faces of the dead.

Translated from the German by Christopher Middleton

JOSEPH LEE

German Prisoners

When first I saw you in the curious street,
Like some platoon of soldier ghosts in grey,
My mad impulse was all to smite and slay,
To spit upon you – tread you 'neath my feet.
But when I saw how each sad soul did greet
My gaze with no sign of defiant frown,
How from tired eyes looked spirits broken down,
How each face showed the pale flag of defeat,
And doubt, despair, and disillusionment,
And how were grievous wounds on many a head,
And on your garb red-faced was other red;
And how you stooped as men whose strength was spent,
I knew that we had suffered each as other,
And could have grasped your hand and cried, 'My brother'!

RENÉ ARCOS

The Dead

In the wind that blows
The veils of widows
All float on one side

And the mingled tears
Of a thousand sorrows
In one stream glide.

Pressing each other close the dead
Who own no hatred and no flag,
Their hair veneered with clotted blood,
The dead are all on the same side.

In the one clay where endlessly
Beginnings blend with the world that dies
The brothered dead lain cheek to cheek
Today atone for the same defeat.

Divided sons, fight on, fight on,
You lacerate humanity
And tear the earth apart in vain,
The dead are all on the same side;

Under the earth no more than one,
One field, one single hope abide,
As for the universe can only be
One combat and one victory.

Translated from the French by Christopher Middleton

HAMISH HENDERSON

Ninth Elegy: Fort Capuzzo

For there will come a day
when the Lord will say
– Close Order!

One evening, breaking a jeep journey at Capuzzo
I noticed a soldier as he entered the cemetery
and stood looking at the grave of a fallen enemy.
Then I understood the meaning of the hard word 'pietas'
(a word unfamiliar to the newsreel commentator
as well as to the pimp, the informer and the traitor).

His thought was like this. – Here's another 'Good Jerry'!
Poor mucker. Just eighteen. Must be hard-up for Manpower.
Or else he volunteered, silly bastard. That's the fatal.
the – fatal – mistake. Never volunteer for nothing.
I wonder how he died? Just as well it was him, though,
and not one of our chaps . . . Yes, the only good Jerry,
as they say, is your sort, chum.
                    Cheerio, you poor bastard.
Don't be late on parade when the Lord calls 'Close Order'.
Keep waiting for the angels. Keep listening for Reveille.

JORGE LUIS BORGES

Juan Lopez and John Ward

It was their fate to live in a strange time.
The planet had been carved into different countries,
each one provided with loyalties, with loved memories.
with a past which doubtless had been heroic, with
ancient and recent traditions, with rights, with grievances,
with its own mythology, with
forebears in bronze, with anniversaries, with demagogues and
with symbols.
Such an arbitrary division was favourable to war.

Lopez had been born in the city next to the motionless
river; Ward, in the outskirts of the city
through which
Father Brown had walked. He had studied Spanish so as
to read the Quixote.
The other professed a love of Conrad, revealed
to him in a class in Viamonte Street.
They might have been friends, but they saw each other just
      once,
face to face, in islands only too well-known,

and each one was Cain, and each one, Abel.
They buried them together. Snow and corruption
know them.
The story I tell happened in a time we cannot
understand.

   Translated from the Spanish by Rodolfo Torragno

WALT WHITMAN

Reconciliation

Word over all, beautiful as the sky,
Beautiful that war and all its deeds of carnage must in time be
      utterly lost,
That the hands of the sisters Death and Night incessantly
      softly wash again, and ever again, this soil'd world;
For my enemy is dead, a man divine as myself is dead,
I look where he lies white-faced and still in the coffin – I draw
      near,
Bend down and touch lightly with my lips the white face in the
      coffin.

The Bereaved

There is little or no comfort for the bereaved: a lost son, or lover, or husband, is a dreadful price to pay. The grief is all the greater if it has come about as the result of vengeful slaughter, as happened at Culloden (1746), when a thousand Highlanders were killed and many hundreds more executed by the 'Butcher' Cumberland. 'Tell it not in Gath,' cries David in his lament for Jonathan. Or, as Anne Finch, Countess of Winchilsea, wrote at the time of Marlborough's campaigns: 'Trail all your Pikes, dispirit every Drum, / March in a slow Procession from afar.'

ANONYMOUS (HEBREW)

from 2 Samuel 2

The beauty of Israel is slain upon thy high places: how are the
    mighty fallen!
Tell it not in Gath, publish it not in the streets of Askelon; lest
    the daughters of the Philistines rejoice, lest the daughters
    of the uncircumcised triumph.
Ye mountains of Gilboa, let there be no dew, neither let there
    be rain, upon you, nor fields of offerings: for there the
    shield of the mighty is vilely cast away, the shield of Saul,
    as though he had not been anointed with oil.
From the blood of the slain, from the fat of the mighty, the
    bow of Jonathan turned not back, and the sword of Saul
    returned not empty.
Saul and Jonathan were lovely and pleasant in their lives, and
    in their death they were not divided: they were swifter
    than eagles, they were stronger than lions.

Ye daughters of Israel, weep over Saul, who clothed you in
    scarlet, with other delights, who put on ornaments of gold
    upon your apparel.
How are the mighty fallen in the midst of the battle! O
    Jonathan, thou wast slain in thine high places.
I am distressed for thee, my brother Jonathan: very pleasant
    has thou been unto me: thy love to me was wonderful,
    passing the love of women.
How are mighty fallen, and the weapons of war perished!

HOMER

from The Iliad, Book XVIII

So mourn'd Pelides his late loss, so weighty were his moans,
Which, for their dumb sounds, now gave words to all his
        Myrmidons:
'O Gods,' said he, 'how vain a vow I made, to cheer the mind
Of sad Menœtius, when his son his hand to mine resign'd,
That high tow'r'd Opus he should see, and leave ras'd Ilion
With spoil and honour, ev'n with me! But Jove vouchsafes to
        none
Wish'd passages to all his vows; we both were destinate
To bloody one earth here in Troy; nor any more estate
In my return hath Peleüs or Thetis; but because
I last must undergo the ground, I'll keep no fun'ral laws,
O my Patroclus, for thy corse, before I hither bring
The arms of Hector and his head to thee for offering.
Twelve youths, the most renown'd of Troy, I'll sacrifice beside,
Before thy heap of funeral, to thee unpacified.
In mean time, by our crooked sterns lie, drawing tears from me
And round about thy honour'd corse, these dames of
        Dardanie,
And Ilion, with the ample breasts (whom our long spears and
        pow'rs

And labours purchas'd from the rich and by-us-ruin'd tow'rs,
And cities strong and populous with divers-languag'd men)
Shall kneel, and neither day nor night be licens'd to abstain
From solemn watches, their toil'd eyes held hope with endless
    tears.'

    Translated from the Greek by George Chapman

ANNE FINCH, COUNTESS OF WINCHILSEA

from All Is Vanity

A *bolder Youth*, grown capable of Arms,
Bellona courts with her prevailing Charms;
   Bids th' inchanting Trumpet sound,
   Loud as Triumph, soft as Love,
   Striking now the Poles above,
   Then descending from the Skies,
   Soften every falling Note;
As the harmonious *Lark* that sings and flies,
When near the Earth, contracts her narrow Throat,
   And warbles on the Ground:
Shews the proud Steed, impatient of the Check,
   'Gainst the loudest Terrors Proof,
Pawing the Valley with his steeled Hoof,
With Lightning arm'd his Eyes, with Thunder cloth'd his
    Neck;
   Who on th' advanced Foe, (the Signal giv'n)
Flies, like a rushing Storm by mighty Whirlwinds driv'n;
   Lays open the Records of Fame,
No glorious Deed omits, no Man of mighty Name;
   Their Stratagems, their Tempers she'll repeat,
   From *Alexander's*, (truly stil'd the GREAT)
   From *Cæsar's* on the World's Imperial Seat,
   To *Turenne's* Conduct, and to *Conde's* Heat.

'Tis done! and now th' ambitious Youth disdains
 The safe, but harder Labours of the Gown,
 The softer pleasures of the Courtly Town,
The once lov'd rural Sports, and Chaces on the Plains;
 Does with the Soldier's Life the Garb assume,
 The gold Embroid'ries, and the graceful Plume;
 Walks haughty in a Coat of Scarlet Die,
 A Colour well contrived to cheat the Eye,
Where richer Blood, alas! may undistinguisht lye.
 And oh! too near that wretched Fate attends;
 Hear it ye Parents, all ye weeping Friends!
 Thou fonder Maid! won by those gaudy Charms,
 (The destin'd Prize of his Victorious Arms)
 Now fainting Dye upon the mournful Sound,
That speaks his hasty Death, and paints the fatal Wound!
 Trail all your Pikes, dispirit every Drum,
 March in a slow Procession from afar,
 Ye silent, ye dejected Men of War!
 Be still the Hautboys, and the Flute be dumb!
 Display no more, in vain, the lofty Banner;
 For see! where on the Bier before ye lies
 The pale, the fall'n, th' untimely Sacrifice
To your mistaken Shrine, to your false Idol Honour!

ROBERT BURNS

Lament for Culloden

The lovely lass o' Inverness,
Nae joy nor pleasure can she see;
For e'en and morn she cries, Alas!
And aye the saut tear blins her ee:
Drumossie moor – Drumossie day –
A waefu' day it was to me!

For there I lost my father dear,
My father dear, and brethren three.

Their winding-sheet the bluidy clay,
Their graves are growing green to see:
And by them lies the dearest lad
That ever blest a woman's ee!
Now wae to thee, thou cruel lord,
A bluidy man I trow thou be,
For mony a heart thou hast made sair
That ne'er did wrang to thine or thee.

ROBERT SOUTHEY

The Soldier's Wife

Weary way-wanderer, languid and sick at heart,
Travelling painfully over the rugged road,
Wild-visaged Wanderer! God help thee wretched one!

Sorely thy little one drags by thee bare-footed,
Cold is the baby that hangs at thy bending back,
Meagre and livid and screaming for misery.

Woe-begone mother, half anger, half agony,
As over thy shoulder thou lookest to hush the babe,
Bleakly the blinding snow beats in thy haggèd face.

Ne'er will thy husband return from the war again,
Cold is thy heart and as frozen as Charity!
Cold are thy children. – Now God be thy comforter!

WALT WHITMAN

Come Up from the Fields Father

Come up from the fields father, here's a letter from our Pete,
And come to the front door mother, here's a letter from thy
    dear son.

Lo, 'tis autumn,
Lo, where the trees, deeper green, yellower and redder,
Cool and sweeten Ohio's villages with leaves fluttering in the
    moderate wind,
Where apples ripe in the orchards hang and grapes on the
    trellis'd vines,
(Smell you the smell of the grapes on the vines?
Smell you the buckwheat where the bees were lately buzzing?)
Above all, lo, the sky so calm, so transparent after the rain, and
    with wondrous clouds,
Below too, all calm, all vital and beautiful, and the farm
    prospers well.
Down in the fields all prospers well,
But now from the fields come father, come at the daughter's
    call,
And come to the entry mother, to the front door come right
    away.

Fast as she can she hurries, something ominous, her steps
    trembling,
She does not tarry to smooth her hair nor adjust her cap.

Open the envelope quickly,
O this is not our son's writing, yet his name is sign'd,
O a strange hand writes for our dear son, O stricken mother's
    soul!
All swims before her eyes, flashes with black, she catches the
    main words only,

Sentences broken, *gunshot wound in the breast, cavalry
    skirmish, taken to hospital,*
At present low, but will soon be better.

Ah now the single figure to me,
Amid all teeming and wealthy Ohio with all its cities and
    farms,
Sickly white in the face and dull in the head, very faint,
By the jamb of a door leans.

Grieve not so, dear mother, (the just-grown daughter speaks
    through her sobs,
The little sisters huddle around speechless and dismay'd,)
See dearest mother, the letter says Pete will soon be better.

Alas poor boy, he will never be better, (nor may-be needs to be
    better, that brave and simple soul,)
While they stand at home at the door he is dead already,
The only son is dead.

But the mother needs to be better,
She with thin form presently drest in black,
By day her meals untouch'd, then at night fitfully sleeping,
    often waking,
In the midnight waking, weeping, longing with one deep
    longing,
O that she might withdraw unnoticed, silent from life escape
    and withdraw,
To follow, to seek, to be with her dear dead son.

STEPHEN CRANE

'Do not weep, maiden, for war is kind'

Do not weep, maiden, for war is kind.
Because your lover threw wild hands toward the sky
And the affrighted steed ran on alone,

Do not weep.
War is kind.

Hoarse, booming drums of the regiment,
Little souls who thirst for fight,
These men were born to drill and die.
The unexplained glory flies above them,
Great is the Battle-God, great, and his Kingdom –
A field where a thousand corpses lie.

Do not weep, babe, for war is kind.
Because your father tumbled in the yellow trenches,
Raged at his breast, gulped and died,
Do not weep.
War is kind.

Swift blazing flag of the regiment,
Eagle with crest of red and gold,
These men were born to drill and die.
Point for them the virtue of slaughter,
Make plain to them the excellence of killing
And a field where a thousand corpses lie.

Mother whose heart hung humble as a button
On the bright splendid shroud of your son,
Do not weep.
War is kind.

SIEGFRIED SASSOON

Glory of Women

You love us when we're heroes, home on leave,
Or wounded in a mentionable place.
You worship decorations; you believe
That chivalry redeems the war's disgrace.
You make us shells. You listen with delight,

By tales of dirt and danger fondly thrilled.
You crown our distant ardours while we fight,
And mourn our laurelled memories when we're killed.
You can't believe that British troops 'retire'
When hell's last horror breaks them, and they run,
Trampling the terrible corpses – blind with blood.
    O German mother dreaming by the fire,
    While you are knitting socks to send your son
    His face is trodden deeper in the mud.

KATHERINE MANSFIELD

To L. H. B. (1894–1915)

Last night for the first time since you were dead
I walked with you, my brother, in a dream.
We were at home again beside the stream
Fringed with tall berry bushes, white and red.
'Don't touch them: they are poisonous,' I said.
But your hand hovered, and I saw a beam
Of strange, bright laughter flying round your head
And as you stooped I saw the berries gleam.
'Don't you remember? We called them Dead Man's Bread!'
    I woke and heard the wind moan and the roar
Of the dark water tumbling on the shore.
Where – where is the path of my dream for my eager feet?
By the remembered stream my brother stands
Waiting for me with berries in his hands . . .
'These are my body. Sister, take and eat.'

FORD MADOX FORD

from Antwerp

This is Charing Cross;
It is midnight;
There is a great crowd
And no light.
A great crowd, all black that hardly whispers aloud.
Surely, that is a dead woman – a dead mother!
She has a dead face;
She is dressed all in black;
She wanders to the bookstall and back,
At the back of the crowd;
And back again and again back,
She sways and wanders.

This is Charing Cross;
It is one o'clock.
There is still a great cloud, and very little light;
Immense shafts of shadows over the black crowd
That hardly whispers aloud . . .
And now! . . . That is another dead mother,
And there is another and another and another . . .
And little children, all in black,
All with dead faces, waiting in all the waiting-places,
Wandering from the doors of the waiting-room
In the dim gloom.

These are the women of Flanders.
They await the lost.

They await the lost that shall never leave the dock;
They await the lost that shall never again come by the train
To the embraces of all these women with dead faces;
They await the lost who lie dead in trench and barrier and foss,

In the dark of the night.
This is Charing Cross; it is past one of the clock;
There is very little light.

There is so much pain.

BERNARD SPENCER

Passed On

Some of his messages were personal
almost as his lost face; they showed he knew
about their pets, the life that went on beating
in desks and scrapbooks, and each particle

of the family language: the young engineer,
who had put khaki on and died in the mud,
at times would almost touch them.
                              Yet he was
(But how?) the sing-song spirit-gospeller;

the irrelevance, the baby-talk and spout
of 'Vera,' the Control; and stagey things,
a bell, a violin, an Indian chief;
even what crashed the furniture about.

But then he was their son. That love, that birth
made the old couple blind enough to bear
the medium's welcome, taking no offence,
and haunt his room that opened clean off earth.

JACQUES PRÉVERT

Familial

The mother does knitting
The son fights the war
She finds this quite natural the mother
And the father what does he do the father?
He does business
His wife does knitting
His son the war
He business
He finds this quite natural the father
And the son and the son
What does the son find the son?
He finds absolutely nothing the son
His mother does knitting his father business he war
When he finishes the war
He'll go into business with his father
The war continues the mother continues she knits
The father continues he does business
The son is killed he continues no more
The father and the mother go to the graveyard
They find this quite natural the father and mother
Life continues life with knitting war business
Business war knitting war
Business business business
Life with the graveyard.

Translated from the French by Lawrence Ferlinghetti

KATHLEEN RAINE

Heroes

This war's dead heroes, who has seen them?
They rise, in smoke above the burning city,
Faint clouds, dissolving into sky.

And who, sifting the Libyan sand, can find
The tracery of a human hand,
The faint impression of an absent mind,
The fade-out of a soldier's day dream?

You'll know your love no more, nor his sweet kisses –
He's forgotten you, girl, and in the idle sun
In long green grass that the east wind caresses
The seed of man is ravished by the corn.

The Fruits of War

It has been said that it was the trench warfare of 1914–18 which first brought home the full psychological horror of war; that until then a romantic and chivalrous haze had been allowed to settle over battlefields, encouraging successive generations blithely to take up the manly pursuit of arms. Not so. George Gascoigne, writing in the reign of Elizabeth I, spoke not just of mangled corpses and maimed limbs, but also, anticipating Owen and Sassoon, of 'The broken sleeps, the dreadful dreams, the woe.'

If victory is often hollow, and memory short, so that even feats of great bravery are 'from the book of honour razed quite', that may be among the very reasons why warfare is endlessly renewed.

WILLIAM SHAKESPEARE

Sonnet 25

Let those who are in favour with their stars
Of public honour and proud titles boast,
Whilst I, whom fortune of such triumph bars
Unlook'd for joy in that I honour most.
Great princes' favourites their fair leaves spread
But as the marigold at the sun's eye,
And in themselves their pride lies buried,
For at a frown they in their glory die.
The painful warrior famoused for fight,
After a thousand victories once foil'd
Is from the book of honour razed quite,
And all the rest forgot for which he toil'd:
    Then happy I, that love and am beloved
    Where I may not remove nor be removed.

JOACHIM DU BELLAY

Rome

O thou new comer who seek'st Rome in Rome
And find'st in Rome no thing thou canst call Roman;
Arches worn old and palaces made common,
Rome's name alone within these walls keeps home.

Behold how pride and ruin can befall
One who hath set the whole world 'neath her laws,
All conquering, now conquered, because
She is Time's prey and Time consumeth all.

Rome that art Rome's one sole last monument,
Rome that alone has conquered Rome the town,
Tiber alone, transient and seaward bent,
Remains of Rome. O world, thou unconstant mime!
That which stands firm in thee Time batters down,
And that which fleeteth doth outrun swift time.

Translated from the French by Ezra Pound

GEORGE GASCOIGNE

from The Fruits of War

I set aside to tell the restless toil,
The mangled corpse, the maimed limbs at last,
The shortened years by fret of fever's foil,
The smoothest skin with scabs and scars disgraced,
The frolic favour frounced and foul defaced,
The broken sleeps, the dreadful dreams, the woe,
Which wone with war and cannot from him go.

I list not write, for it becomes me not,
The secret wrath which God doth kindle oft,
To see the sucklings put into the pot,
To hear their guiltless blood send cries aloft,
And call for vengeance unto him, but soft!
The soldiers they commit those heinous acts,
Yet kings and captains answer for such facts.

What need we now at large for to rehearse
The force of Fortune, when she list to frown?
Why should I here display in barren verse
How realms are turned topsy-turvy down,
How kings and Caesars lose both claim and crown,
Whose haughty hearts to hent all honour haunt,
Till high mishaps their doughtiest deeds do daunt?

All these, with more, my pen shall overpass,
Since Haughty Heart has fixed his fancy thus.
'Let chance,' saith he, 'be fickle as it was,
Sit bonus, in re mala, animus.
Nam omne solum viro forti ius.
And fie,' saith he, 'for goods or filthy gain!
I gape for glory; all the rest is vain.'

Vain is the rest, and that most vain of all:
A smouldering smoke which flieth with every wind,
A tickle treasure, like a trendling ball,
A passing pleasure mocking but the mind,
A fickle fee as fancy well can find,
A summer's fruit which long can never last,
But ripeneth soon and rots again as fast.

And tell me, Haughty Heart, confess a truth,
What man was aye so safe in glory's port
But trains of treason (oh, the more the ruth!)
Could undermine the bulwarks of this fort
And raze his ramparts down in sundry sort?

Search all thy books and thou shalt find therein
That honour is more hard to hold than win.

Ask Julius Caesar if this tale be true,
The man who conquered all the world so wide,
Whose only word commanded all the crew
Of Roman knights at many a time and tide,
Whose pomp was thought so great it could not glide –
At last with bodkins dubbed and doused to death,
And all his glory banished with his breath.

JAMES SHIRLEY

from Ajax and Ulysses

The glories of our blood and state
    Are shadows, not substantial things;
There is no armor against fate;
    Death lays his icy hand on kings:
            Sceptre and crown
            Must tumble down,
And in the dust be equal made
With the poor crooked scythe and spade.

Some men with swords may reap the field,
    And plant fresh laurels where they kill:
But their strong nerves at last must yield;
    They tame but one another still:
            Early or late
            They stoop to fate,
And must give up their murmuring breath
When they, pale captives, creep to death.

The garlands wither on your brow;
    Then boast no more your mighty deeds;
Upon Death's purple altar now

See where the victor-victim bleeds:
    Your heads must come
    To the cold tomb.
Only the actions of the just
Smell sweet, and blossom in their dust.

JOHN MILTON

from Paradise Regained, Book III

They err who count it glorious to subdue
By conquest far and wide, to overrun
Large countries, and in field great battles win,
Great cities by assault. What do these worthies
But rob and spoil, burn, slaughter, and enslave
Peaceable nations, neighbouring or remote,
Made captive, yet deserving freedom more
Than those their conquerors, who leave behind
Nothing but ruin wheresoe'er they rove,
And all the flourishing works of peace destroy;
Then swell with pride, and must be titled Gods,
Great Benefactors of mankind, Deliverers,
Worshipped with temple, priest, and sacrifice?
One is the son of Jove, of Mars the other;
Till conqueror Death discover them scarce men,
Rolling in brutish vices, and deformed,
Violent or shameful death their due reward.
But, if there be in glory aught of good,
It may by means far different be attained,
Without ambition, war, or violence –
By deeds of peace, by wisdom eminent,
By patience, temperance.

EBENEZER ELLIOTT

War

The victories of mind,
Are won for all mankind;
But war wastes what it wins,
Ends worse than it begins,
And is a game of woes,
Which nations always lose:
Though tyrant tyrant kill,
The slayer liveth still.

EDWARD FITZGERALD

'War begets Poverty'

War begets Poverty,
Poverty, Peace —
Peace, begets Riches,
Fate will not cease —
Riches beget Pride,
Pride is War's ground —
War begets Poverty,
And so the world goes round.

BERTOLT BRECHT

What Did the Nazi Send His Wife?

And what did she get, the soldier's wife
Out of the town of Prague?

From Prague she got her high-heeled shoes,
That's what she got from Prague.

And what did she get, the soldier's wife,
From Oslo, over the Sound?
From Oslo she got a fur-trimmed cap,
Hope it's becoming, the fur-trimmed cap
From Oslo over the Sound.

And what did she get, the soldier's wife,
From wealthy Amsterdam?
From Amsterdam she's got a hat,
And she looks awfully good in that,
Neat and sweet in her Dutch hat
That came from Amsterdam.

And what did she get, the soldier's wife,
Out of the Belgian land?
From Brussels she got the loveliest lace –
How nicely it sets off her face!
Out of the Belgian land.

And what did she get, the soldier's wife,
From Paris, the City of Light?
Oh, from Paris she got her satin dress;
How the neighbors envy the satin dress
From Paris, the City of Light.

And what did she get, the soldier's wife,
From southward Bucharest?
From there, she got a peasant waist,
Embroidered and laced, a Rumanian waist
From Southward Bucharest!

And what did she get, the soldier's wife,
From the cold Russian land?
Why, from there she got her widow's veil;

Oh, she looks pale in her widow's veil
That she got from the Russian land!

Translated from the German

ROBERT GRAVES

Dead Cow Farm

An ancient saga tells us how
In the beginning the First Cow
(For nothing living yet had birth
But elemental cow on earth)
Began to lick cold stones and mud:
Under her warm tongue flesh and blood
Blossomed, a miracle to believe;
And so was Adam born, and Eve.
Here now is chaos once again,
Primaeval mud, cold stones and rain.
Here flesh decays and blood drips red,
And the Cow's dead, the old Cow's dead.

WALLACE STEVENS

from Phases

This was the salty taste of glory,
That it was not
Like Agamemnon's story.
Only, an eyeball in the mud,
And Hopkins,
Flat and pale and gory!

IOAN ALEXANDRU

The End of the War

When I came into the world the war was endin',
Last orders were shot. On field
Last cannons were hung by their shadows.
In our house presents were shared.

'First to you, John,' said the War to father, from the corner of
    the table,
'Because you have served me so faithfully
I hand you this wooden leg.
Wear it in memory of me, and good health to you.
It's sturdy from the trunk of an old oak;
When you die the woods will rock you
Like a brother in the summits of their eyes.
Your right hand, because it has no book learning anyway,
I wrenched from your elbow and have given it to the earth
To teach it to write.

'For you, Maria,' said the War to my mother –
'Because you watered my horses with your tears
And left two sons on the battlefield
To polish my boots, and brought up
Two maidens with whom I've spent my nights,
Look, I'll give you this beautiful bunch of wakeful nights,
As well as this empty house without a roof.

'To you, George, son of Peter from over the hill, –
For those two hazel eyes, you say you had,
Look, I give you possession of all the boundaries of darkness,
So you can harvest them, you and your wife
Forever.

'For the village I leave only forty orphans
Under six months, ten empty houses and the others in ruins,
Also, the sky towards sunset, half-burned.
The tower without bells; eight women in the cemetery
Hung with heads to the ground, and twenty horses dead from
    the neighbour's farm.

'For you, just born, because we don't know each other very
    well,
I leave the cow's udder dry,
The plum trees burned alive in the garden,
The eye of the well, dead,
And may the sky feed you on its stars.
And I baptize you in the name of the Lord.'

Translated from the Romanian by Andrea Deletant and Brenda Walker

Civil War

Civil wars are the most cruel and vicious of all wars. England has
suffered from them twice, America once, and the Balkans
seemingly forever. I could have chosen several poems but I finally
settled on a single passage of verse drama which depicts the full
horror. It is the harrowing scene from *Henry VI* in which a father
discovers he has killed his son, and a son discovers that he has
killed his father.

WILLIAM SHAKESPEARE

from Henry VI, Part III (Act 3, Scene v)

Son: Ill blows the wind that profits nobody.
This man whom hand to hand I slew in fight
May be possessèd with some store of crowns;
And I, that haply take them from him now,
May yet ere night yield both my life and them
To some man else, as this dead man doth me. –
Who's this? O God! It is my father's face,
Whom in this conflict I, unwares, have killed.
O, heavy times, begetting such events!
From London by the King was I pressed forth;
My father, being the Earl of Warwick's man,
Came on the part of York, pressed by his master;
And I, who at his hands received my life,
Have by my hands of life bereavèd him.
Pardon me, God, I knew not what I did!
And pardon, father, for I knew not thee!
My tears shall wipe away these bloody marks;
And no more words till they have flowed their fill.

King: O, piteous spectacle! O, bloody times!
Whiles lions war and battle for their dens,
Poor harmless lambs abide their enmity.
Weep, wretched man; I'll aid thee tear for tear;
And let our hearts and eyes, like civil war,
Be blind with tears, and break o'ercharged with grief.
  Father: Thou that so stoutly hath resisted me,
Give me thy gold, if thou hast any gold;
For I have bought it with an hundred blows.
But let me see: is this our foeman's face?
Ah, no, no, no, it is mine only son!
Ah, boy, if any life be left in thee,
Throw up thine eye! See, see what showers arise,
Blown with the windy tempest of my heart,
Upon thy wounds, that kills mine eye and heart!
O, pity, God, this miserable age!
What stratagems, how fell, how butcherly,
Erroneous, mutinous, and unnatural,
This deadly quarrel daily doth beget!
O boy, thy father gave thee life too soon,
And hath bereft thee of thy life too late!
  King: Woe above woe! Grief more than common grief!
O that my death would stay these ruthful deeds!
O, pity, pity, gentle heaven, pity!
The red rose and the white are on his face,
The fatal colours of our striving houses;
The one his purple blood right well resembles;
The other his pale cheeks, methinks, presenteth.
Wither one rose, and let the other flourish;
If you contend, a thousand lives must wither.
  Son: How will my mother for a father's death
Take on with me and ne'er be satisfied!
  Father: How will my wife for slaughter of my son
Shed seas of tears and ne'er be satisfied!
  King: How will the country for these woeful chances
Misthink the King and not be satisfied!

Son: Was ever son so rued a father's death?
Father: Was ever father so bemoaned his son?
King: Was ever king so grieved for subjects' woe?
Much is your sorrow; mine ten times so much.
  Son: I'll bear thee hence, where I may weep my fill.
  Father: These arms of mine shall be thy winding-sheet;
My heart, sweet boy, shall be thy sepulchre,
For from my heart thine image ne'er shall go;
My sighing breast shall be thy funeral bell;
And so obsequious will thy father be,
Even for the loss of thee, having no more,
As Priam was for all his valiant sons.
I'll bear thee hence; and let them fight that will,
For I have murdered where I should not kill.

War Poets

Roy Campbell was particularly severe on the civilian poet who pontificated from the safety of his desk; and he is not the only writer to have questioned either the propriety or the effectiveness of poems on the subject of war – whoever the poet might be.

The best war poets may not always have been those who served in the forces and experienced fighting directly, but they most often were. Three of the poets in this section were killed in action – John Jarmain, T. Cameron Wilson and Sidney Keyes – and, in this light, Wilson's own image for the war poet as that bold scavenger, the magpie, has particular poignancy.

WALT WHITMAN

To a Certain Civilian

Did you ask dulcet rhymes from me?
Did you seek the civilian's peaceful and languishing rhymes?
Did you find what I sang erewhile so hard to follow?
Why I was not singing erewhile for you to follow, to
      understand – nor am I now;
(I have been born of the same as the war was born,
The drum-corps' rattle is ever to me sweet music, I love well
      the martial dirge,
With slow wail and convulsive throb leading the officer's
      funeral;)
What to such as you anyhow such a poet as I? therefore leave
      my works,
And go lull yourself with what you can understand, and with
      piano-tunes,
For I lull nobody, and you will never understand me.

W. B. YEATS

On Being Asked for a War Poem

I think it better that in times like these
A poet's mouth be silent, for in truth
We have no gift to set a statesman right;
He has had enough of meddling who can please
A young girl in the indolence of her youth,
Or an old man upon a winter's night.

JOHN JARMAIN

These Poems

You who in evenings by the fire
May read these words of mine,
How let you see the desert bare
In the print-smooth line?

Listen! These poems were not made in rooms,
But out in the empty sand,
Where only the homeless Arab roams
In a sterile land;

They were not at tables written
With placid curtains drawn,
But by candlelight begotten
Of the dusk and dawn.

They had no peace at their creation,
No twilight hush of wings;
Only the tremble of bombs, the guns' commotion,
And destructive things.

ROBERT GRAVES

When I'm Killed

When I'm killed, don't think of me
Buried there in Cambrin Wood,
Nor as in Zion think of me
With the Intolerable Good.
And there's one thing that I know well,
I'm damned if I'll be damned to Hell!

So when I'm killed, don't wait for me,
Walking the dim corridor;
In Heaven or Hell, don't wait for me,
Or you must wait for evermore.
You'll find me buried, living-dead
In these verses that you've read.

So when I'm killed, don't mourn for me.
Shot, poor lad, so bold and young,
Killed and gone – don't mourn for me.
On your lips my life is hung:
O friends and lovers, you can save
Your playfellow from the grave.

T. P. CAMERON WILSON

Magpies in Picardy

The magpies in Picardy
Are more than I can tell.
They flicker down the dusty roads
And cast a magic spell
On the men who march through Picardy,
Through Picardy to hell.

(The blackbird flies with panic,
The swallow goes with light,
The finches move like ladies,
The owl floats by at night;
But the great and flashing magpie
He flies as artists might.)

The magpie in Picardy
Told me secret things —
Of the music in white feathers,
And the sunlight that sings
And dances in deep shadows —
He told me with his wings.

(The hawk is cruel and rigid,
He watches from a height;
The rook is slow and sombre,
The robin loves to fight;
But the great and flashing magpie
He flies as lovers might.)

He told me that in Picardy,
An age ago or more,
While all his fathers still were eggs,
These dusty highways bore
Brown, singing soldiers marching out
Through Picardy to war.

He said that still through chaos
Works on the ancient plan,
And two things have altered not
Since first the world began —
The beauty of the wild green earth
And the bravery of man.

(For the sparrow flies unthinking
And quarrels in his flight.
The heron trails his legs behind,

The lark goes out of sight;
But the great and flashing magpie
He flies as poets might.)

SIDNEY KEYES

War Poet

I am the man who looked for peace and found
My own eyes barbed.
I am the man who groped for words and found
An arrow in my hand.
I am the builder whose firm walls surround
A slipping land.
When I grow sick or mad
Mock me not nor chain me:
When I reach for the wind
Cast me not down:
Though my face is a burnt book
And a wasted town.

DALE R. CARVER

The Poet

With clinical eye and mind alert
he watched the ebb and flow,
saw in live bodies beyond all hurt
dead eyes; saw blood on snow.

He walked with death ever near
beneath an indifferent sky,
knew the sickening taste of fear,
watched the valiant die,

watched the cowardly live on,
knew anguish at broken trees,
saw the mine-slain forest fawn
and proud men on their knees.

He recorded minutely in memory
all that came to pass,
then, ill of soul, wrote poetry
as a sick cat eats grass.

ROY CAMPBELL

The Volunteer's Reply to the Poet

'Will it be so again?'

. . . So the Soldier replied to the Poet,
Oh yes! it will all be the same,
But a bloody sight worse, and you know it
Since you have a hand in the game:
And you'll be the first in the racket
To sell us a similar dope,
Wrapped up in a rosier packet,
But noosed with as cunning a rope.
You coin us the catchwords and phrases
For which to be slaughtered; and then,
While thousands are blasted to blazes,
Sit picking your nose with your pen.
We know what you're bursting to tell us,
By heart. It is all very fine.
We must swallow the Bait that you sell us
And pay for your Hook and your Line.
But when we have come to the Isthmus
That bridges the Slump to the War,
We shall contact a new Father Christmas
Like the one we contacted before,

Deploring the one he replaces
Like you do (it's part of the show!)
But with those same mincing grimaces
And that mealy old kisser we know!
And he'll patent a cheap cornucopia,
For all that our purse can afford,
And rent us a flat in Utopia
With dreams for our lodging and board.
And we'll hand in our Ammo and Guns
As we handed them in once before,
And he'll lock them up safe, till our sons
Are conscripted for Freedom once more.
We can die for our faith by the million
And laugh at our bruises and scars,
But hush! for the Poet-Civilian
Is weeping, between the cigars.
Mellifluous, sweeter than Cadbury's,
The MOI Nightingale (Hush!)
Is lining his funk-hole with Bradburies
So his feelings come out with a rush,
For our woes are the cash in his kitty
When his voice he so kindly devotes
In sentiment, pathos, and pity,
To bringing huge lumps to the throats
Of our widows, and sweethearts, and trollops,
Since it sells like hot cakes to the town
As he doles out the Goitre in dollops
And the public is gulping it down.
Oh well may he weep for the soldier,
Who weeps at a guinea a tear,
For although his invention gets mouldier,
It keeps him his job in the rear.
When my Mrs the organ is wheeling
And my adenoids wheeze to the sky,
He will publish the hunger I'm feeling
And rake in his cheque with a sigh:

And when with a trayful of matches
And laces, you hawk in the street,
O comrades, in tatters and patches,
Rejoice! since we're in for a treat:
For when we have died in the gutter
To safeguard his income and state,
Be sure that the Poet will utter
Some beautiful thoughts on our Fate!

EDWARD BOND

First World War Poets

You went to the front like sheep
And bleated at the pity of it
In academies that smell of abattoirs
Your poems are still studied

You turned the earth to mud
Yet complain you drowned in it
Your generals were dug in at the rear
Degenerates drunk on brandy and prayer
You *saw* the front – and only bleated
The pity!

You survived
Did you burn your generals' houses?
Loot the new millionaires?
No, you found new excuses
You'd lost an arm or your legs
You sat by the empty fire
And hummed music hall songs

Why did your generals send you away to die?
They saw a Great War coming
Between masters and workers

In their own land
So they herded you over the cliffs to be rid of you
How they hated you while you lived!
How they wept over you once you were dead!

What did you fight for?
A new world?
No – an old world already in ruins!
Your children?
Millions of children died
Because you fought for your enemies
And not against them!

We will not forget!
We will not forgive!

EDGELL RICKWORD

Trench Poets

I knew a man, he was my chum,
but he grew blacker every day,
and would not brush the flies away,
nor blanch however fierce the hum
of passing shells; I used to read,
to rouse him, random things from Donne –
like 'Get with child a mandrake-root.'
But you can tell he was far gone,
for he lay gaping, mackerel-eyed,
and stiff and senseless as a post
even when that old poet cried
'I long to talk with some old lover's ghost.'

I tried the Elegies one day,
but he, because he heard me say:
'What needst thou have more covering than a man?'

grinned nastily, and so I knew
the worms had got his brains at last.
There was one thing that I might do
to starve the worms; I racked my head
for healthy things and quoted 'Maud.'
His grin got worse and I could see
he sneered at passion's purity.
He stank so badly, though we were great chums
I had to leave him; then rats ate his thumbs.

The Epic

All epics, since the *Aeneid*, have been concerned with nationalism and propaganda. Just as Virgil's was written to glorify Rome, so was Camoens's to celebrate Portugal's feats of maritime exploration and empire-building. They are one of the mainsprings of national pride. Elizabeth Barrett Browning gives the idea a subversive twist when she suggests that there is epic material to be found in ordinary modern life.

In *Tristram Shandy*, Laurence Sterne sets out the rather more commonplace reasons for war: 'For what is war? What is it, Yorrick, when fought, as ours has been, upon principles of liberty, and upon principles of honour – what is it – but the getting together of quiet and harmless people, with their swords in their hands to keep the ambitious and the turbulent within bounds?'

VIRGIL

from The Aeneid, Book I

Arms, and the Man I sing, who, forc'd by Fate,
And haughty Juno's unrelenting Hate;
Expell'd and exil'd, left the Trojan Shoar:
Long Labours, both by Sea and Land he bore;
And in the doubtful War, before he won
The Latian Realm, and built the destin'd Town:
His banish'd Gods restor'd to Rites Divine,
And setl'd sure Succession in his Line:
From whence the Race of Alban Fathers come,
And the long Glories of Majestick Rome.
    O Muse! the Causes and the Crimes relate,
What Goddess was provok'd, and whence her hate:
For what Offence the Queen of Heav'n began

To persecute so brave, so just a Man!
Involv'd his anxious Life in endless Cares,
Expos'd to Wants, and hurry'd into Wars!
Can Heav'nly Minds such high resentment show;
Or exercise their Spight in Human Woe?

Translated from the Latin by John Dryden

LUIS CAMOENS

from The Lusiads, Canto I

The feats of Arms, and famed heroick Host,
    from occidental Lusitanian strand,
    who o'er the waters ne'er by seaman crost,
    farèd beyond the Taprobane-land,
    forceful in perils and in battle-post,
    with more than promised force of mortal hand;
and in the regions of a distant race
rear'd a new throne so haught in Pride of Place:

And, eke, the Kings of mem'ory grand and glorious,
    who hied them Holy Faith and Reign to spread,
    converting, conquering, and in lands notorious,
    Africk and Asia, devastation made;
    nor less the Lieges who by deeds memorious
    brake from the doom that binds the vulgar dead;
my song would sound o'er Earth's extremest part
were mine the genius, mine the Poet's art.

Cease the sage Grecian, and the Man of Troy
    to vaunt long Voyage made in bygone day:
    Cease Alexander, Trajan cease to 'joy
    the fame of vict'ories that have pass'd away:
    The noble Lusian's stouter breast sing I,
    whom Mars and Neptune dared not disobey:

Cease all that antique Muse hath sung, for now
a better Brav'ry rears its bolder brow. [. . .]

Grant me sonorous accents, fire-abounding,
 now serves ne peasant's pipe, ne rustick reed;
 but blast of trumpet, long and loud resounding,
 that 'flameth heart and hue to fiery deed:
 Grant me high strains to suit their Gestes astounding,
 your Sons, who aided Mars in martial need;
that o'er the world be sung the glorious song,
if theme so lofty may to verse belong.

And Thou! O goodly omen'd trust, all-dear
 To Lusitania's olden liberty,
 whereon assurèd esperance we rear
 enforced to see our frail Christianity:
 Thou, O new terror to the Moorish spear,
 the fated marvel of our century,
to govern worlds of men by God so given,
that the world's best be given to God and Heaven:

Thou young, thou tender, ever-flourishing bough,
 true scion of tree by Christ belovèd more,
 than aught that Occident did ever know,
 'Cæsarian' or 'Most Christian' styled before:
 Look on thy 'scutcheon, and behold it show
 the present Vict'ory long past ages bore;
Arms which He gave and made thine own to be
by Him assumèd on the fatal tree . . .

 Translated from the Portuguese by Richard Burton

GEORGE GORDON, LORD BYRON

from Don Juan, Canto VII

Oh, thou eternal Homer! I have now
  To paint a siege, wherein more men were slain,
With deadlier engines and a speedier blow,
  Than in thy Greek gazette of that campaign;
And yet, like all men else, I must allow,
  To vie with thee would be about as vain
As for a brook to cope with ocean's flood;
But still we moderns equal you in blood;

If not in poetry, at least in fact;
  And fact is truth, the grand desideratum!
Of which, howe'er the Muse describes each act,
  There should be ne'ertheless a slight substratum.
But now the town is going to be attacked;
  Great deeds are doing – how shall I relate 'em?
Souls of immortal generals! Phœbus watches
To colour up his rays from your despatches.

Oh, ye great bulletins of Bonaparte!
  Oh, ye less grand long lists of killed and wounded!
Shade of Leonidas, who fought so hearty,
  When my poor Greece was once, as now, surrounded!
Oh, Cæsar's Commentaries! now impart, ye
  Shadows of glory! (lest I be confounded)
A portion of your fading twilight hues,
So beautiful, so fleeting, to the Muse.

When I call 'fading' martial immortality,
  I mean, that every age and every year,
And almost every day, in sad reality,
  Some sucking hero is compelled to rear,

Who, when we come to sum up the totality
  Of deeds to human happiness most dear;
Turns out to be a butcher in great business,
Afflicting young folks with a sort of dizziness.

Medals, rank, ribands, lace, embroidery, scarlet,
  Are things immortal to immortal man,
As purple to the Babylonian harlot:
  An uniform to boys is like a fan
To women; there is scarce a crimson varlet
  But deems himself the first in Glory's van.
But Glory's glory; and if you would find
What that is — ask the pig who sees the wind!

ELIZABETH BARRETT BROWNING

from Aurora Leigh

The critics say that epics have died out
With Agamemnon and the goat-nursed gods;
I'll not believe it. I could never deem
As Payne Knight did, (the mythic mountaineer
Who travelled higher than he was born to live,
And showed sometimes the goitre in his throat
Discoursing of an image seen through fog,)
That Homer's heroes measured twelve feet high.
They were but men: — his Helen's hair turned gray
Like any plain Miss Smith's who wears a front;
And Hector's infant whimpered at a plume
As yours last Friday at a turkey-cock.
All actual heroes are essential men,
And all men possible heroes: every age,
Heroic in proportions, double-faced,
Looks backward and before, expects a morn
And claims an epos.

Ay, but every age
Appears to souls who live in 't (ask Carlyle)
Most unheroic. Ours, for instance, ours:
The thinkers scout it, and the poets abound
Who scorn to touch it with a finger-tip:
A pewter age, – mixed metal, silver-washed:
An age of scum, spooned off the richer past,
An age of patches for old gaberdines,
An age of mere transition, meaning nought
Except that what succeeds must shame it quite
If God please. That's wrong thinking, to my mind,
And wrong thoughts make poor poems.
                                    Every age,
Through being beheld too close, is ill-discerned
By those who have not lived past it. We'll suppose
Mount Athos carved, as Alexander schemed,
To some colossal statue of a man.
The peasants, gathering brushwood in his ear,
Had guessed as little as the browsing goats
Of form or feature of humanity
Up there, – in fact, had travelled five miles off
Or ere the giant image broke on them.
Full human profile, nose and chin distinct,
Mouth, muttering rhythms of silence up the sky
And fed at evening with the blood of suns;
Grand torso, – hand, that flung perpetually
The largesse of a silver river down
To all the country pastures. 'T is even thus
With times we live in, – evermore too great
To be apprehended near.
                                    But poets should
Exert a double vision; should have eyes
To see near things as comprehensively
As if afar they took their point of sight,
And distant things as intimately deep
As if they touched them. Let us strive for this.

I do distrust the poet who discerns
No character or glory in his times,
And trundles back his soul five hundred years,
Past moat and drawbridge, into a castle-court
To sing – oh, not of lizard or of toad
Alive i' the ditch there, – 't were excusable,
But of some black chief, half knight, half sheep-lifter,
Some beauteous dame, half chattel and half queen,
As dead as must be, for the greater part,
The poems made on their chivalric bones;
And that's no wonder: death inherits death.

Nay, if there 's room for poets in this world
A little overgrown, (I think there is)
Their sole work is to represent the age,
Their age, not Charlemagne's, – this live, throbbing age,
That brawls, cheats, maddens, calculates, aspires,
And spends more passion, more heroic heat,
Betwixt the mirrors of its drawing-rooms,
Than Roland with his knights at Roncesvalles.
To flinch from modern varnish, coat or flounce,
Cry out for togas and the picturesque,
Is fatal, – foolish too. King Arthur's self
Was commonplace to Lady Guenever;
And Camelot to minstrels seemed as flat
As Fleet Street to our poets.
                              Never flinch,
But still, unscrupulously epic, catch
Upon the burning lava of a song
The full-veined, heaving, double-breasted Age.
That, when the next shall come, the men of that
May touch the impress with reverent hand, and say
'Behold, – behold the paps we all have sucked!
This bosom seems to beat still, or at least
It sets ours beating: this is living art,
Which thus presents and thus records true life.'

Arguments for War

War is too important to be left to the politicians, or even to the generals. Each has its own complex causes and justifications, even if some are more potent than others. Fulke Greville, writing at the beginning of the seventeenth century, coolly sets out the reasons why war promotes the virtues more effectively than peace. Wallace Stevens's argument is that the fighter, paradoxically enough, is both 'master of men' and servant of freedom.

FULKE GREVILLE, LORD BROOKE

'What is the cause, why states, that war and win'

What is the cause, why states, that war and win,
Have honour, and breed men of better fame,
Than states in peace, since war and conquest sin
In blood, wrong liberty, all trades of shame?
   Force-framing instruments, which it must use,
   Proud in excess and glory to abuse.

The reason is; peace is a quiet nurse
Of idleness, and idleness the field,
Where wit and power change all seeds to the worse,
By narrow self-will upon which they build,
   And thence bring forth captiv'd inconstant ends,
   Neither to princes, nor to people friends.

Besides, the sins of peace on subjects feed,
And thence wound power, which for it all things can,
With wrong to one despairs in many breed,
For while laws' oaths, power's creditors to man,
   Make humble subjects dream of native right,
   Man's faith abus'd adds courage to despite.

Where conquest works by strength, and stirs up fame,
A glorious echo, pleasing doom of pain,
  Which in the sleep of death yet keeps a name,
  And makes detracting loss speak ill in vain.

For to great actions time so friendly is,
As o'er the means (albeit the means be ill)
It casts forgetfulness; veils things amiss,
With powers and honour to encourage will.

Besides things hard a reputation bear,
To die resolv'd though guilty wonder breeds,
Yet what strength those be which can blot out fear,
And to self-ruin joyfully proceeds,
  Ask them that from the ashes of this fire,
  With new lives still to such new flames aspire.

WALLACE STEVENS

from Phases

What shall we say to the lovers of freedom,
Forming their states for new eras to come?
Say that the fighter is master of men.

Shall we, then, say to the lovers of freedom
That force, and not freedom, must always prevail?
Say that the fighter is master of men.

Or shall we say to the lovers of freedom
That freedom will conquer and always prevail?
Say that the fighter is master of men.

Say, too, that freedom is master of masters,
Forming their states for new eras to come.
Say that the fighter is master of men.

Pacifism

The idea that pacifism should be respected has developed significantly over the past hundred years. Although Quakers, among others, have always opposed the taking up of arms, this was never used as a public argument against the press gangs and there were no debates about it during either the Napoleonic Wars or any of the other wars of the nineteenth century. It requires a degree of political sophistication and tolerance for a society to allow some of its members to refuse the call to arms, especially when the very existence of the state and its freedoms is under threat. Conscientious objection was respected by British governments in both World Wars – though many individuals who proclaimed it were ostracized and subject to personal abuse.

Conscientious objectors have often had to display courage and resilience, since the view they take is at odds with that of most of their fellow countrymen. Some have chosen to serve in non-combative roles in the field of battle – as stretcher-bearers, for instance – showing, through acts of great bravery, that their objection was based not on fear but on principle.

George Orwell's poem, attacking pacifism so eloquently, was dashed off in reply to the one by Alex Comfort. Writing as 'Obadiah Hornbrooke', Comfort, a pacifist and socialist, had published his poem in the magazine *Tribune* in 1943.

HILAIRE BELLOC

The Pacifist

Pale Ebenezer thought it wrong to fight,
But Roaring Bill (who killed him) thought it right.

T. W. H. CROSLAND

The White Feather Legion

Yes, somehow and somewhere and always,
   We're first when the shoutings begin,
We put up a howl for Old England
   The Kaiser can hear in Berlin,
                    Dear boys!
   He hears it and quakes in Berlin.
Yes, a health to ourselves as we scatter
   In taxis to get the last train,
Cheer oh, for the White Feather Legion
   Goes back to its females again,
                    Regards!
   Goes back to its slippers again,
                    Hurrah!
   The Bass and the lager again,
                    Here's how!

HENRY NEWBOLT

The Non-Combatant

Among a race high-handed, strong of heart,
Sea-rovers, conquerors, builders in the waste,
He had his birth; a nature too complete,
Eager and doubtful, no man's soldier sworn
And no man's chosen captain; born to fail,
A name without an echo: yet he too
Within the cloister of his narrow days
Fulfilled the ancestral rites, and kept alive
The eternal fire; it may be, not in vain;
For out of those who dropped a downward glance

Upon the weakling huddled at his prayers,
Perchance some looked beyond him, and then first
Beheld the glory, and what shrine it filled,
And to what Spirit sacred: or perchance
Some heard him chanting, though but to himself,
The old heroic names: and went their way:
And hummed his music on the march to death.

EDNA ST VINCENT MILLAY

Conscientious Objector

I shall die, but that is all that I shall do for Death.

I hear him leading his horse out of the stall; I hear the clatter on
    the barn-floor.
He is in haste; he has business in Cuba, business in the Balkans,
    many calls to make this morning.
But I will not hold the bridle while he cinches the girth.
And he may mount by himself; I will not give him a leg up.

Though he flick my shoulders with his whip, I will not tell him
    which way the fox ran.
With his hoof on my breast, I will not tell him where the
    black boy hides in the swamp.
I shall die, but that is all that I shall do for Death; I am not on
    his pay-roll.

I will not tell him the whereabouts of my friends nor of my
    enemies either.
Though he promise me much, I will not map him the route to
    any man's door.

Am I a spy in the land of the living, that I should deliver men to
     Death?
Brother, the password and the plans of our city are safe with
     me; never through me
Shall you be overcome.

R. F. PALMER

The Conchie

He came to the depot a figure of shame,
    A 'conchie' refusing to fight,
Who said 'twas no glory to kill and to maim,
    To see who was wrong and who right!

We thought it a slight on the Medical Corps
    When they drafted the 'conchie' to us,
And thought it an insult that in time of war,
    A soldier should make so much fuss.

We called him a coward and laughed him to scorn,
    Each evening when he knelt to pray,
We said he was yellow and should have been born
    As a woman, but nought would he say.

In the African desert one hot August day,
    When the fighting was heavy and grim,
A messenger came from headquarters to say,
    That our chance of survival was dim.

When darkness descended our stretchers we took
    To bring in the wounded and slain.
Tho' Jerry was shelling, by hook or by crook
    We went out again and again.

At last when we'd finished our task for the night
    We reported and answered our roll,

The 'conchie' was absent. We guessed that in fright,
  He'd bolted and missed the recall.

Another day passed in the tropical heat
  And when the sun sank in the west,
Another six miles we'd been forced to retreat
  And the enemy gave us no rest.

As we lay under cover the following night
  And stared out across 'No Man's Land',
We saw in the glare of a stray Verey Light
  Two men creeping in, hand-in-hand.

The 'conchie' 'd returned. He was wounded and worn,
  And was leading a man who was blind,
His face was blood-spattered, his clothing was torn,
  And his leg dragging useless behind.

All day he had tended the shell-blinded man
  In the glare of the African sun,
And as darkness fell the long journey began,
  And collapsed in our lines when 'twas done.

Our 'conchie' now wears a VC on his breast,
  We call him a coward no more.
He still says his prayers e'er going to rest,
  The pride of the Medical Corps.

ALEX COMFORT

Letter to an American Visitor

Columbian poet, whom we've all respected
  From a safe distance for a year or two,
Since first your *magnum opus* was collected –
  It seems a pity no one welcomed you
  Except the slippery professional few,

Whose news you've read, whose posters you've inspected;
　　Who gave America Halifax, and who
Pay out to scribes and painters they've selected
　　　　Doles which exceed a fraction of the debts
　　　　Of all our pimps in hardware coronets.

You've seen the ruins, heard the speeches, swallowed
　　The bombed-out hospitals and cripples' schools –
You've heard (on records) how the workers hollowed
　　And read in poker-work GIVE US THE TOOLS:
　　You know how, with the steadfastness of mules,
The Stern Determination of the People
　　Goes sailing through a paradise of fools
Like masons shinning up an endless steeple –
　　　　A climb concluding after many days
　　　　In a brass weathercock that points all ways.

The land sprouts orators. No doubt you've heard
　　How every buffer, fool and patrioteer
Applies the Power of the Spoken Word
　　And shoves his loud posterior in your ear;
　　So Monkey Hill competes with Berkeley Square –
The BBC as bookie, pimp and vet
　　Presenting Air Vice-Marshals set to cheer
Our raided towns with vengeance (though I've yet
　　　　To hear from any man who lost his wife
　　　　Berlin or Lubeck brought her back to life).

You've heard of fighting on the hills and beaches
　　And down the rabbit holes with pikes and bows –
You've heard the Baron's bloody-minded speeches
　　(Each worth a fresh Division to our foes)
　　That smell so strong of murder that the crows
Perch on the Foreign Office roof and caw
　　For German corpses laid in endless rows,
'A Vengeance such as Europe never saw' –
　　　　The maniac Baron's future contribution
　　　　To peace perpetual through retribution . . .

You've heard His Nibs decanting year by year
   The dim productions of his bulldog brain,
While homes and factories sit still to hear
   The same old drivel dished up once again –
   You heard the Churches' cartwheels to explain
That bombs are Christian when the English drop them –
   The Union bosses scrapping over gain
While no one's the temerity to stop them
     Or have the racketeers who try to bleed 'em
     Flogged, like the Indians for demanding freedom.

They found you poets – quite a decent gallery
   Of painters who don't let their chances slip;
And writers who prefer a regular salary
   To steer their writings by the Party Whip –
   Hassall's been tipped to have Laureateship:
Morton is following Goebbels, not St Paul.
   There's Elton's squeaky pump still gives a drip,
And Priestley twists his proletarian awl
     Cobbling at shoes that Mill and Rousseau wore
     And still the wretched tool contrives to bore.

They found you critics – an astounding crowd:
   (Though since their work's living, I won't say
Who howled at Eliot, hooted Treece, were loud
   In kicking Auden when he slipped away
   Out of the looney-bin to find, they say,
A quiet place where men with minds could write:
   But since Pearl Harbour, in a single day
The same old circus chase him, black is white,
     And once again by day and night he feels
     The packs of tripehounds yelling at his heels).

I say, they found you artists, well selected,
   Whom we export to sell the British case:
We keep our allied neighbours well protected
   From those who give the thing a different face –
   One man's in jail, one in a 'medical place';

Another working at a farm with pigs on:
　　We take their leisure, close their books, say grace,
And like that bus-conducting lad Geoff Grigson
　　　　We beat up every buzzard, kite and vulture,
　　　　And dish them out to you as English Culture.

Once in a while, to every Man and Nation,
　　There comes, as Lowell said, a sort of crisis
Between the Ministry of Information
　　And what your poor artistic soul advises:
　　They catch the poets, straight from Cam or Isis:
'Join the brigade, or be for ever dumb –
　　Either cash in your artistic lysis
Or go on land work if you won't succumb:
　　　　Rot in the Army, sickened and unwilling':
　　　　So you can wonder that they draw their shilling?

You met them all. You don't require a list
　　Of understrapping ghosts who once were writers –
Who celebrate the size of Britain's fist,
　　Write notes for sermons, dish out pep to mitres,
　　Fake letters from the Men who Fly our Fighters.
Cheer when we blast some enemy bungalows –
　　Think up atrocities, the artful blighters,
To keep the grindstone at the public's nose –
　　　　Combining moral uplift and pornography,
　　　　Produced with arty paper and typography.

They find their leisure to fulfil their promise,
　　Their work is praised, *funguntur vice cotis*;
And Buddy Judas cracks up Doubting Thomas.
　　Their ways are paved with favourable notice
　　(Look how unanimous the Tory vote is).
They write in papers and review each other,
　　You'd never guess how bloody full the boat is;
I shan't forgive MacNeice his crippled brother
　　　　Whom just a year ago on New Year's Day
　　　　The Germans murdered in a radio play.

O for another Dunciad – a POPE
  To purge this dump with his gigantic boot –
Drive fools to water, aspirin or rope –
  Make idle lamp-posts bear their fitting fruit:
  Private invective's far too long been mute –
O for another vast satiric comet
  To blast this wretched tinder, branch and root.
The servile stuff that makes a true man vomit –
    Suck from the works to which they cling like leeches,
    Those resurrection-puddings, Churchill's speeches.

God knows – for there is libel – I can't name
  How many clammy paws of these you've shaken,
Been told our English spirit is the same
  From Lord Vansittart back to pseudo-Bacon –
  Walked among licensed writers, and were taken
To Grub Street, Malet Street, and Portland Place,
  Where every question that you ask will waken
The same old salesman's grin on every face
    Among the squads of columbines and flunkeys,
    Set on becoming Laureate of Monkeys.

We do not ask, my friend, that you'll forget
  The squirts and toadies when you were presented,
The strength-through-joy brigades you will have met
  Whose mouths are baggy and whose hair is scented –
  Only recall we were not represented.
We wrote our own refusals, and we meant them.
  Our work is plastered and ourselves resented –
Our heads are bloody, but we have not bent them.
    We hold no licences, like ladies' spaniels;
    We live like lions in this den of Daniels.

O friend and writer, deafened by the howls
  That dying systems utter, mad with fear
In darkness, with a sinking of the bowels,
  Where all the devils of old conscience leer –
  Forget the gang that met you on the pier,

Grinning and stuffed with all the old excuses
    For starving Europe, and the crocodile tear
Turned on for visitors who have their uses.
      We know the capers of the simian crew.
      We send our best apologies to you.

GEORGE ORWELL

As One Non-Combatant to Another

O poet strutting from the sandbagged portal
Of that small world where barkers ply their art,
And each new 'school' believes itself immortal,
Just like the horse that draws the knacker's cart:
O captain of a clique of self-advancers,
Trained in the tactics of the pamphleteer,
Where slogans serve for thoughts and sneers for answers –
You've chosen well your moment to appear
And hold your nose amid a world of horror
Like Dr Bowdler walking through Gomorrah.

In the Left Book Club days you wisely lay low,
But when 'Stop Hitler!' lost its old attraction
You bounded forward in a Woolworth's halo
To cash in on anti-war reaction;
You waited till the Nazis ceased from frightening,
Then, picking a safe audience, shouted 'Shame!'
Like a Prometheus you defied the lightning,
But didn't have the nerve to sign your name.
You're a true poet, but as saint and martyr
You're a mere fraud, like the Atlantic Charter.

Your hands are clean, and so were Pontius Pilate's,
But as for 'bloody heads', that's just a metaphor;
The bloody heads are on Pacific islets
Or Russian steppes or Libyan sands – it's better for

The health to be a CO than a fighter,
To chalk a pavement doesn't need much guts,
It pays to stay at home and be a writer
While other talents wilt in Nissen huts;
'We live like lions' – yes, just like a lion,
Pensioned on scraps in a safe cage of iron.

For a while you write the warships ring you round
And flights of bombers drown the nightingales,
And every bomb that drops is worth a pound
To you or someone like you, for your sales
Are swollen with those of rivals dead or silent,
Whether in Tunis or the BBC,
And in the drowsy freedom of this island
You're free to shout that England isn't free;
They even chuck you cash, as bears get buns,
For crying 'Peace!' behind a screen of guns.

In 'seventeen to snub the nosing bitch
Who slipped you a white feather needed cheek,
But now, when every writer finds his niche
Within some mutual-admiration clique,
Who cares what epithets by Blimps are hurled?
Who'd give a damn if handed a white feather?
Each little mob of pansies is a world,
Cosy and warm in any kind of weather;
In such a world it's easy to 'object',
Since that's what both your friends and foes expect.

At times it's almost a more dangerous deed
Not to object: I know, for I've been bitten.
I wrote in nineteen-forty that at need
I'd fight to keep the Nazis out of Britain;
And Christ! how shocked the pinks were! Two years later
I hadn't lived it down; one had the effrontery
To write three pages calling me a 'traitor',
So black a crime it is to love one's country.

Yet where's the pink that would have thought it odd of me
To write a shelf of books in praise of sodomy?

Your game is easy, and its rules are plain:
Pretend the war began in 'thirty-nine,
Don't mention China, Ethiopia, Spain,
Don't mention Poles except to say they're swine;
Cry havoc when we bomb a German city,
When Czechs get killed don't worry in the least,
Give India a perfunctory squirt of pity
But don't inquire what happens further East;
Don't mention Jews – in short, pretend the war is
Simply a racket 'got up' by the Tories.

Throw in a word of 'anti-Fascist' patter
From time to time, by way of reinsurance,
And then go on to prove it makes no matter
If Blimps or Nazis hold the world in durance;
And that we others who 'support' the war
Are either crooks or sadists or flag-wavers
In love with drums and bugles, but still more
Concerned with cadging Brendan Bracken's favours;
Or fools who think that bombs bring back the dead,
A thing not even Harris ever said.

If you'd your way we'd leave the Russians to it
And sell our steel to Hitler as before;
Meanwhile you save your soul, and while you do it,
Take out a long-term mortgage on the war.
For after war there comes an ebb of passion,
The dead are sniggered at – and there you'll shine,
You'll be the very bull's-eye of the fashion,
You almost might get back to 'thirty-nine,
Back to the dear old game of scratch-my-neighbour
In sleek reviews financed by coolie labour.

But you don't hoot at Stalin – that's 'not done' –
Only at Churchill; I've no wish to praise him,

I'd gladly shoot him when the war is won,
Or now, if there was someone to replace him.
But unlike some, I'll pay him what I owe him;
There was a time when empires crashed like houses,
And many a pink who'd titter at your poem
Was glad enough to cling to Churchill's trousers.
Christ! how they huddled up to one another
Like day-old chicks about their foster-mother!

I'm not a fan for 'fighting on the beaches',
And still less for the 'breezy uplands' stuff,
I seldom listen-in to Churchill's speeches,
But I'd far sooner hear that kind of guff
Than your remark, a year or so ago,
That if the Nazis came you'd knuckle under
And peaceably 'accept the *status quo*'.
Maybe you would! But I've a right to wonder
Which will sound better in the days to come,
'Blood, toil and sweat' or 'Kiss the Nazi's bum'.

But your chief target is the radio hack,
The hired pep-talker – he's a safe objective,
Since he's unpopular and can't hit back.
It doesn't need the eye of a detective
To look down Portland Place and spot the whores,
But there are men (I grant, not the most heeded)
With twice your gifts and courage three times yours
Who do that dirty work because it's needed;
Not blindly, but for reasons they can balance,
They wear their seats out and lay waste their talents.

All propaganda's lying, yours or mine;
It's lying even when its facts are true;
That goes for Goebbels or the 'party line',
Or for the Primrose League or PPU.
But there are truths that smaller lies can serve,
And dirtier lies that scruples can gild over;

To waste your brains on war may need more nerve
Than to dodge facts and live in mental clover;
It's mean enough when other men are dying,
But when you lie, it's much to know you're lying.

That's thirteen stanzas, and perhaps you're puzzled
To know why I've attacked you – well, here's why:
Because your enemies all are dead or muzzled,
You've never picked on one who might reply.
You've hogged the limelight and you've aired your virtue,
While chucking sops to every dangerous faction,
The Left will cheer you and the Right won't hurt you;
What did you risk? Not even a libel action.
If you would show what saintly stuff you're made of,
Why not attack the cliques you *are* afraid of?

Denounce Joe Stalin, jeer at the Red Army,
Insult the Pope – you'll get some come-back there;
It's honourable, even if it's barmy,
To stamp on corns all round and never care.
But for the half-way saint and cautious hero,
Whose head's unbloody even if 'unbowed',
My admiration's somewhere near to zero;
So my last words would be: Come off that cloud,
Unship those wings that hardly dared to flitter,
And spout your halo for a pint of bitter.

E. E. CUMMINGS

'i sing of Olaf glad and big'

i sing of Olaf glad and big
whose warmest heart recoiled at war:
a conscientious object-or

his wellbelovéd colonel(trig
westpointer most succinctly bred)
took erring Olaf soon in hand;
but—though an host of overjoyed
noncoms(first knocking on the head
him)do through icy waters roll
that helplessness which others stroke
with brushes recently employed
anent this muddy toiletbowl,
while kindred intellects evoke
allegiance per blunt instruments—
Olaf(being to all intents
a corpse and wanting any rag
upon what God unto him gave)
responds,without getting annoyed
'I will not kiss your fucking flag'

straightway the silver bird looked grave
(departing hurriedly to shave)

but—though all kinds of officers
(a yearning nation's blueeyed pride)
their passive prey did kick and curse
until for wear their clarion
voices and boots were much the worse,
and egged the firstclassprivates on
his rectum wickedly to tease
by means of skilfully applied
bayonets roasted hot with heat—
Olaf(upon what were once knees)
does almost ceaselessly repeat
'there is some shit I will not eat'

our president,being of which
assertions duly notified
threw the yellowsonofabitch
into a dungeon, where he died

Christ(of His mercy infinite)
i pray to see;and Olaf,too

preponderatingly because
unless statistics lie he was
more brave than me:more blond than you.

ERNEST CROSBY

The Military Creed

The American Admiral in command at Samoa
was asked what he thought of expansion. He is
reported to have answered, 'I do not think; I
obey orders.'

'Captain, what do you think,' I asked,
    'Of the part your soldiers play?'
The captain answered, 'I do not think –
    I do not think – I obey.'

'Do you think you should shoot a patriot down
    And help a tyrant slay?'
The captain answered, 'I do not think –
    I do not think – I obey.'

'Do you think that your conscience was meant to die
    And your brains to rot away?'
The captain answered, 'I do not think –
    I do not think – I obey.'

'Then if this is your soldier's code,' I cried,
    'You're a mean, unmanly crew,
And with all your feathers and gilt and braid
    I am more of a man than you;

'For whatever my lot on earth may be,
    And whether I swim or sink,
I can say with pride, "I do *not* obey –
    I do *not* obey – *I think!*" '

EDWARD YOUNG

'One to destroy, is murder by the law'

One to destroy, is murder by the law,
And gibbets keep the lifted hand in awe;
To murder thousands, takes a specious name,
War's glorious art, and gives immortal fame.

The Religious Blessing

It is always helpful to have God on your side, and armies were regularly blessed by priests before the butchery began. On the enlistment form for the British Army most soldiers, when asked to state their religion, put 'C of E' – which did not necessarily signify any strong pious inclination, but was meant to let the army know which burial service should be used if they were killed.

A simple and heartfelt prayer was uttered by Sir Jacob Astley, the Sergeant-Major General who commanded the Royalist infantry at the battle of Edgehill, the first engagement of the English Civil War in 1643: 'O Lord, thou knowest how busy I must be this day: if I forget thee, do not thou forget me.'

ANONYMOUS (HEBREW)

from Exodus 15

I will sing unto the LORD, for he hath triumphed gloriously:
    the horse and his rider hath he thrown into the sea.
The LORD is my strength and song, and he is become my
    salvation: he is my God, and I will prepare him an
    habitation; my father's God, and I will exalt him.
The LORD is a man of war: the LORD is his name.
Pharaoh's chariots and his host hath he cast into the sea: his
    chosen captains also are drowned in the Red sea.
The depths have covered them: they sank into the bottom as a
    stone.
Thy right hand, O LORD, is become glorious in power: thy
    right hand, O LORD, hath dashed in pieces the enemy.
And in the greatness of thine excellency thou hast overthrown
    them that rose up against thee: thou sentest forth thy
    wrath, which consumed them as stubble.

And with the blast of thy nostrils the waters were gathered
together, the floods stood upright as an heap, and the
depths were congealed in the heart of the sea.
The enemy said, I will pursue you, I will overtake, I will divide
the spoil; my lust shall be satisfied upon them; I will draw
my sword, my hand shall destroy them.
Thou didst blow with thy wind, the sea covered them: they
sank as lead in the mighty waters.
Who is like unto thee, O LORD, among the gods? who is like
thee, glorious in holiness, fearful in praises, doing
wonders?
Thou stretchedst out they right hand, the earth swallowed
them.
Thou in thy mercy hast led forth the people which thou hadst
redeemed: thou hast guided them in thy strength unto thy
holy habitation.

SEDULIUS SCOTTUS

from The Defeat of the Norsemen

Battle is joined on the open plain,
brightness of weapons glints in the air,
warriors' manifold voices shake
    the frame of the sky.

Opposing armies shower their spears,
the unhappy Dane counts his wounds,
a mighty army aims and strikes
    with showers of iron.

Those who have thirsted through the years
drink the blood of a raving tyrant
and find a sweetness in sating their breast
    with slaughter of men.

Diggers of pitfalls tumble in;
an overweening tower tumbles;
a swelling enemy host – behold –
    is crushed by Christ.

A people great and powerful humbled,
a cursed mass ground utterly down
– death's mouth has swallowed an evil stock:
    praise, Christ, to Thee.

Reckon that overthrow of people:
not counting the humble and lesser kinds
more on that hideous field in blood
    than thrice three thousand.

The judge is just, the world's ruler,
Christ the glory of Christian people,
prince of glory, subduer of evil,
    in rule supreme.

A strong tower, salvation's shield,
he worsts the mighty giants in battle,
He whose name exceeds all others
    and is blessed.

Avenger of a faithful people,
Who drove the sea in swollen tempest
in Egypt once, on chariots and riders
    and whelmed all.

Translated from the Latin by James Carney

ANONYMOUS

from The Poem of the Cid

'Gentlemen, for this day's work our chance has not been ill,
To-morrow with God's blessing we shall do better still;

Our Bishop, good Don Jerom, an early mass shall say
And give us absolution before the dawn of day.
Then we shall sally forth and assault them in the names
Of the Lord and his Apostle our worthy good St James.'
There was an answer all at once, one answer from the whole:
'With all our hearts,' the knights replied, 'with all our hearts
    and soul.'
Minaya was in haste, and thus he spake his mind:
'Cid, since you so determine, leave six score men behind;
Go forward with the rest, and let the battle join,
And God will send us succour on your side or on mine.'
'Let it be so!' the Cid replied. The night was coming on.
The Christians all were arm'd betimes, accoutred every one.
At the second cock-crow, before the dawn of day,
The Bishop Don Jeronimo was ready mass to say.
He sang the mass full solemnly in the cathedral quire,
And gave them absolution, perfect and entire.
'He that falls in battle, his face against the foe,
I make him clean of all his sins, his soul to heaven shall go.
And now, right worthy Cid, for the mass that has been
    chanted,
I shall require a boon and it must needs be granted.
– The foremost place in battle and the first stroke of the fight.'
'Let it be yours,' the Cid replied, 'it is a claim of right.'

    Translated from the Spanish by John Hookham Frere

LUIS CAMOENS

from The Lusiads, Canto I

With glad reception our Commander meets
    the Moorish chieftain and his whole convóy;
    whom with a gift of richest gear he greets
    whereof a store was shipped for such employ:

He gives him rich conserves, he gives, rare treats,
    the liquors hot which fill man's heart with joy.
Good be the gifts the Moor contented thinks,
but more the sweetmeats prizes, most the drinks.

The sailor-people sprung from Lusus' blood
    in wond'ering clusters to the ratlines clung;
    noting the stranger's novel mode and mood
    with his so barb'arous and perplexèd tongue.
    Sometime the wily Moor confusèd stood
    eyeing the garb, the hue, the fleet, the throng;
and asked, with questions manifold assailing,
if they from Turkey-land, perchance, were hailing.

He further tells them how he longs to see
    what books their credence, law and faith contain;
    if these conforming with his own agree
    or were, as well he ween'd, of Christian grain:
    Nay more, that hidden naught from him may be,
    he prayed the Captain would be pleased t' ordain
that be displayèd every puissant arm
wherewith the for'eigners work their foemen harm.

To this the doughty Chieftain deals reply,
    through one that óbscure jargon knowing well: –
    'Illustrious Signior! I fain will try
    all of ourselves, our arms, our creed to tell.
    Nor of the country, kith or kin am I
    of irksome races that in Turkey dwell;
my home is warlike Europe and I wend
seeking the far-famed lands of farthest Inde.

'I hold the law of One by worlds obey'd,
    by visible things and things invisible;
    He who the hemispheres from naught hath made,
    with sentient things and things insensible:
    Who with vitup'erate foul reproach bewray'd
    was doomed to suffer death insufferable;

And who, in fine, by Heav'n to Earth was given,
that man through Him might rise from Earth to Heaven.

'Of this GOD-MAN most highest, infinite,
    The books thou wouldst behold I have not brought;
    we stand excused of bringing what men write
    on paper, when in sprite 'tis writ and wrought.
    But an with weapons wouldst refresh thy sight,
    As thou hast askèd, I deny thee nought;
A friend to friends I show them; and I vow
ne'er wouldst be shown their temper as my foe.'

This said, he bids his armourers diligent
    bring arms and armour for the Moorman viewer:
    Come sheeny harness, corselets lucident,
    the fine-wove mail-coat and plate-armour sure;
    shields decorate with 'scutcheons different,
    bullets and spingards, th' ice-brook's temper pure;
bows, quivers furnisht with the grinded pile,
the sharp-edged partizan, the good brown bill:

Brought are the fiery bombs, while they prepare
    sulph'urous stink-pots and grenades of fire:
    But them of Vulcan biddeth he to spare
    their dread artill'ery belching flames in ire;
    naught did that gentle gen'erous spirit care
    with fear the few and fearful folk t' inspire,
and right his reas'oning: 'Twere a boast too cheap
to play the Lyon on the seely Sheep.

But from whate'er th' observant Moorman heard,
    and from whate'er his prying glance could see,
    a settled deadly hate his spirit stir'd,
    and evil crave of treach'erous cowardrie:
    No sign of change he showed in gest or word;
    but with a gay and gallant feigning he

vowèd in looks and words to treat them fair,
till deeds his daring purpose could declare.

Translated from the Portuguese by Richard Burton

RUDYARD KIPLING

Hymn before Action

The earth is full of anger,
    The seas are dark with wrath,
The Nations in their harness
    Go up against our path:
Ere yet we loose the legions —
    Ere yet we draw the blade,
Jehovah of the Thunders,
    Lord God of Battles, aid!

High lust and forward bearing,
    Proud heart, rebellious brow —
Deaf ear and soul uncaring,
    We seek Thy mercy now!
The sinner that forswore Thee,
    The fool that passed Thee by,
Our times are known before Thee —
    Lord, grant us strength to die!

For those who kneel beside us
    At altars not Thine own,
Who lack the lights that guide us,
    Lord, let their faith atone!
If wrong we did to call them,
    By honour bound they came;
Let not Thy Wrath befall them,
    But deal to us the blame.

From panic, pride, and terror,
    Revenge that knows no rein –
Light haste and lawless error,
    Protect us yet again.
Cloke Thou our underserving,
    Make firm the shuddering breath,
In silence and unswerving
    To taste Thy lesser death.

Ah, Mary pierced with sorrow,
    Remember, reach and save
The soul that comes to-morrow
    Before the God that gave!
Since each was born of woman,
    For each at utter need –
True comrade and true foeman –
    Madonna, intercede!

E'en now their vanguard gathers,
    E'en now we face the fray –
As Thou didst help our fathers,
    Help Thou our host to-day.
Fulfilled of signs and wonders,
    In life, in death made clear –
Jehovah of the Thunders,
    Lord God of Battles, hear!

GERARD MANLEY HOPKINS

The Soldier

Yes. Why do we all, seeing of a soldier, bless him? bless
Our redcoats, our tars? Both these being, the greater part,
But frail clay, nay but foul clay. Here it is: the heart,
Since, proud, it calls the calling manly, gives a guess
That, hopes that, makesbelieve, the men must be no less;

It fancies, feigns, deems, dears the artist after his art;
And fain will find as sterling all as all is smart,
And scarlet wear the spirit of war there express.

Mark Christ our King. He knows war, served his soldiering
       through;
He of all can reeve a rope best. There he bides in bliss
Now, and seeing somewhere some man do all that man can do,
For love he leans forth, needs his neck must fall on, kiss,
And cry 'O Christ-done deed! So God-made-flesh does too:
Were I come o'er again' cries Christ 'it should be this.'

W. T. STEAD

from War against War in South Africa

Now that War is in the air, e'en the parson in his lair
Is seized with wild desirings for the sight of spurting blood.
And he pitches it so strong to his sanctimonious throng
That they almost hear in fancy bodies falling with a thud . . .
Be upon them with the sword — 'tis the mandate of the Lord —
And expose your neighbour's vitals to the healthful
       atmosphere;
Do not misapply your skill to the doct'ring of his bill,
But just cleave him through the skull with a gash from ear to
       ear.
       Don't put water in his milk,
       Nor mix cotton with his silk,
       But just bash him like a Christian-Brother dear.

W. N. EWER

The Only Way

'Conscription will lead the way to the higher life.'
                              The Dean of Exeter, 1916

Through the slow succeeding ages
Priests and prophets, saints and sages
Have waged a long, incessant strife,
Seeking for the higher life.
Hindus wrapt in contemplation,
Hebrews voicing revelation,
Greeks, Egyptians, and Chinese,
Moslems, Christians, and Parsees,
All have held the ancient quest,
All have sought to find the best;
All of them have gone astray —
None have found the narrow way.

Buddha lived, and preached, and died,
Christ was scourged and crucified,
Socrates and Plato taught,
St Francis prayed, Mahomet fought.
All their labour, all their pain,
All their strivings were in vain;
Vain the work of every master
From Bergson back to Zoroaster,
Vain the toil of every teacher
From Moses down to Friedrich Nietzsche.
No hope for man can ever be
In faith or in Philosophy.

Gloomy is the prospect then
For the stricken sons of men,
Doomed the lower life to live;
None has any help to give.

When, hark! there comes a voice from Devon!
The Dean has found the keys of heaven,
Has found the path that none could find,
Has seen where all the saints were blind.
Marlborough is come to bring salvation
And Higher Life to all the nation.
Sure and simple his prescription:
All mankind needs is – Conscription!

C. WRIGHT

May God Go with You, Son

You said 'May God go with you, Son
And may you soon come safely home
Remember that where'er you go
You'll never be alone'
Well I carried those thoughts with me, Mum
But when the aeroplane took me higher
I couldn't see the Angels, Mum
And I never heard their choir

I looked for signs of Holiness
Wherever I was sent
And 'though I saw all kinds of men
They knew not what love meant
I saw the bodies of children, Mum
And oil wells set on fire
But I couldn't see the Angels, Mum
And I never heard their choir

I tried to find a reason
For laying to waste Mankind
And always, Mum, your parting words
Were present in my mind

It's not that I wasn't looking, Mum
Or that I'm calling you a liar
But I couldn't see the Angels, Mum
And I never heard their choir

Gods and Spirits of Warfare

The gods, spirits and demons of war have taken many forms and been given many names. Homer warned about warfare that 'at first she is but small, / Yet after, but a little fed, she grows so fast and tall.' This view was echoed by Winston Churchill, who compared savouring danger to sipping champagne: 'A single glass of champagne imparts a feeling of exhilaration . . . The nerves are braced; the imagination is agreeably stirred; the wits become more nimble. A bottle produces a contrary effect. So it is with war, and the quality of both is best discovered by sipping.'

ERNEST BRYLL

Nike

– And such exactly she should be: whatever is superfluous
has been hewed away by wind. Ailerons of wings
were long ago devoured by the sea. Why would she steer
her course worthy of a thunderbolt? Her hands are cut off
– there is no one deserving of her wreath . . .

                                   Under her feet
(perhaps shadowed by a fold of her dress) survived
the prow of the Rhodes trireme – preserving a scent of tar,
of oarsmen's sweat, of well-jointed wood.
And that's quite enough. From it we write on,
How the ship in full foam, catching up with the arrows
darted to the enemy's broadside, crossed the waters of the
    Styx;
how the sound of bronze died out, how fire consumed the tints.
– And such exactly she should be. Washed by earth,
her breast bereft of the warmth of nipples,
goddess of a sterile river. It is proper

that we see her as she is – without a head.
For to whom did she ever give a scrap of laurel to keep?
Victory was the beginning of defeats. Nothing but the rapture
    of the race
was left; the echo of shouts, pursuing
our ships faster than ever she did.

Translated from the Polish by Czeslaw Milosz

ARTHUR RIMBAUD

Evil

Whilst the red spittle of the grape-shot sings
All day across the endless sky, and whilst entire
Battalions, green or scarlet, rallied by their kings,
Disintegrate in crumpled masses under fire;

Whilst an abominable madness seeks to pound
A hundred thousand men into a smoking mess –
Pitiful dead in summer grass, on the rich ground
Out of which Nature wrought these men in holiness;

He is a God who sees it all, and laughs aloud
At damask altar-cloths, incense and chalices,
Who falls asleep lulled by adoring liturgies

And wakens when some mother, in her anguish bowed
And weeping till her old black bonnet shakes with grief
Offers him a big sou wrapped in her handkerchief.

Translated from the French by Norman Cameron

S. T. COLERIDGE

Fire, Famine and Slaughter

Famine: Sisters! sisters! who sent you here?
Slaughter: I will whisper it in her ear.
Fire: No! no! no!
Spirits hear what spirits tell:
'Twill make an holiday in Hell.
     No! no! no!
Myself, I named him once below,
And all the souls, that damned be,
Leaped up at once in anarchy,
Clapped their hands and danced for glee.
They no longer heeded me;
But laughed to hear Hell's burning rafters
Unwillingly re-echo laughters!
     No! no! no!
Spirits hear what spirits tell:
'Twill make an holiday in Hell!
  Famine: Whisper it, sister! so and so!
In a dark hint, soft and slow.
  Slaughter: Letters four do form his name –
And who sent you?
  Both: The same! the same!
  Slaughter: He came by stealth, and unlocked my den,
And I have drank the blood since then
Of thrice three hundred thousand men.
  Both: Who bade you do it?
  Slaughter: The same! the same!
Letters four do form his name.
He let me loose, and cried Halloo!
To him alone the praise is due.
  Famine: Thanks, sister, thanks! the men have bled,
Their wives and their children faint for bread.

I stood in a swampy field of battle;
With bones and skulls I made a rattle,
To frighten the wolf and carrion-crow
And the homeless dog — but they would not go.
So off I flew: for how could I bear
To see them gorge their dainty fare?
I heard a groan and a peevish squall,
And through the chink of a cottage-wall —
Can you guess what I saw there?
   Both: Whisper it, sister! in our ear.
   Famine: A baby beat its dying mother:
I had starved the one and was starving the other!
   Both: Who bade you do 't?
   Famine: The same! the same!
Letters four do form his name.
He let me loose, and cried Halloo!
To him alone the praise is due.
   Fire: Sisters! I from Ireland came!
Hedge and corn-fields all on flame,
I triumph'd o'er the setting sun!
And all the while the work was done,
On as I strode with my huge strides,
I flung back my head and I held my sides,
It was so rare a piece of fun
To see the sweltered cattle run
With uncouth gallop through the night,
Scared by the red and noisy light!
By the light of his own blazing cot
Was many a naked Rebel shot:
The house-stream met the flame and hissed,
While crash! fell in the roof, I wist,
On some of those old bed-rid nurses,
That deal in discontent and curses.
   Both: Who bade you do 't?
   Fire: The same! the same!
Letters four do form his name.

He let me loose, and cried Halloo!
To him alone the praise is due.
   All: He let us loose, and cried Halloo!
How shall we yield him honour due?
   Famine: Wisdom comes with lack of food.
I'll gnaw, I'll gnaw the multitude,
Till the cup of rage o'erbrim:
They shall seize him and his brood –
   Slaughter: They shall tear him limb from limb!
   Fire: O thankless beldames and untrue!
And is this all that you can do
For him, who did so much for you?
Ninety months he, by my troth!
Hath richly catered for you both;
And in an hour would you repay
An eight years' work? – Away! away!
I alone am faithful! I
Cling to him everlastingly.

JOSHUA SYLVESTER

'War is the mistress of enormity'

War is the mistress of enormity,
Mother of mischief, monster of deformity;
Laws, manners, arts she breaks, she mars, she chases,
Blood, tears, bowers, towers, she spills, smites, burns, and
    razes.
Her brazen teeth shake all the earth asunder:
Her mouth a firebrand, and her voice a thunder,
Her looks are lightning, every glance a flash,
Her fingers guns that all to powder smash;
Fear and despair, flight and disorder, post
With hasty march before her murderous host.
As burning, waste, rape, wrong, impiety,

Rage, ruin, discord, horror, cruelty,
Sack, sacrilege, impunity and pride are still stern consorts
    by her barbarous side;
And poverty, sorrow, and desolation
Follow her armies' bloody transmigration.

GEOFFREY CHAUCER

from The Knight's Tale

On t'other side there stood Destruction bare;
Unpunished Rapine, and a waste of war;
Contest, with sharpened knives, in cloisters drawn,
And all with blood bespread the holy lawn.
Loud menaces were heard, and foul disgrace,
And bawling infamy, in language base;
Till sense was lost in sound, and silence fled the place.
The slayer of himself yet saw I there;
The gore congealed was clottered in his hair:
With eyes half closed and gaping mouth he lay,
And grim, as when he breathed his sullen soul away.
In midst of all the dome Misfortune sat,
And gloomy Discontent, and fell Debate,
And Madness laughing in his ireful mood,
And armed complaint on theft, and cries of blood.
There was the murdered corpse, in covert laid,
And violent death in thousand shapes displayed;
The city to the soldier's rage resigned;
Successless wars, and poverty behind;
Ships burnt in fight, or forced on rocky shores,
And the rash hunter strangled by the boars;
The newborn babe by nurses overlaid;
And the cook caught within the raging fire he made.
All ills of Mars his nature, flame, and steel;
The gasping charioteer, beneath the wheel

Of his own car, the ruined house that falls
And intercepts her lord betwixt the walls;
The whole division that to Mars pertains,
All trades of death that deal in steel for gains,
Were there: the butcher, armourer, and smith,
Who forges sharpened fauchions, or the scythe.
The scarlet conquest on a tower was placed,
With shouts and soldiers' acclamations graced;
A pointed sword hung threatening o'er his head,
Sustained but by a slender twine of thread.
There saw I Mars his ides, the Capitol,
The seer in vain foretelling Caesar's fall;
The last triumvirs, and the wars they move,
And Antony, who lost the world for love.
These, and a thousand more, the fane adorn;
Their fates were painted ere the men were born,
All copied from the heavens, and ruling force
Of the red star, in his revolving course.

Translated from the Middle English by John Dryden

HOMER

from The Iliad, Book IV

Rude Mars had th' ordering of their spirits; of Greeks, the
        learned Maid.
But Terror follow'd both the hosts, and Flight, and furious
        Strife
(The sister, and the mate, of Mars) that spoil of human life;
And never is her rage at rest, at first she is but small,
Yet after, but a little fed, she grows so vast and tall
That, while her feet move here in earth, her forehead is in
        heaven;

And this was she that made even then both hosts so deadly
    given.
Through every troop she stalk'd, and stirr'd rough sighs up
    as she went;
But when in one field both the foes her fury did content,
And both came under reach of darts, then darts and shields
    oppos'd
To darts and shields; strength answer'd strength; then
    swords and targets clos'd
With swords and targets; both with pikes; and then did
    tumult rise
Up to her height; then conquerors' boasts mix'd with the
    conquer'd's cries;
Earth flow'd with blood. And as from hills rain-waters
    headlong fall,
That all ways eat huge ruts, which, met in one bed, fill a vall
With such a confluence of streams that on the mountain
    grounds
Far off, in frighted shepherds' ears, the bustling noise
    rebounds:
So grew their conflicts, and so show'd their scuffling to the ear,
With flight and clamour still commix'd, and all effects of fear.

    Translated from the Greek by George Chapman

HOMER

from The Iliad, Book II

          Through the host with this the Goddess ran,
In fury casting round her eyes, and furnish'd every man
With strength, exciting all to arms, and fight incessant. None
Now liked their lov'd homes like the wars; and as a fire upon
A huge wood, on the heights of hills, that far off hurls his light,
So the divine brass shin'd on these, thus thrusting on for fight.

Their splendour through the air reach'd heaven; and as about
    the flood
Caïster, in an Asian mead, flocks of the airy brood,
Cranes, geese, or long-neck'd swans, here, there, proud of their
    pinions fly,
And in their falls lay out such throats, that with their spiritful
    cry
The meadow shrieks again; so here, these many-nation'd men
Flow'd over the Scamandrian field, from tents and ships; the
    din
Was dreadful that the feet of men and horse beat out of earth;
And in the flourishing mead they stood, thick as the odorous
    birth
Of flowers, or leaves bred in the spring; or thick as swarms of
    flies
Throng then to sheep-cotes, when each swarm his erring wing
    applies
To milk dew'd on the milk-maid's pails; all eagerly dispos'd
To give to ruin th' Ilians. And as in rude heaps clos'd,
Though huge goatherds are at their food, the goatherds easily
    yet
Sort into sundry herds; so here the chiefs in battle set
Here tribes, here nations, ordering all.

    Translated from the Greek by George Chapman

Old Battlefields Revisited

Battlefields exert a peculiar attraction. Old comrades visit them to remember; students to verify reports and consider tactics *in situ*; tourists to evoke romantic ghosts and imagine the clash of arms. On some, mementoes can be found; on others, flowers spring up – as perhaps they do even at El Alamein. Even when grass is the only thing to be seen, there is plenty for the mind to work on.

In Southey's poem, Old Kaspar can tell his grandchildren, who find a skull at the battlefield of Blenheim, little more than that it was 'a famous victory'. He could not recall that Blenheim resulted from a brilliant march by Marlborough across Europe which surprised his enemies; that his tactics in the battle were superb; that at the end 50,000 men lay dead and wounded; and that in this, the greatest battle in the War of the Spanish Succession, the prestige and power of France, under its Sun King, Louis XIV, were shattered. All these things were forgotten; only the skull remained.

LI HO

An Arrowhead from the Ancient Battlefield of Ch'ang-p'ing

Lacquer dust and powdered bone and red cinnabar grains:
From the spurt of ancient blood the bronze has flowered.
White feathers and gilt shaft have melted away in the rain,
Leaving only this triple-cornered broken wolf's tooth.

I was searching the plain, riding with two horses,
In the stony fields east of the post-station, on a bank where
    bamboos sprouted,
After long winds and brief daylight, beneath the dreary stars,
Damped by a black flag of cloud which hung in the empty
    night.

To left and right, in the air, in the earth, ghosts shrieked from
    wasted flesh.
The curds drained from my upturned jar, mutton victuals were
    my sacrifice.
Insects settled, the wild geese swooned, the buds were blight-
    reddened on the reeds,
The whirlwind was my escort, puffing sinister fires.

In tears, seeker of ancient things, I picked up this broken barb
With snapped point and russet flaws, which once pierced
    through flesh.
In the east quarter on South Street a pedlar on horseback
Talked me into bartering the metal for a votive basket.

Translated from the Chinese by A. C. Graham

BASIL BUNTING

from Briggflatts

Loaded with mail of linked lies,
what weapon can the king lift to fight
when chance-met enemies employ sly
sword and shoulder-piercing pike,
pressed into the mire,
trampled and hewn till a knife
– in whose hand? – severs tight
neck cords? Axe rusts. Spine
picked bare by ravens, agile
maggots devour the slack side
and inert brain, never wise.
What witnesses he had life,
ravelled and worn past splice,
yarns falling to staple? Rime
on the bent, the beck ice,
there will be nothing on Stainmore to hide

void, no sable to disguise
what he wore under the lies,
king of Orkney, king of Dublin, twice
king of York, where the tide
stopped till long flight
from who knows what smile,
scowl, disgust or delight
ended in bale on the fellside.

ROBERT SOUTHEY

The Battle of Blenheim

I

It was a summer evening,
  Old Kaspar's work was done,
And he before his cottage door
  Was sitting in the sun,
And by him sported on the green
His little grandchild Wilhelmine.

II

She saw her brother Peterkin
  Roll something large and round,
Which he beside the rivulet
  In playing there had found;
He came to ask what he had found,
That was so large, and smooth, and round.

III

Old Kaspar took it from the boy,
  Who stood expectant by;
And then the old man shook his head,

And, with a natural sigh,
''Tis some poor fellow's skull,' said he,
'Who fell in the great victory.

IV

'I find them in the garden,
    For there's many here about;
And often when I go to plough,
    The ploughshare turns them out!
For many thousand men,' said he,
'Were slain in that great victory.'

V

'Now tell us what 'twas all about,'
    Young Peterkin, he cries;
And little Wilhelmine looks up
    With wonder-waiting eyes;
'Now tell us all about the war,
And what they fought each other for.'

VI

'It was the English,' Kaspar cried,
    'Who put the French to rout;
But what they fought each other for,
    I could not well make out;
But everybody said,' quoth he,
'That 'twas a famous victory.

VII

'My father lived at Blenheim then,
    Yon little stream hard by;
They burnt his dwelling to the ground,
    And he was forced to fly;

So with his wife and child he fled,
Nor had he where to rest his head.

VIII

'With fire and sword the country round
   Was wasted far and wide,
And many a childing mother then,
   And new-born baby died;
But things like that, you know, must be
At every famous victory.

IX

'They say it was a shocking sight
   After the field was won;
For many thousand bodies here
   Lay rotting in the sun;
But things like that, you know, must be
After a famous victory.

X

'Great praise the Duke of Marlbro' won,
   And our good Prince Eugene.'
'Why 'twas a very wicked thing!'
   Said little Wilhelmine.
'Nay . . . nay . . . my little girl,' quoth he,
'It was a famous victory.

XI

'And everybody praised the Duke
   Who this great fight did win.'
'But what good came of it at last?'
   Quoth little Peterkin.
'Why that I cannot tell,' said he
'But 'twas a famous victory.'

JOHN MCCRAE

In Flanders Fields

In Flanders fields the poppies blow
Between the crosses, row on row
  That mark our place; and in the sky
  The larks, still bravely singing, fly
Scarce heard amid the guns below.

We are the Dead. Short days ago
We lived, felt dawn, saw sunset glow,
  Loved and were loved, and now we lie
    In Flanders fields.

Take up our quarrel with the foe:
To you from failing hands we throw
  The torch; be yours to hold it high.
  If ye break faith with us who die
We shall not sleep, though poppies grow
    In Flanders fields.

PHILIP JOHNSTONE

High Wood

Ladies and gentlemen, this is High Wood,
Called by the French, Bois des Fourneaux,
The famous spot which in Nineteen-Sixteen,
July, August and September was the scene
Of long and bitterly contested strife,
By reason of its High commanding site.
Observe the effect of shell-fire in the trees
Standing and fallen; here is wire; this trench
For months inhabited, twelve times changed hands;

(They soon fall in), used later as a grave.
It has been said on good authority
That in the fighting for this patch of wood
Were killed somewhere above eight thousand men,
Of whom the greater part were buried here,
This mound on which you stand being . . .

                                        Madame, please,
You are requested kindly not to touch
Or take away the Company's property
As souvenirs; you'll find we have on sale
A large variety, all guaranteed.
As I was saying, all is as it was,
This is an unknown British officer,
The tunic having lately rotted off.
Please follow me – this way . . .

                              the *path* sir, *please*,
The ground which was secured at great expense
The Company keeps absolutely untouched,
And in that dug-out (genuine) we provide
Refreshments at a reasonable rate.
You are requested not to leave about
Paper, or ginger-beer bottles, or orange-peel,
There are waste-paper baskets at the gate.

JOHN JARMAIN

El Alamein

There are flowers now, they say, at Alamein;
Yes, flowers in the minefields now.
So those that come to view that vacant scene,
Where death remains and agony has been
Will find the lilies grow –
Flowers, and nothing that we know.

So they rang the bells for us and Alamein,
Bells which we could not hear:
And to those that heard the bells what could it mean,
That name of loss and pride, El Alamein?
— Not the murk and harm of war,
But their hope, their own warm prayer.

It will become a staid historic name,
That crazy sea of sand!
Like Troy or Agincourt its single fame
Will be the garland for our brow, our claim,
On us a fleck of glory to the end:
And there our dead will keep their holy ground.

But this is not the place that we recall,
The crowded desert crossed with foaming tracks,
The one blotched building, lacking half a wall,
The grey-faced men, sand powdered over all;
The tanks, the guns, the trucks,
The black, dark-smoking wrecks.

So be it: none but us has known that land:
El Alamein will still be only ours
And those ten days of chaos in the sand.
Others will come who cannot understand,
Will halt beside the rusty minefield wires
And find there — flowers.

CARL SANDBURG

Grass

Pile the bodies high at Austerlitz and Waterloo.
Shovel them under and let me work —
       I am the grass; I cover all.

And pile them high at Gettysburg
And pile them high at Ypres and Verdun.
Shovel them under and let me work.
Two years, ten years, and passengers ask the conductor:

> What place is this?
> Where are we now?

> I am the grass.
> Let me work.

The Dead

The war dead, considered collectively, are nearly always looked upon as heroes, whether their sacrifice has been worthwhile or in vain. This tradition is at least as old as the fourth century BC, when 300 Spartans died defending the pass at Thermopylae. But much the same sentiment was expressed by Emily Dickinson, writing twenty-two centuries later, after the American Civil War, when she rewarded those who had died in battle with divinity. The Japanese poem I have included describes the spirit in which Second World War kamikaze pilots met their own deaths, the very word 'kamikaze' meaning 'divine wind'.

Each death is a single event but the pale battalions soon mount up. At Albuera, the bloodiest battle of the Peninsular War (1808–14), only a third of the front-line troops survived. On the first day of the Battle of the Somme in July 1916, 19,000 were killed before thirty minutes were up. Since 1900, more than 108 million people – civilian as well as military – have died as a result of war.

Those who have won laurels often do not have the opportunity to wear them. As Walt Whitman says, 'They themselves were fully at rest, they suffer'd not, / The living remain'd and suffer'd.'

SIMONIDES

The Greek Dead at Thermopylae

Great are the fallen of Thermopylae,
Nobly they ended, high their destination –
Beneath an altar laid, no more a tomb,
Where none with pity comes or lamentation,
        But praise and memory –
        A splendour of oblation
No rust shall blot nor wreckful Time consume.

The ground is holy: here the brave are resting,
And here Greek Honour keeps her chosen shrine.
Here too is one the worth of all attesting –
Leônidas, of Sparta's royal line,
Who left behind a gem-like heritage
   Of courage and renown,
    A name that shall go down
    From age to age.

  Translated from the Greek by T. F. Higham

W. M. THACKERAY

The Due of the Dead

I sit beside my peaceful hearth,
 With curtains drawn and lamp trimmed bright
I watch my children's noisy mirth;
 I drink in home, and its delight.

I sip my tea, and criticise
 The war, from flying rumours caught;
Trace on the map, to curious eyes,
 How here they marched, and there they fought.

In intervals of household chat,
 I lay down strategetic laws;
Why this manœuvre, and why that;
 Shape the event, or show the cause.

Or, in smooth dinner-table phrase,
 'Twixt soup and fish, discuss the fight;
Give to each chief his blame or praise;
 Say who was wrong and who was right.

Meanwhile o'er Alma's bloody plain
 The scathe of battle has rolled by –

The wounded writhe and groan – the slain
   Lie naked staring to the sky.

The out-worn surgeon plies his knife,
   Nor pauses with the closing day;
While those who have escaped with life
   Find food and fuel as they may.

And when their eyes in sleep they close,
   After scant rations duly shared,
Plague picks his victims out, from those
   Whom chance of battle may have spared.

Still when the bugle sounds the march,
   He tracks his prey through steppe and dell;
Hangs fruit to tempt the throats that parch,
   And poisons every stream and well.

All this with gallant hearts is done;
   All this with patient hearts is borne:
And they by whom the laurel's won
   Are seldom they by whom 'tis worn.

No deed, no suffering of the war,
   But wins us fame, or spares us ill;
Those noble swords, though drawn afar,
   Are guarding English homesteads still.

Owe we a debt to these brave men,
   Unpaid by aught that's said or sung;
By leaders from a ready pen,
   Or phrases from a flippant tongue.

The living, England's hand may crown
   With recognition, frank and free;
With titles, medals, and renown;
   The wounded shall our pensioners be.

But they, who meet a soldier's doom –
   Think you, it is enough, good friend,

To plant the laurel at their tomb,
   And carve their names – and there an end?

No. They are gone: but there are left
   Those they loved best while they were here –
Parents made childless, babes bereft,
   Desolate widows, sisters dear.

All these let grateful England take;
   And, with a large and liberal heart,
Cherish, for her slain soldiers' sake,
   And of her fullness give them part.

Fold them within her sheltering breast;
   Their parent, husband, brother, prove.
That so the dead may be at rest,
   Knowing those cared for whom they love.

WALT WHITMAN

from When Lilacs Last in the Dooryard Bloom'd

And I saw askant the armies,
I saw as in noiseless dreams hundreds of battle-flags,
Borne through the smoke of the battles and pierced with
     missiles I saw them,
And carried hither and yon through the smoke, and torn and
     bloody,
And at last but a few shreds left on the staffs, (and all in
     silence,)
And the staffs all splinter'd and broken.

I saw battle-corpses, myriads of them,
And the white skeletons of young men, I saw them,
I saw the debris and debris of all the slain soldiers of the war,
But I saw they were not as was thought,
They themselves were fully at rest, they suffer'd not,

The living remain'd and suffer'd, the mother suffer'd,
And the wife and the child and the musing comrade suffer'd,
And the armies that remain'd suffer'd.

EMILY DICKINSON

'It feels a shame to be Alive'

It feels a shame to be Alive –
When Men so brave – are dead –
One envies the Distinguished Dust –
Permitted – such a Head –

The Stone – that tells defending Whom
This Spartan put away
What little of Him we – possessed
In Pawn for Liberty –

The price is great – Sublimely paid –
Do we deserve – a Thing –
That lives – like Dollars – must be piled
Before we may obtain?

Are we that wait – sufficient worth –
That such Enormous Pearl
As life – dissolved be – for Us –
In Battle's – horrid Bowl?

It may be – a Renown to live –
I think the Men who die –
Those unsustained – Saviours –
Present Divinity –

CHARLES HAMILTON SORLEY

'When you see millions of the mouthless dead'

When you see millions of the mouthless dead
Across your dreams in pale battalions go,
Say not soft things as other men have said,
That you'll remember. For you need not so.
Give them not praise. For, deaf, how should they know
It is not curses heaped on each gashed head?
Nor tears. Their blind eyes see not your tears flow.
Nor honour. It is easy to be dead.
Say only this, 'They are dead.' Then add thereto,
'Yet many a better one has died before.'
Then, scanning all the o'ercrowded mass, should you
Perceive one face that you loved heretofore,
It is a spook. None wears the face you knew.
Great death has made all his for evermore.

VICE-ADMIRAL OHNISHI

Blossoms in the Wind

In blossom today, then scattered:
Life is so like a delicate flower.
How can one expect the fragrance
To last forever?

ANONYMOUS

Hymn to the Fallen

'We hold our flat shields, we wear our jerkins of hide;
The axles of our chariots touch, our short swords meet.
Standards darken the sun, the foe roll on like clouds;
Arrows fall thick, the warriors press forward.
They have overrun our ranks, they have crossed our line;
The trace-horse on the left is dead, the one on the right is
    wounded.
The fallen horses block our wheels, our chariot is held fast;
We grasp our jade drum-sticks, we beat the rolling drums.'

Heaven decrees their fall, the dread Powers are angry;
The warriors are all dead, they lie in the open fields.
They set out, but shall not enter; they went but shall not
    come back.
The plains are empty and wide, the way home is long.
Their tall swords are at their waist, their bows are under
    their arm;
Though their heads were severed their spirit could not be
    subdued.
They that fought so well – in death are warriors still;
Stubborn and steadfast to the end, they could not be
    dishonoured.
Their bodies perished in the fight; but the magic of their
    souls is strong –
Captains among the ghosts, heroes among the Dead.

Translated from the Chinese by Arthur Waley

G. K. CHESTERTON

The English Graves

Were I that wandering citizen whose city is the world,
I would not weep for all that fell before the flags were furled;
I would not let one murmur mar the trumpets volleying forth
How God grew weary of the kings, and the cold hell in the
    north.
But we whose hearts are homing birds have heavier thoughts
    of home,
Though the great eagles burn with gold on Paris or on Rome,
Who stand beside our dead and stare, like seers at an eclipse,
At the riddle of the island tale and the twilight of the ships.

For these were simple men that loved, with hands and feet
    and eyes,
Whose souls were humbled to the hills and narrowed to the
    skies,
The hundred little lands within one little land that lie,
Where Severn seeks the sunset isles or Sussex scales the sky.

And what is theirs, though banners blow on Warsaw risen
    again,
Or ancient laughter walks in gold through the vineyards of
    Lorraine,
Their dead are marked on English stones, their loves on
    English trees,
How little is the prize they win, how mean a coin for these —
How small a shrivelled laurel-leaf lies crumpled here and
    curled:
They died to save their country and they only saved the world.

THOMAS HARDY

Albuera

They come, beset by riddling hail;
They sway like sedges in a gale;
They fail, and win, and win, and fail. Albuera!

They gain the ground there, yard by yard,
Their brows and hair and lashes charred, ·
Their blackened teeth set firm and hard.

Their mad assailants rave and reel,
And face, as men who scorn to feel,
The close-lined, three-edged prongs of steel,

Till faintness follows closing-in,
When, faltering headlong down, they spin
Like leaves. But those pay well who win Albuera.

Out of six thousands souls that sware
To hold the mount, or pass elsewhere,
But eighteen hundred muster there.

Pale Colonels, Captains, ranksmen lie,
Facing the earth or facing sky; –
They strove to live, they stretch to die.

Friends, foemen, mingle; heap and heap. –
Hide their hacked bones, Earth! – Deep, deep, deep,
Where harmless worms caress and creep.

Hide their hacked bones, Earth! – deep, deep, deep,
Where harmless worms caress and creep. –
What man can grieve? what woman weep?
Better than waking is to sleep! Albuera!

ANONYMOUS

Dead on the War Path

This very day, a little while ago, you lived
But now you are neither man nor woman,
Breathless you are, for the Navahos killed you!
Then remember us not, for here and now
We bring you your food. Then take and keep
Your earth-walled place: once! twice!
Three times! four times! Then leave us now!

Translated from the Pueblo Indian by H. J. Spinden

ROBERT GRAVES

Corporal Stare

Back from the line one night in June,
I gave a dinner at Béthune –
Seven courses, the most gorgeous meal
Money could buy or batman steal.
Five hungry lads welcomed the fish
With shouts that nearly cracked the dish;
Asparagus came with tender tops,
Strawberries in cream, and mutton chops.
Said Jenkins, as my hand he shook,
'They'll put this in the history book.'
We bawled Church anthems *in choro*
Of Bethlehem and Hermon snow,
With drinking-songs, a mighty sound
To help the good red Pommard round.
Stories and laughter interspersed,
We drowned a long La Bassée thirst –

Trenches in June make throats damned dry.
Then through the window suddenly,
Badge, stripes and medals all complete,
We saw him swagger up the street,
Just like a live man – Corporal Stare!
   Stare! Killed last month at Festubert,
Caught on patrol near the Boche wire,
Torn horribly by machine-gun fire!
He paused, saluted smartly, grinned,
Then passed away like a puff of wind,
Leaving us blank astonishment.
The song broke, up we started, leant
Out of the window – nothing there,
Not the least shadow of Corporal Stare,
Only a quiver of smoke that showed
A fag-end dropped on the silent road.

MICHAEL GREENING

Missing – Believed Drowned

Alone, quite alone now;
Only the slap of the hump-backed wave
Can reach him here,
Washing away his manhood, far away.

Awake, all agape his face,
Stabbing surprise at the sea-stretched sky
That saw him fall.
And O his mouth but a cut for the tide.

His was no newspaper death.
No high-explosive slogan-burst
Heightened his heart, nor did the singing lead
Write headlines in the prophet-sky for him.

Merely the heart of the world
Turned cold; and he was erased; his head
Is a seed that never took root,
A stub that is crushed before it's alight.

Do not watch, do not watch;
This is the issue, the pay-book, the number,
This is not him;
Too casually he slips and ebbs with the running tide.

O, do not look for an answer.
The birds of the drowned as they mew,
Do not know, do not know.
And under all the sea lies, vast and menacing.

Remembrance

It is important for both individuals and the nation to cherish and respect the memory of the dead. Every village in France has a well cared-for memorial listing the names of the villagers who died in the two World Wars, and Britain still observes Remembrance Sunday, with the monarch paying homage at the Cenotaph in Whitehall, on behalf of her subjects. Ceremonies of remembrance may be public and religious or private and agnostic. What is never forgotten is the debt owed to those who laid down their lives for their country.

WALT WHITMAN

Ashes of Soldiers

Ashes of soldiers South or North,
As I muse retrospective murmuring a chant in thought,
The war resumes, again to my sense your shapes,
And again the advance of the armies.

Noiseless as mists and vapours,
From their graves in the trenches ascending,
From cemeteries all through Virginia and Tennessee,
From every point of the compass out of the countless graves,
In wafted clouds, in myriads large, or squads of twos or threes
    or single ones they come,
And silently gather round me.

Now sound no note O trumpeters,
Not at the head of my cavalry parading on spirited horses,
With sabres drawn and glistening, and carbines by their thighs,
    (ah my brave horsemen!

My handsome tan-faced horsemen! what life, what joy and
 pride,
With all the perils were yours.)

Nor you drummers, neither at reveillé at dawn,
Nor the long roll alarming the camp, nor even the muffled beat
 for a burial,
Nothing from you this time O drummers bearing my warlike
 drums.

But aside from these and the marts of wealth and the crowded
 promenade,
Admitting around me comrades close unseen by the rest and
 voiceless,
The slain elate and alive again, the dust and debris alive,
I chant this chant of my silent soul in the name of all dead
 soldiers.

Faces so pale with wondrous eyes, very dear, gather closer yet,
Draw close, but speak not.

Phantoms of countless lost,
Invisible to the rest henceforth become my companions,
Follow me ever – desert me not while I live.

Sweet are the blooming cheeks of the living – sweet are the
 musical voices sounding,
But sweet, ah sweet, are the dead with their silent eyes.

Dearest comrades, all is over and long gone,
But love is not over – and what love, O comrades!
Perfume from battle-fields rising, up from the fœtor arising.
Perfume therefore my chant, O love, immortal love,
Give me to bathe the memories of all dead soldiers,
Shroud them, embalm them, cover them all over with tender
 pride.

Perfume all – make all wholesome,
Make these ashes to nourish and blossom,
O love, solve all, fructify all with the last chemistry.

Give me exhaustless, make me a fountain,
That I exhale love from me wherever I go like a moist perennial
        dew,
For the ashes of all dead soldiers South or North.

LAWRENCE BINYON

from Poems for the Fallen

They went with songs to the battle, they were young,
Straight of limb, true of eye, steady and aglow.
They were staunch to the end against odds uncounted,
They fell with their faces to the foe.

They shall grow not old, as we that are left grow old:
Age shall not weary them, nor the years condemn.
At the going down of the sun and in the morning
We will remember them.

WILFRED OWEN

Anthem for Doomed Youth

What passing-bells for these who die as cattle?
    Only the monstrous anger of the guns.
    Only the stuttering rifles' rapid rattle
Can patter out their hasty orisons.
No mockeries now for them; no prayers or bells,
    Nor any voice of mourning save the choirs, –
The shrill, demented choirs of wailing shells;
    And bugles calling for them from sad shires.

What candles may be held to speed them all?
    Not in the hands of boys, but in their eyes
Shall shine the holy glimmers of good-byes.

The pallor of girls' brows shall be their pall;
Their flowers the tenderness of silent minds,
And each slow dusk a drawing-down of blinds.

PHILIP LARKIN

MCMXIV

Those long uneven lines
Standing as patiently
As if they were stretched outside
The Oval or Villa Park,
The crowns of hats, the sun
On moustached archaic faces
Grinning as if it were all
An August Bank Holiday lark;

And the shut shops, the bleached
Established names on the sunblinds,
The farthings and sovereigns,
And dark-clothed children at play
Called after kings and queens,
The tin advertisements
For cocoa and twist, and the pubs
Wide open all day;

And the countryside not caring:
The place-names all hazed over
With flowering grasses, and fields
Shadowing Domesday lines
Under wheat's restless silence;
The differently-dressed servants
With tiny rooms in huge houses,
The dust behind limousines;

Never such innocence,
Never before or since,
As changed itself to past
Without a word – the men
Leaving the gardens tidy,
The thousands of marriages
Lasting a little while longer:
Never such innocence again.

KEITH DOUGLAS

Simplify Me When I'm Dead

Remember me when I am dead
and simplify me when I'm dead.

As the processes of earth
strip off the colour and the skin:
take the brown hair and blue eye

and leave me simpler than at birth,
when hairless I came howling in
as the moon entered the cold sky.

Of my skeleton perhaps,
so stripped, a learned man will say
'He was of such a type and intelligence,' no more.

Thus when in a year collapse
particular memories, you may
deduce, from the long pain I bore

the opinions I held, who was my foe
and what I left, even my appearance
but incidents will be no guide.

Time's wrong-way telescope will show
a minute man ten years hence
and by distance simplified.

Through that lens see if I seem
substance or nothing: of the world
deserving mention or charitable oblivion,

not by momentary spleen
or love into decision hurled,
leisurely arrive at an opinion.

Remember me when I am dead
and simplify me when I'm dead.

GEOFFREY HILL

The Distant Fury of Battle

Grass resurrects to mask, to strangle,
Words glossed on stone, lopped stone-angel;
But the dead maintain their ground –
That there's no getting round –

Who in places vitally rest,
Named, anonymous; who test
Alike the endurance of yews
Laurels, moonshine, stone, all tissues;

With whom, under licence and duress,
There are pacts made, if not peace.
Union with the stone-wearing dead
Claims the born leader, the prepared

Leader, the devourers and all lean men.
Some, finally, learn to begin.
Some keep to the arrangement of love
(Or similar trust) under whose auspices move

Most subjects, toward the profits of this
Combine of doves and witnesses.
Some, dug out of hot-beds, are brought bare,
Not past conceiving but past care.

MARTIN BELL

Reasons for Refusal

Busy old lady, charitable tray
Of social emblems: poppies, people's blood –
I must refuse, make you flush pink
Perplexed by abrupt No-thank-you.
Yearly I keep up this small priggishness,
Would wince worse if I wore one.
Make me feel better, fetch a white feather, do.

Everyone has list of dead in war,
Regrets most of them, e.g.

Uncle Cyril; small boy in lace and velvet
With pushing sisters muscling all around him,
And lofty brothers, whiskers and stiff collars;
The youngest was the one who copped it.
My mother showed him to me,
Neat letters high up on the cenotaph
That wedding-caked it up above the park,
And shadowed birds on Isaac Watts' white shoulders.

And father's friends, like Sandy Vincent;
Brushed sandy hair, moustache, and staring eyes.
Kitchener claimed him, but the Southern Railway
Held back my father, made him guilty.
I hated the khaki photograph,
It left a patch on the wallpaper after I took it down.

Others I knew stick in the mind,
And Tony Lister often –
Eyes like holes in foolscap, suffered from piles,
Day after day went sick with constipation
Until they told him he could drive a truck –
Blown up with Second Troop in Greece:
We sang all night once when we were on guard.

And Ken Gee, our lance-corporal, Christian Scientist –
Everyone liked him, knew that he was good –
Had leg and arm blown off, then died.
Not all were good. Gross Corporal Rowlandson
Fell in the canal, the corrupt Sweet-water,
And rolled there like a log, drunk and drowned.
And I've always been glad of the death of Dick Benjamin,
A foxy urgent dainty ballroom dancer –
Found a new role in military necessity
As RSM. He waltzed out on parade
To make himself hated. Really hated, not an act.
He was a proper little porcelain sergeant-major –
The earliest bomb made smithereens:
Coincidence only, several have assured me.

In the school hall was pretty glass
Where prissy light shone through St George –
The highest holiest manhood, he!
And underneath were slain Old Boys
In tasteful lettering on whited slab –
And, each November, Ferdy the Headmaster
Reared himself squat and rolled his eyeballs upward,
Rolled the whole roll-call off an oily tongue,
Remorselessly from A to Z.

Of all the squirmers, Roger Frampton's lips
Most elegantly curled, showed most disgust.
He was a pattern of accomplishments,
And joined the Party first, and left it first,

At OCTU won a prize belt, most improbable,
Was desert-killed in '40, much too soon.

His name should burn right through that monument.

No poppy, thank you.

TOM PAULIN

Peacetime

We moved house
in '63.

My brother cried
quietly in his room.

Stuff in the loft,
my dad said burn it.

I cut the brass buttons
from his khaki tunic,

sploshed petrol,
felt in the back pocket

of the heavy trousers —
no wallet,

only four sheets
of folded bog-roll

(he'd been an officer
and planned ahead).

I chucked a match.
Whap!

ANNA AKHMATOVA

from In 1940

At the burial of an epoch
no psalm is heard at the tomb.
Soon nettles and thistles
will decorate the spot.
The only busy hands are those
of the gravediggers. Faster! Faster!
And it's quiet, Lord, so quiet
you can hear time passing.

Some day it will surface again
like a corpse in a spring river;
but no mother's son will claim her,
and grandsons, sick at heart,
will turn away.
                    Sorrowing heads . . .
The moon swinging like a pendulum . . .

And now, over death-struck Paris,
such silence falls.

Translated from the Russian by Stanley Kunitz and Max Hayward

BORIS PASTERNAK

Courage

I will remember
the countless unnamed men of besieged cities
who stood firm when the paving blocks
leaped from their beds, when the bricks
of their homes crashed about their heads,
and death sang its shrill monotonous whine.

I will remember them
on the hasty barricades in the quiet suburbs
where the cherry tree lived peaceably in the garden.
They lay on the roads, shouting for reinforcements
with no one near enough to hear.

I will remember
the chunk of bread they sank their teeth into
crossing the torn wheat field
to the burned house.
They made their fingers familiar
with the sleek rifle butt
not for praise or power, but the cold
knowledge of the job that must be done.

It was not enough to be angry.
It was not enough to be thirsty
for blood to match your child's blood
darkening the ground behind the roofless schoolhouse.
They needed quiet eyes and iron hands.

I will remember
the yammer of machine-guns at their shelter,
and how they lived always with whispering ears
from the bullets' passing;
how they came back from the outpost,
walking carefully like dead men reborn,
told the commander where to find the enemy;
how they went back again to the dangerous corner
among the pockmarked bricks.

I will say
how they died in the fullness of their lives
and became part of our songs
and walked among the thunderbolts and eagles.

Translated from the Russian

SA'DI YUSUF

Hamra Night

A candle in a long street
A candle in the sleep of houses
A candle for frightened shops
A candle for bakeries
A candle for a journalist trembling in an empty office
A candle for a fighter
A candle for a woman doctor watching over patients
A candle for the wounded
A candle for plain talk
A candle for the stairs
A candle for a hotel packed with refugees
A candle for a singer
A candle for broadcasters in their hideouts
A candle for a bottle of water
A candle for the air
A candle for two lovers in a naked flat
A candle for the falling sky
A candle for the beginning
A candle for the ending
A candle for the last communiqué
A candle for conscience
A candle in my hands.

Translated from the Arabic by Abdullah al-Udhari

Peace

At last.

ANONYMOUS (HEBREW)

from Micah 4

But in the last days it shall come to pass, that the mountain
  of the house of the LORD shall be established in the top
  of the mountains, and it shall be exalted above the hills;
  and people shall flow unto it.
And many nations shall come, and say, Come, and let us go
  up to the mountain of the LORD, and to the house of the
  God of Jacob; and he will teach us of his ways, and we
  will walk in his paths: for the law shall go forth of Zion,
  and the word of the LORD from Jerusalem.
And he shall judge among many people, and rebuke strong
  nations afar off; and they shall beat their swords into
  plowshares, and their spears into pruninghooks: nation
  shall not lift up a sword against nation, neither shall they
  learn war any more.
But they shall sit every man under his vine and under his fig
  tree; and none shall make them afraid: for the mouth of
  the LORD of hosts hath spoken it.

RALPH KNEVET

The Vote

The helmet now an hive for bees becomes,
And hilts of swords may serve for spiders' looms;

    Sharp pikes may make
    Teeth for a rake;
And the keen blade, th'arch enemy of life,
Shall be degraded to a pruning knife.
    The rustic spade
    Which first was made
For honest agriculture, shall retake
Its primitive employment, and forsake
    The rampires steep
    And trenches deep.
Tame conies in our brazen guns shall breed,
Or gentle doves their young ones there shall feed.
    In musket barrels
    Mice shall raise quarrels
For their quarters. The ventriloquious drum,
Like lawyers in vacations, shall be dumb.
    Now all recruits,
    But those of fruits,
Shall be forgot; and th'unarmed soldier
Shall only boast of what he did whilere,
    In chimneys' ends
    Among his friends.

If good effects shall happy signs ensue,
I shall rejoice, and my prediction's true.

JOHN GOWER

from To Henry IV

Peace is the chief of all the worldes wealth,
    And to the heaven it leadeth eke the way;
Peace is of man's soul and life the health,
    And doth with pestilence and war away.
    My liege lord, take heed of what I say,

If war may be left off, take peace on hand,
Which may not be unless God doth it send.

With peace may every creature dwell at rest;
   Withoute peace there may no life be glad;
Above all other good peace is the best;
   Peace hath himself when war is all bestead;
   Peace is secure, war ever is adread;
Peace is of all charity the key,
That hath the life and soule for to weigh.

For honour vain, or for the worldes good,
   They that aforetimes the strong battles made,
Where be they now? – bethink well in thy mood!
   The day is gone, the night is dark and fade,
   Their cruelty which then did make them glad,
They sorrow now, and yet have nought the more;
The blood is shed, which no man may restore.

War is the mother of the wronges all;
   It slayeth the priest in holy church at mass,
Forliths the maid, and doth her flower to fall;
   The war maketh the great city less,
   And doth the law its rules to overpass,
There is no thing whereof mischief may grow,
Which is not caused by the war, I trow.

ANONYMOUS

'A soldier stood at the pearly gate'

A soldier stood at the pearly gate,
His face was scarred and old.
He stood before the man of fate
For admission to the fold.

'What have you done,' St Peter asked,
'To gain admission here?'
'I've been a soldier, sir,' he said,
'For many and many a year.'

The pearly gate swung open wide
As Peter touched the bell.
'Inside', he said, 'and choose your harp.
You've had your share of hell.'

Acknowledgements

Many of the poems in this book are lucky to have survived, either because they were written on the field of battle or because they first appeared in small and ephemeral volumes of wartime verse. I was fortunate to find copies of a number of these endangered publications, among them a slender paperback printed in Calcutta in 1945, *Muses in Exile*, which collected poems that had first seen the light of day in the forces' newspaper of South East Asia Command. The Vietnam War produced far more prose commentaries than poetic ones, but I came across some vivid poems written by American soldiers in a book called *Winning Hearts and Minds*, published in Brooklyn in 1972. Another valuable collection, this time by nurses who had served in that war, is *Visions of War, Dreams of Peace*. I am grateful to the editors of all these volumes, as I am to Martin Page, who set out to preserve the bawdy songs and poems of the Second World War, many passed down and refined or embellished through oral tradition, in *Kiss Me Goodnight, Sergeant Major* and *For Gawdsake Don't Take Me*.

I also wish to pay tribute to the Salamander Oasis Trust for the thorough work it has done in collecting and publishing many poems from the Second World War, a body of work hitherto much underrated. Closer to today, there are the poems of immediate witness to the war in Bosnia which were published by Bloodaxe Books in a volume under the title *Klaonika* (1993). I could not have compiled this anthology without drawing upon such books – and indeed many more.

K.B.

The editor and publishers gratefully acknowledge the following for permission to reproduce copyright material in this book.

ANNA AKHMATOVA: to the Harvill Press for 'Alexander at Thebes', 'Cleopatra', and 'In 1940', from *Poems of Akhmatova*, selected, translated and introduced by Stanley Kunitz and Max Hayward. First published in 1973 by Little, Brown and Company. First

Custodio and Ad Donker Publishers for 'The Volunteer's Reply to the Poet', from *Collected Works: 1* (Bodley Head, 1955). JAMES CARNEY: to Colin Smythe Ltd for an excerpt from 'The Defeat of the Norsemen', trans. James Carney, from *Medieval Irish Lyrics* (Dolmen Press, 1981). CHARLES CAUSLEY: to David Higham Associates Ltd for 'H.M.S. *Glory*' and 'Song of the Dying Gunner AA1', from *Collected Poems* (Macmillan, 1992). C. P. CAVAFY: to Random House UK Ltd for 'Waiting for the Barbarians', trans. Edmund Keeley and Philip Sherrard, from *Collected Poems*, ed. George Savidis (Chatto, 1990). ALEX COMFORT: to the author for 'Letter to an American Visitor', from *Tribune* (4 June 1943). JOY CORFIELD: to the Salamander Oasis Trust for 'Morse Lesson', from *The Voice of War* (Michael Joseph, 1995). E. E. CUMMINGS: to W. W. Norton & Company Ltd for 'I sing of Olaf glad and big', from *Complete Poems 1904–1962* by E. E.Cummings, ed. George J. Firmage, copyright © 1931, 1959, 1979, 1991 by the Trustees for the E. E. Cummings Trust and George James Firmage. R. N. CURREY: to Routledge Publishers Ltd for 'Unseen Fire' from *This Other Planet* (1945). JAMES DICKEY: to University Press of New England for 'The Performance', from *Poems 1957–1967* (Wesleyan University Press), copyright © 1967 by James Dickey. EMILY DICKINSON: to Harvard University Press and the Trustees of Amherst College for 'My Portion is Defeat – today', from *The Poems of Emily Dickinson*, ed. Thomas Johnson, Cambridge, Mass.: The Belknap Press of Harvard University Press, copyright © 1951, 1955, 1979, 1983 by the President and Fellows of Harvard College; and to Little, Brown & Company, from *The Complete Poems of Emily Dickinson* (Poem 639), ed. Thomas H. Johnson, copyright 1929 by Martha Dickinson Bianchi; copyright renewed 1957 by Mary L. Hampson. KEITH DOUGLAS: to Oxford University Press for 'How to Kill', 'Aristocrats', 'Vergissmeinnicht' and 'Simplify Me when I'm Dead', from *The Complete Poems of Keith Douglas*, ed. Desmond Graham (1978). GAVIN EWART: to Random House UK Ltd for 'Officers Mess' and 'A Personal Footnote', from *The Collected Ewart 1933–1980* (Hutchinson, 1980). FORD MADOX FORD: to David Higham Associates Ltd for an excerpt from 'Antwerp', from *Ford Madox Ford*, Volume 1 (Bodley Head, 1972). ROBERT GARIOCH: to the Saltire Society for 'Property', '1941' and 'Phooie!', from *Complete Poetical Works*, ed. Robin Fulton (Macdonald Publishers, 1983). WILFRID GIBSON: to Mrs Dorothy Gibson and Macmillan General Books for 'In the Ambulance' and 'Breakfast', from *Collected Poems 1905–1925* (Macmillan, 1926). W. S. GRAHAM: to Faber & Faber Ltd for 'The Conscript Goes' and 'What's the News?', from *Aimed at Nobody*, eds. Margaret Blackwood and Robin Skelton (1993). ROBERT GRAVES: to Carcanet Press for 'David and Goliath', '1915', 'The Leveller', 'Dead Cow Farm', 'Sergeant-Major Money', 'When I'm Killed' and 'Corporal Stare', from *Collected Poems*. MICHAEL GREENING: to R. N. Currey for 'Missing – Believed Drowned', from *Poems from India*, eds. R. N. Currey and R. V. Gibson (Oxford University Press, 1945). IVOR GURNEY: to Oxford University Press for 'The Bohemians' and 'Strange Hells', from *Collected Poems of Ivor Gurney*, ed. P. J. Kavanagh (1982). IAN HAMILTON: to Faber & Faber Ltd for 'The Newscast', from *Fifty Poems* (1988). TONY HARRISON: to the author for 'The Cycles of Donji Vakuf', published in *the Guardian*. ALFRED HAYES: to Peter Owen Ltd for 'The City of Beggars'. RICHARD HELLER: to the author for 'The Minister Has All His Notes In Place'. HAMISH HENDERSON: to Polygon for 'Opening of an Offensive' and 'Ninth Elegy', from *Elegies for the Dead* (Edinburgh University Press, 1979). HO XUAN HONG: to *The Spectator* for 'The General's Plaque', trans. Graeme Wilson. TED HUGHES: to Faber & Faber Ltd for 'Out', from *Wodwo* (1967). VICTOR HUGO: to Faber & Faber Ltd for 'Russia 1812', trans. Robert Lowell, from *Imitations* (1962). VERA INBER: to University of California Press for 'Leningrad, 1943', an excerpt from 'The Pulkovo Meridian', from *Soviet Poets and Society* by Alexander Kaun, copyright © 1943 The Regents of the University of California. DAVID JONES: to Faber & Faber Ltd for an excerpt from *In Parenthesis*. SIDNEY KEYES: to Routledge Publishers for 'Dunbar, 1650' and 'War Poet', from *Collected Poems* (1988). THOMAS KINSELLA: to the translator for 'The world laid low . . .', from *An Duanaire: Poems of the Dispossessed* (Dolmen Press, 1981). STANLEY KUNITZ: to W. W. Norton & Co Inc for 'Careless Love', from *The Poems of Stanley Kunitz 1928–1978*, copyright 1930, 1944 by Stanley Kunitz. PHILIP LARKIN: to Faber & Faber Ltd for 'MCMXIV', from *Collected Poems*, ed. Anthony Thwaite (1988). PRIMO LEVI: to Faber & Faber Ltd for 'Shema', trans. Ruth Feldman and Brian

Swann, from *Collected Poems* (1988). ALUN LEWIS: to Seren Books for an excerpt from 'The Jungle', from *Collected Poems*, ed. Cary Orchard (1994). CHRISTOPHER LOGUE: to Faber & Faber Ltd for 'The Song of the Dead Soldier', from *Selected Poems*, and extracts from *War Music*. HUGH MACDIARMID: to Carcanet Press for 'Another Epitaph on an Army of Mercenaries' and 'Under the Greenwood Tree', from *Complete Poems* (1985). SORLEY MACLEAN: to Carcanet Press for 'Death Valley' and 'Heroes', from *Collected Poems* (1989). JOHN MANIFOLD: to University of Queensland Press for 'Fife Tune', from *Collected Verse* (University of Queensland Press, St Lucia, 1978). CHRISTOPHER MIDDLETON: to the translator for 'Brothers' by Heinrich Lersch, and 'The Dead' by René Arcos, from *Ohne Hass und Fahne* (Hamburg, 1959). EDNA ST VINCENT MILLAY: to Elizabeth Barnett, literary executor, for 'Conscientious Objector', from *Collected Poems* (Harper Collins), copyright © 1934, 1962 by Edna St Vincent Millay and Norma Millay Ellis. ADRIAN MITCHELL: to the Peters Fraser & Dunlop Group for 'To Whom It May Concern', from *Love Songs of World War III* (Allison & Busby, 1989). PAUL MULDOON: to Faber & Faber Ltd for 'Truce', from *Why Brownlee Left* (1980). GEORGE ORWELL: to A. M. Heath & Company Ltd for 'As One Non-Combatant to Another', from *Tribune* (18 June 1943), copyright © The Estate of the late Sonia Brownell Orwell and Martin Secker & Warburg Ltd. PAO CHAO: to Constable Publishers Ltd for 'The Scholar Recruit', trans. Arthur Waley, from *A Hundred and Seventy Chinese Poems* (1987). DOROTHY PARKER: to Duckworth Publishers Ltd for 'Penelope', from *The Collected Dorothy Parker* (1974). TOM PAULIN: to Faber & Faber Ltd for 'Peacetime', from *Fivemiletown* (1987). MERVYN PEAKE: to David Higham Associates Ltd for an excerpt from 'The Rhyme of the Flying Bomb', from *The Rhyme of the Flying Bomb* (Dent, 1962). EZRA POUND: to Faber & Faber Ltd for translations of 'Song of the Bowmen of Shu', 'A War Song' and 'Rome', from *Translations* (1953). TOM RAWLING: to the author for 'Gas Drill', from *The Poetry Book Society Anthology 1989–1990*, ed. Christopher Reid (Hutchinson, 1989). HERBERT READ: to David Higham Associates Ltd for 'The Happy Warrior' (from 'The Scene of War'), from *Selected Poetry* (Sinclair-Stevenson, 1992). OLIVER REYNOLDS: to Faber & Faber Ltd for 'Hazel', from *The Player*

Queen's Wife (1987). EDGELL RICKWORD: to Carcanet Press for
'Trench Poets' and 'Winter Warfare', from *Collected Poems*
(1991). ANNE RIDLER: to Carcanet Press Ltd for 'At Parting', from
Collected Poems. RAINER MARIA RILKE: to Devin-Adair Publishers
Inc for 'The Last Evening', trans. C. F. MacIntyre, from *War and
the Poet* by Eberhart and Rodman (1945), copyright by Devin-
Adair Publishers, Old Greenwich, Connecticut 06870. ARTHUR
RIMBAUD: to Anvil Press Poetry for 'Evil' and 'The Rooks', trans.
Norman Cameron, from *A Season in Hell and Other Poems* (Anvil
Press Poetry, 1994). JOHN RIMINGTON: to the Salamander Oasis
Trust for 'God of the Flies', from *Return to Oasis* (Shepheard
Walwyn, 1980). CARL SANDBURG: to Harcourt Brace & Company
for 'Grass', from *Cornhuskers* by Carl Sandburg, copyright 1918
by Holt, Rinehart & Winston Inc, and renewed 1946 by Carl
Sandburg. PETER SANDERS: to the Salamander Oasis Trust for
'Tripoli', from *Return to Oasis* (Shepheard Walwyn, 1980).
SIEGFRIED SASSOON: to George Sassoon for 'Suicide in the
Trenches', 'The General' and 'Glory of Women', from *Collected
Poems 1908–1956* (Faber, 1984). VERNON SCANNELL: to the
author and Robson Books for 'Bayonet Training', from *Collected
Poems* (1993). OSBERT SITWELL: to David Higham Associates Ltd
for 'Judas and the Profiteer', from *Collected Poems and Satires*
(Duckworth, 1931). BERNARD SPENCER: to Oxford University
Press for 'A Thousand Killed', 'The Invaders' and 'Passed On',
from *Collected Poems of Bernard Spencer*, ed. Roger Bowen
(1981). STEPHEN SPENDER: to Faber & Faber Ltd for 'Ultima
Ratio Regum', from *Collected Poems 1928–1985*. WALLACE
STEVENS: to Faber & Faber Ltd for an excerpt from 'Phases', from
Opus Posthumous (1990). DOUGLAS STREET: to the Salamander
Oasis Trust for 'Love Letters of the Dead', from *Poems of the
Second World War: The Oasis Selection* (Dent/Everyman, 1985).
HOLGER TESCHKE: to the translator, Margitt Lehbert, for 'The
Minutes of Hasiba' from *Klaonika* (Bloodaxe Books, 1993).
DYLAN THOMAS: to David Higham Associates Ltd for 'The hand
that signed the paper felled a city' and 'A Refusal to Mourn the
Death, by Fire, of a Child in London', from *The Poems of Dylan
Thomas* (Dent, 1971). MICHAEL THWAITES: to the author for
extracts from 'The Jervis Bay', from *The Voice of War* (Michael
Joseph, 1995). H. H. TILLEY: to R. N. Currey for 'From Citizen

B.O.R. Speaking', from *Poems from India*, eds. R. N. Currey and R. V. Gibson (Oxford University Press, 1945). N. J. TRAPNELL: to the Salamander Oasis Trust for 'Lament of a Desert Rat', from *The Voice of War* (Michael Joseph, 1995). VIRGIL: to Carcanet Press for an excerpt from 'The Aeneid' (Book II) by Virgil, trans. C. H. Sisson. PAUL WIDDOWS: to R. N. Currey for 'Minutiae 3', from *Poems from India*, eds. R. N. Currey and R. V. Gibson (Oxford University Press, 1945). C. WRIGHT: to Warner Books/New York for 'May God Go with You, Son', from *Visions of War, Dreams of Peace*, copyright © 1991 by Lynda Van Devanter.

Additional bibliographical information: MADELINE IDA BEDFORD: 'Munition Wages', from *The Young Captain: Fragments of War and Love* (London: Erskine Macdonald, 1917). F. W. D. BENDALL: 'Outposts', from *Front Line Lyrics* (1918). RONALD FREDERICK PALMER: 'The Conchie', from *Military Moments: Some Modern Barrack Room Ballads* (Ilfracombe: Arthur H. Stockwell, 1951). JESSIE POPE: 'The Beau Ideal', from *More War Poems* (London: Grant Richards, 1915). DONALD THOMPSON: 'On the Relative Merit of Friend and Foe, Being Dead', from *Spring Sacrifice: Poems* (London: John Lane, The Bodley Head, 1945).

Every effort has been made to trace or contact copyright holders, but in some cases this has proved impossible. The editor and publishers would like to hear from any copyright holders not acknowledged.

Index of Authors

Adkins, Geoffrey, 211, 450
Aeschylus, 198
Akhmatova, Anna, 409, 430
Albizzi, Niccolo Degli, 431
Alexandru, Ioan, 490
Amichai, Yehuda, 237, 391
Amiel, Barry Conrad, 131
Apollinaire, Guillaume, 231
Aragon, Louis, 16, 302
Arcos, René, 465
Aristophanes, 38
Aschilochus, 175
Asquith, Herbert, 163
Auden, W. H., 15, 79, 393

Bedford, Madeline Ida, 43
Bell, Martin, 579
Bellay, Joachim Du, 483
Belloc, Hilaire, 230, 514
Bendall, F. W. D., 171
Bensley, Connie, 240
Betjeman, John, 41
Binyon, Lawrence, 575
Blok, Alexander, 258
Blunden, Edmund, 104
Bond, Edward, 502
Borges, Jorge Luis, 467
Brecht, Bertolt, 487
Bridges, Thomas, 31
Brodsky, Joseph, 401
Brooke, Fulke Greville, Lord, 512
Brooke, Rupert, 119
Brooks, John, 180
Browning, Elizabeth Barrett, 55, 509
Bryll, Ernest, 216, 543
Bunno, 80
Bunting, Basil, 553
Burgoyne, John, 29
Burns, Robert, 472
Butterfield, F. G., 452
Byron, George Gordon, Lord, 179, 268, 278, 508

Camoens, Luis, 319, 506, 534
Campbell, Roy, 500
Carver, Dale R., 499

Causley, Charles, 333, 350
Cavafy, C. P., 435
Chaucer, Geoffrey, 548
Chesterton, G. K., 201, 288, 568
Churchill, Charles, 199
Clare, John, 115, 437
Clough, A. H., 2, 405
Coleridge, S. T., 398, 545
Comfort, Alex, 518
Corfield, Joy, 99
Cowper, William, 200
Crane, Stephen, 475
Crosby, Ernest, 168, 230, 529
Crosland, T. W. H., 515
Cummings, E. E., 527
Currey, R. N., 236

Davenant, William, 28
De Born, Bertrand, 12
Deloney, Thomas, 358
Dibdin, Thomas, 227
Dickey, James, 383
Dickinson, Emily, 432, 565
Donne, John, 337
Douglas, Keith, 45, 165, 172, 577
Doyle, F. H., 117
Drayton, Michael, 284
Dryden, John, 20, 162, 341

Elliott, Ebenezer, 487
Ellis, R. H., 49
Ewart, Gavin, 106, 424
Ewer, W. N., 540

Fenton, James, 407
Fitzgerald, Edward, 487
Ford, Ford Madox, 187, 478
Frankau, Gilbert, 74

Garioch, Robert, 69, 249, 403
Garrick, David, 9
Gascoigne, George, 304, 483
Gibson, Wilfred, 130
Gifford, William, 47
Gower, John, 586
Graham, W. S., 333, 440

Graves, Robert, 78, 129, 164, 178, 489, 497, 570
Greening, Michael, 571
Grenfell, Julian, 13
Gurney, Ivor, 90, 447
Gutteridge, Bernard, 463

Hamilton, Ian, 402
Hardy, Thomas, 36, 120, 162, 242, 266, 331, 460, 569
Harrison, Tony, 428
Hayes, Alfred, 433
Heine, Heinrich, 183
Heller, Richard, 204
Henderson, Hamish, 232, 466
Henley, W. E., 213
Hill, Geoffrey, 397, 403, 578
Ho Xuan Hong, 192
Homer, 33, 134, 206, 207, 270, 311, 325, 367, 470, 549, 550
Hopkins, Gerard Manley, 538
Housman, A. E., 19, 62, 443
Hughes, Ted, 448
Hugo, Victor, 184
Hunt, G. W., 10

Inber, Vera, 365

Jarmin, John, 248, 381, 496, 558
Jarrell, Randall, 394
Johnson, Samuel, 419
Johnstone, Philip, 557
Jones, David, 260
Jonson, Ben, 13, 59
Juvenal, 418

'K', 250
Kenevet, Ralph, 585
Keyes, Sidney, 431, 499
Kipling, Rudyard, 75, 77, 81, 88, 102, 121, 188, 193, 200, 217, 228, 275, 373, 382, 452, 537
Krige, Uys, 173
Kunitz, Stanley, 218

Landor, W. S., 192
Larkin, Philip, 576
Lawrence, D. H., 231
Lee, Joseph, 465
Lee, Nathaniel, 410
Lermontov, Mikhail, 295
Lersch, Heinrich, 464

Levi, Primo, 396
Lewis, Alun, 253
Li Ho, 552
Logue, Christopher, 56, 169, 313
Longfellow, Henry Wadsworth, 348, 368
Lovelace, Richard, 27

Macaulay, Thomas Babington, Lord, 135, 293
McCrae, John, 557
MacDiarmid, Hugh, 62, 336
Mackintosh, Ewart Alan, 23
Maclean, Sorley, 4, 166
MacNeice, Louis, 233
Manifold, John, 21
Mansfield, Katherine, 457, 477
Marlowe, Christopher, 241, 356, 414, 422
Marvell, Andrew, 341
Meddemmen, J. G., 130
Melville, Herman, 18, 87, 348
Millay, Edna St Vincent, 516
Milton, John, 222, 486
Mitchell, Adrian, 400
Moore, Thomas, 9
Morant, Harry, 76
Morris, William, 380
Muldoon, Paul, 461

Neruda, Pablo, 201
Newbolt, Henry, 116, 118, 515
Nisbet, Hume, 301

Ohnishi, Vice Admiral 566
Orwell, George, 523
Owen, Wilfred, 3, 122, 127, 247, 445, 459, 575

Pacquet, Basil T., 442
Paley, Grace, 390
Palmer, R. F., 517
Pao Chao, 85
Parker, Dorothy, 41
Parker, Martin, 454
Pasternak, Boris, 582
Paulin, Tom, 581
Peacock, Thomas Love, 427
Peake, Mervyn, 234
Platke, Stan, 375
Pope, Jessie, 441
Prévert, Jacques, 480

Qasim, Samih al-, 441

Raine, Kathleen, 481
Rawling, Tom, 67
Read, Herbert, 171
Reed, Henry, 65
Reynolds, Oliver, 72
Rickword, Edgell, 254, 503
Ridler, Anne, 37
Rilke, Rainer Maria, 30
Rimbaud, Arthur, 257, 544
Rimington, John, 259
Rosenberg, Isaac, 259
Ross, Alan, 105, 254, 451

Sandburg, Carl, 559
Sanders, Peter A., 105
Sankichi, Toge, 238
Sassoon, Siegfried, 192, 194, 377, 476
Scannell, Vernon, 63
Scarfe, Francis, 220
Scott, John, 25
Scott, Sir Walter, 22, 209, 323
Scottus, Sedulius, 532
Scurfield, George, 251
Seegar, Alan, 126
Shakespeare, William, 6, 71, 86, 96, 160,
    175, 176, 190, 246, 315, 444, 482,
    492
Shirley, James, 485
Short, John, 108
Shuster, Dana, 375
Simonides, 561
Sitwell, Osbert, 204
Slutsky, Boris, 387
Sorley, Charles Hamilton, 566
Southey, Robert, 473, 554
Spencer, Bernard, 399, 434, 479
Spender, Stephen, 203
Stead, W. T., 539

Stevens, Wallace, 489, 513
Street, Douglas, 463
Swift, Jonathan, 1
Sylvester, Joshua, 547

Tasso, Torquato, 93
Tennant, Edward, 194
Tennyson, Alfred, Lord, 91, 280, 299
Teschke, Holger, 392
Thackeray, W. M., 562
Thien, Ho, 388
Thomas, Dylan, 202, 386
Thomas, Edward, 246
Thompson, Donald, 462
Thwaites, Michael, 344
Tilley, H. H., 83
Trapnell, N. J., 125

Ungaretti, Giuseppe, 264

Virgil, 353, 354, 505
Vulgarius, Eugenius, 221

Waldinger, Ernst, 385
Wallace, Edgar, 371
Warner, Sylvia Townsend, 52
West, Arthur Graeme, 262
Whitman, Walt, 24, 369, 468, 474, 495,
    564, 573
Whittier, J. G., 362
Widdows, Paul, 107
Wilson, T. P. Cameron, 497
Winchilsea, Anne Finch, Countess of, 471
Wolfe, Charles, 265
Woodhouse, Peter, 83
Wright, C., 541

Yeats, W. B., 163, 496
Young, Edward, 530
Yusuf, Sa'di, 584